Visual Basic® 5 Fundamentals

UNLEASHED

Mike Amundsen
Rob Bernavich
John Charlesworth
John D. Conley III
Paul Kimmel
Rick Ladymon
Lowell Mauer
Mike McMillan
Greg Perry
Alex Reich

SAMS
PUBLISHING

201 West 103rd Street
Indianapolis, IN 46290

Overview

Contents

Tell Us What You Think!

As a reader, you are the most important critic and commentator of our books. We value your opinion and want to know what we're doing right, what we could do better, what areas you'd like to see us publish in, and any other words of wisdom you're willing to pass our way. You can help us make strong books that meet your needs and give you the computer guidance you require.

Do you have access to the World Wide Web? Then check out our site at http://www.mcp.com.

> **NOTE**
>
> If you have a technical question about this book, call the technical support line at 317-581-3833 or send e-mail to support@mcp.com.

As the team leader of the group that created this book, I welcome your comments. You can fax, e-mail, or write me directly to let me know what you did or didn't like about this book—as well as what we can do to make our books stronger. Here's the information:

Fax: 317-581-4669

E-mail: programming_mgr@sams.mcp.com

Mail: Christopher Denny
           Comments Department
           Sams Publishing
           201 W. 103rd Street
           Indianapolis, IN 46290

I

PART

Exploring Visual Basic 5 Features

New Features in Visual Basic 5

by John W. Charlesworth

IN THIS CHAPTER

CHAPTER

1

This chapter offers a high-level overview of the new features and changes in Visual Basic 5. For ease of reference, it is organized to correspond with the content matter of this book's companion, *Visual Basic 5 Development Unleashed.* By referring to the table of contents for each book, you should be able to easily find the detailed sections you want.

You'll also see indications to tell you which version of Visual Basic supports the new features. Features are supported in all editions, in the Professional and Enterprise editions only, or in the Enterprise Edition only.

Exciting Times Are Ahead: An Overview

Exciting times are ahead for Visual Basic users. Whether you are a VB dabbler knowing just enough to create basic user interface prototypes or a seasoned expert able to magically create applications in VB using tips and tricks not generally known, you'll find this version of Visual Basic an exciting step forward for you and your projects.

For novices, VB 5 offers easier ways to create programs that perform functions only advanced or expert programmers could build before now. Wizards that aid you step-by-step were added throughout the product. These wizards help build the fundamental base from which you can add your own specific code. Project, forms, and class templates provide a head start to creating your own style application while maintaining Windows design guidelines.

For intermediate and expert users, Microsoft has added many of the tools you need that previously required lower-level languages such as C++. You can now build your own controls directly in Visual Basic. Adding Internet access and making your programs Internet-aware using ActiveX technology could hardly be easier. Features included in the Enterprise Edition to control remote objects make workgroup and enterprise-wide application development easier and more robust.

New language elements give all users the capability to add functions such as drag and drop to applications. Another language enhancement needed by advanced developers and now supported is Windows callbacks. You can choose to compile your application into interpreted code or as native code. This offers significant performance advantages. These new features, along with many other language enhancements, make Visual Basic a solid and viable tool for just about any application development.

Yes, exciting times are ahead. Visual Basic is no longer only a learning tool or a prototyping tool with the final product ultimately written in another language. Visual Basic is now a fully function-rich environment for creating small utilities and large enterprise-wide computing applications for private or commercial use.

The Fundamentals

This section discusses new features and enhancements of Visual Basic 5 affecting everyday development and more commonly used VB components. Here you will find the primary changes to the development environment, the Visual Basic language, and fundamental development methods.

Refer to the section "Advanced Programming Topics" later in this chapter for information relating to topics such as databases, Internet and ActiveX support, setup programs, and enterprise computing tools and methods.

A Better Way to Work Using the New IDE

Perhaps the most significant improvements to Visual Basic 5 come in the development environment itself. Microsoft made great strides in creating a development environment to fully accommodate your development needs. In fact, you might notice that Visual Basic's IDE enhancements bring it closer to the development environment of Microsoft's other development tools such as Visual C++. This was a deliberate effort by Microsoft to provide a consistent and functionally rich set of tools for your use regardless of your programming language of choice.

General Design Enhancements

Several new, important design enhancements make the development environment more flexible. Foremost, Microsoft made the development environments of its various development tools more consistent. In fact, Microsoft's Development Studio approach merges the development environments so that you can use different language tools within the same development environment. Specific design enhancements (included in all editions) for Visual Basic 5 include the following:

- **Project options include MDI, SDI, and Explorer-style interfaces.** There are now three basic frameworks for a project. You use the multiple-document interface (MDI) when you want to have multiple document windows open simultaneously. The single-document interface (SDI) provides a single-window application. The Explorer framework is similar to the file explorer and provides a tree view on the left side of the application and a document view on the right side. The Explorer style is useful for viewing information in an organized way, allowing the user to select the data and the detail level of the data to view. The information and icons represented in the tree view can easily be altered.

- **Multiple projects can exist in a single instance of Visual Basic.** You can now have multiple projects open at the same time in the same instance of Visual Basic. You no longer need to run multiple copies of VB when creating and debugging multiple projects (as was the case when developing add-ins). This can be helpful when debugging ActiveX, add-in, and enterprise applications. A new capability to build project groups also allows you to batch-compile selected projects active within the current workspace.

- **Online Internet help within VB offers additional resources.** Within the VB help menus, you can find shortcuts to many informative development sites online. This is a great resource for frequently asked questions (FAQs), software updates, or knowledge-base information not included in VB's local help files or the local *Visual Basic Books Online.*

- **Development environment windows and toolbars are dockable and linkable.** The various development environment windows (Project Explorer, Properties, Form Layout, Locals, Immediate, Watch, Object Browser, and the color palette) along with the toolbox and toolbars can be docked, undocked, and linked to each other.

- **New command-line options run VB from DOS.** You can now use the /RUNEXIT option to execute Visual Basic from the DOS command line. Using /? as a parameter when launching Visual Basic from the command line (DOS prompt) displays all the valid command-line options.

Program Editor Updates

Significant Program Editor updates make your job easier. The primary changes (for all editions) include the following:

- **Auto Quick Info provides statement and function syntax.** Within the code window, Quick Info provides the syntax for statements and functions as you type. This tooltip display not only shows the correct syntax but also highlights the parameter to be entered next as you type. If a given parameter has fixed options, a drop-down list shows the options you can choose. This simple tool can save you from looking up function parameters and constant values and can also help you avoid the typing errors that can occur when manually entering parameters and constants.

- **Drop-down lists of parameters, properties, methods, and constants save time and avoid errors.** If turned on through the Options | Editor tab (as Auto Quick Info), this tool provides a drop-down box list of object, control, or function information including parameters, properties, methods, and valid constants. As you type a statement containing an object, control, or function reference, the drop-down list displays the valid options applicable to the reference. As with Quick Info, this tool helps you prevent errors by showing all the valid options applicable to what you are doing.

- **Complete Word automatically finishes words you type.** As a time saver, Visual Basic can automatically identify and complete a word you are entering in the code window once you've entered enough characters for it to recognize the word you want.

■ **Data tips show variable and property values.** Placing the mouse over a variable or property name in the Code window while in break mode displays a tooltip that shows the current variable or property's value.

■ **Dragging and dropping to the Watch window reduces errors in typing while debugging.** To maintain a continuous display of a variable's contents, you can add that variable to the Watch window. In addition to using the old methods for adding Watch window variables, you can drag and drop to the Watch window directly from the Code window.

■ **Margin indicators help debugging.** In the left margin of the code window, you have margin indicators to set breakpoints, show call stack pointers, indicate bookmarks, and show the next statement to execute. You can easily set and toggle breakpoints by clicking in the margin to the left of the statement. Changing the next statement to execute is as easy as dragging the next statement marker to a new Code window location.

■ **Procedure View and Full Module view let you decide how procedures display in the Code window.** You can choose to display either a single selected procedure or all a module's procedures in the Code window. Choosing Procedure View displays only the selected procedure in the Code window. Full Module View displays all procedures in the module, allowing you to easily scroll through them.

■ **The capability to block and unblock comments aids debugging.** You can now select a group of lines and add or remove the comment character with a single command. This timesaving feature is particularly useful during debugging, when you might want to temporarily disable a section of your program.

IDE Windows Enhancements

Major improvements to the Integrated Development Environment (IDE) will make your job easier. The primary enhancements (included in all editions) follow:

■ **The Object Browser is more helpful and useful.** The Object Browser contains improvements that enable you to jump directly to references in your code and provide more descriptive information in the description pane of the Object Browser window. The descriptions are useful as a reminder of an object's purpose. Jumping to references and objects from the Object Browser saves you from digging through big projects when looking for a particular reference.

■ **The debug window is replaced.** The old style debug window is replaced by the Locals, Immediate, and Watch windows. One of the best advantages of this enhancement is that the Locals window automatically displays all local variables and values in the currently active procedure without your having to manually add them.

■ **The Properties window is organized by category or alphabetically.** You can now display the Properties window by category or alphabetically. A description window provides a short description of the highlighted property, serving as a reminder of its purpose. Prior versions of Visual Basic contained only an alphabetical listing of properties. The category display organizes properties into logical groups such as appearance, behavior, data, position, scale, font, miscellaneous, list, text, and DDE groups. With VB, you often set positioning, appearance, font, or data properties as a group, which means you set more than one related property at a time. Grouping related properties means you don't have to bounce around in the Properties window looking for each property.

- **The Project Explorer tree view shows project structure.** The Project Explorer window is now more like that used for compilers such as Microsoft's Visual C++. The project structure is displayed in a tree view form, allowing you to expand and close folders as desired. Folders represent groupings of projects, forms, modules, class modules, property pages, user controls, user documents, and designers. This new project window style is tremendously helpful for larger projects when you don't want to see all components at the same time.

- **The New Project dialog helps you select project types.** The New Project dialog allows you to select a specific project type or the Project Application Wizard, which helps you define a new application. Supported project types include standard EXE, ActiveX EXE, ActiveX DLL, ActiveX control, ActiveX document EXE, ActiveX document DLL, and add-in. You can also select project templates from the Existing and Recent tabs of the New Project dialog. Notice that Visual Basic 5 includes many new project types. Previously, some of these project types could be created only in a language such as Visual C++.

- **The new Form Layout window lets you position forms visually.** You can now visually position all forms at design time by using the new Form Layout window. Based on where you place the form in the layout window, the form properties are automatically updated with the appropriate positioning values. This a simple but timesaving feature.

- **Palette improvements give better control and performance.** The enhanced palette support provides more flexibility and control while maintaining backward compatibility. Windows's halftone palette is also supported.

Toolbar Enhancements

You'll like the significant enhancements to Visual Basic's toolbars, available in all editions:

- **General toolbar enhancements.** New buttons on existing toolbars and new toolbars reflect many of the new features in Visual Basic 5. New features common to all the toolbars and to the toolbox are docking and undocking and linking toolbars to each other. You might also notice the new CommandBar concept applied to the Standard and Forms Editor toolbars. The CommandBar combines toolbars and menus into a single entity. When you select the drop-down arrow associated with a particular button, a drop-down menu displays various options related to that toolbar button. Whatever you select from the menu options becomes the default option for the button on the toolbar.

- **New Add-In toolbar.** The new Add-In toolbar displays icons for some of the wizards and utilities new in VB 5. The Application Wizard, Class Builder Utility, Data Form Wizard, ActiveX Migration Wizard, ActiveX Control Wizard, and Property Page Wizard are included by default. One nice aspect of this toolbar is that you can add any executable or add-in DLL. This gives you the flexibility to add your own tools or other software tools you find useful in development directly onto a toolbar.

- **New Form Editor toolbar.** A new Form Editor toolbar provides buttons for easy control alignment and sizing, control locking, and form organization. Notice that the options for alignment include aligning more than one control by their left sides, the center of the controls, or their right sides. You can also align by top sides, vertical middle, and bottom sides, and you can simply align controls to the standard form grid. You can also center a group of controls horizontally or vertically on a form. The sizing button lets you adjust groups of controls to have the same height, width, or both height and width. Locking controls prevents you from inadvertently changing control placement once you've finalized how you want the form to look. The Bring to Front and Send to Back buttons help you organize controls on a form. This toolbar is actually a good example of the concept of command bars. It combines a standard-type toolbar with menu-type options. You'll notice, for example, that there is a drop-down arrow to the right of several buttons on this toolbar. By selecting the arrow, you see a drop-down menu of options associated with that toolbar button. When you select one of these options, it then becomes the default option for that toolbar button.

- **Standard toolbar changes.** For the most part, the standard toolbar is the same as it was in prior VB versions. Additions include buttons for adding new projects, adding new components, and accessing the new Form Layout window. Notice that this toolbar incorporates the new CommandBar style. As described previously, the CommandBar combines the toolbar buttons with menu options.

- **Personalized IDE toolbars.** When you access the View | Toolbars menu, you see a Customize option, which has become a standard option on Windows applications. From the Customize dialog, you can choose which toolbars to display, add new toolbars, delete toolbars, and alter what is included on each toolbar. You can also change button size, set whether shortcut keys should be included in button tooltips, set whether tooltips should be shown with toolbars, and set menu animation styles (none, random, unfold, or slide). One of the best features here is the capability to customize shortcut menus. Shortcut menus are usually accessed via right-clicking the mouse or pressing Shift+F10 on the keyboard. These shortcut menus are context sensitive to what is active or selected in the development environment. You can customize these shortcut menus to best reflect how you work.

■ **Customizable toolbox.** The toolbox contains icons for all the controls you've made available to the project through the Project | Components menu. The Components dialog allows you to select which controls, designers, and insertable objects to include in the toolbox. (Only controls were valid toolbox objects in prior versions of Visual Basic.) You can also organize and categorize those toolbox objects by adding tabs on the toolbox itself.

CAUTION

ActiveX controls included with Visual Basic 5 are 32 bit only. Some companies sell ActiveX controls for development that are 16-bit controls. These controls do not work with Visual Basic 5.

Your Choice: Native Code or Interpreted

In the past, one of the inherent barriers to using Visual Basic for commercial development was its creation of programs using interpreted code (p-code). When running a Visual Basic program, you needed runtime DLL modules to interpret VB's pneumonic codes and translate them into code understandable by the computer. You don't need this extra step with the native code that most other languages generate within their EXEs. Interpreted code can have a significant negative effect on performance.

Visual Basic 5 solves the problem of interpreted code and gives you the option to choose whether to use interpreted code or native code for the Professional and Enterprise Editions. You can also apply compiler optimization settings, allowing VB to tune your programs to run most efficiently on your targeted platform. You can optimize for small code or fast code and even set an option to favor the Pentium Pro chip. Visual Basic 5 offers a number of advanced optimization settings as well.

Wizards, Wizards Everywhere

Perhaps the most significant advancement in Visual Basic 5 is its addition of numerous wizards to help both novices and advanced users alike create useful applications. Functions previously created by only advanced developers (such as building your own classes and controls) are straightforward and easier to implement when you use the wizards.

Frankly, I can't say enough about how useful these tools are. Many people who used VB for only basic prototyping in the past might feel more comfortable creating real applications. Many of the intimidating aspects of programming were alleviated in Visual Basic, and although there is still a learning curve involved with building useful applications, VB helps you get started and take on relatively complex functions with ease. It's also helpful to use templates to build tedious functions included with many Windows applications (splash screens, login dialogs, about boxes, Internet browsers, option dialogs, tip-of-the-day dialogs, and so on) so that you can focus your time on the specifics of your own tool.

The Application Wizard

The Application Wizard takes you through an interview process that asks questions and lets you select options you want in your project. It then builds a complete application that meets the requirements you designated. It also provides a summary report upon completion that gives instructions on what to do next. The application created by the Application Wizard is complete and can run as is. From this framework created for you, you can add code to perform the specific functions of your application.

You cannot invoke the Application Wizard to change settings in your project. It builds an initial application framework only. If you want to add additional features later, you need to use another wizard or add them manually.

The ActiveX Control Interface Wizard

The ActiveX Control Interface Wizard (available in the Professional and Enterprise Editions) helps you create the interface and function elements of your own ActiveX controls. You use it after you create the elements that make up the physical appearance of your control. You then use the wizard to connect the physical interface with the program interface (the properties, events, and methods). Primarily, the wizard helps you identify all the properties, events, and methods to be included in your control and how they functionally map to other controls you include within your control. This tool makes creating your own ActiveX controls easy.

The ActiveX Document Migration Wizard

The ActiveX Document Migration Wizard (provided with the Professional and Enterprise Editions) helps you convert forms in your project into ActiveX documents. This wizard does not convert your whole project into an ActiveX application; it merely converts forms for you. Why would you want to migrate your forms to ActiveX documents? If you want to have users run your program from a document container such as Microsoft's Internet Explorer or Microsoft Binder, your forms must conform to their structure. For example, ActiveX documents don't contain all the same properties as their equivalent forms because the ActiveX document container application handles those properties on behalf of the document itself. Also, navigation between ActiveX documents generally relies on hyperlink objects, whereas forms use many other methods.

After selecting the forms within the current project you want converted, you can select options for the conversion, including whether to comment out invalid code during the conversion and whether to remove the original forms after converting. The wizard can produce a summary report after the conversion is finished that provides further instructions on completing your application conversion and how to test your ActiveX documents.

The Data Form Wizard

If you want to build an application that accesses local or remote databases, the Data Form Wizard might be helpful to you. This wizard, which comes with the Professional and Enterprise Editions, creates forms that are data bound to a database you specify.

First, you select the database you want to access and choose the form type to create (single record, grid, or master/detail). If you select a remote database, you can also set the remote database connection parameters. You then define which tables and fields to include on the form. After you provide this information, the wizard does its magic and creates the form for you, including all appropriate data-bound controls.

Don't overlook this wizard if you work with databases. If you've built VB database applications before, you know how tedious it is to add individual controls, bind each one to a database, and add database-specific maintenance code (add, modify, delete, refresh, and so on). The wizard does this work for you. It adds standard code for the form, such as scaling datagrids and changing the mouse pointer to an hourglass as needed. Most likely, you'll change the form created by this wizard, but it creates a good base from which to work and definitely saves you time.

The Property Page Wizard

The Property Page Wizard (part of the Professional and Enterprise Editions) helps you create property pages for your own user controls. To use this wizard, you must have your own user control. The wizard uses your control to identify all the possible properties that can be set on your property pages. Although the wizard suggests standard property pages based on properties you include, you can override these values. The wizard suggests some standard pages based on common Windows guidelines that will make your control property pages consistent with others having the same properties. The Property Page Wizard asks you which properties to include and how they should be organized on the property pages. It then builds the property pages for you.

If you create your own controls, use this wizard. Developers using your controls will appreciate the ease with which they can use your property pages to set property values.

Setup Wizard Enhancements

The Setup Wizard and Setup Toolkits were included in prior VB versions, but these tools have been enhanced in several areas. Setup Toolkits come with all editions of Visual Basic. You can now do the following:

- **Create your own dependency files.** You can create your own dependency files for controls and applications. These dependency files identify what runtime modules are required for each component in your application.

- **Distribute your applications across the Internet.** Using ActiveX technology, you can distribute your applications across the Internet with automatic code-download features supported in Microsoft's Internet Explorer (version 3.0 or newer).

■ **Install remote components using remote automation.** You can also install remote components using the Enterprise Edition remote automation and the Distributed Component Object Model (DCOM). The Setup Wizard supports building both client and server setup programs.

■ **Use a setup directory structure for distribution on CD-ROM or a network.** You can copy setup programs to a network or CD-ROM using a standard disk directory install structure (disk1, disk2, and so on). You can then run setup from the network or CD-ROM without making disk media changes. Instead, the setup program looks through the SETUP launch path and finds the appropriate install directories.

The Setup Wizard is an easy, standardized way of creating distribution media for your applications. It automatically identifies components to include, recompiles your application for you if desired, compresses files, and builds the distribution software on the specified media. If the standard wizard options are not sufficient for your application, you can also modify the setup program itself.

The Wizard Manager

The Wizard Manager is a feature of the Professional and Enterprise Editions that helps you create your own wizards. It does this by building a basic wizard framework and managing the step-by-step screens of your wizard. You can add, edit, and delete steps. If you intend to include wizards in your applications, this is a great tool to use during development. One important benefit of using this tool is that your wizards maintain a consistent style with other Windows wizards.

The Class Builder Utility

Although it is not a wizard, the Class Builder Utility (provided with the Professional and Enterprise Editions) does make it easier to create classes and collections. This tool helps you build classes and collection hierarchies by generating base code and including the properties, events, and methods. You can base your classes on other existing classes or create new ones. The great benefit of this tool is that building object models is simpler, and you can finish all the steps within a single tool. The utility itself does a good job of showing your object model hierarchies and defined properties, events, and methods. It also generates all the base code for you and highlights the procedures where you need to add code specific to your object model. It even has the option of generating debugging code for initialize and terminate events and can include its own error-raising handlers for processing errors. You have many options for defining the scope or availability of your object to applications. You can create private classes and collections or global multiuse objects that anyone can create and use.

If you aren't familiar with classes and collections, take some time to learn about them. They can help your applications be more modular, enable you to reuse more components, and isolate code and data from your application that is needed within the object itself. These capabilities are some of the keys to object-oriented programming.

Templates Are for You

In addition to all the wizards, Visual Basic also includes many templates. *Templates* (available for all editions) are prebuilt functions you can individually add to your project that contain all the basic components needed to perform their job. For example, if you want to add an about box to your project, you can manually build one, or you can use the function-rich About Box forms template and then customize it for your application.

Dialogs common to many Windows applications require tedious efforts to build manually. By using templates, it is easy to include these dialogs in your project. In fact, many of the wizards (such as the Setup Wizard) use templates themselves. The Wizard Manager uses wizard templates to help you build your own wizards.

The biggest benefit of using templates is that you can save time creating the basic frameworks of functions and focus your efforts on the specifics of your own application. Templates include significant programming that you don't have to write. You can also be sure that your application's behavior is consistent with other Windows applications.

When you want to share components of your project with others to include in their own projects, you can create your own templates. You then place your templates in the appropriate directories so they are automatically shown in template dialogs and the Application Wizard.

Project Templates

Defining your project has two important parts. First, you must decide what type of project to create (standard EXE, ActiveX control or document EXEs and DLLs, add-ins, and so on). The type of project determines how your application will ultimately be used.

The second aspect of defining your project is selecting the interface style. You can have an SDI, MDI, or Explorer-style interface. If you don't specifically select an interface style through a wizard, you'll probably end up with an SDI application being used by default.

When creating new projects, either manually or through one of the wizards, you must choose your project's type. Rather than build your project interface from a blank starting form, project templates provide for you the base structure for the project type and interface. This is not only a timesaving feature but also helps you keep the overall presentation of your application consistent with other applications.

Forms Templates

Forms templates are useful when you add common Windows-type dialogs such as about boxes, splash screens, login dialogs, options dialogs, Internet browsers, tips of the day, or your own reusable forms.

These templates are functionally complete forms that you can customize for your specific application. For example, the about box is complete with controls and code in place. It even provides system information for you by launching the Sysinfo program via the Sysinfo control.

What you customize on the about box is the application name, version number, your logo, and any licensing information or disclaimers. You can also add other controls or remove those provided by the template. As its name implies, a template is a framework from which you can build and customize your own functions.

Class and Module Templates

When you want to add classes or collections to your project, you can manually build them by directly manipulating forms and code, you can use the Class Builder Utility, or you can use class module templates. This is an opportunity to reuse object models you want to share among multiple applications you create. There really is only one class module template provided with VB, and that is for add-ins.

Enriching Your Language Skills

Several new language enhancements were added to Visual Basic 5. Many of the enhancements increase capabilities for object-oriented development and enterprise development.

Some capabilities that severely limited prior VB versions but are now included are Windows callbacks. Supporting Windows callbacks means you can use the full spectrum of API calls and process responses asynchronously.

Several key language improvements include the capability to pass arrays as arguments, support for enumerate types, debugging support of asserts, drag-and-drop support within controls, improved data type handling, and the capability to declare, raise, and handle your own events. You'll find that not only did Microsoft spend significant effort improving the development environment, but it also made dramatic improvements to the Visual Basic language itself.

New Language Elements

Microsoft went to great lengths to add new language features for the Professional and Enterprise Editions, which are described here:

- **Enumerated types group constants.** You can create an enumerated type for grouping related named constants. This is useful for having a defined set of constants such as the days of the week and using them by name rather than by an integer-equivalent value. If you own the Visual Basic Enterprise Edition, you can also include enumerations in your own ActiveX component type libraries. They can then be shared by other developers using your components.

- **Optional arguments for procedures can be data typed.** In prior VB versions, optional arguments were declared as variant data types. You can now define the data type for optional arguments. This saves memory space, potentially improves performance based on calculations and comparison operations, and helps you catch erroneous data type conversions during debugging. You can use optional arguments in any procedure. You can set default values for optional arguments for cases where a value is not passed to the procedure.

■ **Property procedures support optional arguments.** Property procedures including Let and Get can have optional arguments.

■ **Asserts help debugging.** Asserts, used in other languages such as Visual C++ to aid debugging, are supported in Visual Basic 5. Asserts allow you to conditionally pause program execution at the statement where the assert method is located. This debug object method is useful to verify assumptions you make about values of variables or properties. Use the assert to check that the value falls within the expected range. If at any time it does not, the program enters break mode and highlights the assert statement where your assumption failed. This method only works in design mode and does not affect your application when run outside the development environment.

■ **Raise and handle your own events.** Your components' objects can raise events to be handled by other applications and can also handle events raised by your objects or other applications.

■ **New decimal data type is based on variant.** The variant data type handles decimals as 96-bit unsigned integers scaled by a power of 10, designating the number of digits to the right of the decimal. The number of digits to the right of the decimal can be from 0 to 28. The maximum value with no decimals to the right of the decimal point is +/-79,228,162,514,264,337,593,543,950,335. With the maximum 28 decimals places, the largest value is +/-7.9228162514264337593543950335, and the smallest value is +/-0.0000000000000000000000000001.

■ **Class modules can have default properties.** When creating your own controls, you can specify a property or method as the default. There can be only one property or method as the default for a control. The default property is equivalent to the old value property.

■ **Get and Put file operations support arrays.** You can use arrays for the Get and Put file I/O operations.

■ **Calendar property.** The calendar property lets you specify (SET) or retrieve (GET) the type of calendar: Gregorian (the default) or Hijri (the Islamic calendar based purely on lunar cycles). This property is an enumerated list that is part of the Visual Basic for Applications (VBA) object library.

Windows Callbacks Are Here

One of the limitations of prior VB versions was that you could not use the full spectrum of Windows or DLL functions that required callbacks. *Callbacks* are messages resulting from initial function calls that are asynchronous, meaning that the messages sent to you don't necessarily come in direct response to the initial request. You may receive multiple messages at a later time, and you don't want to wait for those messages. The Professional and Enterprise Editions of Visual Basic now support these callbacks by providing the AddressOf keyword, which you place in front of your callback function's name in the initial calling argument list.

Using this new feature provides great opportunities for using all the Windows functions along with any of your own DLL callbacks, but it also introduces some risks of which you need to be aware. Debugging becomes more complicated when using callbacks in VB because even while in break mode, you might get callbacks from DLL functions. These callbacks will be handled and will ignore any breakpoints you set. Also, you cannot reset your program while a callback function is on the stack. You need to exit the application and restart. If you edit or delete a callback function while it is active, you might get unpredictable termination of your application if a callback is received. If you use callbacks, save your work often just in case you experience callback errors. Thoroughly understand the use of callbacks before jumping in, and you'll save yourself many headaches while enjoying their benefits.

Easy Drag and Drop

One of the great new features provided with all editions of Visual Basic 5 is that most controls support drag-and-drop operations between OLE applications. This feature lets you do things such as dragging text or graphics from one control to another or from a control to another OLE application. You can also drag and drop from other applications to yours.

There are different levels of drag-and-drop support within controls. Although some controls support fully automatic drag-and-drop operations (most of the controls provided with the Professional and Enterprise editions), others support only manual drag-and-drop operations requiring your own code. You can find out if a control you want to use supports automatic drag and drop by looking for the `OLEDragMode` and `OLEDropMode` properties. If the `OLEDragMode` property doesn't exist but the control does have an `OLEDrag` method, it can support OLE dragging, but only through manual support of your code. Some controls support dragging but not dropping.

Many new properties, events, and methods support drag and drop. They are easy to use and implement and make your applications more complete, particularly for mouse users.

New Forms Properties

Several new forms properties were added for all VB editions:

■ **`Palette` and `PaletteMode` properties give more control over color.** Better control and performance along with backward compatibility are provided by two new palette properties. The new `Palette` property lets you set what palette to use for a control or object based on a provided image. The `PaletteMode` property lets you select which palette to reference based on several options: Use the halftone palette, use the palette from the top owning control or object having a palette, use the palette specified by the `Palette` property, use the container's palette for user controls supporting the ambient `Palette` property, use no palette (for user controls only), or use the ActiveX designer's palette.

■ **`StartUpPosition` property controls forms positioning when loaded.** The `StartUpPosition` property applies to forms and lets you set where on the screen the form displays based on the following choices: no setting, center form within parent window, center form on screen, or position form at the top-left corner of the screen.

New Graphics Formats

If you've worked with images in Visual Basic, you were probably frustrated that it didn't support more image formats. BMP files were just too big and bulky to load but were the only realistic choice at times because of the limited image format choices available. Not only do the large BMP files take a long time to load, but they also take up a great deal of memory while loaded. With all editions of Visual Basic 5, you can use GIF and JPG images with the picture and image controls and also with the picture object. These formats are much more efficient than BMP files. Sometimes these files can be 1/10 or less the size of the equivalent BMP file. With smaller sized images, load time is shorter and memory usage is smaller. This is good stuff!

Tooltips Text in All Controls

The ToolTipsText property exists for all controls. It sets or returns a string containing the text that displays when the user's mouse is placed over a control.

An Easier Job with New Controls

In addition to enjoying the enhancements to existing controls such as OLE drag and drop, new graphics file formats, and tooltip text for all controls, you can also create your own ActiveX controls (using the VB Professional and Enterprise Editions). You can combine existing controls or create your own directly within the VB development environment. Your controls can have properties, events, methods, data binding, built-in licensing, property pages for setting options, and Internet capabilities. This is just scratching the surface. In addition to making existing controls richer and creating your own controls in VB, you'll want to explore six new controls.

Spicing Up Applications with the Animation Control

If you want to add neat animations such as those in the Windows copy and move dialogs that show files flying between folders, the animation control is for you. It lets you play silent video (AVI) files that run as separate threads so they don't directly impact functions you perform in your application. The video files must not contain audio, or you will receive an error from the control.

Data Comes Alive with the MSChart Control

The MSChart control provides graphical representations of data contained within a data grid. Based on the data and labels contained within the data grid, the chart control can build all major chart types, including three-dimensional charts. The charts are fully customizable, even down to the backdrop or axis walls and floor colors.

Getting Tabular with the `MSFlexGrid` Control

The `MSFlexGrid` control is a step up from the old grid control. It displays tabular data including both strings and pictures and lets you format, merge, and sort cells. The control can be bound to a database for read-only display.

Speaking Internet Protocol Using the Internet Transfer Control

The Internet transfer control connects to the Internet using a method you specify and downloads files based on either the Hypertext Transfer Protocol (HTTP), File Transfer Protocol (FTP), or Gopher. The control can be useful in many ways, such as providing automatic file downloads from public FTP sites, parsing Web page contents and building your own dynamic displays, and adding FTP browsing capabilities to your applications.

The Updown Control: Sticking with Your Buddy

The updown control is a big advancement over the old spin control. It performs the standard function of incrementing or decrementing values as in its old form, but there's more. The great part of this new control is its built-in buddy features that allow you to directly associate a buddy control and its properties with the updown control. You can explicitly assign a buddy or allow the control to use tab order to select its own buddy. Not only can you tell the updown control which buddy property to use, but you can also use its alignment properties to define how the control aligns itself with its buddy. The control has many flexible features and is worth exploring.

Getting Connected Using the WinSock Control

When needing to connect to remote machines and exchange data using the User Datagram Protocol (UDP) or the Transmission Control Protocol (TCP), use the WinSock control. If you've dabbled in this area before, you know that programming directly to the Windows sockets APIs is cumbersome and fraught with errors due to customization of the sockets' DLLs by various vendors. The WinSock control makes it easier to program your own connection-management tools. You can use this control for creating both the client and server components of your application.

The Custom Web Browser and Internet Explorer Object

The Application Wizard allows you to add a custom browser to your application. The custom browser provides very basic browser features but lets you programmatically control its access of Web sites on the Internet. This browser is based on the Internet Explorer 3.0 program, which installs the HTML control needed for the browser's Internet connectivity. Internet Explorer must be installed on your machine in order to be included in the Application Wizard interview.

If you have Internet Explorer installed on your machine, you can also use the `InternetExplorer` object, which lets you create and control an instance of Internet Explorer itself.

Advanced Programming Topics

The previous sections summarize new features and enhancements of Visual Basic 5 that affect everyday development and more commonly used VB components.

This section highlights new features and enhancements relating to more complex topics, such as

- Customizing VB's IDE using the extensibility model
- Object-oriented programming enhancements
- Implementing Internet and ActiveX features
- Using database tools and objects
- Debugging and performance tools and techniques
- Building software distribution programs
- Creating interactive help
- Implementing Enterprise Edition tools and methods
- Using the repository
- Working with Visual Sourcesafe

Making the IDE Work the Way You Do

In addition to all the great new features in Visual Basic, which provide overwhelming opportunities for enriching your applications, Microsoft's Visual Basic extensibility model offers the capability to fully extend and customize VB's IDE for the Professional and Enterprise Editions. You can customize the environment in two ways: by manually setting options or programmatically controlling the environment using extensibility model objects. Using the extensibility model lets you control virtually all aspects of the development environment. Adding to the environment is easy with enhanced add-in features, flexible add-in registration, component management using the new repository, and adding your own wizards. There is a lot to learn when you take on the extensibility model, but if you find that the development environment just doesn't handle working the way you do, it is well worth your effort to check it out.

Easy Object-Oriented Development

For years, object-oriented programming (OOP) tools and methods were available only for programming languages like C++. Then with Visual Basic 4 came the basic groundwork for objects in the way of classes. With Visual Basic 5, more complete tools and methods bring Visual Basic object-oriented programming to a new level. Not only has the whole foundation of Visual Basic moved to an object basis, but also the typical characteristics of object-oriented components are supported.

Polymorphism Supported by the `Implements` Method

Polymorphism, an important element of object-oriented programming, is supported in all Visual Basic editions through the use of the `Implements` method. This method provides early binding of interfaces at compile time without specifying the implementing object. *Early binding* is when you specify interfaces (including properties, methods, and events) for compiler resolution without identifying the actual object in code that implements the characteristics defined by the interface. Although using the `Implements` method is available in all editions, creating new interfaces that you can refer to with the `Implements` method requires the Professional or Enterprise Edition.

Communicating with Your Friend

Just as procedures can be `public` or `private`, they can also be `Friend`. `Friend` functions (provided in all editions) allow internal component communication, sharing information within the component's own objects while not giving access to that information externally. Because a `Friend` procedure isn't part of the component's interface (properties, events, or procedures), applications using the component don't have access to it. To use `Friend` members, you must early-bind variables at compile time. `Friend` members are particularly useful for passing user-defined types between objects.

Sharing Your Components as Global Objects

As you build your own classes (using the Professional and Enterprise Editions), you can designate the instancing property as `GlobalMultiUse`. Doing so tells Visual Basic to add your class to a project's global name space when first referenced in that project. This property value is different from the normal `MultiUse` property because `GlobalMultiUse` does not require explicit declaration in code as does `MultiUse`. `GlobalMultiUse` creates a separate instance of the class for each user. If you use the `GlobalSingleUse` property instead, it still has the benefits of being global but creates one shared instance for all user applications.

Global objects are displayed in the Globals section of the Object Browser.

Specifying Default Class Properties

You can designate a property or method as the default property for your class or control. The designated property or method is invoked when operations are performed using an instance of your object and when the object doesn't contain an explicit value or reference to a property or method.

Creating Unattended Mode Operations

When your ActiveX objects have no user interaction, you can use a special Unattended Execution mode that suppresses message boxes and dialogs (even those from the operating system).

Unattended operations can run locally or on remote computers and require no user intervention. Log files can record any system messages. This feature can be particularly useful for enterprise applications where you might want to perform automatic software updates for all the client workstations. If you are creating applications for LAN administrators, this can be a handy feature for you. Unattended mode features are available with the Professional and Enterprise Editions.

Debugging Classes with Error Handlers

You can step directly into your error handler when an error occurs by pressing Alt+F8 from break mode. To do this, you must have debugging options set to either Break On All Errors or Break in Class Module. If there is no error handler in the current procedure where the error occurred, Alt+F8 raises the error in the calling procedure. If you prefer to run the error handler rather than step into it, you can press Alt+F5 instead.

For...Each with Collection Classes

If you add a hidden NewEnum method containing the correct procedure ID, your collection classes will work with the For...Each operation. For...Each is a looping method for repeating groups of statements—in this case, for each element in a collection.

Energizing Your Applications with ActiveX

Besides being a buzzword thrown around by marketing types to attract your attention, ActiveX is actually an important component model for your applications. Once known as OLE, ActiveX takes object development a step further by allowing your objects to be Internet aware. Your objects may be documents, executables, resources such as databases and local language translation objects, and controls used to encapsulate functions in a tight, modular way.

Building Your Own ActiveX Controls

Create your own ActiveX controls, use existing ones, or subclass existing ones to create your own custom variations. Prior to VB 5, you had to build controls using a development language such as Visual C++. Now, you can do it all without leaving the comfort of VB's Professional or Enterprise Edition development environment. Your controls can have

- Properties
- Events
- Methods
- Data binding with local or remote databases
- Property pages
- Licensing support
- Internet support, including connection and transfer functions

Special features include asynchronous download of data and also hyperlinking. *Asynchronous download* means you can retrieve files, images, or other data directly through your controls.

ActiveX Control Interface Wizard Makes Control Building Easy

It's hard to imagine making ActiveX control building any easier than using the ActiveX Control Interface Wizard. After building the basis (forms) of your control, this wizard helps you tie it all together by associating properties, methods, and events with the functions of the control itself.

Creating ActiveX Documents

At first, ActiveX documents may seem a bit complicated to understand as a concept. ActiveX documents are more than a document that you use in a word processor; they are actually applications that tightly integrate with your Internet or intranet browser or other container application. They require a container application such as a browser in which they can operate. They are simple to create using standard VB forms.

Just like parts of HTML pages, ActiveX documents can be automatically downloaded or upgraded when a user accesses or navigates to them. They can have a user interface that looks like its own application and not just a document. They can incorporate hyperlink object properties and methods that let users jump to specific URLs or navigate through the history list. ActiveX documents also negotiate menus with their container application. This is the capability to merge menus that are part of the ActiveX document application with the menus of their host application. Finally, you can maintain or persist data using the `PropertyBag` object in Internet Explorer.

The bottom line is that ActiveX documents let you interact with the Internet using rich functional interfaces that can include forms, message boxes, ActiveX controls, and your specialized code functions.

Adding Hyperlinking Functions Using the `Hyperlink` Object

Add ActiveX hyperlinking functions to your controls using the `Hyperlink` object. This object lets your ActiveX document application request its container to jump to a specific URL or to navigate through the history list.

Debugging ActiveX DLLs in Process

You can step directly into your ActiveX DLLs during debugging. The DLLs you create in VB can be debugged in the VB environment at the same time as the calling application (standard EXE). This is because VB supports loading multiple projects into the development environment simultaneously.

Modeless Forms in ActiveX DLLs

Client applications can show modeless forms or dialogs contained within in-process components formerly known as OLE DLLs.

New Tools and Techniques for Database Development

Data-access capabilities in Visual Basic 5 were greatly enhanced with new extensions to the Data Access Objects (DAO) and Remote Data Objects (RDO) models. Of particular note is the new event-driven data access methodology that will change the way you work with your databases. The event-driven concept lets you make database requests and asynchronously receive status or completion through events.

See the section "Enterprise Edition Specific Enhancements" later in this chapter for details about new RDO database features available only in the Visual Basic Enterprise Edition.

ODBCDirect Gives Direct Access Using Minimal Resources

You can more efficiently access server data by using ODBCDirect. ODBCDirect uses the DAO object model on top of the ODBC API to establish connections, create cursors, and execute complicated requests. The ODBCDirect mode does not require using the JET database engine. This was accomplished by adding a `DefaultType` property to the DBEngine and by adding a new `Connection` object. ODBCDirect also allows DAO to use RDO. The primary benefits of using ODBCDirect are

- Direct data access with the server handling query processing
- Minimum client resources because the JET database engine is not loaded
- Use of server-specific functions prohibited by the JET database engine
- Asynchronous queries, which allow your application to perform other operations without waiting for the query request to finish
- Batch optimistic update lets you hold `Recordset` changes locally and then submit them in batches to the server

The DAO/JET Architecture Is Segmented to Improve Resource Management

By segmenting DAO/JET objects used most often from less frequently used objects, unnecessary loading of objects is reduced. This means that your application won't load architectural components that it doesn't need. Specifically, the `DBEngine`, `Workspace`, `Connection`, `Recordset`, `QueryDef`, `Parameter`, and `Field` objects are separated from other objects less frequently used.

The DAO Triggers Trappable Errors

Within the DAO object model, you cannot use features with objects that don't support them. For example, if you attempt to use a method with an object that doesn't support that method, a trappable error is triggered.

Partial Replication Supports Testing Relations

A new property in the JET workspace, `PartialReplica`, sets or returns a `Relation` object value telling you whether that relation should affect creation of a partial replica from a full replica.

By the way, there is a Replication Manager application you can use within Visual Basic if you've installed Microsoft Access. This tool lets you create and maintain replica databases. The DAO object supports most of the methods and properties provided in the Replication Manager utility if you don't have Microsoft Access.

Searching Forward-Only Recordset Object

You can choose to perform Recordset searches in a forward direction only. This is useful for quickly searching a Recordset from its beginning to end without moving backward. While performing forward-only searches, only one row is accessible at a time.

Setting the Maximum Number of Records Returned in a Query

When using ODBC databases, you can specify the maximum number of rows or records to return for a query by using the MaxRecords property. When the number of records specified by MaxRecords is reached, no additional records are returned for the requested query. This new property can be useful when you have limited memory for handling queries, but you must be careful because limiting the number of returned records might result in useful data not being returned.

The SetOption Method Overrides JET Registry Settings

Default Registry settings for the JET database engine can be temporarily overridden. You can change settings such as the page timeout, shared and exclusive asynchronous delays, user and implicit commit sync keys, maximum buffer size, flush buffer transaction timeout, and other values. The runtime settings stay in effect until either you change them again or the DBEngine is closed. It is unlikely that you will use this new feature; however, you might find specific situations while working with databases when you want to adjust the settings. Note that changing these Registry settings can affect other applications that might use the JET database engine that your users launch while yours is still running.

Data Binding Links Your Controls to Databases

The Data Bindings collection lets you bind or connect properties of an ActiveX user control to database fields. You can bind more than one property of a control to database fields. Specifically, this means that when you build your own ActiveX controls, you can build in the support for connecting to your local or remote databases and manipulating database information in whatever way you choose.

The Visual Data Manager

The Visual Data Manager is an add-in tool that demonstrates all the DAO methods and is also a useful application. You can create new databases, manage existing ones, perform SQL queries, and even use the Data Form Designer within this tool to create VB forms based on your database definition. Another neat feature of the Visual Data Manager is its global replace function. At times, this can be very useful. Besides providing useful functions, the complete source project is provided and serves as a great program reference for performing virtually all the DAO functions.

The Setup Wizard and Internet Downloads

In addition to creating standard setup programs for your applications, VB 5 adds the capability to package your applications for Internet download using the Professional or Enterprise Editions. Your application must be an ActiveX control, EXE, or DLL to be packaged for Internet download. The Setup Wizard creates cabinet files that can be downloaded and installed from a browser. Unlike prior setup programs, the Internet download only transfers and installs the component files that do not already exist on the user's system. This new feature is particularly useful for minimizing download times for setup programs that contain all the VB runtime modules associated with your application.

Enterprise Edition–Specific Enhancements

The Visual Basic Enterprise Edition offers many features beyond the Standard and Professional editions. Primarily, its focus is on enterprise and distributed applications. It does, however, include tools such as Visual Sourcesafe that no serious developer should be without even if you never create enterprise applications. You'll see in this section that a great deal of work and emphasis was placed on extending Visual Basic as a viable tool for creating applications usable by small workgroups, company-wide enterprises, and remote access.

Migration to COM in a Distributed Environment

The Component Object Model (COM) supports distributed components. Rather than use the remote automation tools usable for 16-bit environments, 32-bit applications can directly use the Component Object Model. The COM is really the replacement for OLE and now allows you to access remote components.

Distributed Application Configuration Utilities for Network Interactivity

Tools included with the Enterprise Edition help you set up and register your ActiveX components to work across the network. These tools allow you to encapsulate application functions into ActiveX components, which can be distributed locally or across the network.

Multithreaded and Thread-Safe ActiveX Components

Multithreaded and thread-safe ActiveX features allow you to build multithreaded ActiveX components that can be used for unattended execution, meaning that no user interface and no user interaction is required. Object instances can be allocated across multiple threads for more reliable and efficient operation.

Optimizing with the Application Performance Explorer

The Application Performance Explorer is really several tools in one. It provides the capability to fine-tune your client/server applications by helping with design and performance optimization of your application. You can even create "what if" tests to verify performance based on possible network configuration scenarios.

The source project that is included is an excellent example of a distributed application. You can use this example as a template for your own distributed applications.

Enhanced Database Development Using RDO and DAO

The enhanced Remote Data Object and Remote Data Control support local cursors, query objects, standalone connections, and optimistic batch updates. The Connection Designer helps you create freestanding connection objects containing your own queries and stored procedures. There are additional asynchronous operation options allowing query responses as events. Components can be marked for background processing so they'll run asynchronously on remote computers. You can create queries as methods and utilize stored procedure parameter management. Finally, you can debug SQL transaction statements directly within Visual Basic.

Repository Magic

The repository is a new tool in Visual Basic that gives you the capability to manage information about your project. The `Repository` object lets you save, organize, search, and retrieve data from your projects. Using the `Extensibility` object and APIs, you can add full repository access programmatically. You can also create new object models for managing software tools.

Visual Sourcesafe: Control Your Software

Although you can buy Sourcesafe separately, this important product is included with the Visual Basic Enterprise Edition. If you are a serious developer creating real applications, you need this tool to help control your software. Visual Sourcesafe is like a library for your software: You can check projects and components in and out. It manages versioning and histories of iterative changes you've made to your applications. This is not a new product, but several important enhancements were made:

- **Archival.** You can archive unneeded parts of your software database for better efficiency.

- **Web management.** For users managing HTML and Internet-related files, Sourcesafe can create site maps and help move components to Web servers.

- **Merging changes.** When a file is checked in that was updated by multiple people at the same time, Sourcesafe provides a visual merge window to help you merge changes and resolve conflicts. This not only applies to files, but you can manipulate project differences as well by moving files from one place to another.

- **Cloaking.** Cloaking lets you hide projects so they can't be affected by certain operations.

■ **Direct file editing.** By double-clicking a file listed in the Sourcesafe Explorer, you can activate the file for editing without switching back to your development environment and manually loading the file.

Summary

As you can see, Visual Basic 5 is a substantial upgrade that offers many new tools for both the novice and the expert developer. The wizards give you a jump start on adding features to your applications that were not available in prior versions of Visual Basic. The improvements to the development environment itself make it easier to fine-tune and debug your projects. Object-oriented enhancements such as support for polymorphism and the Friend functions allow you to take advantage of object-oriented programming concepts. These, along with Windows call-backs and native mode code compilation, remove the limitations that kept Visual Basic from truly being a suitable option for real product development in prior VB versions.

ActiveX enhancements and support for Internet integration and distributed Internet setup are key components you'll use in your applications.

Visual Basic has come to the point of being an easy-to-learn and easy-to-use development tool that you can use to create commercially viable applications. If you are already doing VB development but haven't yet purchased a copy of VB 5, do it now. It is well worth your money. If you haven't before done Windows development but are ready to jump in, there is no better way to learn Windows programming than by starting with Visual Basic.

CHAPTER 2

Conquering the Integrated Development Environment

by Rick Ladymon

IN THIS CHAPTER

The Integrated Development Environment (IDE) of Visual Basic (VB) 5.0 was completely redesigned from previous versions of Visual Basic. Those readers who are familiar with Visual Basic 4.0 will be quite surprised when they first see VB 5.0. The IDE of VB 5.0 is one complete window that contains all the tools needed for developing VB projects. This arrangement is completely different from the VB 4.0 IDE, in which each window acts independently of each other.

Figure 2.1 shows an example of the new screen layout of VB 5.0 when the user selects the Standard EXE option when first starting Visual Basic.

FIGURE 2.1.

The Visual Basic Integrated Development Environment window.

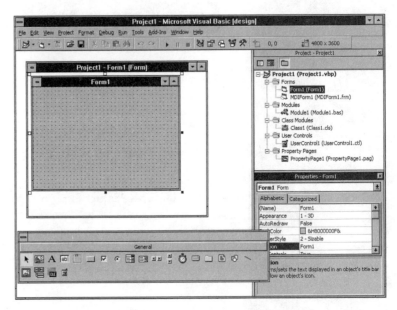

The main window of VB 5.0 contains several other windows that aid in creating and managing projects; I describe and explain these windows in this chapter. This chapter is designed to provide an overview of the IDE, not to be a complete guide to everything that you can do in Visual Basic 5.0. I explain the following windows and tools in this chapter:

Project Explorer window

Properties window

Code and Form windows

Form Layout window

Debug windows

Toolbox window

Toolbar windows

Color palette

IDE Menus

Getting Help

The Project Explorer Window

The Project Explorer window is the window you use to manage the files for any given project. The window is displayed in the upper-right corner of the main working area of VB 5.0, and it displays all the forms, modules, user controls, and property pages that are currently included in the project. (Refer to Figure 2.1.) This window provides an easy way to navigate through the project objects. One important improvement in Visual Basic 5.0 is that you can work on multiple projects at the same time.

The Project Explorer Window Layout

The three icons in the upper-left corner of the Project Explorer window are the View Code icon, the View Object icon, and the Toggle Folders icon. Clicking the View Code icon displays the code in the Code window for the highlighted object, and clicking the View Object icon displays the form associated with the object in the Form window. The View Object icon is available only to those objects that have forms associated with them.

The Project Explorer window defaults to the folder tree view (shown in Figure 2.1), which displays all the objects contained in the current project in tree view. The name of the project is followed by the Forms folder, the Modules folder, the Class Modules folder, the User Controls folder, and the Property Pages folder. Each folder contains a list of all the appropriate objects contained in the project, in alphabetical order.

You can change the view by clicking the Toggle Folders icon on the toolbar of the Project Explorer window. Clicking this icon toggles the view from a folder view to a list of all the objects in alphabetical order regardless of their type.

One of the major differences between Visual Basic 5.0 and earlier releases is that the name of the form or module is displayed first, followed by the name of the file saved on disk in parentheses. Visual Basic 4.0 displayed these two names in the reverse order. As the developer, you have the option to name the modules differently from how they are saved. I have found that when working on large projects with multiple people, it is better to keep the two names the same to avoid confusion when trying to track down bugs. You can change the names of the forms and modules by using the Properties window (Name property). You can change the names of the saved files for the forms and modules when you save the project or the file. If you create or add a new form or module, Visual Basic prompts you for the name of the file when you save the project or file.

2

THE INTEGRATED
DEVELOPMENT
ENVIRONMENT

I want to mention one last thing about the Project Explorer window. When you right-click one of the forms or modules in a project, you see a pop-up menu like the one in Figure 2.2.

FIGURE 2.2.

The Project Explorer window's pop-up menu.

This pop-up menu contains the following shortcuts

- Choosing View Code is the same thing as clicking the View Code button at the top of the Project Explorer window. It automatically sends you to the Code window and shows the code of the selected form or module.
- Selecting View Object is the same thing as clicking the View Object button at the top of the Project Explorer window. It automatically sends you to the Form window and shows the selected form. If the object you clicked does not contain a form, you do not see this option.
- Choosing Properties automatically sets focus to the Properties window and shows the properties of the selected form or module. This option can be useful if you do not currently have the Properties window open because it automatically opens the Properties window, sets focus to it, and fills it with the information about the selected object.
- Selecting Add displays the types of forms, modules, and objects that you can add to the project: Form, MDI Form, Module, Class Module, User Control, Property Page, User Document, Active X Designer, and Add File. Selecting the Add File option opens the Add File dialog, which allows you to select which file you want to add to the project from one of the connected disk drives.
- Selecting Save *form/module name* automatically saves the selected object to disk. If you have not previously saved the object, the Save As dialog opens to allow you to name the file.
- Selecting Save *form/module name* As opens the Save File As dialog, which allows you to name the file and choose where you want to save it.
- Selecting Print opens the Print dialog, which allows you to print the selected code of the form or module.
- Selecting Dockable toggles the capability to dock the active window. A window is docked when it is attached or "anchored" to one edge of the screen, application

window, or another dockable window. When you move a dockable window, it snaps to the location. A window is not dockable when you can move it anywhere on the screen and leave it there.

■ Selecting Hide hides the Project Explorer window.

The Properties Window

You use the Properties window to display all the properties you can set at design time for any given form or control. It is displayed on the right side of the screen; by default, it is displayed under the Project Explorer window. You can size this window according to your preferences.

The Properties window contains several components. The title bar contains the word Properties followed by the name of the current form or control. Below the title bar is a drop-down combobox that shows all the objects on the form with the name of the current object displayed in the text portion of the combobox. You can easily navigate to an object by clicking the down arrow of the combobox and selecting the object you want.

Below the Objects combobox are two tab groups that display the properties for the selected object. The first tab group, Alphabetic, displays all the properties of the object in alphabetical order. The second tab group, Categorized, displays all the properties of the object by category. This second tab group is useful for locating certain types of actions you might want to perform, such as positioning the object.

Below the tab groups is a dynamic textbox that displays help on a selected property. To receive help on a given property, click one of the properties.

To show the properties for any given control on a form, click the control. The Properties window reflects the properties that you can set at design time for that control. This provides an easy way to modify the properties for the control. Figure 2.1 shows an example of a newly created form that has no controls associated with it yet.

The Properties window allows you to change the properties for a control at design time. Some properties of controls are available only at runtime. The difference between design time and runtime is quite simple. If you can change the properties using the Properties window, you are changing it at design time. If you have to write code in a subroutine or function in the code window, you are modifying the property at runtime. You can press the F1 key to get detailed help on any property of a control. The help available in VB 5.0 is very extensive, and it will tell you if properties are available only at design time or runtime or both.

Visual Basic has many types of properties associated with all kinds of controls; I cannot describe them all in this chapter. You should review and experiment with the properties that are provided with each type of form and control you want to use.

2

THE INTEGRATED
DEVELOPMENT
ENVIRONMENT

The Code and Form Windows

The Code window on the left side of the screen displays the code associated with the current form or module. The Code window is very important because you use it to add and modify the code for all the objects that are part of the project. Without the Code window, you would not be able to write code for your controls. Some controls, especially pushbuttons, need to have code written for them when they are clicked. The Code window is designed to give programmers an easy-to-use way of adding and modifying code for their controls. Figure 2.3 shows an example of the Code window.

FIGURE 2.3.

The Code window.

The Code window contains several components. The Object drop-down combobox is displayed in the upper-left corner of the Code window. This combobox contains all the objects on the form for which the code can be modified. The first object listed is the (General) objects group, which contains all the code that is not part of a given control on a form, such as a pushbutton. If you view the code for a module, the (General) objects group is the only object available for selection because modules do not have forms. If you view the code for a form, at least one other object is listed in the Objects combobox—the name of the current form.

The Code window contains one other drop-down combobox, the Procedure combobox, which is displayed in the upper-right corner. This combobox contains all the procedures associated with the selected object in the Object combobox. If the (General) object is selected, the first procedure listed in the Procedure combobox is the (Declarations) procedure. The Declarations procedure section of a form contains all the variables that were defined as global to that module or form. When the (General) object is selected, the Procedure combobox contains all the user-defined subs and functions that are part of the current module or form. If you select a control object, such as a pushbutton, in the Object combobox, the Procedure combobox contains all the events associated with the selected control object. The first event with added code is displayed in the Code window. Any event that contains code is displayed in bold so you can easily tell which events have code in them.

The main function of the Code window is to allow you to add and modify the code for a form or module. The code section of the Code window is displayed below the Object and Procedure comboboxes, and it contains vertical and horizontal scrollbars to allow you to view the code more easily. It also has two pushbutton icons in the lower-left corner that change the view of the code from Procedure view (the left pushbutton icon) to Full Form view (the right pushbutton icon). When you are viewing code in Procedure view, you will see only the code that is part of the procedure. When you are viewing code in Full Form view, you will see code for the procedure, plus any other code that can be displayed on the screen that will fit into the Code window. These procedures will be separated by underlines so you can tell when one procedure ends and another begins.

The Form Window

The Form window is displayed whenever you click the View Object button of the Project Explorer window with a form selected. The Form window allows you to easily add, modify, or remove controls on your forms. Figure 2.1 shows an example of the Form window with some sample controls.

The form inside the Form window represents the way the form appears onscreen. You can modify the controls on the form by clicking an object and then performing an action, such as dragging it to a new location or changing the size by dragging the edges. When you double-click an object, the code for that object is automatically displayed in the Code window for that form. The Properties window automatically reflects the properties associated with the selected control.

You can copy the control to the Clipboard by selecting the control, selecting the Edit pull-down menu, and then selecting either Cut (Ctrl+X) or Copy (Ctrl+C). You can then paste the control to another form by selecting the Paste option from the Edit pull-down menu or by pressing Ctrl+V. You can move objects from one form to another quite easily this way.

The Form Layout Window

The Form Layout window is new to Visual Basic 5.0, and is designed to give you more control over the screen positioning of forms. The Form Layout window is displayed on the right side of the screen; its default position is below the Properties window.

The Form Layout window gives you the ability to easily control the position of forms onscreen. An icon representing a computer screen is shown in the main portion of the Form Layout window. You can select which form you want to move by clicking the form with the left mouse button; by holding the button down, you can move the form wherever you want onscreen. You can also click the form with the right mouse button to open the Form Layout window's menu. You can explore the help available on the Form Layout window to get more information about how to move your forms.

The Debug Windows

You use the three different Debug windows—Immediate, Locals, and Watch—to debug the code for your projects. The Immediate window gives you the ability to print or modify the value of a given variable. The Locals window shows all the local variables for a given procedure. The Watch window lets you set which variables you want to watch. Figure 2.4 shows examples of the Debug windows.

FIGURE 2.4.

Two of the Debug windows.

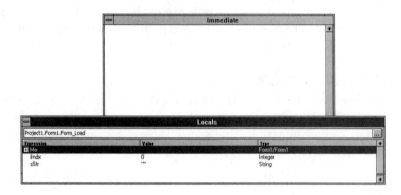

The Immediate Debug Window Layout

The Immediate Debug window automatically opens empty in break mode. The break mode in Visual Basic is the temporary suspension of code execution in the development environment. A powerful tool, break mode lets you examine and reset variables and continue program execution. Whenever the program is in break mode, you have access to the Immediate window, and a statement is executed in the context or scope that is displayed in the Procedure box.

From the Immediate Debug window, you can type or paste a line of code and press Enter to run it. You can also copy and paste the code from the Immediate window into the Code window, but you cannot save code in the Immediate window. You can position this window anywhere on your screen unless you make it a dockable window from the Docking tab of the Options dialog box.

The Locals Debug Window

The Locals Debug window automatically displays all the declared variables and their values in the current procedure. When the Locals window is visible, it is automatically updated every time there is a change from run to break mode or you navigate in the stack display.

The first component of the Locals Debug window is the Calls Stack textbox and pushbutton displayed below the Local Debug window's title bar. The text displayed in this window shows the current procedure that is executing; if the project is in run mode, you see <Running>. The Calls Stack pushbutton opens the Calls Stack dialog box, which lists the procedures in the calls stack. You can use this window to go backward through the calls stack and set breakpoints to aid in project debugging.

Below the Calls Stack textbox and pushbutton are the column headers Expression, Value, and Type. When you view the Locals Debug window, you can resize the column headers by dragging the border to the right or the left. The Expression column lists all the variables that are local to the current procedure. The first variable in the list is a special module variable that can be expanded to display all module-level variables in the current module. For a class module, the system variable Me is defined. For standard modules, the first variable is the name of the current module. Global variables and variables in other projects are not accessible from the Locals window. You cannot edit the data in this column because the variables were defined before the project was run.

The Value column displays the value of the expression. When you click a value in the Value column, the cursor changes to an I-beam. You can edit a value and then press Enter, the up arrow, the down arrow, Tab, or Shift+Tab or click the screen to validate the change. If the value is illegal, the Edit field remains active, and the value is highlighted. You also see a message box describing the error. You cancel a change by pressing Esc. All numeric variables must have a value listed because by default, a numeric variable must be something. (String variables can have an empty value list.) You can expand and collapse variables that contain subvariables, such as a user-defined type. Collapsed variables do not display a value, but each subvariable does. The expand and collapse icons appear to the left of the variable.

You cannot edit data in the Type column, which displays the variable type.

The Watch Debug Window

The Watch Debug window displays all the variables that have a watch set on them. It contains a listbox with the column headers Expression, Value, Type, and Context. You can change the size of the column headers by dragging the border to the right or left. You can also drag a selected variable to the Immediate window.

The Expression column displays the watch expression with the Watch icon on the left. The Value column displays the value of the expression at the time of the transition to break mode. You can edit a value and then press Enter, the up arrow, the down arrow, Tab, or Shift+Tab or click somewhere on the screen to validate the change. If the value is illegal, the Edit field remains active, and the value is highlighted. You also see a message box describing the error. Cancel a change by pressing Esc. The Type column displays the type of the element, such as integer. The Context column displays the context of the watch expression. If the context of the expression isn't in scope when going to break mode, the current value isn't displayed.

The Toolbox Window

The Toolbox window contains all the controls, both standard and custom, that are included in the project. The Toolbox window automatically displays whenever you open a project in design mode. Figure 2.1 shows an example of the Toolbox window. This window is not visible in run mode.

The Toolbox window contains the standard toolbox controls that come with Visual Basic 5.0:

■ The Pointer icon is the only item in the toolbox that doesn't draw a control. When you select the pointer, you can only resize or move a control that is already on a form. The pointer icon also allows you to click a control object and thereby display the properties for that control in the Properties window. You can also double-click on a control to bring up the Code window to display the code that has been written for the control.

■ The Picture Box icon displays a graphical image (either decorative or active) as a container that receives output from graphics methods or as a container for other controls.

■ The Label icon allows you to create a control that displays text you don't want the user to change, such as a caption under a graphic.

■ The Textbox icon allows you to create a control that holds text the user can either enter or change.

■ The Frame icon creates a control so you can create a graphical or functional grouping for controls. To group controls, draw the frame first and then draw controls inside the frame.

■ The Command Button icon creates a button the user can choose to execute a command.

■ The Checkbox icon creates a checkbox that displays multiple choices when the user can choose more than one.

■ The Option Button icon (also known as a radio button) allows you to create options so the user can make only one selection between multiple choices.

■ The Combobox icon allows you to draw a combination listbox and textbox. The user can either choose an item from the listbox or enter a value in the textbox.

■ The Listbox icon lets you create a display list of items from which the user can choose one. The list can be scrolled if it has more items than what can be displayed at one time.

■ The HScrollBar icon creates a horizontal scrollbar for quickly navigating through a long list of items or a large amount of information. You can also use it as an input device or to indicate the current position on a scale.

■ The VScrollBar icon creates a vertical scrollbar for quickly navigating through a long list of items or a large amount of information. You can also use it as an input device or to indicate the current position on a scale.

■ The Timer icon lets you create a timer that generates timer events at set intervals. This control is invisible at runtime.

■ The DriveListBox icon lets you create a control that displays all the valid disk drives available to the user so he can select a drive.

■ The DirListBox icon creates a control that displays a directory listbox showing the directories and paths for a given drive.

■ The FileListBox icon creates a control that displays a list of files from a given directory.

■ The Shape icon creates a control that can draw a variety of shapes on your form at design time. You can choose a rectangle, a rounded rectangle, a square, a rounded square, an oval, or a circle.

■ The Line icon lets you create a control to draw a variety of line styles on your form at design time.

■ The Image icon creates a control that displays a graphical image from a bitmap, icon, or metafile on your form. Images displayed in an Image control, which can only be decorative, use fewer resources than a picture box.

■ The Data icon creates a control that provides access to data in databases through bound controls on your form.

■ The OLE icon allows you to create a control that links and embeds objects from other applications in your Visual Basic application.

■ You can easily add new controls to the toolbox by selecting the Custom Controls option from the Tools menu. This will bring up the Custom Controls dialog, which will allow you to select or remove which custom controls you want in the toolbox. If you buy a custom control from an outside vendor, you can add this control to the toolbox by browsing for it and then selecting it.

The Toolbars

The four standard toolbars that come with Visual Basic 5.0 are the Debug toolbar, the Edit toolbar, the Form Editor toolbar, and the Standard toolbar. Visual Basic 5.0 also lets you customize the existing toolbars and create and customize your own toolbars. The Debug toolbar contains all the icons that aid in debugging your projects. The Edit toolbar contains the icons that edit the code of your project. The Form Editor toolbar contains the icons that let you edit your forms. The Standard toolbar contains the standard icons that are displayed under the menu bar at the top of the screen. Figure 2.5 shows the Debug, Edit, and Form Editor toolbars.

FIGURE 2.5.

The Debug, Edit, and Form Editor toolbars.

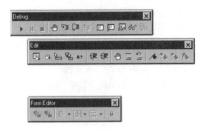

The Standard Toolbar

The Standard toolbar defaults to an open state whenever you open a new or an existing project. It contains buttons that are shortcuts to some commonly used menu items. You can click a toolbar button once to execute the action represented by that button. You can select the Show Tooltips option (which is the default setting) in the General tab of the Options dialog box if you want to display tooltips for the toolbar buttons.

The Debug Toolbar

The Debug toolbar contains buttons that are shortcuts to some commonly used menu items frequently used in debugging code. You can click a toolbar button once to execute the action represented by that button. You can select the Show Tooltips option in the General tab of the Options dialog box if you want to display tooltips for the toolbar buttons in the same way you can for any of the debug windows.

The Edit Toolbar

The Edit toolbar contains the buttons that are shortcuts to some commonly used menu items frequently used when editing code. You can click a toolbar button once to execute the action represented by that button. You can select the Show Tooltips option in the General tab of the Options dialog box if you want to display tooltips for the toolbar buttons.

The Form Editor Toolbar

The Form Editor toolbar contains the buttons that are shortcuts to some commonly used menu items useful for working with forms. You can click a toolbar button once to execute the action represented by that button. You can select the Show Tooltips option in the General tab of the Options dialog box if you want to display tooltips for the toolbar buttons.

Customizing the Toolbars

Visual Basic 5.0 provides the capability to customize the existing toolbars supplied by Visual Basic or create your own toolbars. To customize the toolbars, select the Customize option from the Toolbars menu option on the View pull-down menu. This opens the Customize dialog, as shown in Figure 2.6.

FIGURE 2.6.

The Customize dialog.

The Customize dialog is a great tool for adding, removing, or modifying existing toolbars for your projects. This dialog contains three major tab groups: Toolbars, Commands, and Options. Once you create a custom toolbar, it automatically shows up in the menu of the Toolbars option on the View pull-down menu. The following sections explain the Customize dialog so you can create your own custom toolbars.

The Toolbars Tab Group

The Toolbars tab group displays a list of all the toolbars that are currently available to the project. A checkmark indicates each of the toolbars that are open at that time. You can check or uncheck the checkboxes to open or close them. The only one you cannot uncheck is the menu bar because if you did so, you could not do very much with Visual Basic.

On the right side of the list of toolbars are four pushbuttons:

- Clicking the New pushbutton opens the New Toolbar menu, which allows you to name a new toolbar to customize. Go ahead and click this pushbutton, and name the toolbar anything you want. After you click OK, you see your new custom toolbar in the list of toolbars, and it is visible onscreen. Click the toolbar and drag it off the Customize dialog so it remains visible.

- The Rename pushbutton is available only if you select a custom toolbar; clicking it opens the Rename toolbar dialog, which allows you to rename the toolbar. Go ahead and click the Rename pushbutton, and change the name of the toolbar to something else. Click OK. Notice that the toolbar changes names.

- The Delete pushbutton is available only if you select a custom toolbar; clicking it allows you to delete customized toolbars. Go ahead and click the Delete pushbutton, and then click OK. Notice that the custom toolbar is deleted. Now, click the New pushbutton and create a new toolbar.

- The Reset pushbutton allows you to undo the changes you made to any of the toolbars.

The Commands Tab Group

The Commands tab group allows you to add toolbar buttons to your custom toolbar, and I believe you are really going to like this tab because it is so powerful. The Commands tab contains two listboxes, Categories and Commands. The Categories listbox contains a list of all the categories available. The Commands listbox contains a list of all the commands available under each category. Select a category and look at the type of commands available. For example, click the File category; you see all the available commands that relate to the File category. Click the New Project command with the left mouse button, hold it down, and drag it on top of the new custom toolbar that you created earlier. Notice that the command button is automatically added to the custom toolbar. Now add a few other command buttons from other categories. To delete commands from the custom toolbar, just grab them with the left mouse button and pull them off the custom toolbar. It's that easy.

The Modify Selection pushbutton is enabled when you select a toolbar command on your custom toolbar. Select one of the toolbar buttons on your custom toolbar and then click the Modify Selection pushbutton. A pop-up menu allows you to customize the toolbar command almost any way you want. Play around with the menu options and create the toolbar of your choice.

The Options Tab Group

The Options tab group contains three checkboxes and one pull-down listbox that allow you to change the style of your toolbars. Experiment with these options and choose the ones that best suit your programming style and preferences. When you finish modifying your custom toolbar, click the Close pushbutton of the Customize Toolbar dialog and then select the View pull-down menu and click the Toolbars option. You will see your new custom toolbar in the list.

The Color Palette

You use the Color palette to change the colors of a form or control and set up a custom color scheme. The image at the upper-left corner of the Color palette displays the currently selected foreground and background colors for the form or control. The image below this displays the currently selected foreground and background colors for any text in the form or control.

> **NOTE**
>
> If the text and background colors that you selected are not displayed, one of the colors you selected might be dithered, which is a color comprising up to three differently colored pixels.

Next to these two images is a set of colors that you can select for the text on a form or a control. The two pushbuttons to the right of the selectable colors are the default pushbutton, which displays the default color tables, and the Define Colors pushbutton, which lets you define your own custom color patterns.

> **NOTE**
>
> You can also set the colors for forms and controls with the `BackColor` or `ForeColor` property.

Summary

This chapter deals with the Integrated Development Environment of Visual Basic 5.0 and covers the most commonly used functions of the IDE. The IDE is a powerful tool that was explicitly designed to help the VB developer create expert visual applications as well as projects that can be maintained and developed in a timely manner. The IDE can be modified to fit your own style or the style of a particular company. You can develop either large or small projects and multiple projects simultaneously.

One of the major differences between Visual Basic 5.0 and earlier releases is the improvement of the IDE. It no longer looks and feels as though several windows act independently of each other because the IDE is fully contained in one main window. The IDE was improved by the addition of the toolbars that give you quick access to commonly used functions.

2

THE INTEGRATED DEVELOPMENT ENVIRONMENT

PART

II

Getting Started with Development

Getting Started with the Application Wizard

by Mike McMillan

IN THIS CHAPTER

CHAPTER 3

One of the biggest improvements in Visual Basic 5 over previous versions of VB is the number of wizards available to the developer. There is a wizard for creating ActiveX controls, another for connecting your application to a database, and yet another for helping you create an application: the Application Wizard.

The Application Wizard creates an application shell that includes many features you want in your applications: a toolbar, a menu, a login box, an about box, and several other features. This chapter explores how to use the Application Wizard to create an application shell from which you can add custom features to turn it into a full-fledged Visual Basic application.

Using the Application Wizard

You use the Application Wizard to create an application shell that provides you with the basic features of an application. You are expected to fill in the details to make the application fully functional. The Application Wizard creates menus, toolbars, about and login boxes, and even access to the Internet by presenting you with a series of dialogs asking you to provide the wizard with some information about what kind of application you want to create. You still have to add a lot of code and controls to the application, but the wizard does take a lot of the drudgery out of the initial building of an application.

The three ways to load the wizard are

■ Start it when you first start Visual Basic. (See Figure 3.1.)

■ Select File | New Project from the VB menu bar.

■ Add it to the Add-Ins menu using the Add-Ins Manager and then select it from the Add-Ins menu.

FIGURE 3.1.

The Application Wizard icon is visible when you start Visual Basic.

The opening dialog of the wizard simply identifies the program as the Application Wizard, tells you that to go back and change a selection you can click the Back button, and instructs you to click Next to move to the next dialog.

The screen also has a checkbox you can check if you don't want to see the opening screen of the wizard. Because this screen doesn't make any changes to the application, feel free to check this box.

At the bottom of the screen are the wizard's command buttons. These buttons are used to perform the following:

■ Help provides an explanation of what function is available with that particular screen.

■ Cancel exits the Application Wizard.

■ Back takes you back one screen.

■ Next moves you to the next screen.

■ Finish stops the wizard and creates the application shell with the choices you have made before that point.

Choosing the Interface Type

The next dialog in the wizard asks you to choose an interface type. The wizard gives you the option of creating one of the following three interface types:

■ Multiple-document interface (MDI)

■ Single-document interface (SDI)

■ Explorer-style interface

The multiple-document interface type is the standard Visual Basic application interface that is created if you don't use the Application Wizard. An MDI application has one parent window or form, and other windows that are created later are child windows contained within the parent window.

The single-document interface type creates just one window (form). If you create other forms later, they are independent forms that have no relationship to the parent form.

The Explorer-style type creates an application that looks just like the Windows Explorer application that comes with Windows 95. (See Figure 3.2.)

The Interface Type dialog also provides you with a visual hint if you want to know what any of the three interface types looks like. In the left corner of the dialog is a graphic representation of the interface type that is currently selected. If you choose the Single Document Interface type, the graphic changes to show what a Single Document Interface type looks like. Figure 3.3 shows the Interface Type dialog with the Multiple Document Interface type selected, which is the default.

FIGURE 3.2.

The Windows Explorer interface, which you can emulate in your Visual Basic application.

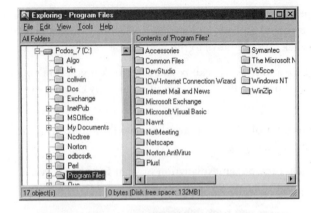

FIGURE 3.3.

The Interface Type dialog with the Multiple Document Interface type selected.

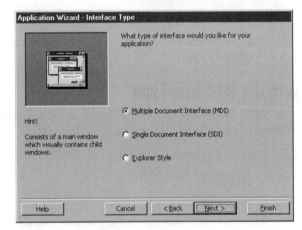

This chapter discusses how to create an application using all three interface types, but for this first example, choose the MDI interface type and click the Next button to move to the next dialog.

Creating a Menu

The next dialog in the Application Wizard is the Menus dialog. This dialog lets you create a menu system with up to five menus on the menu bar. The menus you can create are standard Windows menus that are found in most Windows applications.

The menus you can create with the wizard are

- File
- Edit
- View

■ Window

■ Help

When the Menus dialog is displayed, all but the View menu are selected as default menus. The wizard is suggesting that these menus are part of most Windows applications and that you should provide them in your application. The View menu is not selected because View functions are the least common types of functions to be found in applications and can be left out of many applications without affecting the usability of the program.

Figure 3.4 displays the Menus dialog of the Application Wizard. Besides the checkboxes for the different menus and the command buttons at the bottom of the dialog, the only other controls on the dialog are two command buttons, Select All and Clear All. Select All, as its name implies, selects all the menu choices without making you check each box, and Clear All clears all the checkboxes automatically.

FIGURE 3.4.

Choose your menus in the Menus dialog.

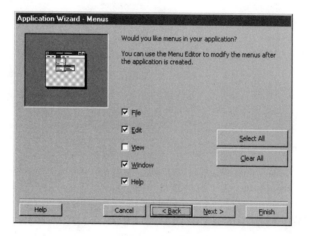

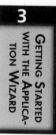

For the sample application you'll create in this chapter, the default selections are sufficient. If you clicked either Select All or Clear All, check all the default menu choices and click Next to move to the next wizard dialog.

Creating a Resource File

A *resource file* is a file that can store text strings, graphics, and sound files. You use a resource file if you create an international application that displays text in another language. For every other language you want displayed in your application, you create a resource file for that language.

If you are creating an international application, select Yes and then enter the full path name of the resource file you want to store your information; otherwise, select No. Then click Next to move to the Internet Connectivity dialog.

Connecting Your Application to the Internet

The Internet Connectivity dialog adds a custom Web browser to your application. To add Internet connectivity to an application, you must have Microsoft Internet Explorer (IE) 3.0 installed on your computer system, and you must have a connection to the Internet.

If you do have IE 3.0 installed and access to the Internet, you can select Yes in the dialog. The wizard then allows you to enter a start page to load or you can select the default, which is http:// www.microsoft.com. (See Figure 3.5.)

FIGURE 3.5.

You can add a custom Web browser in the Internet Connectivity dialog.

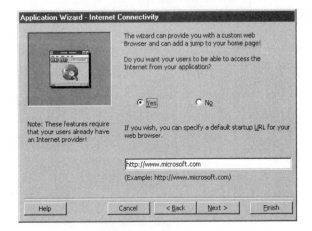

For this example, select Yes, leave the default start page as it is, and click Next to move to the next wizard dialog—the Standard Forms dialog.

Adding Standard Forms to Your Application

The Standard Forms dialog allows you to select several different forms that are often found in applications. These forms include

- A splash screen at application startup
- A login dialog box for ID and password
- An options dialog box for custom settings
- An about box

A *splash screen* is a screen that appears when an application is first loaded. The screen might display your company's logo or a welcome message from your company. It is common to display a splash screen for larger applications while all the forms and other objects of the application are being loaded into memory.

A login dialog box contains two textboxes that let the user enter an ID and a password. If you are creating secure applications, you want to select this form.

An Options dialog box gives your users the chance to make certain changes to the application environment, such as text fonts, background colors, and other such settings.

An about box is the least necessary of these forms but one that most applications have. An about box can tell the user what version of the program he is using and any other system information you want to provide to him. Also, most about boxes also provide a button to let the user see information about the computer system, such as how much memory it has, how physical resources are used, and so on.

Figure 3.6 displays the Standard Forms dialog. Besides the standard form selections, it also contains a button that lets you choose form templates you have already created. If you have already created a splash screen form or a login form, for example, you can choose it by clicking the Form Templates button.

FIGURE 3.6.
Choose standard forms for your application in the Standard Forms dialog.

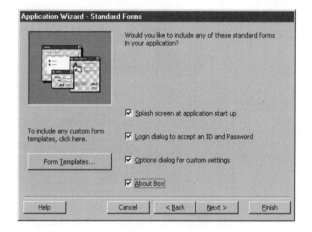

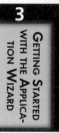

To see how these forms are created for an application, select all the forms for this example. Then click Next to move to the next dialog.

Creating Data Access Forms

The Application Wizard can create forms that are automatically connected to a database you can access. There are other ways of connecting your application to a database (such as the Data Form Wizard), but if you want a simplified data access form, you can create one on this dialog.

If you select Yes on the Data Access Forms dialog, you must tell the wizard what type of database you want to connect. The database types the wizard can connect include

- Microsoft Access
- dBASE III and IV

■ FoxPro 2.0, 2.5, 2.6, and 3.0

■ Paradox 3.*x*, 4.*x*, and 5.*x*

If the database type you want to connect is in this list, you can use the wizard to create a form that is connected to it. If the database type you want to connect is not on the list because it is an ODBC database, such as Microsoft SQL Server or Oracle, you must use another method to create data access forms, such as the Data Form Wizard.

Figure 3.7 shows the Data Access Forms dialog with a Microsoft Access database type chosen and a path name to the Biblio database that is included with Visual Basic 5. You can type the pathname or use the Browse button to find the database.

FIGURE 3.7.

Specify your database in the Data Access Forms dialog.

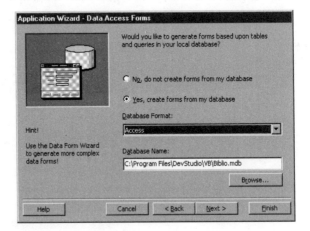

When you have entered these selections in the Data Access Forms dialog, click Next to move to the next dialog, Select Tables.

Selecting Tables to View with Data Access Forms

Because this application is going to be connected to a database, the wizard wants to know what tables and queries to use for the forms. For example, if you want your application to display all the data from the Titles table in your application, you select the Titles table. If you want to display a custom set of data from a table or tables, you can select a query that is already written.

The Select Tables dialog displays the list of tables associated with the database you selected in the last step. (See Figure 3.8.) This is the default. If you want to see a list of the queries for the database, select the Queries option button. If you want to see all the table names and all the queries, select the Both option button.

Figure 3.8.

Choose the table(s) to be used from your database in the Select Tables dialog box.

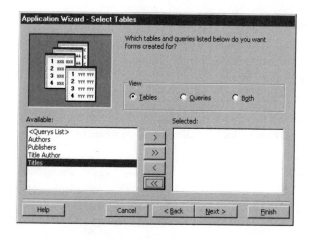

To select which tables or queries you want for a form, highlight the table or query in the Available listbox and click the right arrow button. This moves the highlighted item to the Selected listbox. You can move all the Available items over to the Selected listbox by clicking the double right-arrow button. You can remove items from the Selected listbox by highlighting the item and clicking the left-arrow button. You can remove all the items from the Selected listbox by clicking the double left-arrow button. Figure 3.9 shows the Selected listbox with the `Titles` table selected, the table that is used for this example.

Figure 3.9.

The Select Tables dialog with the `Titles` table selected.

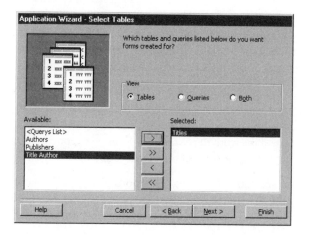

When you have added `Titles` to the Selected listbox, click the Next button to move to the last dialog of the Application Wizard.

Finishing Up the Application

The last dialog of the Application Wizard is the Finished! dialog (see Figure 3.10). On this dialog, you give your application a name, indicate whether the settings you have chosen during this session of the Application Wizard should be used as the default settings for the next time you use the wizard, and decide whether you want to view a report telling you what the wizard has done.

For this example, give the application the name Sample, choose Yes for viewing the closing report, and don't select the checkbox for changing the default settings.

FIGURE 3.10.

Name your database in the Finished! dialog.

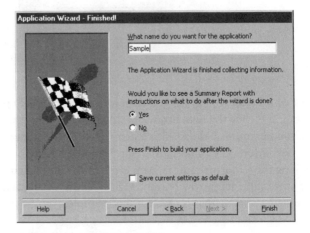

Click the Finished button, and Visual Basic will crank away at creating all the forms you specified. The forms are created immediately, and then the Application Wizard displays the Application Created dialog to let you know the wizard is finished.

Because you asked the Application Wizard to provide you a report telling you what it did in creating your application, the Summary Report dialog appears next. This dialog tells you that the wizard is finished and adds code comments to your application to give you hints on how you can extend the work the wizard has done. The report also provides a list of the other wizards you can use to add more functionality to your application. The report is shown in Figure 3.11.

When you are finished viewing the report, you can click either the Close button to close the dialog or the Save button to save the report to a file. For this example, click the Close button and go to the Visual Basic IDE to view the work the wizard did.

The next section displays the forms created by the Application Wizard and reviews the functionality each form provides. There is also a discussion of the things you must do to complete the work started by the wizard.

FIGURE 3.11.

The Application Wizard's summary report tells you what the wizard has done and suggests changes you can make.

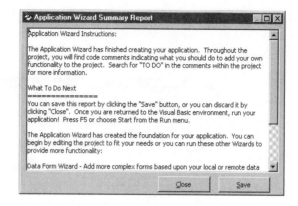

Exploring the Finished Application

The best way to explore the forms created by the Application Wizard is to look at them at design time in the IDE. Each form that was created by the wizard is listed in VB's project window. The project window for the sample application is shown in Figure 3.12.

FIGURE 3.12.

The project window for the sample application.

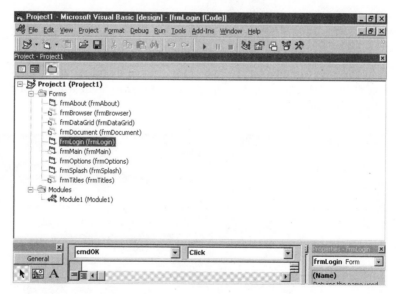

To view one of the forms, double-click it in the project window. For example, you can make changes to the login form in the same way you change any other form created in VB. To see the code that is written behind the command buttons, double-click the command button to view the Click event in a code window. (See Figure 3.13.) In the code, there is a To-Do comment to remind you that the login form does not work until some code is written to check for a correct password.

FIGURE 3.13.

The cmdOK_Click() *event code.*

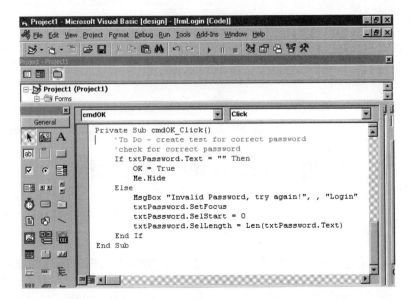

Another form to explore is the main form created by the wizard. This form, named frmMain, has all the menus and the toolbars on it and is the parent window of the MDI application. frmMain is displayed in Figure 3.14.

FIGURE 3.14.

frmMain—*the parent window of the sample application.*

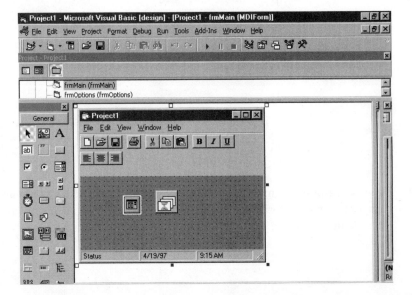

On the menu bar, you see the menus you selected on the Menus dialog of the Application Wizard. You also see a standard document toolbar below the menu bar. This toolbar was automatically added by the wizard and provides your application with the functionality most standard Windows applications have.

Once you've examined the program in design mode, running the program displays more of the features developed by the wizard. For example, one of the choices you selected while the Application Wizard was running was a form that is connected to a database. You chose the table `Titles` as the one you wanted displayed on the form. Figure 3.15 shows the form that the wizard created.

FIGURE 3.15.

The data access form created by the Application Wizard.

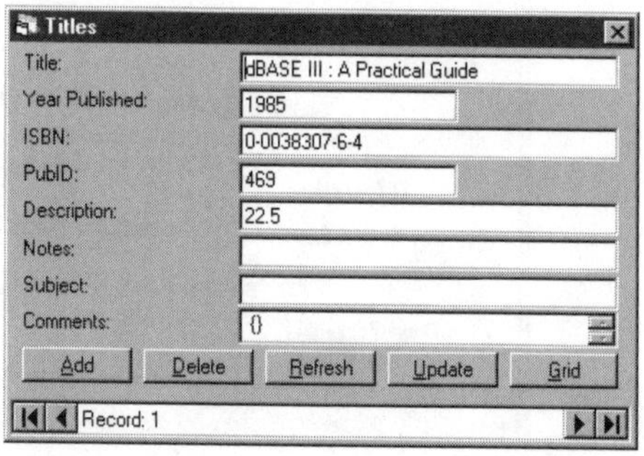

To display this form, after you have the sample program running, select View | Data Form | Titles on the menu. This form is a database front-end application that can be used to browse the database table, add items to the table, delete items, and edit items.

NOTE

You can also create this type of data access form by using the Data Form Wizard.

Another feature you selected using the wizard is a Web browser. To view the Web browser, choose View | Web Browser from the menu. The browser the wizard developed, although not as feature-packed as Microsoft Internet Explorer 3.0, gives you the following command buttons:

- ■ Forward
- ■ Back
- ■ Stop
- ■ Refresh
- ■ Home
- ■ Search

Figure 3.16 shows the Web browser within the sample parent window, with the window maximized to display the Microsoft Web page using the full screen.

FIGURE 3.16.

The Web browser created by the Application Wizard.

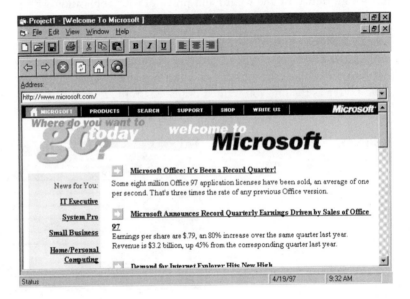

If you want to add more features to the Web browser created by the wizard, Microsoft provides a Web Browser ActiveX control, which is an add-in to VB if you have Microsoft Internet Explorer 3.0. To learn more about the Web Browser control, see Microsoft's Web Browser documentation on the Internet at `http://www.microsoft.com/accessdev/doc/bapp97/chapters/ba21_5.htm`. This information is posted with information for developing applications using Microsoft Access in Office 97, but it applies equally well to Visual Basic 5.

Now that you have seen some of what the Application Wizard does to create an application for you, explore the application further to get a better idea of how much work the wizard did and how much work is left for you to do. You'll be surprised at how many of the gritty details of the application can be handled by the wizard.

Using the Application Wizard to Create a Single-Document Interface Application

The first example you created with the Application Wizard built a multiple-document interface application, which was evident immediately when a blank document was loaded when the program was first run. One of the other interface types the wizard can create is a single-document interface application.

To create an SDI application using the Application Wizard, follow the same steps and make the same selections you did for the MDI application, but choose Single Document Interface on the Interface Type dialog. The other dialogs will have the same choices for you to make as they did when you created the MDI application.

When you finish the wizard, making the same selections as you did for the MDI application, you end up in the VB IDE. Click the Run button on the toolbar, and your application looks like the application in Figure 3.17.

FIGURE 3.17.

The sample application created using the SDI type.

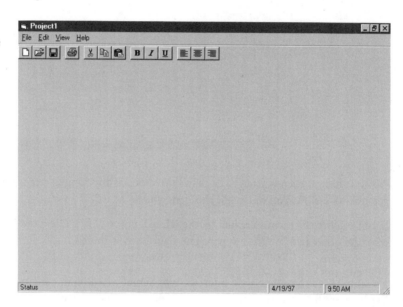

The first thing you notice is that there is only one form. That's because you created an SDI, not an MDI, application. Other than this difference, however, this application has the same functionality as the MDI application. There is a data form that browses the Titles table, a Web browser, and all the other choices that were selected in the wizard.

If you don't need or want the functionality of a multiple document interface, choose the SDI option when using the Application Wizard.

Creating an Explorer-Style Application

When you select Explorer Style on the Interface Type dialog of the Application Wizard and make the same choices for the other dialogs as you did in the previous two examples, you end up with a main form that looks like the form in Figure 3.18.

FIGURE 3.18.

The sample application with the Explorer-style interface.

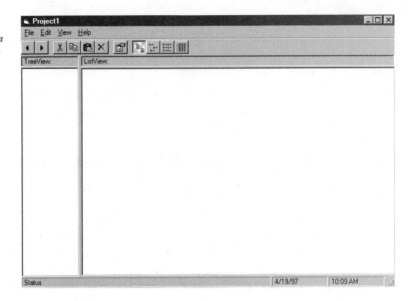

No code has yet been written to display a directory or anything in tree view or list view, so you get a blank screen. You must add this code yourself.

If you explore the menus created by the wizard, you will find the same functionality you had with the other two interface types. The data form is there, as are the Web browser and the other options.

To see what the Explorer-style interface type actually looks like, remember that the Windows Explorer application has this interface. If you want to create an application with this type of interface, the Explorer-style interface type is the choice you want to make.

Summary

The Application Wizard can handle a lot of the details that are involved in first creating an application. For someone first starting out with VB, this wizard is invaluable for learning how an application should be created from the beginning. As you become more familiar with VB, you will want to experiment with modifying the interface created by the wizard to make things look and act as you want. Eventually, you might find that creating an application is easier without using the wizard. When you get to that point, remember to thank the wizard for making you a Visual Basic application interface expert.

Using the ActiveX Document Migration Wizard

by Paul Kimmel

IN THIS CHAPTER

CHAPTER 4

The ActiveX Document Migration Wizard converts new or existing forms into ActiveX documents. An ActiveX document has the same relationship to a program capable of containing an ActiveX document as a Microsoft Word document has to MS Word. The ActiveX document is a reusable program resource to its container; without the container, the document is out of context.

This chapter demonstrates how to use the ActiveX Document Migration Wizard by offering you an opportunity to work along while a database and data-aware form are created. You'll see a step-by-step example of using the Add-In Manager to add the Migration Wizard to Visual Basic and using the wizard to convert the data-aware form to an ActiveX document. You will also learn how to incorporate that ActiveX document into Microsoft's Internet Explorer.

In this chapter you will learn how Visual Basic forms can be converted to reusable ActiveX documents by doing the following:

- Creating a personnel lookup form
- Going through a step-by-step example demonstrating how to use the ActiveX Document Migration Wizard
- Learning how non-ActiveX code is manipulated
- Learning how an ActiveX document is used

This chapter teaches you how to use the ActiveX Document Migration Wizard to convert a regular application form into an ActiveX document. ActiveX documents can be used in the original applications that inspired their creation, and the added benefit is that they can be used in many other contexts. Visual Basic 5 can be used to originate and test business solutions that have an ultimately different purpose. The World Wide Web is arguably the most exciting development environment right now. Visual Basic 5 will help you develop ActiveX documents that are usable on the Web and in any other program or system that has adopted the ActiveX document protocol.

Creating the Demonstration Form

Here's the scenario presented in this chapter: An information systems manager has determined that the corporate intranet will include a centrally updatable company personnel phone directory. The Internet Explorer browser is used as the intranet browser and is an ActiveX container.

The objective of the directory browser is to maintain a centrally maintainable database that can be updated as personnel changes occur. The directory will be updated as employee records are updated, resulting in no distribution of hard-copy directory lists. A feasibility study is requested, and you must demonstrate that current technology is capable of supporting the requirement. The feasibility study is a functional demonstration of the technology, which if successful will be built on the existing personnel database and incorporated into the intranet.

A *vertical slice program* is a program that demonstrates that a particular architectural solution can technically satisfy the problem domain. For the example in this chapter, you will need to create a sample database containing some sample personnel records. At your disposal are Microsoft's Visual Basic 5, its Visual Data Manager, and Microsoft Internet Explorer 3.0 (or an ActiveX document–capable Web browser).

Using the Visual Data Manager to Create a Database

You will need to create a test database for the demonstration application defined in this chapter. For our purposes here, you will need a database containing fields for first name, last name, and phone number extension. The examples illustrated in this chapter are included on this book's CD-ROM.

Creating a Database

Starting with the Visual Data Manager depicted in Figure 4.1, you quickly define a database and subsequently a table using the following steps:

FIGURE 4.1.

The Visual Data Manager, used to create the demo database.

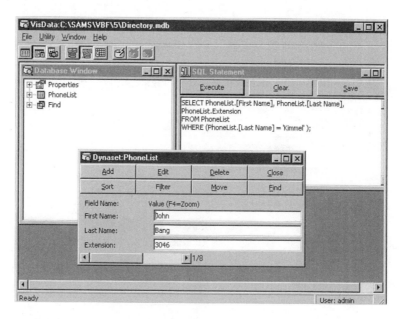

1. From the Visual Basic 5 menu (the Developer Studio), select Add-Ins | Visual Data Manager.

2. In the Visual Data Manager, to create the `Directory.mdb` database, select File | New | Microsoft Access, Version 7.0 MDB.

3. In the Select Microsoft Access Database to Create dialog, choose the directory in which you want to create the database and name the database `Directory.mdb`.

4. In the Database window (which is subsequently opened), click the right mouse button and select New Table from the speed menu.

5. You will finish creating the database table, PhoneList, in the Table Structure dialog shown in Figure 4.2; begin by entering the table name, PhoneList.

FIGURE 4.2.

The Table Structure dialog, used to define the demo table.

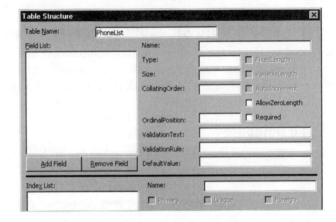

6. Click Add Field.

7. Use the Add Field dialog, shown in Figure 4.3, to add three fields with the following definitions:

Field	Definition
First Name	Text, 12
Last Name	Text, 22
Extension	Text, 14

FIGURE 4.3.

The Add Field dialog, used to define the table fields.

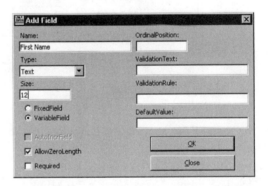

8. Click Close.

9. In the Table Structure dialog, click Add Index.

10. In the Add Index dialog (shown in Figure 4.4), create a non-unique index on the Last name field; name the index Last Name as well.

11. In the Table Structure dialog, click Build the Table.

4

THE ACTIVEX
DOCUMENT
MIGRATION
WIZARD

FIGURE 4.4.

The Add Index dialog, used to create an index for the Last Name *field.*

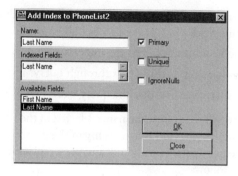

You will be returned to the Database window, and the PhoneList table will appear in the Database window list. The sample Directory.mdb provided for you on this book's CD-ROM contains some sample records. You can use the book's database or add some records to the database. To add records, double-click in the Database window on the PhoneList table.

In the next section you will use the Visual Data Manager to define and test a SQL query that will enable you to perform a dynamic search on the indexed Last Name field.

Defining the SQL Query

The Visual Data Manager is not as powerful as Microsoft's Access 97, but it certainly will suffice. You use the Query Builder (shown in Figure 4.5) to define the last name search query.

FIGURE 4.5.

The Query Builder.

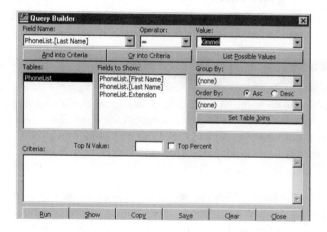

The following steps walk you through the process:

1. In the Database window, click the right mouse button and select New Query.
2. In the Query Builder (shown in Figure 4.5), select the PhoneList table from the Tables listbox.
3. In the Field Name combobox, select the PhoneList.Last Name. field.
4. Use the default operator, =.

5. Click the List Possible Values button to fill the Value combobox with values from the Last Name field.

6. Click the Run button to test the query.

7. A dialog that asks, Is this a pass through query? is displayed. Click No.

8. After you have verified that the query works, click Save and save the query as Find.

The Find query will return just the name selected in the Query Builder dialog. When you take the time to complete the find functionality of the demonstration application, you might want to replace the equal operator with LIKE and use a replaceable parameter. The revised query can be rewritten as follows:

```
SELECT PhoneList.[First Name], PhoneList.[Last Name], PhoneList.Extension
FROM PhoneList
WHERE (PhoneList.[Last Name] Like 'K*' );
```

You replace the 'K*' portion of the SQL, perhaps from the Text property of a textbox control. The database is now complete. Close the Visual Database Manager, returning to the Developer Studio.

Having added data to the table, defined an index, and tested the find query, you are ready to build the application. If you are familiar with the steps involved in building a data-bound form, you can skip to the section "Using the Migration Wizard Step-by-Step."

Designing the Interface

If you are familiar with some of the steps of the Migration Wizard, but not all of them, feel free to skip ahead to only those sections that cover steps unfamiliar to you.

> **NOTE**
>
> I often use the terms *Visual Basic* and *Developer Studio* interchangeably. The Developer Studio is the development platform that all Microsoft developers use for all language tools. This is true whether you are programming in Visual Basic, C++, or J++. When Visual Basic is running, I use *Developer Studio* and *Visual Basic* to mean the same thing.

To create the form, which you will convert to an ActiveX document in the section titled "Using the Migration Wizard Step-by-Step," you need to begin by selecting File | New Project in the Developer Studio. From the New Project dialog, select the default Standard EXE project type and click OK.

The objective is to create a Windows 95 database application. The application (shown in Figure 4.6) will be a single form browser that enables you to browse through all fields of the PhoneList table. For navigation purposes, the program will be defined to have a single menu, Record. The Record menu will have five items: First, Previous, Next, Last, and Find. For simplicity, you will use a data control, but it will not be visible to the end user. This section contains the remaining compartmentalized steps for creating and testing the data-bound application.

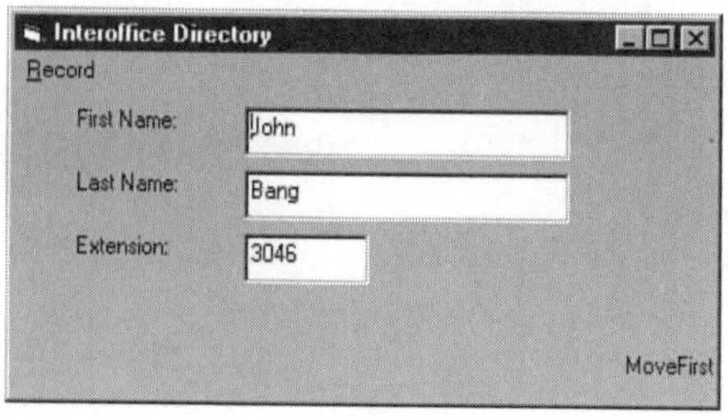

FIGURE 4.6.

*The Interoffice
Directory application.*

Your goal at this juncture is to build a robust standard Visual Basic application. You should focus on that objective when you are designing forms, even if you know that their ultimate configuration will result in an ActiveX document. If a form will ultimately be converted to an ActiveX document, you can mitigate the need for reengineering by avoiding those things that cannot be used in ActiveX documents, such as OLE controls. For the most part, the Migration Wizard will filter out or warn you of those things that will not be retained in your ActiveX document.

Adding Controls and a Menu

Here, we will treat the design process as if we were going to stop once the Windows application is complete. The ActiveX Document Migration Wizard alleviates the burden of focusing on the end result so you can focus on the process of producing a robust application first.

> **NOTE**
>
> OLE controls cannot be used in ActiveX documents. If part of your form's functionality depends on an OLE control, you need to find an alternative way to solve the problem that does not include the OLE control.

The controls we need consist of four label controls, three textbox controls, and a data control. Place the controls on the form in the configuration shown in Figure 4.6, or be creative and choose an alternate configuration.

Click on the Menu Editor toolbar button, or select Tools | Menu Editor to display the Menu Editor, shown in Figure 4.7. Define the menu by following these steps:

1. Add a Record menu by entering &Record in the Caption textbox and RecordMenu in the Name textbox. (Adopting a convention such as this one—adding the word Menu to the phrase you put in the Caption field to contrive the control name—simplifies the need to contrive unique names.)
2. Click the right-arrow button.

4

THE ACTIVEX
DOCUMENT
MIGRATION
WIZARD

3. Add the following menus: First, Previous, Next, Last, - (separator), and Find. Use the convention described in step 1.

4. For each submenu, in the Shortcut combobox select Ctrl+the first letter of the menu caption.

FIGURE 4.7.

You create the Record menu by filling out the Menu Editor dialog, as shown here.

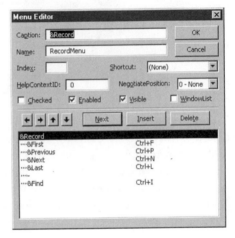

The first four menus simply borrow the control's method names. Using method names for menu names makes it easy to contrive menu captions and match captions to actions in the underlying code. If you have not added the data control, do so now.

Modifying the Control Properties

The concept of rapid application development (RAD) is derived from the notion that you can perform a lot of the tasks necessary to visually create an application in the Visual Developer Studio. Just five or so years ago, even simple tasks such as naming dialogs were done programmatically, requiring the programmer to write a lot of additional constructor code. Unfortunately, even fundamental coding like that requires debugging and maintenance. Visual Basic mitigates the need for writing code to define the way controls look. In keeping with the notion of RAD, let's perform as many tasks as possible visually, or at design time.

The next thing you need to do to complete the application is modify each of the controls. I will name the control and the property or properties that require modification. We will use the default properties for the most part:

1. Change the Caption property from Label1 to First Name:.

2. Change the Caption property from Label2 to Last Name:.

3. Change the Caption property from Label3 to Extension:.

4. Change the data control's BOFAction property to MoveFirst.

5. Change the data control's Connect property to Access.

6. Change the data control's DatabaseName property to the Directory.mdb. You can use the ellipsis button in the Property dialog to search for the database.

7. Change the Data control `EOFAction` property to `MoveLast`.

8. Change the Data control `ReadOnly` property to `True`.

9. Change the Data control `RecordSet` property to `PhoneList`.

10. Change the Data control `Visible` property to `False` because you will be offering the Record menu for navigation.

11. Change the `Text1` control `DataSource` property to `Data1`. This will cause the available fields to appear in the DataField combobox.

12. Change the `Text1` control's `DataField` property to `First Name`. Select it from the DataField combobox to avoid misspellings.

13. Change the `Text2` control's `DataSource` property to `Data1`.

14. Change the `Text2` control's `DataField` property to `Last Name`.

15. Change the `Text3` control's `DataSource` property to `Data1`.

16. Change the `Text3` control's `DataField` property to `Extension`.

17. Change the form's `Name` property to `DirectoryForm`.

18. Change the form's `Caption` property to `Interoffice Directory`.

19. Set the `Label4` `Alignment` property to `1 - Right Justify`.

After you have completed these steps, half the job is done. The majesty of Visual Basic development is that it alleviates the necessity of writing code to perform cumbersome tasks. In the next section, you will see how little code is necessary to get the database browser up and running.

Adding Code

In the last section you added `Label4`, an extraneous label. `Label4` will be used to record the last `RecordSet` action taken. The first thing you will want to do is to add code to ensure that `Label4`—the record action label—is aligned to the bottom of the form.

> **NOTE**
>
> As we complete the browser with code, there are a few sidebar issues to keep in mind. When prototyping, naming conventions are secondary. Because prototype code should be discarded, or at a minimum reworked, before being released into production, using the default names is sufficient. You can skip comments, too. When prototyping, which is what our feasibility demonstration is, you can hack away, not doing all those things you are supposed to do when developing a production system.

Adding the following call to `Move` in the `Form_Resize` event will ensure that the label hugs the bottom of the form all the time:

```
Call Label4.Move(0, ScaleHeight - Label1.Height, ScaleWidth, Height)
```

4

THE ACTIVEX
DOCUMENT
MIGRATION
WIZARD

The remaining code is shown in Listing 4.1, followed by a detailed description of the action it performs.

Listing 4.1. directoryForm.frm from personnel.vbp—The browser form code.

```
1: Private Sub FindMenu_Click()
2:    MsgBox "Under Construction!", vbExclamation
3: End Sub
4:
5: Private Sub FirstMenu_Click()
6:    Data1.Recordset.MoveFirst
7:    Call RefreshRecordSetAction("MoveFirst")
8: End Sub
9:
10: Private Sub Form_Initialize()
11:    Call FirstMenu_Click
12:   End Sub
13:
14: Private Sub Form_Resize()
15:    Call Label4.Move(0, ScaleHeight - Label1.Height, ScaleWidth, Height)
16: End Sub
17:
18: Private Sub LastMenu_Click()
19:    Data1.Recordset.MoveLast
20:    Call RefreshRecordSetAction("MoveLast")
21: End Sub
22:
23: Private Sub NextMenu_Click()
24:    If (Data1.Recordset.EOF = False) Then
25:        Data1.Recordset.MoveNext
26:        Call RefreshRecordSetAction("MoveNext")
27:    Else
28:        Beep
29:    End If
30: End Sub
31:
32: Private Sub PreviousMenu_Click()
33:    If (Data1.Recordset.BOF = False) Then
34:        Data1.Recordset.MovePrevious
35:        Call RefreshRecordSetAction("MovePrevious")
36:    Else
37:        Beep
38:    End If
39: End Sub
40:
41: Public Sub RefreshRecordSetAction(ByVal Action As String)
42:    Label4.Caption = Action
43: End Sub
```

Remember that each two-line pair defining the boundaries of a function is generated for you; it is apparent that a small amount of code is capable of producing a Windows application significantly more powerful than the few lines of code that guide it. Lines 1, 2, and 3 display a message box letting the user know that the find feature is under construction. When you implement find, simply remove MsgBox and add the code that provides the functionality.

All the subroutines ending in `Click` provide the remaining menu functionality. For example, selecting Record | First calls the `Data1.RecordSet.MoveFirst` method. You can easily discern how each of the remaining menu items is implemented. The final thing each `Click` does is call the `RefreshRecordSetAction` function. You could easily refer to `Label4` directly, but using a function is more extensible. Why? The interface could easily remain the same—that is, the `RefreshRecordSetAction` function could remain the same while the underlying implementation changes. For example, you might ultimately decide to use a different control to display the `RecordSet` action.

`PreviousMenu_Click` and `NextMenu_Click` offer a little conditional checking that will reduce the likelihood that the recordset is moved past the beginning or end of the file. In a production application, you might even want to add one level of indirection to the functionality behind the event handlers. By defining functions to perform the action, you can provide meaningful names to the functions, such as `SetFirstRecord`, which when called from anywhere proffer the correct semantic meaning and intent.

Testing the Application

A convenience of having the ActiveX Document Wizard is the ease with which you can develop forms destined to be ActiveX documents. Further, even after the conversion process, the old form is maintained, enabling you to easily extend and retest the form in its Windows executable state.

Any testing process requires that all code paths be exercised. A rigorous application of this rule is less necessary when prototyping, but still necessary. Test the `DirectoryForm` form by pressing F5 and selecting each of the Record menu items. The recordset is read only, so testing beyond the menus is unnecessary. After ensuring that each feature of the prototype works correctly, implement the find functionality or continue to the next section, "Using the Migration Wizard Step-by-Step." To implement the Find menu, use the `InputBox` function, prompting the user for the `Last Name` token to search for, and setting the `RecordSet` property equal to the SQL string defined in the database as `Find`. Make sure you save the project at this point.

Using the Migration Wizard Step-by-Step

The form you will convert to a document is `DirectoryForm`, created in the previous section. This section includes a step-by-step demonstration of how to convert an existing form. The first thing you need to do is ensure that the Migration Wizard is available. To do that, select the Add-Ins menu and click on the Add-Ins Manager menu item. In the Add-In Manager dialog (shown in Figure 4.8), check VB ActiveX Document Migration Wizard and click OK. The ActiveX Document Migration Wizard is now a menu item in the Add-Ins menu.

The Migration Wizard converts individual forms to ActiveX documents, but does not convert a Windows application to an ActiveX document–based application. Remember that the benefit is that you can create and test your forms as standard executables, but you can only

4

THE ACTIVEX
DOCUMENT
MIGRATION
WIZARD

convert individual forms to ActiveX documents. The following sections walk you through each step of that process.

FIGURE 4.8.

Using the Add-In Manager to add the ActiveX Document Migration Wizard to the Add-Ins menu.

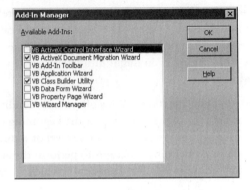

The Introduction Dialog

After you have added the Migration Wizard to the Add-Ins menu, you can use it. Select Add-Ins | ActiveX Document Migration Wizard to begin the process of converting `DirectoryForm` to an ActiveX document. The Introduction page is shown in Figure 4.9.

FIGURE 4.9.

The Introduction page of the ActiveX Document Migration Wizard.

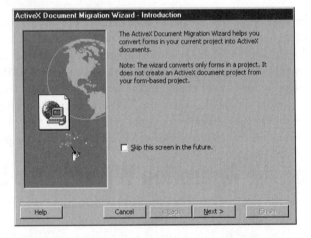

The Introduction screen reminds you that the ActiveX Document Migration Wizard only converts forms. Check the Skip this screen in the future option, and click Next.

The Form Selection Page

The ActiveX Document Migration Wizard Form Selection page, shown in Figure 4.10, lists the forms in the current project. Checking any or all forms will target the selected forms to be converted to document-based (`.DOB`) forms.

FIGURE 4.10.

The Form Selection dialog of the ActiveX Document Migration Wizard.

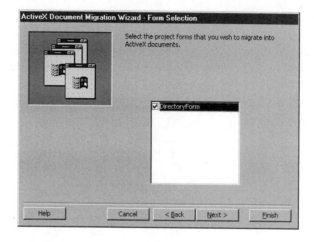

To complete the migration process using all the remaining defaults, click Finish. If you click the Finish button, the forms you selected will be converted to files using the following convention:

```
DocFormName.dob
```

In other words, Doc is prefixed to the name, and the .dob extension is added to the new file. If you intend to diverge from the default selections on the remaining dialog, click Next.

Selecting Options

The ActiveX Document Migration Wizard's Options screen enables you to have the wizard comment out all invalid code. Letting the wizard comment out invalid code will save you from having to do so when you try to compile the project. For example, using the Move method during form load is invalid. By selecting the option to comment out invalid code, the Form_Load event handler will be rewritten, as in the following example:

```
Private Sub Form_Load()
  '[AXDW] The following line was commented out by the ActiveX Document
➥Migration Wizard.
  '    Me.Move 0, 0
End Sub
```

> **NOTE**
>
> The ActiveX Document Migration Wizard uses the [AXDW] tag as a convention for commenting out invalid code.

Other examples of invalid code that will need to be commented out include method calls to Hide, Show, Load, Unload, and End.

The second option, the Remove the original forms after conversion checkbox (see Figure 4.11), instructs the wizard to remove the original forms from the application on which the ActiveX documents are based. The next page of the dialog is Finished!. You can click Finish at this point or continue to the next page if you are using the wizard for the first time.

Figure 4.11.

The Options page of the ActiveX Document Migration Wizard.

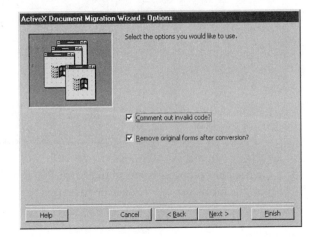

Finishing Up

The Finished! page of the ActiveX Document Migration Wizard has two options (see Figure 4.12). The first option is Yes, by default. Leave it Yes, perhaps for the first couple conversions, because the instructions provided by the wizard will remind you how you can test and use the converted document.

Figure 4.12.

When you are familiar with converting forms to ActiveX documents, click No and check Save current settings as default.

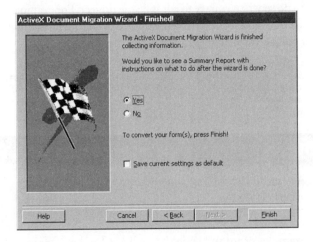

After you are familiar with the steps for converting, testing, and using ActiveX documents, you might want to select No in the Finished! dialog and save the current settings as the default. The instructions are useful, but you will not need them after a few document conversions.

Reading the Summary Report

The Finished! dialog described in the last section suggests that new users leave the default options selected. The last thing the wizard will do is display a summary report (see Figure 4.13), which will provide invaluable steps for using the ActiveX document in the context of several different ActiveX document–capable programs.

FIGURE 4.13.

The summary report from the ActiveX Document Wizard gives a list of other ActiveX document–creation resources available.

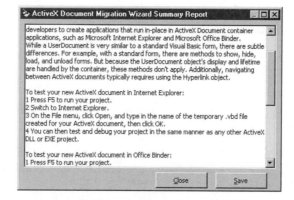

The output from the documentation wizard is a `.dob` file for each form created. In this example, you will end up with `DocDirectoryForm.dob` and a summary report if you requested one. (The summary report from this chapter is included on the CD-ROM as `AXDOCWIZ.TXT`.) The next section gives instructions that demonstrate how to use the ActiveX document.

Testing and Using the ActiveX Document

The simplest way to test forms that will ultimately be converted to ActiveX documents is to test them as part of a Windows application in the context in which they were developed. However, once the document is converted to an ActiveX document, you can still execute it from the Developer Studio, open the document in the container, and test it by exercising the document features.

> **NOTE**
>
> ActiveX document menus are merged into the container's menu. In this example, Ctrl+N was used to move to the next record. However, because the Internet Explorer already uses Ctrl+N, you would need to change the shortcut in your ActiveX document to get the fit and finish just right.

For this sample program, you tested the features as part of the original program in which it was developed. Then, when `DirectoryForm` was converted to an ActiveX document, the wizard converted the application to an ActiveX EXE project. Follow these steps to test the ActiveX document in Microsoft Internet Explorer:

1. In the Developer Studio, press F4.

2. Run Internet Explorer.

3. Choose File | Open, which opens the Visual Basic document file `DirectForm.vbd`.

The ActiveX document shown executing in Internet Explorer in Figure 4.14 works just the same as it does as a Windows application. You can add an Hypertext Markup Language (HTML) `HREF` command to incorporate access in an HTML page. Here's an example that allows you to test the program as part of any Web page:

```
<HTML>
<HEAD>
<TITLE>Microsoft Internet Explorer</TITLE>
</HEAD>
<BODY>
<A HREF="c:\sams\vbf\5\DirectoryForm.vbd">Company Directory</A>
</BODY>
</HTML>
```

FIGURE 4.14.

The sample ActiveX document, executing in Internet Explorer.

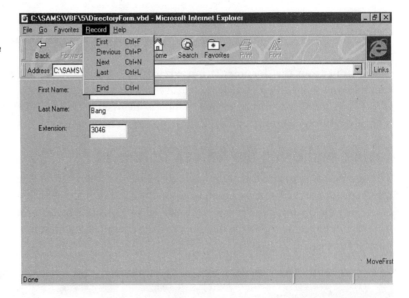

Summary

The ActiveX Document Migration Wizard enables you to easily develop visual forms and convert them almost automatically to ActiveX documents. The Migration Wizard comments out code that is unusable and replaces code that has direct substitutions in the UserDocument object. Most Visual Basic code can either be used directly or substituted. If event handlers, such as Form_Load, cannot be used directly, they can still be used as regular functions called from UserDocument event handlers.

In this chapter you have learned all the steps necessary to create reusable ActiveX documents. To learn more about developing applications and database programming in Visual Basic, refer to the following chapters:

- Chapter 3, "Getting Started with the Application Wizard," will help you get a jump start on application development.

- Chapter 5, "Designing Forms: Your Look and Feel," provides you expert tips and tricks for designing forms.

- Chapter 6, "Using Form Templates," introduces a plethora of pre-created, reusable forms.

4

THE ACTIVEX
DOCUMENT
MIGRATION
WIZARD

Designing Forms: Your Look and Feel

by Alex Reich

IN THIS CHAPTER

CHAPTER 5

The most visible aspect of an application to users is the user interface. This certainly makes it one of the most important aspects of an application. Not only do successful applications (applications that are well received by the targeted users) have well-written and optimized code, but also the interface is intuitive for the audience. Regardless of how much sweat and pain is put into writing an application, if the GUI is gooey, the application is as good as dead.

You must address several questions before designing your interface. Should your application use the multiple-document style, single-document style, or the Explorer style? How many forms do you plan to use in your application? Which commands will you include in your menus, and which functions do you plan to incorporate into toolbars for commonly used functions? Do you plan on using dialog boxes to communicate with users at various events? If so, which standard look and feel do you plan to give your dialog boxes? What kind of help assistance do you plan to give users? Are you going to write a help file? How about help links on an intranet or Internet site?

The first step in designing the user interface is to assess the aim of your application.

Generally, Visual Basic programs are written for two needs of an application: displaying information and acquiring information. Within these applications is the scope of their need: Will the applications be used constantly for your target users, or will the application be run only occasionally? Each of these applications addresses its own needs and requires a different mindset during design.

Your target audience of users should always be at the front of your mind when you design applications. If your application is primarily targeted for beginning or novice users, the design must be simple, whereas if your target audience is primarily advanced users, the design can be more complex. For export use of your application, you must consider international language, symbols, and culture as part of your interface design. Dialog boxes such as the one in Figure 5.1 illustrate an ambiguous message to the user.

Figure 5.1.

A dialog box with an ambiguous message.

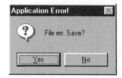

Designing a good user interface is an evolving process. The best guide is to take a look at existing office applications that you find easy to use yourself. In this chapter, I take a look at some of the tools you can use in your user interface design and how they affect your application.

User Interface Styles

As mentioned previously, the three styles of user interfaces are the *single-document interface*, or *SDI*, the *multiple-document interface*, or *MDI*, and the new *Explorer-style interface*. The most common application you have probably seen is the single-document interface design. The highly regarded Notebook.exe application is a good example of an SDI application. (See Figure 5.2.) SDI is perfect for narrow and focused-feature applications. Programs such as Notepad and Clock have a limited feature set and therefore require either one form to interact with the user or very few forms altogether.

FIGURE 5.2.

*Microsoft Notepad, an
SDI application.*

Microsoft Word, Excel, and VB itself are examples of MDI interface applications that enable users to use several documents simultaneously. With MDI, each document gets its own window, which allows users to interact with the application with a greater degree of control. (See Figure 5.3.) MDI applications typically have a Window menu on the right side of the menu bar that allows users to switch between windows and documents. Another common feature of the Window menu is to allow users to cascade, tile, and arrange the windows.

FIGURE 5.3.

*Microsoft Word, an
MDI application.*

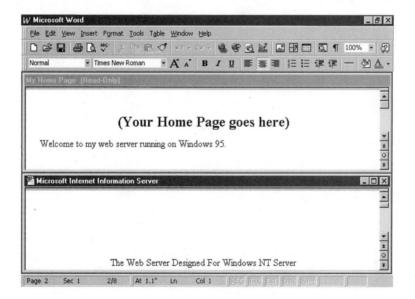

The purpose of the application determines the style. Certain applications' purposes naturally lend themselves to a particular style; for others, you must make a strategic decision about which style to use. Applications that use several forms, such as joint tax returns, may need multiple copies of similar forms; this seems to lend itself to the MDI style. Dedicated applications such as an alarm clock are usually best adapted to the SDI style, although another copy of the application may run in tandem.

Because the SDI style is common and generally easy to use, it is featured throughout the book in many of the examples. You must carefully plan and develop MDI applications. Later in this chapter, I explore many of the details you might want to consider when developing an MDI application.

The newest interface to be introduced is the *Explorer-style* interface. (See Figure 5.4.) The Explorer-style interface consists of two regions, or panes, of information. The left pane, or navigation pane, consists of a tree view control that determines where the user will navigate. The user may drill down through a hierarchy of information. The right pane, or main window, is basically an SDI window that is only one part of the entire application and that is controlled entirely by the navigation pane. The Explorer-style interface is naturally best suited for browsing through a large amount of information such as databases, libraries of pictures, documents, or files.

FIGURE 5.4.

Windows Explorer interface, an Explorer-style application combining a tree view with an SDI-like main window.

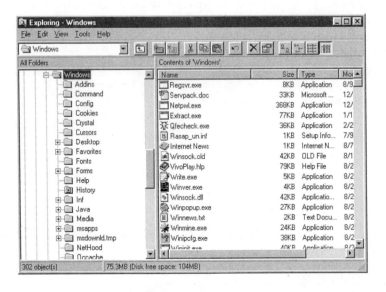

In addition to examining the examples in this chapter, the best way to compare each of the different styles is to use the Application Wizard. The wizard generates frameworks of each style and creates the forms and code to drive the interface.

MDI in Depth

MDI allows the creation of applications that are capable of maintaining several forms within one container form. Applications such as Microsoft Word, Excel, and even VB itself are examples of applications that use MDI. MDI is by far the most popular interface for content creation.

Documents, or *child forms*, are contained in the *parent form*, which is the workspace that houses all the child forms within the application. For instance, Microsoft Word provides the capability to display and create several documents simultaneously in multiple windows, each with a different type. However, no child form can leave the boundaries of the Word parent form. When the parent form is minimized, all the children are automatically minimized. Also, only the parent form's icon appears in the taskbar.

Parent Forms

As the main container forms for an application, parent forms or MDI form objects have certain restrictions. An application can have only one parent form. Parent forms cannot be converted into normal forms or even child forms, nor can normal or child forms be converted into a parent form. In addition, parent forms can never be modal. Look at the two windows in Figure 5.5. The different shading in the body of the parent form (MDIForm1) indicates its ability to contain other forms and its inability to contain controls other than the menu and picture box controls.

Normal Forms

Your first Hello, World! program most likely was built on a normal form, which is Visual Basic's default form type. Normal forms can be converted to child forms and vice versa; however, they can never become parent forms. This can be important in the circumstance that your program contains both parent forms with their children and normal forms. Consider the situation where the user minimizes the parent form while one of your normal forms is still displayed. You will have to code yourself in order to force all forms to minimize if the user minimizes one such as the parent form.

Modal Forms

One of the most common (although frustrating) examples of a modal form is the General Protection Fault, or GPF, dialog. If you are the unfortunate recipient of one of these dialogs, you will find you cannot continue operating the application until you acknowledge the message. Keep in mind that while this can be a useful form of communicating with the user, it can also provide an annoying method of interrogating and informing the user: Use modal forms sparingly.

5

DESIGNING
FORMS: YOUR
LOOK AND FEEL

FIGURE 5.5.

Normal and parent forms.

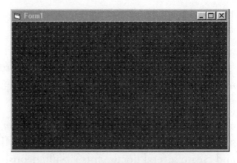

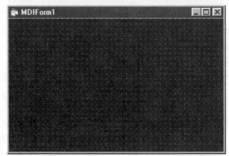

To create a parent form, you must use the Project menu or submenu because an MDI form is a special class of form in itself. Select the Add MDI Form command to create the parent form within the project. Notice in Figure 5.5 that the body of the form is a shade different from that of a conventional form. This difference occurs because the parent form is itself a container object whose *workspace* (the area within the borders of the parent form and underneath the title and menu bars) is reserved and cannot contain many of the standard controls that normal forms can contain.

TIP

Parent forms can only contain the menu and picture box controls or any controls that have an Align property. If you need other controls within your parent form, simply create a picture box control and place your other controls inside your picture box. Because the picture box control is itself a container object, you can include any other controls you need within the MDI form.

Designing Child Forms

Creating a child form is simple compared to creating its parent. A child form is merely a conventional form with its MDIChild property set to True. Any application can contain many different child forms of similar or different types. At design time, child forms are not limited to the boundaries of their parent form. You can add controls, set properties, and use methods and events in code; for all intents and purposes, at design time, child forms are just like any other conventional VB form.

You have two methods to determine at a glance whether a form is an MDI child: by checking the `MDIChild` property in the properties window or by looking at the project window. Visual Basic creates special icons for each type of form, as shown in Figure 5.6.

FIGURE 5.6.

Project window icons depict the standard, MDI, and child forms.

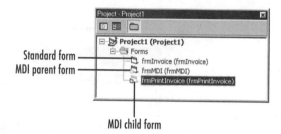

Standard form
MDI parent form
MDI child form

Child Forms' Runtime Attributes

Child forms at runtime take on several new attributes that you must keep in mind while designing MDI applications:

- Child forms, when minimized, appear within the parent form rather than the operating system taskbar. When the parent form is minimized, all the child forms are contained within the one parent icon. When a parent form is restored or maximized, all the children return to their last states.

- Child forms cannot be moved outside the boundaries of their parent form.

- Maximized child form captions are combined with their parent form's caption. (See Figure 5.7.)

- Child forms cannot be invisible or hidden.

- The `AutoShowChildren` property of the parent form allows you to indicate whether child forms are shown automatically when the parent form is shown (`True`) or hidden until in use (`False`).

- If a child form uses a menu, its menu becomes the dominant menu. (There can be only one menu on the screen at a time—either the parent's menu or the child's.)

Identifying Child Forms and Controls at Runtime

When creating module and class-level code, you will probably want to create subroutines and functions that use child forms and controls as arguments. You must be able to differentiate the active child form control on that form from other active child forms and controls and be able to pass a handle to it from the calling form. Several methods accomplish this using global variables, the `Me` keyword, and the `ActiveForm` and `ActiveControl` properties.

5

DESIGNING
FORMS: YOUR
LOOK AND FEEL

FIGURE 5.7.
Child forms.

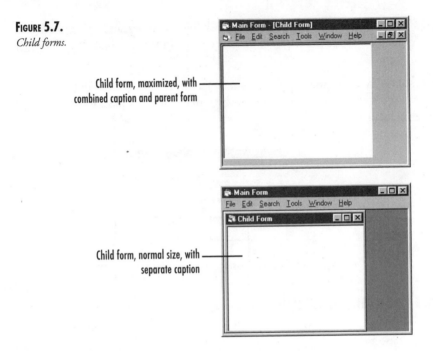

Child form, maximized, with ——
combined caption and parent form

Child form, normal size, with ——
separate caption

The Global Variable Method and the Me Keyword

Global variables have their obvious trade-offs: Overhead is one and maintenance is another. However, by using global variables, you can ensure that you will always point to the correct child forms. For example, you set a global variable such as `gblActiveInvoice` to the `Me` keyword:

```
Set gblActiveInvoice = Me
```

This allows the global variable `gblActiveInvoice` to act as a pointer to the current invoice. Whenever the user changes the focus from the invoice form to another form, the application knows which child had the last focus and can reference it accordingly. The `Me` keyword within the context of a form behaves as an implicitly declared variable, which makes for more readable code.

ActiveForm and ActiveControl

If a function simply needs the form or control handle passed to it, the `ActiveForm` and `ActiveControl` properties (which are intrinsic properties of the `Screen` object) will suffice. The `ActiveForm` property returns a handle to the currently active form, whereas the `ActiveControl` property returns a handle to the currently selected control. They can also be used in tandem:

```
Msgbox ActiveForm.ActiveControl.SelLength
```

> **NOTE**
>
> The parent form must have at least one child form visible before the `ActiveForm` or `ActiveControl` property can be accessed.

Closing Child Forms with `QueryUnload`

What happens to an MDI application when a user who is filling out a maximized child form invoice accidentally closes the application instead of the invoice? By default, the parent form automatically closes all the children and closes the application. To ensure that users are asked whether they want to save their work, you use the `QueryUnload` event on the parent form.

The `QueryUnload` event fires first for the parent form and then for every child form that is open. This event is perfect for centralized code that can access every member in the MDI application. For example, using the invoice application, you create a public variable in the child:

```
Public boolInvoiceChanged as boolean
```

You then set the variable equal to `True` if the users make any changes to the current invoice and `False` if the users save the invoice or cancel their changes. Because each of the public form-level variables is accessible from the `QueryUnload` event, you can check `boolInvoiceChanged` and query the users about whether they want to save changes.

The `QueryUnload` event contains two arguments, `Cancel` and `UnloadMode`. `Cancel` prevents the unload event from continuing and, if applicable, the application from ending. If the value of `Cancel` is nonzero, the form is *not* unloaded. The most common use of the `Cancel` event is for the user to be queried, "Would you like to save this first?" with the options of Yes, No, and Cancel. The Cancel option might set your `Cancel` argument to a nonzero value, say `123`, which would allow the user to continue working on the form.

The `UnloadMode` argument of the `QueryUnload` event designates what is causing the form to be unloaded. The constants are `VbFormControlMenu`, `vbAppWindows`, `vbAppTaskManager`, `vbFormCode`, and `vbFormMDIForm`, with the first three controlled by the user, by code, and per the parent's form closing, respectively. This argument is particularly useful for allowing for a graceful exiting depending on your application's internal states:

```
Private Sub Form_QueryUnload(Cancel as Integer, UnloadMode as Integer)
    If boolInvoiceChange Then
        If msgbox("Would you like to save your invoice?",
        ➥vbQuestion+vbYesNo , "Order Entry Application") = vbYes Then
            'Calls FileSave Routines
        EndIf
    EndIf
End Sub
```

5

DESIGNING FORMS: YOUR LOOK AND FEEL

Advanced MDI Techniques

The child–parent relationship has its faults; however, if you ever need to create a modal child form, you are out of luck. You can address this limitation by using the .Tag property of the child form. The .Tag property is a user-definable property found in all forms that you, the programmer, can use however you want. With the .Tag property workaround, the main form waits until the .Tag property is set by the child, thus forcing control to remain with the child form. The following code segment demonstrates use of this by allowing the parent to wait for the child to exit by looping with a DoEvents statement to allow other process to continue while waiting for the user:

```
Parent Form (frmMain.frm):
    Private Sub mnuModalChild_Click()
            ' Pseudo-Modal Dialog Box Demo
            frmChild.Show
    Do
        DoEvents
    Loop Until frmChild.Tag <> ""
    Unload frmChild
    MsgBox "Modal Child finished."
End Sub
Child Form (frmChild.frm):
    Private Sub cmdClose_Click()
    ' Set the tag for the form,
    ' the Do loop back in frmMain will finish execution.
    Me.Tag = "Close"
End Sub
```

Several other workarounds use the .Tag property with MDI forms. For example, you generally use global variables to keep track of which child is in use. With a .Tag property workaround, a child is immediately distinguishable by using a virtual index. Other uses include the .Tag property as temporary storage for SQL statements or for use in an Undo function.

Startup Form

In Visual Basic, by default, the first form designed in an application is the *startup form*. When an application begins execution, the form's Form_Initialize is fired and the form is displayed. If you want a different form to be the first form when the application starts, you must change the startup form:

1. In the Project menu, choose Project Properties.
2. Navigate to the General tab.
3. Select the desired form in the Startup Object listbox.
4. Select OK.

Of course, you don't always want to use a startup form, especially if you prefer a splash screen to describe your application and who wrote it. Splash screens are especially useful for applications that take a long time to load. By creating a Sub Main procedure in a conventional VB module, you can control the startup as well.

If you have ever seen an application partially paint the screen while processing something extremely complex, you will understand why it is better to do your heavy processing outside events such as `Form_Load` and `Form_Activate`. A common example you may have seen is loading a large file into an application and then attempting to switch applications. The `Repaint` of the second application is failing to occur because the first application is still processing. This can happen to your own applications unless you do much of your application initialization with routines such as the `Sub Main` procedure:

```
Sub Main()
    Dim gblDatabase as database

    'Show the user the splash screen before anything else.
    frmSplash.Show

'Code to Load forms, initialize recordsets, etc.

    ...

    'Application is initialized,
    'begin displaying required forms and unload the splash screen.
    frmMain.show
    Unload frmSplash
End Sub
```

This illusion makes the users think something is happening, and they imagine the application is loading faster. When the preloading and initialization routines are completed, you can display the first form and unload the splash screen from memory.

TIP

You can double your splash screen as an About box by using form-level variables as arguments to the form's function. This way, you can show more information to the user than what can be digested in the time span of a splash screen.

Of course, don't go overboard with splash screens. Fancy graphics and large bitmaps with tons of controls will slow down your application. If a splash screen is too burdensome, you might need a second splash screen while the first splash screen is loading!

Prebuilt Forms

Prebuilt forms free you from much of the drudgery of creating commonly used forms such as log-in forms, splash screens, and so on. By choosing one of the prebuilt forms when adding a form to a project, you save time by starting with a template that can be altered to your own specification.

Because the prebuilt forms are created only in memory, if you begin working with one, you can remove it any time without worrying about a corresponding file in your project directory.

This floating template functionality of prebuilt forms gives you the flexibility of trying differ-ent prebuilt forms without worrying about creating a mess on your hard drive. By beginning with one of these forms (see Figure 5.8), you can be hours ahead in doing development.

FIGURE 5.8.

The Add Form dialog shows numerous prebuilt forms that eliminate the drudgery of creating commonly used forms.

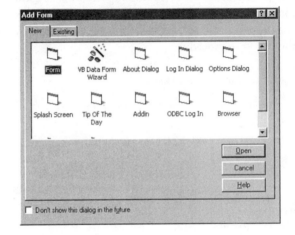

Using standards is a major factor in development, especially on large projects. The prebuilt forms adhere to commonly used Visual Basic standards that have evolved over the past several years. Using standards such as variable-naming conventions allows the programmer to easily remember both the function of a variable and its type.

The Data Form Wizard

The Data Form Wizard lets you automatically generate Visual Basic forms complete with bound controls and procedures to manage data from database tables, queries, and forms. You can use the Data Form Wizard for both single-source queries and tables with master/detail forms for one-to-many relationships. For optimization, the Data Form Wizard provides the Data con-trol, which uses JET technology, and the RemoteData control, which uses Remote Data Object (RDO) technology.

Creating a single-source form is relatively simple. You must select a database type using either installed JET drivers or an ODBC connection for remote connectivity. If you choose ODBC, the user must provide additional information for logins to the database. Once you determine the type, you select a database.

Next, you determine the form type: single, grid, or master/detail. As the name implies, a single form is dedicated to a single source, either a table or query. The grid layout uses the same source as a single layout but displays the information in a DBGrid control that is bound to the data-base. This is particularly useful when the database source contains large amounts of informa-tion the user can iterate through. The master/detail layout combines two related sources of data on one form.

Once you determine the layout, you select the individual fields. This creates the body of the record source statement, essentially building a SQL string behind the scenes of the wizard. With the master/detail layout, you have an additional step of choosing the relationship between the master data source and the detail data source. (See Figure 5.9.)

Figure 5.9.

The master data source is connected to the detail source via a relating field.

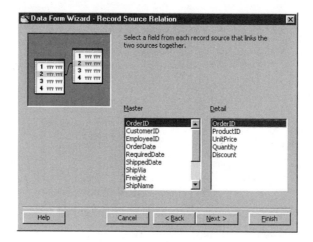

Finally, you choose the default controls, which determine the functionality of the form. Keep in mind when using the wizard that you might want the wizard to develop the functionality first so you can then limit this functionality through code, either by making invisible certain controls or limiting their capabilities based on other events.

Summary

Designing forms' looks and feels is an art that you should not take either too lightly or too seriously. The best programs are sometimes overlooked in praise because they have a user interface only a programmer could love. On the flip side, many applications provide a great deal of fluff with elegant menus of several levels and yet offer little substance to drive the interface. Designing an MDI, SDI, or Explorer-style interface, which is certainly less important than providing the functionality behind it, leaves a lasting impression on users, particularly those who use the application on a regular basis.

Technologies such as the prebuilt forms and Data Form Wizard allow you to quickly build prototypes of applications on the database. This step literally saves hours of labor that produces completely functional but bare forms. Once you determine the look and feel of the forms in your applications, the rest of the job is to simply tie together all the loose ends.

Using Form Templates

by John W. Charlesworth

IN THIS CHAPTER

Form Templates Overview

With each new version of Visual Basic, Microsoft adds features to make program development easier. One of the new features in Visual Basic 5 that will prove itself a timesaver for you is the addition of form templates. Form templates are predesigned and prebuilt forms that represent commonly used dialogs in many applications. The following are the standard form templates delivered with Visual Basic:

- About box
- Splash Screen dialog
- Tip of the Day dialog
- ODBC Logon dialog
- Security Login dialog
- Options dialog
- Internet browser
- Add-ins dialog
- Data grid
- Querys

Using these templates reduces the tedium of manually building them. This chapter tells you about

- Adding form templates to your project
- Using the form templates provided with Visual Basic
- Personalizing form templates for your application

To help illustrate the use of form templates, you'll create a project using them. You see by the end of the chapter that there is opportunity for you to create your own form templates specific to your business and applications. This can not only save you time but also provide standardization and consistency to your applications.

TIP

Form templates can help your project development by

- Saving time you otherwise spend manually building standard forms and dialogs and creating the programming for each of them
- Giving your applications a consistent presentation style, a consistent appearance, and a behavior consistent with other Microsoft Windows applications

Adding Form Templates to Your Project

There are three main ways to add form templates to your project:

- Use the Project | Add File menu to manually add files.
- Insert them using the standard Add Form methods.
- Ask for them during the Application Wizard interview.

Adding Forms Using the Project | Add File Menu

Using the Project | Add File menu is an acceptable way of adding a form template to your project; however, this is not the most preferred way and does not automatically update template object references in your project. Because the Add File method always defaults to the last directory opened, you might have to take extra steps to find and select the form templates directory. This method is generally used for adding files other than templates to projects.

Using the Standard Add Form Method

If you already have an existing project and want to use a form template, the preferred method is to use the Project | Add Form menu. Selecting this menu item brings up the Add Form selection dialog, as shown in Figure 6.1.

FIGURE 6.1.

*The Add Form dialog
used to select form
templates.*

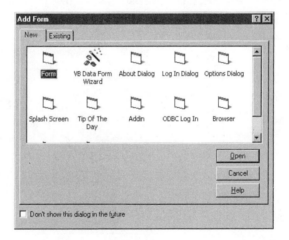

If you want to use a form template or file from a directory other than the form template directory, you can use the Existing tab on the same Add Form dialog, as shown in Figure 6.2. Notice that this tab gives you the normal file-browsing facility to locate your desired form template. You use this if you have a number of your own customized templates that you don't want stored in the main Visual Basic templates directory.

FIGURE 6.2.

You use the Existing tab on the Add Form dialog to search for templates outside the normal form template directory.

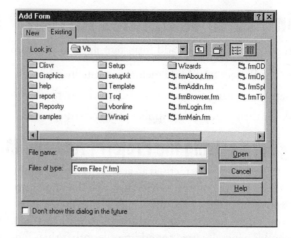

> **NOTE**
>
> If you don't see the Add Form dialog after selecting Project | Add Form, that means you turned off the display of form templates. To turn this display back on, select Tools | Options in Visual Basic and choose the Environment tab. Within the Show Templates For frame, make sure the Forms option is selected. This is shown in Figure 6.3.

FIGURE 6.3.

The Options dialog lets you choose whether to show form templates when selecting Project | Add Form.

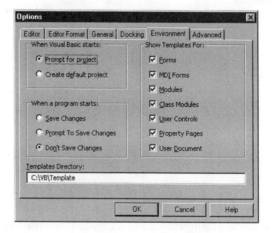

As mentioned before, you can only use the Add Form method of adding templates when you have an existing project.

> **NOTE**
>
> There is one additional item listed in the Add Form dialog that is not a template. This is the VB Data Form Wizard. The VB Data Form Wizard is discussed in detail in *Visual Basic 5 Development Unleashed*.

Other form templates come with Visual Basic but are specifically used by other wizards. An example of this is the Wizard Template for creating your own wizards. Other examples are the main program templates used to create your SDI, MDI, or Explorer-style form interfaces. These examples and others are discussed throughout this book.

Adding Forms Using the Application Wizard

When you do not have an existing project and intend to use the Application Wizard, you have the opportunity to select the form templates listed previously as part of the wizard interview process. Related to this chapter, there are three areas in the interview process where you can select form templates:

- Internet Connectivity
- Standard Forms
- Form Templates

Figure 6.4 shows the Internet Connectivity section of the Application Wizard interview. By selecting that you want Internet connectivity, you add a custom browser form to your project. A menu is built from the main form to access the browser form, and all associated programming to make the browser work is included.

FIGURE 6.4.

The Application Wizard Internet Connectivity section lets you add the Internet Web browser form to your project.

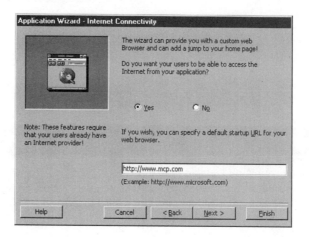

Figure 6.5 shows the Standard Forms section of the Application Wizard interview. Here you can choose to include the more general dialogs associated with many Windows applications.

FIGURE 6.5.

The Application Wizard Standard Forms section lets you add common form templates to your project.

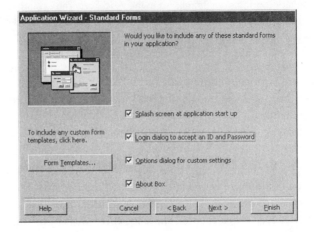

You can add form templates that are more uncommon or that you've created and placed in the standard form templates directory by clicking the Form Templates button on the Standard Forms section of the Application Wizard interview and then choosing the desired templates to add, as shown in Figure 6.6.

FIGURE 6.6.

Add uncommon or your own custom form templates by selecting the Form Templates dialog in the Application Wizard interview.

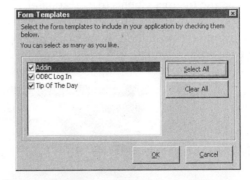

> **NOTE**
>
> Another way to add templates to a project is by using the `AddFromTemplate` method. You use this method to create project components dynamically, which is an advanced topic beyond the scope of this chapter. Consult *Visual Basic Books Online* for more information.

What Do the Form Templates Do for You?

Now that you know how to add form templates to your project, I'll discuss each of them to give you an understanding of their purpose and the depth of the programming behind the scenes, as well as some pointers on customizing the forms to best meet your needs.

I'll approach understanding templates by building a project using the Application Wizard and including most of the form templates related to this chapter. I'll also discuss some of the templates such as add-ins and ODBC security separately. After creating the project, you'll see how much these templates do for you without your having to do much programming.

I won't review all the steps for using the Application Wizard because that is covered in Chapter 3, "Getting Started with the Application Wizard." To build the sample project, follow these steps:

1. Start the Application Wizard and choose to create a Single Document Interface (SDI).

2. Select all menu options.

3. Leave the no default for using a resource file for strings. This isn't relevant to our sample.

4. Choose yes to add Internet connectivity. Go ahead and change the default startup URL to `http://www.mcp.com/sams/home.html`.

5. Choose all the standard forms (splash screen, login dialog, options dialog, and about box) and then click the Form Templates button.

6. Select the ODBC Log In and Tip of the Day templates. Click OK to return to the Standard Forms dialog and then click Next.

7. Choose "Yes, create forms from my database" on the Data Access Forms page. Choosing this invokes other interview pages that allow you to include the Data Grid and Query templates and also pages that build forms for you based on database tables you select. Select Access as the database format and `BIBLIO.MDB` as the database name. `BIBLIO.MDB` is provided with Visual Basic and, depending on your install options, is placed in the main Visual Basic directory. You can also find it in the Chapter 6 source materials directory on the CD-ROM provided with this book.

8. On the Select Tables page, choose to view both tables and queries. Go ahead and move the <Query List> and all table names from the Available column to the Selected column. This results in building the Data Grid, Query, and custom table forms for your project. After making these selections, go to the next step.

9. Call your project `TEMPLATES`, and then click Finish to build the application.

After you follow these steps, Visual Basic creates your new application. This might take several minutes. You start to see how powerful the form templates are when you run the program. Go ahead and play with the program. Notice how the overall application style, including menus, toolbar, and status bar, was created; how some common dialogs were implemented, and that the templates were added to this application. Look in particular at the View menu and its submenu items. You'll see the various form templates in action.

CAUTION

After adding templates either manually or through the Application Wizard, you might get an error (as shown in Figure 6.7) when trying to run the project.

This error is generally a result of the template referencing an object that does not exist in your project. You see what the error refers to because the unknown reference is highlighted in the Code window when the error is displayed. To correct this problem, add a reference for the object by selecting the Project | References menu and then adding the missing object to the project.

It might take some digging to determine which object contains the missing reference. The less apparent object references are for the add-in objects and data-access objects. For example, if you are missing a reference for a VBIDE object or method, add the Microsoft Visual Basic 5 Extensibility object, the connect class template, or the add-in module template. For data access, add in the appropriate DAO or database object library.

FIGURE 6.7.

This error message can be caused by referencing an object not formally added to the project.

Figure 6.8 shows the Visual Basic Project Explorer window, which lists the forms and module created by the Application Wizard. You can examine each form by double-clicking its entry in the Explorer window.

The following sections discuss each of the form templates in detail. The Add-Ins template is also discussed, although it is not included in the project sample created previously. You'll notice that the ODBC Logon and Tip of the Day templates are in the project but are not accessible from the sample application built. You must manually integrate these templates into your application.

6

FIGURE 6.8.

*The Project Explorer
window shows the list
of forms created for the
sample project by the
Application Wizard.*

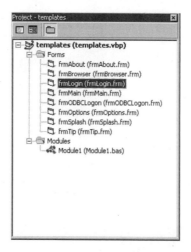

The About Box

Most Windows programs today contain an about box. About boxes display several important pieces of information, which may include

- Company name and application icon
- Copyright and legal trademarks
- Software title and EXE name
- Version numbers (major, minor, and revisions)
- An application description
- Comments (such as credits, license, terms of agreement, warnings, and disclaimers)
- System information
- Technical support information

Not all these pieces of information are included in the About Box template, however. The template as shown in Figure 6.9 includes only the

- Application icon
- Application title
- Version numbers
- Application description
- Warnings or disclaimers

FIGURE 6.9.

The About Box form template contains only a subset of the information available to you.

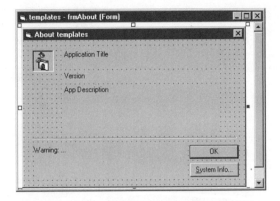

> **TIP**
>
> The About Box is a perfect example of a form template that you will want to customize and then resave (using a different name) as a standard template for your applications. This saves time and also ensures that legal notices, copyrights, and trademarks are standardized for all your applications.

You can modify the information contained on this form in several ways. You could choose to hard-code values on the form itself or in the form code; however, this usually leads to erroneous information in the about box because programmers sometimes forget to update version numbers and such. The preferred method for using the about box is to perform the following steps:

1. Decide what information you want on your about box.
2. Make any necessary visual changes to the form based on those decisions.
3. Set project properties for the application at design time using the Project | Properties dialogs, as shown in Figures 6.10 and 6.11.
4. Try to use application object properties to retrieve the content displayed on the about box, as shown in Listing 6.1.

Table 6.1 shows a list of some of the application object (APP) properties you may want to use in your about box.

6

FIGURE 6.10.

*The Project Properties
dialog lets you set
application properties
(such as Project Name
and Description), that
you can then use in the
about box.*

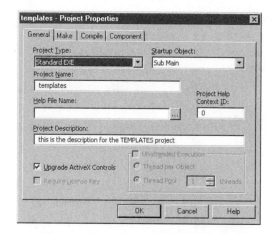

FIGURE 6.11.

*The Make tab of the
Project Properties
dialog is where you set
most of the application
properties for use in the
about box.*

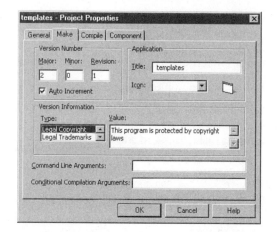

Table 6.1. Application object properties useful for an about box.

Property	Description
Comments	General purpose. Can be used to display whatever text you desire.
CompanyName	Your company name.
EXEName	The name of the executable program.
FileDescription	A description statement about a specific file.
LegalCopyright	Your copyright statement.

continues

Table 6.1. continued

Property	Description
LegalTrademarks	Your trademarks statements.
Major	Major software version number.
Minor	Minor software version number.
Path	Physical disk path from where this application was launched.
ProductName	Your product name.
Revision	A revision number within a particular major and minor software version.
Title	The title of this application.

Most of the application object properties shown in Table 6.1 directly correlate to the Project Properties dialogs shown in Figures 6.10 and 6.11. You can set these properties at design time using the Project Properties dialogs or at runtime by manually setting their values.

To retrieve the application object properties at runtime for use on the about box, add form load statements to the about box form, as shown in Listing 6.1.

Listing 6.1. Retrieving application object properties for your about box.

```
Private Sub Form_Load()
    lblVersion.Caption = "Version " & App.Major & "."
    ➥& App.Minor & "." & App.Revision
    lblTitle.Caption = App.Title
    lblDescription.Caption = App.Comments
    lblDisclaimer.Caption = App.LegalCopyright
lblFileDescription.Caption = App.FileDescription
End Sub
```

Figure 6.12 shows the modified about box. You can, of course, make your about box more complete and meaningful. My intent was purely to illustrate the use of application object properties. For the most part, that is all there is to about boxes.

The final part of the About Box template is the capability to display system information. This simple button you can see on the previous figures actually launches Microsoft's MSINFO program. This is a handy feature for users and is becoming a standard on most about boxes. The best part of the template is that all code for accessing the Registry and tracking down the location for this program, along with handling errors if it does not exist, is built into the template. You do not have to do any extra work to add this feature. Figure 6.13 shows the System Information program as launched by the about box.

FIGURE 6.12.

The about box, modified to display application object properties.

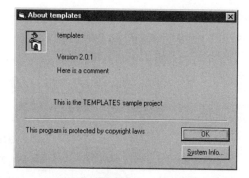

FIGURE 6.13.

The Microsoft System Information program as launched from the about box.

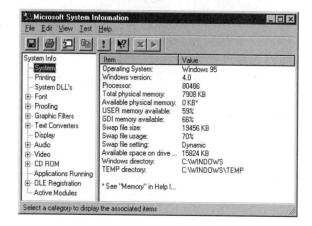

The Splash Screen

The splash screen serves two purposes: First, it serves as a quick startup screen identifying your application; second, it gives the user something to look at while the application loads. Splash screens can give the impression of a faster startup because the user sees something happening during the load.

Splash screens are similar to about boxes and often use the same type of information. Figure 6.14 shows the Splash Screen template.

There really isn't much to the Splash Screen template, and rightly so. Its purpose as mentioned previously, is to give the appearance of progress during the initial program load. With this in mind, don't get too caught up in entertaining the user with CPU-intensive graphics when you personalize this template for your application. It is easy to lose sight of this template's purpose. When you choose to use a splash screen, make sure you

■ Identify your purpose in adding a splash screen (providing performance perception, disclaimers, and licensing information or some introductory information).

- Stay focused on that purpose in customizing the form.

- Consider providing an option to turn off the splash screen, particularly if the splash screen includes any multimedia capabilities.

FIGURE 6.14.

The Splash Screen template used while launching an application.

As mentioned for about boxes, not all the application object properties are included on the Splash Screen template. This template includes placeholders for the following pieces of information:

- Application icon or logo
- Application title and name
- Version numbers
- Company name
- Copyright statement
- Warnings or disclaimers
- License to...
- Platform

The default text on the template is suggestive only, and you can add or replace these labels. As with the about box, you must provide values for the labels on the splash screen. No programming is built into the form to identify any values other than product name and software version.

> **TIP**
>
> The splash screen is another perfect example of a form template that you will want to customize and then resave (using a different name) as a standard template for your applications. This is a good form for introducing "market branding" into your application. The splash screen is the first thing your users see, and by using consistent splash-screen styles, you can give the appearance of a cohesive product line.

Figure 6.15 shows the Splash Screen template at runtime. No changes were made to the template or the use of application object properties.

FIGURE 6.15.

The splash screen at runtime, using some of the application object properties.

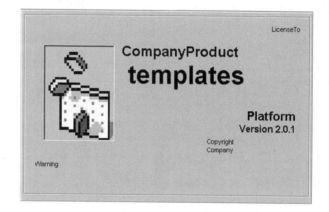

The Tip of the Day

The Tip of the Day template provides a useful way of offering very short tips to your users. You did not see this form in the sample application because, although it was included in the project, it must be manually integrated into your application.

You have two ways to integrate this template into your application: Invoke it during product launch within the main form's load code or provide a toolbar button or menu item to allow the user to invoke it on demand. You might also want to include an Options setting for turning the form on or off. Unless you provide an Options setting, the user does not have a way to turn the form back on if he turns it off using the checkbox on the tips form itself.

This template has several important aspects you should notice:

- The template is hard-coded to use TIPOFDAY.TXT as its tip file.
- The TIPOFDAY.TXT file contains all the tips and must reside in the directory where the application is launched.

- There must be one tip per line in the TIPOFDAY.TXT file. This means your tips must be very concise.

- This template is not practical unless you have more than 30 tips due to the frequency that users would see repeated tips.

- Because tip-of-the-day functions are generally turned off by users within the first few weeks of product use, don't rely on them as a primary source of help for users. Also, tip-of-the-day forms do not offer help search capabilities.

- The template includes code to support either random or consecutive tips display.

Figure 6.16 shows the Tip of the Day template. Notice how it provides an appealing way to give users information one manageable chunk at a time. It is unlikely that you need to modify the form itself. Personalization of this template comes in adding your own tip file.

FIGURE 6.16.

The Tip of the Day template is useful for providing very short tips to users.

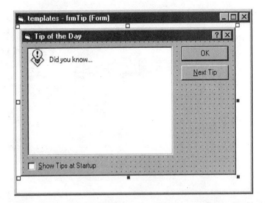

> **CAUTION**
>
> Due to the way the application object Path method works, the Tip of the Day template does not work if you put your application and tips file in the root directory. The Path method does not return a trailing \ unless the application was launched from a drive's root directory. The template presumes that it was not launched from a root directory and automatically appends a trailing \. Attempting to read the tips file from the root directory results in a filename of *drive letter*:\\TIPOFDAY.TXT, which is invalid due to the double \.

You must create your own tips file. Some people use this template to offer cute quotables or sayings, whereas others provide helpful tips and tricks for using the particular application. You should use it because it makes sense for your application and not because it's an easy-to-add, cute feature. It does have its drawbacks as written. The primary drawback is that the code fully loads all tips into memory before displaying any tips.

> **CAUTION**
>
> The Tip of the Day template, as written, loads all tips in the `TIPOFDAY.TXT` file into memory at one time. If you have a large number of tips, this can take significant load time and significant memory usage. Be cautious about how large you make the tips file.
>
> On the other hand, the tip-of-the-day feature really doesn't offer much benefit if fewer than 30 tips are included. With fewer than 30 tips, users frequently see repeated tips, and therefore its value is diminished.

Figure 6.17 shows the tip-of-the-day form at runtime. In this case, it is reporting that the tip file is missing, although this is in itself a good example of the information that can be shown to the user.

FIGURE 6.17.

An example of the tip-of-the-day feature during runtime. In this case, it reports that the tips file is missing.

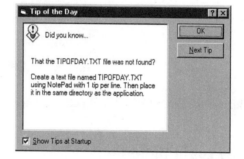

The ODBC Logon Dialog

As with the Tip of the Day template, you did not see the ODBC Logon form when playing with the sample project even though it was included in the project. You must manually integrate this form into your project. Figure 6.18 shows the ODBC Logon template.

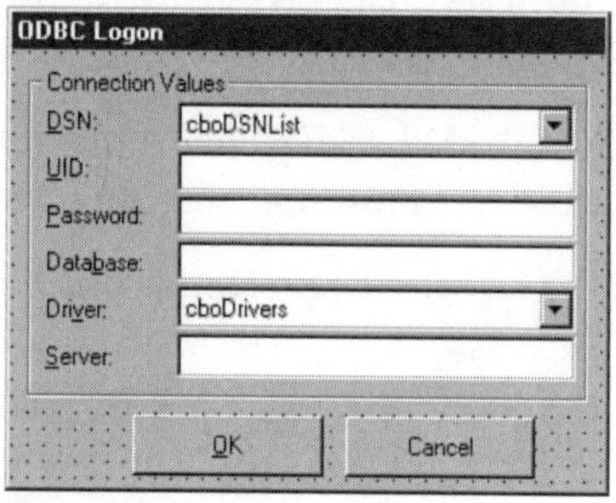

FIGURE 6.18.

The ODBC Logon template helps your users get connected to a database.

The ODBC Logon dialog is just what its name implies. It converses with the ODBC drivers you set up on the user's machine and fills its comboboxes with the available choices for database server names (DSNs) and available drivers. The user then has the capability to enter connect information. When the dialog is complete, it proceeds to connect to the database using the parameters specified by the user.

Unless ODBC is set up on the user's machine, this template offers no value. Also, it communicates strictly with the 32-bit ODBC drivers. Figure 6.19 shows the ODBC Logon dialog at runtime, filled in with sample connect information.

FIGURE 6.19.

The ODBC Logon dialog at runtime, with sample connect data.

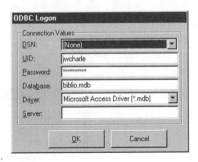

For more information about ODBC and getting connected, see *Visual Basic 5 Development Unleashed.*

The Security Login Dialog

The Security Login template is not quite as sophisticated as the ODBC Logon template. The Security Login template merely provides password-protected access to the application itself, based on password-checking code you add to the template. This template does not require changes to the template form itself, but you must add the programming behind the scenes.

One feature of this dialog is that it retrieves the user name for the user logged on to Windows and then sets the User Name field on the dialog. It also suppresses the password by replacing input characters with asterisks.

You must add the password-checking code in the template. By default, it expects a null password, meaning that the user must not enter a password.

Figure 6.20 shows the Security Login template at runtime.

FIGURE 6.20.

This Login template provides security access to your application.

The Options Dialog

Unlike some of the other templates, the Options template requires modification to personalize it for your application. It is not useful unless you do so, as you can see in Figure 6.21. The template provides general characteristics and behavior for setting applications options, but you must add the controls and programming for each options setting.

FIGURE 6.21.

The Options template has property pages that you can categorize and customize to control settings for your application.

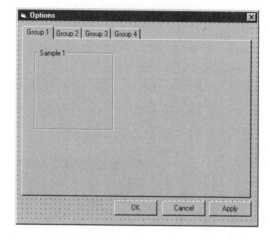

The only programming included in the template is for moving between the property pages and managing display of the controls on each page.

To customize this template, you need to

- Determine what settings you want your users to control for your application.
- Decide how best to organize the settings on property pages along with how many property pages you need.
- Add controls to the property pages for the settings.
- Add programming to manage the individual settings, apply them during runtime, and save them for subsequent use of the application.

TIP

Avoid writing directly to an INI file to save your application settings. Rather, for Windows 95 and NT applications, use the Registry functions to save, retrieve, and delete your Options settings. See this chapter and also *Visual Basic 5 Development Unleashed*, for more information.

The standard Registry location for storing program information for Visual Basic applications is

```
HKEY_CURRENT_USER\Software\VB and VBA Program Settings\appname\section\key
```

Table 6.2 shows the preferred functions you should use for setting or retrieving your application's Options settings.

Table 6.2. Registry functions for setting and retrieving Options settings.

Procedure	Description
GetSetting	Retrieves Registry settings
SaveSetting	Saves or creates Registry settings
GetAllSettings	Returns an array containing multiple Registry settings
DeleteSetting	Deletes Registry settings

Figure 6.22 shows a great example of an Options dialog. It is Visual Basic's own Tools | Options dialog. Note how you can organize the information and property pages in any way you choose.

Figure 6.22.

Visual Basic's own Tools | Options dialog is a good example of how you can customize the Options template.

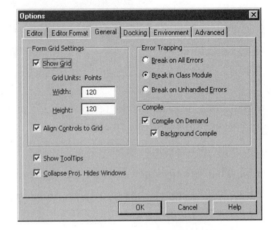

The Internet Browser

One of the nicest templates available in Visual Basic 5 is the Internet Browser. This template lets you provide Internet access to users directly from your application. The many possible uses for adding this template to your projects include

- Getting online technical support
- Downloading software updates
- Getting feedback directly from the users
- Taking the opportunity to show users your other products
- Directly connecting to knowledge bases, Frequently Asked Questions (FAQs), and online help

6

USING FORM
TEMPLATES

■ Increasing the percentage of users who register their software because of online convenience

■ Offering online purchasing

You can probably think of many other possible uses. The Internet Browser template presumes you already have an Internet connection established and uses that connection by default. One nice feature is that the browser inherits certain properties from your other browsers, such as Options settings for showing pictures or playing sounds.

Although the Application Wizard places access to the Internet Browser in the View | Web Browser menu, you can move it to another location, rename it, add multiple menus that start the browser using different URLs, or even automatically start the browser when your application is launched.

Behind the scenes, the browser manages its own window characteristics and page (URL) settings. It is very basic, providing only the most fundamental features such as forward, back, refresh, stop, and search functions. Figure 6.23 shows the Internet Browser template in action.

FIGURE 6.23.

The Internet Browser template, connected to the Sams Web site.

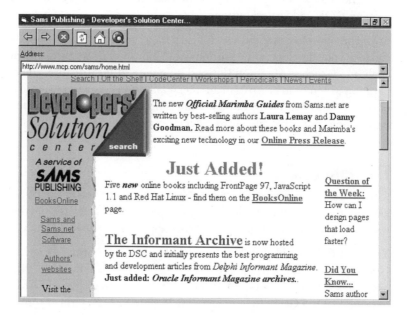

If you want, you can add your own toolbar buttons and menu features to the browser. You can change most aspects of its appearance to be consistent with the style of your own applications.

One thing to keep in mind, however, is that if you provide the Internet Browser as a fundamental component of your application, you might have to provide support when users call you asking how to set up their Internet connection. This can become a significant effort.

Add-ins

In order to use the Add-Ins form template, you also need to use the Add-Ins module and Connect class templates. These different types of templates are not intended to be used separately, and it is not recommended that you add the Add-In form template from either the Application Wizard or the Project | Add Form menus. Rather, because an add-in is its own program type, you should use the Add-In project template by choosing New Project from the Visual Basic File menu.

> **NOTE**
>
> Add-ins can be fairly complicated to fully understand and implement and are beyond the scope of this chapter; however, you can learn more about them in Chapter 3 and in *Visual Basic 5 Development Unleashed*.

I have not included a figure here for the Add-Ins form template because it is merely a blank form with OK and Cancel buttons.

As you become more proficient with Visual Basic, you'll start to see ways that add-ins can greatly enhance your development environment. You can also use them to add functions to other applications such as Microsoft Office. Using the add-ins structure, you can integrate your application to appear to be a part of another application—you can make it appear as a menu item or toolbar button or even a hotkey within other programs. The trend for Windows programs is to become more integrated with other programs, and add-ins help you do just that with your application.

The Data Grid

The Data Grid form template is not specifically mentioned in the Application Wizard interview but is added automatically when you choose to add database functions and select that you want to see specific database tables or lists. Figure 6.24 shows a Data Grid template.

The Data Grid is added to forms created by the Data Forms Wizard. You can see the Data Grid in the sample application by choosing View | Data Forms and then selecting one of the listed tables. You'll see a Grid button on the data form displayed. When you select the Grid button, the Data Grid displays. Figure 6.25 shows a Data Grid at runtime.

The Data Grid manages accessing your particular database and allows users to refresh, sort, or filter table data. Other than customizing the data sets you display, there isn't much to customize on this template. The template even supports columnar adjustments (changing column widths).

To learn more about databases and how to access them, refer to *Visual Basic 5 Development Unleashed*.

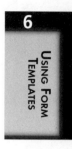

FIGURE 6.24.

The Data Grid form template helps you display database table records in an organized way.

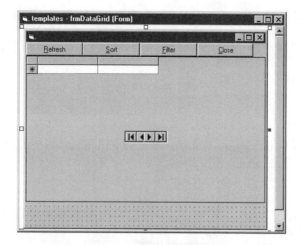

FIGURE 6.25.

The Data Grid template lets you easily display and organize table data.

Title	ISBN	Author
Microsoft Office Developer's Guide (Sams Developer's Guide	0-6723064-7-6	Glisic, Savo G.
Teach Yourself Game Programming in 21 Days/Book and Cd-Rom	0-6723056-2-3	Lamothe, Andre
Master Visual Basic 3/Book and Cd-Rom	0-6723051-4-3	Gurewich, Ori
Teach Yourself Database Programming With Delphin in 21 Days	0-6723085-1-7	Gurewich, Ori
Top Secret : Data Encryption Techniques/Book and Disk	0-6723029-3-4	Held, Gilbert
Programming Sound for DOS and Windows/Book and Disk	0-6723030-9-4	Gurewich, Ori
Word for Windows 6 Super Book/Book and Disk	0-6723038-4-1	Kerr, James
Essential Sybase	0-6723091-5-7	Herbert, Simon
Programming Mapi/Book and Disk	0-6723074-8-0	Lampton, Christophe
Os/2 2.211 Unleashed/Book and Cd-Rom	0-6723044-5-7	Gloor, Peter A.
Teach Yourself Graphics Programming in 21 Days	0-6723059-1-7	Lampton, Christophe
Delphi Developer's Guide/Book and Cd-Rom	0-6723070-4-9	Gurewich, Nathan
Networking Windows : Netware Edition/Book and Disk	0-6723020-6-3	Marks, Howard
Programming Tapi/Book and Disk	0-6723062-5-5	Lampton, Christophe
Tricks of the Game-Programming Gurus/Book and Cd-Rom	0-6723050-7-0	Lamothe, Andre
C Programmer's Guide to Graphics	0-6722278-4-3	Holmes, Geoffrey
Absolute Beginners Guide to Memory Management/International	0-6723035-6-6	Goodner, Brenda
Quick C Programming	0-6722272-1-5	Helman, Paul
32-Bit Programming	0-6723076-2-6	Lampton, Chris
Tricks of the Game Programming Gurus/Book and Cd-Rom	0-6723084-6-0	Lamothe, Andre
Os/2 2.211 Unleashed/Book and Cd-Rom	0-6723044-5-7	Kerr, David
Lotus 1-2-3 in Business : Release 2.3/Book and 5 1/4 Disk	0-6722280-3-3	Griffin, Michael P.
Foxpro Unleashed/Book and Cd	0-6723075-8-8	Khoshafian, Setrag
Teach Yourself Visual dBASE 5.5 Programming in 21 Days	0-6723067-3-5	Gurewich, Nathan
The Waite Group's C Programming Using Turbo C++/Book and Disk	0-6723039-9-X	Lafore, Robert
Programming Sound for DOS and Windows/Book and Disk	0-6723030-9-4	Gurewich, Nathan
Turbo Pascal 6 : Programming for the Pc/Book and 5 1/4 Disk	0-6722281-1-4	Hergert, Douglas

Querys

The Querys form template is not specifically mentioned in the Application Wizard interview, but is added automatically when you choose to add database functions and select that you want to see specific query lists. Figure 6.26 shows a query template.

The Querys template is added to the project by the Data Forms Wizard. You can see the Querys dialog in the sample application by choosing View | Data Forms and then selecting Querys.

FIGURE 6.26.

The Querys form template lists queries saved within a database and lets you execute them.

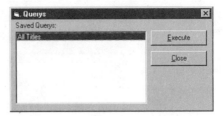

The Querys dialog lists all queries stored within the selected database and lets you select a query and execute it. Figure 6.27 shows the result of executing a selected query; yes—it is a data grid as described in the previous section.

FIGURE 6.27.

This data grid is the result of executing a query.

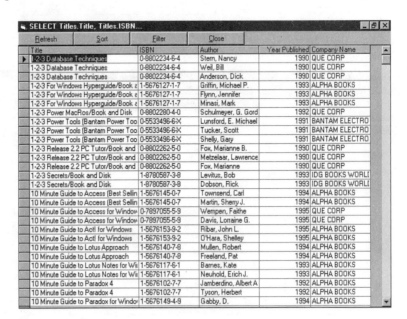

To learn more about databases and how to access them, refer to *Visual Basic 5 Development Unleashed.*

Using Your Own Form Templates

To add your own form templates, you merely need to follow these steps:

1. Create your desired form (including controls, menus, toolbars, status bars, accelerators, help IDs, and so on).

2. Add all navigation and event-handling support.

3. Add programming to your form to perform the functions you want to share.

4. Test your form under all the conditions in which you intend it to be used.

5. Place the form template in the standard Visual Basic form templates directory or in a shared directory from which others can access it.

As you become more advanced, you might prefer to store your form templates in Visual Sourcesafe, as discussed in *Visual Basic 5 Development Unleashed* (also from Sams Publishing). This gives you full version control and helps you better manage shared components between multiple applications.

TIP

Keep a central repository of your customized forms, whether in a shared directory or in Microsoft's Visual Sourcesafe. This helps you and your colleagues avoid adding outdated or incorrect templates to projects.

Also, don't overwrite the Visual Basic–provided templates. If you choose to use one of these templates as the basis for your own customized template, save the new template under a different name to avoid future confusion for yourself or others.

Summary

This chapter describes how form templates can help your project development by

- Saving time you would otherwise spend manually building standard forms and dialogs and creating the programming for each of them

- Giving your applications a consistent presentation style, a consistent appearance, and a behavior consistent with other Microsoft Windows applications

I hope you now have an understanding of form templates and can use them to enrich your projects. Perhaps the most significant benefits of using form templates include the capability to share your own customized templates for purposes of creating product branding, product integration with other applications, and consistency within your own product lines.

Property Pages and the Property Page Wizard

by Mike McMillan

IN THIS CHAPTER

One of the new features of the Visual Basic IDE in version 5.0 is the property page. In previous versions of Visual Basic, the properties of a form, control, or project were displayed in a standard properties window. The properties window is a two-column window with the property name on the left and a textbox or a combobox on the right for viewing or changing the property setting. You are familiar with using the Properties window if you read the preceding chapters of this book.

Not all properties, however, are best displayed in the properties window. Take the Font property, for example. You can set many different attributes for a font, such as the size, style, and whether to make the font bold, underlined, or italic. Because these attributes won't fit easily into the properties window, changing the Font property of a control involves a dialog box with all the different attribute settings. (See Figure 7.1.) Presenting the Font attributes in this manner is fairly awkward, so a better way to do it is the property page.

FIGURE 7.1.

The Font *property dialog box.*

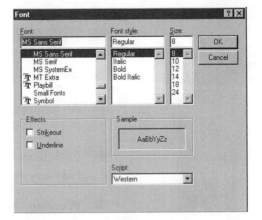

An Overview of the Property Page

VB provides a standard property page design in the shape of a tabbed form. A form can have several tabs, each containing a group of similar properties. Figure 7.2 shows the property page for a newly created project file.

To view a project's property page, you select it from the Project menu. The menu selection is named after your project's name, such as Project1 Properties if you are still using the default name for your project. Figure 7.2 shows the property page that is loaded when you select Project1 Properties.

A project's property page has four tabs—General, Make, Compile, and Component. Notice in Figure 7.2 that the Project Type setting is a combobox. This type of control is necessary because you can choose from several project types. (See Figure 7.3.) It is not convenient to cram these choices into a properties window.

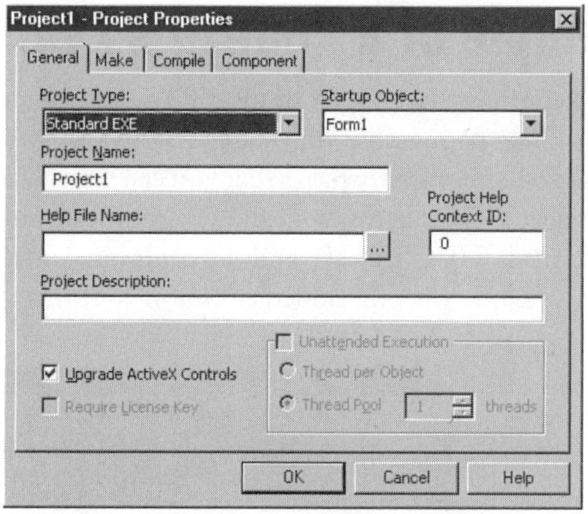

FIGURE 7.2.

A project property page.

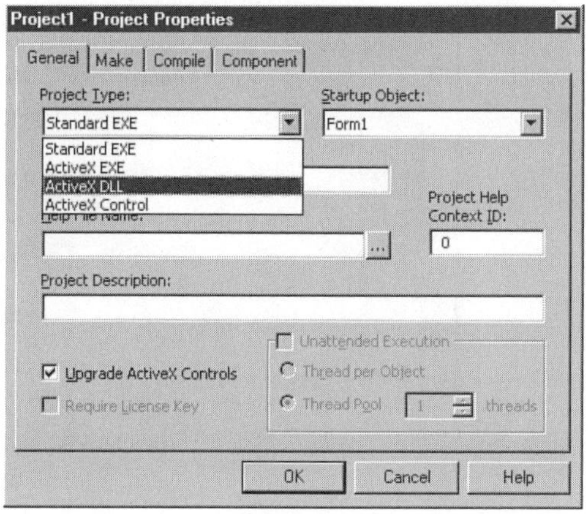

FIGURE 7.3.

An example of a combobox on a property page.

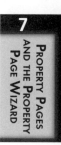

There are other choices on this tab and the other tabs that use comboboxes to present multiple choices for a property setting.

Another aspect to using property pages has a greater benefit than merely making more choices available to the user. Using property pages to present property settings is a more user-friendly way to present the user with the information about the properties. The properties window was a cramped, narrow window that was never the right width. It seemed that the one property you wanted to change or view was just off the screen, requiring scrolling.

Property pages present property settings in an easy-to-view, easy-to-use format. The settings are conveniently grouped so that you don't have to scroll around just to change the placement of a control on the screen. As a developer, you also have the freedom to present property attributes in any way you want. This means that changing the Font property doesn't require a dialog box; all the attributes can easily fit on one property page.

An Example of a Control's Property Page

The standard controls that are part of the VB toolbox are not equipped with property pages in order to keep them compatible with past versions of VB. However, the new Windows common controls do have property pages that you can view by adding the controls to your project. To do this, select Components from the Project menu and check the box marked Microsoft Common Controls 5.0. Click OK, and the common controls are added to the toolbox. Figure 7.4 shows the toolbox with the added common controls.

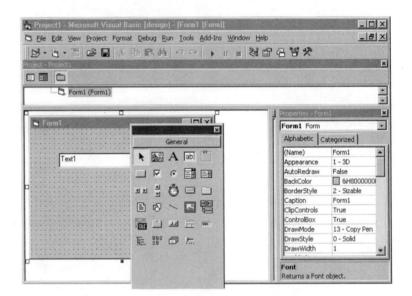

To view the property page of one of the common controls, add one of the controls to a form. For this example, the progress bar is placed on a blank form.

Once the control is on the form, you have two ways to view the progress bar's property pages. One way is to click the control and then select View | Property Pages from the menu. The other way is to double-click the Custom setting in the properties window. Using one of the two methods, open the progress bar's property pages on the screen, as shown in Figure 7.5.

If you compare the properties on the General and Picture tabs in the property pages with the properties in the progress bar's properties window, you discover an important fact about property pages: Not all the properties that a control can have are found in the property pages. The developer always decides which properties should be placed in the property pages, which properties belong in the properties window, and which properties belong in both places.

FIGURE 7.5.

*The progress bar's
property pages.*

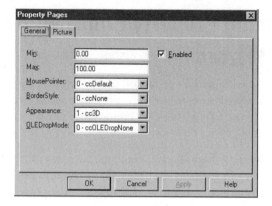

FIGURE 7.6.

*The error message
generated from trying to
view a standard
control's property pages.*

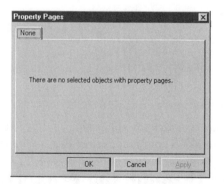

The first rule to use when deciding where to place properties is that properties which are difficult to set in the properties window belong in the property pages. You saw a clear example of such a property already—a property with many settings that should be presented to the user with a combobox.

The second rule of using property pages is to place the most commonly set and changed properties in both the property pages and the properties window. Of course, this rule is subjective, but as a developer, you will know which properties are adjusted the most. Put these properties in the property pages and the properties window.

Remember that the standard VB controls in the toolbox do not have property pages associated with them. If you try to view the property pages of a standard control, such as a textbox, you get an error message like the one shown in Figure 7.6.

You can create your own property pages only for the controls you design yourself. To make things easier for you, VB provides the Property Page Wizard. The next section describes using the Property Page Wizard to create property pages for a user-designed control.

Designing Property Pages with the Property Page Wizard

You can use the Property Page Wizard to step through the creation of property pages for your control. The wizard saves you time over designing the property pages yourself, and it keeps track of things you might have a hard time remembering, such as which properties you defined for your control.

To use the Property Page Wizard, you must have two things in place—a control to set properties for and the properties to set. Other chapters of this book help you create a control and use the ActiveX Interface Control Wizard to create the properties for the control. This example works with a control that is ready to go, properties and all. The RegControl, shown in Figure 7.7, is a control for working with the Registry.

FIGURE 7.7.

The RegControl ActiveX control.

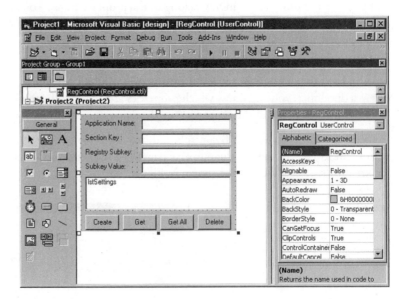

This control allows you to make application-specific Registry entries using a predefined Registry subkey where all VB applications store Registry information.

Working Through the Property Page Wizard Screens

The Property Page Wizard is loaded from the VB Add-Ins menu. If the wizard is not available directly from this menu, use the Add-Ins Manager to add it to your Add-Ins menu. Select the Property Page Wizard, and the Introduction screen appears. (See Figure 7.8.)

FIGURE 7.8.

The Property Page Wizard Introduction screen.

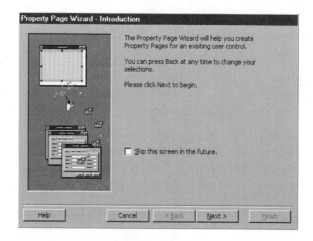

As with the other VB wizards, the Introduction screen simply tells you what the Property Page Wizard can do. The usual wizard command buttons are available at the bottom of this and all other screens of the wizard. There is also a checkbox you can check if you don't want to see the Introduction screen the next time you run the wizard.

To continue with the wizard, click the Next button.

Selecting the Property Pages for Your Control

The next screen is titled Select the Property Pages. You use this screen to create the property pages that appear with your control. The wizard creates as many pages as it can, but you must create most of the pages yourself. Figure 7.9 shows the Select the Property Pages screen.

FIGURE 7.9.

The Select the Property Pages screen.

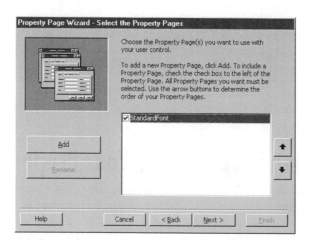

The only property page the wizard created for this control is the StandardFont page. Of course, the RegControl control has more properties than just Font properties, so you must create more property pages.

To create a new page, click the Add button. The wizard asks you for a new property page name. Enter the name and click OK. The new property page name is displayed directly below the StandardFont page that the wizard created.

Figure 7.10 shows two new property pages added for the RegControl: Appearance and Behavior. I chose these names because they mirror categories used in the properties window. Of course, you can use any name you want. Keep in mind that this name will appear on a property page tab, so the name should reflect the properties that will appear on the page.

FIGURE 7.10.

The Appearance and Behavior property pages added to the Select the Property Pages screen.

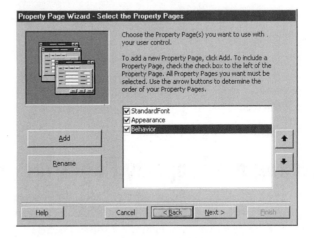

The order in which the property pages appear in the screen's listbox is the order in which they will appear on the property pages the user sees when he is working with the control. If you want to change the order, highlight a property page name and click the up or down arrow. This moves the name up or down in the list and changes the order in which the names will appear.

When you add the property pages you want and put them in the proper order, click the Next button to move to the next screen.

Adding Properties to Your Property Pages

The next step in the wizard is to add properties to your property pages. The Add Properties screen presents a listbox with all the properties on the left of the screen and your property pages as a blank tabbed form on the right of the screen. For each property page, you add properties to the page by highlighting a property and clicking the right arrow to move the property from the listbox to the blank form. Figure 7.11 shows the Appearance property page after its properties were added.

FIGURE 7.11.

Adding properties to a property page.

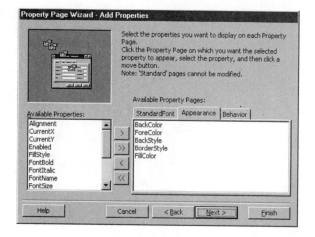

Follow the same procedure to add properties to the other property pages. Figure 7.12 shows the properties that were added to the Behavior property page.

FIGURE 7.12.

The Behavior properties.

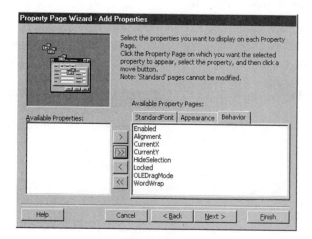

When you add all the properties to their respective property pages, click Next to move to the next step of the wizard.

Finishing Your Property Pages

The next step in the wizard is the Finished screen. This screen lets you know that you are finished with the wizard and asks if you want to see a report of what to do next with your property pages. Figure 7.13 shows the Finished screen of the Property Page Wizard.

FIGURE 7.13.

The Finished screen.

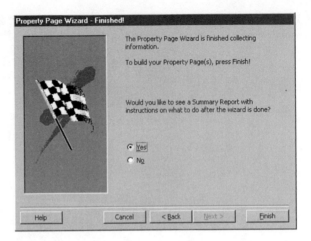

If you want to see the summary report, select the Yes button. Then click Finish, and the wizard will finish its work. A dialog box reports when the property pages are created. Click OK, and the summary report appears.

The summary report is divided into two sections—testing and debugging property pages and making bullet-proof, full-featured property pages. These sections give you hints on what to do next with the property pages created by the wizard. Figure 7.14 shows the summary report.

FIGURE 7.14.

The Property Page Wizard summary report.

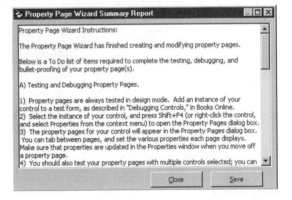

After you view the summary report, you can close it or save it to a file. If you decide to save it, a dialog box appears to let you enter a filename and a directory for the report. After you do this, the Property Page Wizard closes and you return to the Visual Basic IDE. Now you are ready to test your property pages.

Testing the Property Pages Created by the Property Page Wizard

To test the property pages you created, you need to put the control on a form. Once the control is on the form, you can view the property pages in two ways. The first way is to select View | Property Pages from the VB menu when the control is on a form.

The other way to view a control's property pages is to double-click the Custom property setting in the properties window. This also opens the control's property pages.

Figure 7.15 shows the property pages created for RegControl. You can move from page to page by clicking the tab for the page you want. You can set a property by typing in the textbox by the property setting. These settings affect the appearance, behavior, or font attributes of the control just as if the control had been built into VB.

FIGURE 7.15.

Viewing the property pages created by the Property Page Wizard.

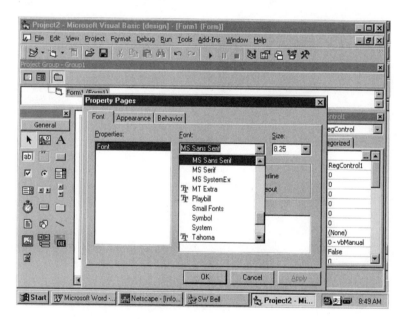

Summary

Property pages provide a user-friendly way to allow the users of your custom-made controls and applications to set properties. Using property pages allows you to create property attributes that can be set from a combobox or displayed all together without including a separate dialog box.

To help you create property pages, Visual Basic provides the Property Page Wizard. The wizard can determine the properties you defined for a control and help you distribute them among different property pages. The wizard also provides you with tips on debugging your property pages and making them more user friendly.

Going Beyond Menu Basics

by Greg Perry

IN THIS CHAPTER

CHAPTER 8

Menus give users options they need to select from one of several alternatives. Visual Basic provides the Menu Editor, a dialog box with which you can create standard menus for your applications. Your application's menus will act and look like most other Windows applications' menus, so your users will feel right at home navigating the menus you create.

Design your applications' menus so they maintain as much consistency with other Windows applications as possible. Most Windows applications contain a File|Exit menu option, for example, and you should create the same menu option so your users can easily terminate the program without hunting for a more obscure (and less common) menu option.

The highlights of this chapter include

- The Menu Editor is a dialog box that gives you an organized view of menu properties.
- Menu bar access keys and menu item shortcut keys let users select menu options from the keyboard.
- Help context IDs ensure that your users get the help they need when they don't understand a particular menu option.
- Menus can dynamically shrink or grow as users run applications.
- You can specify exactly which menu options appear in a container application's menu bar if a user embeds or links your application to another application.
- Pop-up menus are simple to generate, and they provide quick access to common options.

Menu Editor Basics

If you've worked with Visual Basic before, you probably used the Menu Editor to create menus for your applications. In case you are unfamiliar with the Menu Editor and its purpose, this section reviews some of the basic concepts associated with the Menu Editor.

Figure 8.1 shows VB's Menu Editor dialog box, which appears when you press Ctrl+E or select Tools|Menu Editor from VB's development environment menu. The Menu Editor lets you specify your application's menu bar contents as well as the options that appear when your users select a menu bar option. The Menu Editor's controls let you customize the menu so that submenus, shortcut keys, and checked menu options appear in your application.

The Menu Editor gives you a uniform way to enter property values for menu options. An application's menu is nothing more than an object that supports properties (such as the menu name and shortcut keys) and the Click event procedure. When you finish entering menu information in the Menu Editor, the Properties window holds all the menu's property values, and you can modify the menu from the Menu Editor, from the Properties window, or with code at runtime. All the Menu Editor dialog box's fields specify property values for your application's menu.

FIGURE 8.1.

You create the menus for your VB application with the Menu Editor.

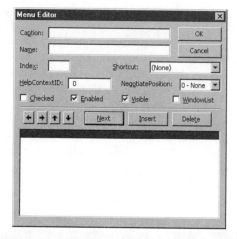

> **NOTE**
>
> Sometimes the items that appear on a menu bar are called *menus* because they become pull-down menus when the user selects that item. The individual items on the pull-down menus are often called *options*. If a menu option produces yet another menu, that secondary menu is called a *submenu*. If a menu option produces a dialog box, such as Visual Basic's File | Open Project... option, ellipses appear after the name to let users know that a dialog box appears for that selection. When your menu options produce dialog boxes, you should also follow this ellipses standard.

As you build your application's menu, the Menu Editor holds the menu's descriptive information. For example, if the first item on your application's menu bar is File, the Menu Editor's Caption text box holds the name `File`. To indicate the access keystroke, insert an ampersand (&) before the designated access key. In other words, the caption `&File` specifies that Alt+F is the access key for the File menu item. The caption `E&xit` specifies that Alt+X is the access key for the Exit menu item. Users can use uppercase or lowercase letters, in conjunction with the Alt key, to trigger the option's access keystroke. When the menu bar appears, Visual Basic underlines the access key instead of showing the ampersand before the letter. The user knows from the underline that Alt+F is the access keystroke for the File menu bar item.

Sometimes VB programmers call access keys *hotkeys*. Define an access key for all menu bar titles so that your users can select any menu option from the keyboard.

WARNING

Don't confuse the term *access key* with *shortcut key*. An access key uses the Alt key in conjunction with another key to display a menu. A shortcut key uses the Ctrl key in conjunction with another key to execute a menu item immediately without first displaying the menu. For example, you can press Ctrl+E, a shortcut key, to display the Menu Editor, or you can press Alt+T (an access key) to display the Tools pull-down menu and then press M to view the Menu Editor. Shortcut keys eliminate menu traversal for some menu options. Although many programmers call shortcut keys *accelerator keys*, Microsoft no longer uses the term accelerator keys in its VB documentation, perhaps because of the similarity between the terms *accelerator* and *access*.

TIP

If you want an ampersand to appear in a menu name without making the subsequent letter an access keystroke, use two ampersands together. In other words, the caption value of Save && Beep produces a menu bar name Save & Beep but provides no access key.

Some menus contain several options. For example, VB's File menu contains 13 or more options depending on the number of files you recently opened. Separator bars help you group menu items together. Figure 8.2 shows VB's File menu with seven separator bars.

FIGURE 8.2.

VB's File menu contains several separator bars that group related items together.

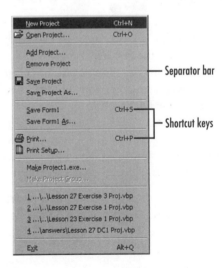

When you want to add separator bars, simply type a single hyphen, -, for the Caption property. Visual Basic places a separator bar at that location.

All menu items, including the separator bars, must have unique names; you place each menu item's name in the Name property. Standard naming conventions dictate that you preface each menu option with the letters mnu to designate that object as a menu object instead of another kind of object such as a command button. Follow the prefix with the name of the menu, as in mnuFile. If the menu is a submenu, continue naming the menu item with the menu names that navigate to that object. For example, mnuFileOpenProject is a good name for a menu item the user selects with File|Open|Project.

Separator bars require unique names, but you don't have to follow the naming convention for separator bars. mnuSep1, mnuSep2, and so on make adequate names for separator bars. Your code rarely manipulates separator bars, so their names are unimportant as long as they are unique.

The Index property holds the menu's subscript value if you create a control array of menus. This property determines the position of the menu item within that control array. Later in this chapter, the section "Runtime Menu Considerations" explains how to use the Index property to create a menu that changes at runtime.

> **NOTE**
>
> Sections that follow this menu-review section describe the Shortcut, HelpContextID, and NegotiatePosition properties.

You'll often manage the Checked, Enabled, and Visible properties from your Visual Basic application's code. When you select Checked (either at design time or at runtime by setting the Checked property to True), the menu item appears with a checkmark beside the item's name. Checked menu items let the user select from one of two menu states, such as turning boldface on or off. The Enabled property lets you turn off a particular item's event response. For example, if a menu item is not currently available due to the program's current settings, you can set the Enabled property to False to dim the menu item and make it unavailable. The Visible property determines whether the menu item is visible when the user displays the menu.

Use the WindowList property when you write MDI (multiple document interface) applications if the menu item is to maintain a list of active windows. For example, if you use Word and open more than one document for editing, Word's Window menu option displays a list of the open document window names. Your own MDI applications need to maintain a similar list so your users can select among the open child windows. Only one menu item can have its WindowList property set to True at any one time.

The second half of the Menu Editor's window controls the addition, deletion, and hierarchy of your menu structure. The four arrow command buttons control the indentation level that determines which menu items appear on the menu bar and which appear on submenus. For example, Menu Editor in Figure 8.3 describes the pull-down menu shown in Figure 8.4. Notice how each item's indentation level in the list determines where that item appears in the final menu.

TIP

If you need fundamental training in creating menus, check out *Teach Yourself Visual Basic in 24 Hours* from Sams Publishing.

FIGURE 8.3.

These Menu Editor options describe the menu in Figure 8.4.

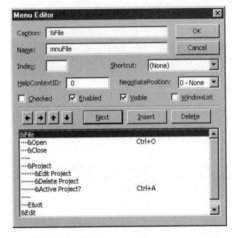

FIGURE 8.4.

The Menu Editor easily creates any menu structure your application requires.

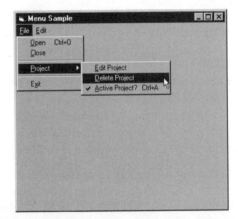

TIP

You don't have to compile and run your entire application to test the menu structure. From Visual Basic's development environment, you can click the Form window's menu bar to display the menu and look at the options that appear.

Menu Events

Menus support only a single event: the `Click` event. Your Visual Basic application knows when the user selects from a menu because that selection generates a `Click` event that corresponds to the menu name. For example, if you need to respond to the File | Open event, you must add code to the event procedure named `mnuFileOpen_Click()`. When the user selects that menu option, the `Click` event automatically triggers, and the code in that event procedure begins executing.

> **WARNING**
>
> Your application cannot respond to separator bars because separator bars do not generate events. The user cannot select a separator bar from a pull-down menu.

Shortcut Keys

Notice that Figure 8.4 shows two shortcut keys, Ctrl+O (for the File | Open menu option) and Ctrl+A (for the File | Project | Active Project? option). Shortcut keys help users select menu options quickly; instead of wading through two or three layers of menus, the user can press the shortcut keystroke combination to execute the menu option immediately.

Add shortcut keystrokes to menu items that the users select frequently. Don't burden your users with too many shortcut keystrokes because too many are difficult to remember. In addition, some shortcut keystrokes may frustrate users. For example, you rarely find a shortcut key for File | Exit because users might accidentally terminate the application when they mean to press a different shortcut key.

The Menu Editor's Shortcut option produces a drop-down listbox of possible shortcut keystrokes from Ctrl+A to Ctrl+Z, the function keys F1 through F12, Ctrl+F1 through Ctrl+F12, Alt+F1 through Shift+F12, Shift+Ctrl+F1 through Shift+Ctrl+F12, Ctrl+Ins, Shift+Ins, Shift+Del, and Alt+Backspace. If you need to remove a shortcut key from a menu item, select the first option in the drop-down list, None.

> **NOTE**
>
> You won't find Alt+ keystrokes listed in the shortcut keystroke list because Visual Basic reserves Alt+ keystrokes for access keys.

Managing Help Context IDs

If you distribute help files with your applications, you might want to include context-sensitive help for your menu options. The user can then request help for a particular menu option by selecting that menu option and then pressing the help request key.

Help context IDs are unique reference numbers that you assign to various help topics within your help file. These IDs form a link to specific help information so that information appears when the user requests help associated with that help context ID.

Suppose your application's help file contains specific help on a menu bar's pull-down menu option named Tools. Your help file will include a special [MAP] section like the following:

```
[MAP]
file_mnu     10
edit_mnu     11
tools_mnu    12
help_mnu     13
edit_cmd     20
exit_cmd     21
list_cmd     22
names_cbo    30
cities_cbo   31
```

Each line in the [MAP] section contains a text link to a help file. (You must create help files with an editor capable of producing .RTF text files.) For example, the link names_cbo might reference help text that describes how to use a combobox on the form. The link tools_mnu would refer to the help project file's text that contains information on the Tools menu. Each unique text link references a different set of text in the help project file. The numbers to the right of the text links, the help context IDs, appear in various controls' HelpContextID property values. For example, the menu item named mnuTools contains a 12 in the item's HelpContextID property. You type the 12 in the Menu Editor's HelpContextID field when creating the Tools menu's properties.

When the user runs the application and displays the Tools menu, he can press F1 to get help. Visual Basic then uses the help context ID value of 12 to cross-reference text in the help file labeled tools_mnu. The application then displays the help text.

> **WARNING**
>
> Your help file will not compile if your help context IDs are not all unique. In this way, the help compiler ensures that each help topic properly appears when requested.

Runtime Menu Considerations

The preceding sections explain how you can manage the following menu properties at runtime:

- ■ `Enabled` determines whether the menu item responds to the user's selection. If disabled, the item's shortcut keystroke is disabled as well. The item is dimmed or fully visible depending on the `Enabled` property's setting.

- ■ `Checked` determines whether a checkmark appears next to the menu item. Use checkmarked menu items to indicate on or off conditions.

- ■ `Visible` determines whether a menu item appears on the menu. If all of a menu is unavailable due to the program's current state, you might want to make the menu bar item invisible so that the user does not see any of the menu items. Any shortcut keystrokes associated with the invisible items are unavailable while the items are invisible.

Depending on the changing conditions of your application at runtime, your program might dynamically set one or more of these properties. (Each property is a boolean property that holds either `True` or `False`.)

In addition to these three runtime properties, your application can manage the menu's contents at runtime. In other words, a menu might grow during the program's execution if more options are required. For example, a recently opened file list grows as the user opens additional data files.

To change a menu's contents dynamically at runtime, the menu item must be part of a control array. When you add a menu item that might grow to additional items, such as a recently used file list, assign an `Index` property value of `0` to that item. When you do, Visual Basic adds a hidden separator bar before the option. If your program adds additional menu items to the control array, the separator bar appears before the first option.

Suppose you want to display a list of recent data files opened from within the current application. You might want to put the file list on your application's File menu bar option. You can create an indexed menu item named `mnuFileData` with an `Index` value of `0`. This first value's array value is named `mnuFileData(0)` using proper array notation, and you should initially (at design time) set this value's `Visible` property to `False` so neither it nor its separator bar appears until your application, at runtime, sets the `Visible` property to `True`.

> **NOTE**
>
> In addition to the `Visible` property, menu items support the `Hide` method, with which you can also make a menu control invisible.

When you create the control array, only one item, the one with the `Index` of 0, appears in the control array. That item does not appear on the menu until your application's code sets the `Visible` property to `True` with code such as this:

```
mnuFileData(0).Caption = strDataFileName
mnuFileData(0).Visible = True
```

As the user opens subsequent data files, you must use the `Load` statement to add new items to the control array before setting the new item's `Caption` property as follows:

```
' Create a new control array element
Load mnuFileData(1)
' Set the new item's caption and make it visible
mnuFileData(1).Caption = strDataFileName
mnuFileData(1).Visible = True
```

You could add a third item using similar code:

```
' Create a new control array element
Load mnuFileData(2)
' Set the new item's caption and make it visible
mnuFileData(2).Caption = strDataFileName
mnuFileData(2).Visible = True
```

Of course, instead of hard-coding the control array subscripts of 1 and 2, you keep track of the control array's highest subscript in a variable (perhaps in a local static variable) and use the variable subscript to add the new items to the menu.

Your application can remove items from a menu by using the `Unload` statement. The following line removes the third item in the menu's file list:

```
Unload mnuFileData(1)    ' Removes the menu item
```

WARNING

You cannot add or remove menu items dynamically at runtime unless the items are part of a menu control array as described here.

Negotiating Menus in Container Applications

You can offer objects from your application's form as embedded or linked objects in other applications inside child windows. If those *container applications* (the applications that borrow the objects) have their own menus, you can determine whether your application's menu item appears in the container application by setting the item's `NegotiatePosition` property when you design the menu inside the Menu Editor dialog box.

You must specify the `NegotiatePosition` property at design time. You cannot, at runtime, change `NegotiatePosition`'s value. The `NegotiatePosition` property supports these values:

- ◼ `0-None`: The item is not displayed on the container's menu bar.
- ◼ `1-Left`: The item appears on the left side of the container's menu bar.
- ◼ `2-Middle`: The item appears in the middle of the container's menu bar.
- ◼ `3-Right`: The item appears on the right side of the container's menu bar.

The active object's menu (the menu from the container) appears with your menu items when the application combines the menus.

WARNING

If the container application's `NegotiateMenus` property is set to `False`, your application's `NegotiatePosition` values have no effect.

Pop-up Menus

A *pop-up menu*, also called a *context menu*, is a floating menu that appears when a user right-clicks the mouse button over a form or other object. Figure 8.5 shows one of VB's pop-up menus that appears when you right-click over a control. Although the Menu Editor appears to create only a single menu for a standard menu bar, you can create one or more pop-up menus that work independently of the application's menu bar by making a top-level (the menu bar level) menu item invisible. All subsequent menu items that fall beneath that menu bar item remain invisible as well and do not appear on the actual menu bar.

FIGURE 8.5.

*Pop-up menus display
available options.*

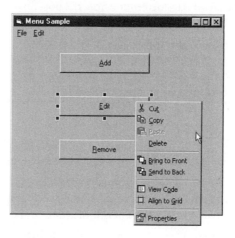

All pop-up menus must contain at least one menu option. Once you create one or more independent pop-up menus with the Menu Editor, you use the `PopupMenu` method to display that menu when appropriate. Here is the `PopupMenu` method's format:

```
object.PopupMenu mnuName [, flags [, x [, y [, boldCommand ]]]]
```

The object's `MouseUp` event is the event most Visual Basic programmers use to respond to a pop-up menu request. For example, suppose the user right-clicks over a form named `frmMain`, and you want to respond to the right-click by displaying the pop-up menu named `mnuGetParams`. The following `MouseUp` event procedure for the form does the trick:

```
Private Sub frmMain_MouseUp (Button As Integer,
    ➡Shift As Integer, X As Single, Y As Single)
  If (Button = 2) Then        ' 2 is right button indicator
    PopupMenu mnuGetParams  ' Display pop-up menu
  End If      ' Do nothing if not right button
End Sub
```

Of course, you must also code the `Click` event procedures for each of the pop-up menu options so that the proper code executes when the user selects one of the pop-up options.

> **NOTE**
>
> The `PopupMenu` method uses the current form as the default object unless you preface the method with a different object.

Table 8.1 lists the various flag values you can specify with the `PopupMenu` method that determines how the pop-up menu appears. Notice that Table 8.1 appears in two parts. The location flags determine where the menu appears in relation to the screen's x and y coordinates that you specify. The behavior flags determine how the pop-up menu responds to the user. If you need to designate a flag from each part of the table, separate the flag with the `Or` keyword in this way:

```
PopupMenu mnuGetParams, vbPopupMenuRightAlign Or
              ➡vbPopupMenuRightButton, intX, intY
```

Table 8.1. Named constants for your pop-up menu flag values.

Name	*Description*
	Location Flags
`vbPopupMenuLeftAlign`	The default value that defines the x coordinate of the pop-up menu's left edge.
`vbPopupMenuCenterAlign`	The value that specifies an x coordinate that determines the center of the pop-up menu.
`vbPopupMenuRightAlign`	The value that defines the x coordinate of the pop-up menu's right edge.

Name	Description
	Behavior Flags
vbPopupMenuLeftButton	The default value that triggers a `Click` event when the user clicks any pop-up menu option with the left button.
vbPopupMenuRightButton	The value that triggers a `Click` event when the user clicks any pop-up menu option with either mouse button.

Summary

This chapter explores some of the more advanced aspects of creating menus for your applications. Once you master the fundamentals of menu development, adding advanced options such as checked menu items, shortcut keys, and help context IDs is simple.

If you write a help script for your application, you will want to incorporate that help into the menu system. To incorporate help topics, you must specify help context ID values for those menu options. The help context ID values make the VB compiler cross-reference the appropriate help topic when the user requests help.

As long as you create a menu control array, you can create menus on-the-fly as your programs execute. Such accordion-like menus benefit applications that must keep track of data file lists that grow as the user uses the application and opens data files. In addition to dynamically changing menus, you can specify negotiating options that determine exactly which menu items appear in container applications that use your application.

Pop-up menus provide special kinds of menus that appear whenever and wherever the user right-clicks over an object such as the form or a control. You can design such pop-up menus to give common options available to the users at that time. For example, if the user right-clicks over a data-entry form, the pop-up menu can offer options that save the form to a disk file or erase the current form's contents so that the user can enter new information.

In conclusion, I suggest you keep in mind the following tips so you can optimize the menus you create with the Menu Editor:

- Begin all menu names with the `mnu` prefix so you can easily distinguish menu items from other controls in your application's code.
- Create menus that mimic popular Windows software, such as Microsoft Word, so that your users have a shorter learning curve with your application.
- Write help topics for all menu bar items as well as for all pull-down menu options so that your users always have help when they don't understand what an option does.
- The more pop-up menu items you supply, the fewer times your users will have to wade through the menu bar's layers of menus looking for an option they need.

Using Message Boxes and Input Dialogs

by Paul Kimmel

IN THIS CHAPTER

CHAPTER 9

Message and input dialogs provide a dimension of interactivity that enables you to add depth to your programs. Programming in Windows enables you to design interactive software with a large variety of options at your users' fingertips. Messages and dialogs enable you to further respond to ad hoc input needs and dynamic program flow.

Some digital code paths can be predicted in advance. When your program needs information from the user to decide which path the code should take, Visual Basic 5 input dialogs and message boxes offer a wide variety of selections for you to capture data on-the-fly.

Visual Basic provides a simplified interface in the `CommonDialog` control, which enables you to capture information about fonts, color, opening and saving files, the Windows printer dialog, and help. The `InputBox` function enables you to capture the most versatile input type, string, providing the ultimate flexibility. When programming in Windows, you have the entire API (Application Programming Interface) at your disposal. If you need acute control beyond what the easy-to-use Visual Basic message boxes and input boxes provide, you can call API functions directly.

In this chapter, you will learn how to apply the `MsgBox`, `InputBox`, `CommonDialog`, and Windows User32 `MessageBox` methods. As an added value, you are presented with a technique that enables you to extend the API to your entire team in a consistent and coherent manner, making the API as easy to use as native Visual Basic functions. Topics discussed in this chapter include the following:

- "Using the `MsgBox` Function" demonstrates this dynamic function, which provides a wide variety of interactive flexibility.
- "Using the `InputBox` Function" teaches you how to capture user input on-the-fly.
- "Using API Message Functions" shows you how to manipulate every aspect of Windows-based messaging.

After completing this chapter, you will have acquired all the fundamental skills necessary for dynamically communicating input needs and programming events to your software users. Secondarily, you will learn how to use message-related API functions and acquire skills that make using any API function a snap for you and your fellow team developers.

Using the MsgBox Function

Historically, computer programs were limited to linear problem solving. A *linear program* solves problems by accepting some initial input values and then processing them with no further input until the result is contrived and the answer is spit out. At Xerox PARC (Palo Alto Research Center) in the '70s, researchers began experimenting with a pointing device—soon referred to as a mouse—that invited a more visual approach to programming. Many innovations, such as languages evolving from binary systems, enabled higher-level *constructs*, or functions, that helped programs become more complex. This ability to aggregate and compound complex algorithms into simple constructs enabled software developers to add depth, imagination, and non-linearity to programs.

Microsoft Windows is arguably a descendant of windowing-type innovations like those at Xerox PARC. Writing Windows programs in Visual Basic 5 makes it easy to add multiple input windows, menus that facilitate spatial interaction between the user and the software, and a third dimension of interaction. This third dimension of interaction is the dialog window. Dialog windows enable you to dynamically alter a program's instructional flow based on dynamic input from the user. Visual Basic and Windows afford the developer a variety of powerful, easy-to-use dialog boxes. In this group are the MsgBox, which I discuss in this section; the InputBox; and a suite of CommonDialog controls. In this section, you learn how to use the flexible MsgBox, each of its five parameters, and the data it returns, and the end of the section offers a demo program that makes it easy for you to practice and gain experience.

Unleashing MsgBox Arguments

The MsgBox function accepts five arguments and returns an integer. Of the five arguments, four are optional, and you are not required to store or use the return value. The MsgBox displays an OK button by default and is capable of displaying a wide variety of buttons. You can evaluate the integer return argument to determine which button the user clicks. The five arguments of the MsgBox function enable you to precisely determine the appearance of the MsgBox, including the text and buttons it displays, and associate a help file and help context.

> **NOTE**
>
> A *help context* is a number that is assigned to some help file information. You may assign these numbers when designing Windows help files or use a utility such as RoboHelp, which assigns them for you.

The return value is discussed in the section "Using the MsgBox Return Argument," later in this chapter. I'll continue the discussion by examining the easiest use of the MsgBox.

The Visual Developer Studio has some unique features that make using new functions or controls easier. There are three ways to get on-the-fly information about the MsgBox function:

- In Visual Basic 5 Code View, you simply type the MsgBox function to display a fly-by hint containing the general syntax of the function.
- In Code View, click once on the function name MsgBox, click the right mouse button, and select Quick Info from the speed menu.
- Press the F1 key to get context-sensitive information.

Any of these steps gives you the syntax information and usually additional details as well. The syntax of the MsgBox function is

```
MsgBox(prompt[, buttons] [, title] [, helpfile, context])
```

NOTE

Notice that the `helpfile` and `context` arguments are bracketed together. This coupling suggests that one of these arguments without the other is meaningless. Although both arguments are optional, if you use one, you must include the name of an `.HLP` file and an integer context number.

Sometimes the syntax is not very clear; that's why the best help files—such as Visual Basic 5's help—also contain examples. A couple things to remember are the function name and that any parameter in brackets ([ ]) is optional. Employing the preceding information, you know that you can call the `MsgBox` function as easily as

```
MsgBox "Hello, World!"
```

This displays the message box shown in Figure 9.1. For those of you using Visual Basic for the first time, follow these steps to reproduce the image in Figure 9.1:

1. Start Visual Basic 5.
2. Select the Standard EXE option from the New Project dialog, or if Visual Basic is already running, select File | New Project.
3. Double-click on the blank form. This implicitly instructs Visual Basic to create a function named `Form_Load` and changes the perspective to Code View.
4. Enter the code `MsgBox "Hello, World!"` between the line containing the `Sub` routine name `Form_Load` and the `End Sub` line. (Don't worry; Visual Basic lets you know if you do something wrong when typing the code.)
5. Press F5 to execute the application.

Figure 9.1.

The most basic use of
`MsgBox`.

The fundamental use of the message box is that easy. Don't underestimate the value of this simple use of the `MsgBox` function. There are two reasons this box exists. The first is that good software development is incremental; that is, it is easiest to develop in small steps. The second reason is that sometimes an unadorned message box is exactly what you need to convey simple information to the user.

> **TIP**
>
> If you want multiple lines of text in your message, concatenate a carriage return represented by `Chr(13)` and a line feed represented by a `Chr(10)` between the strings where you want the line break. `"Hello," + Chr(13) + Chr(10) + "World!"` places each word in the phrase on a separate line.

When you need something more than text to convey your message, you can provide the same `MsgBox` function with more detail, filling in the other optional arguments from left to right and decorating them with a variety of buttons and icons, a title, and individualized help information. The next section contains a table of constant mnemonic values that can satisfy any one of the optional arguments, singly or in combinations.

Using the Optional `MsgBox buttons` Argument

The `prompt` argument is a string argument that can be as large as approximately 1,024 characters. The second argument, `buttons`, is an integer. An *integer argument* means that you can pass a manifest constant integer, such as 1, 2, 3, and so on, or a mnemonic defined as `Const`, such as

```
Const BUTTONS = vbExclamation + vbOKCancel + vbMsgBoxHelpButton
```

Because the argument is itself a variable, you can obviously use a `dim` variable that is neither a constant integer nor a defined constant. Listing 9.1 is an excerpt from `Form1.frm` in `MsgBox.vbp` that shows examples of the `MsgBox` function. (I refer to Listing 9.1 throughout the remainder of this section.)

> **NOTE**
>
> The line numbers in Listing 9.1 are not used in the actual code. They are included for reference purposes only.

> **NOTE**
>
> Visual Basic controls are named `Control1`, `Control2`, `Control3`, and so on. For example, in Listing 9.1 the first command button placed on the form will be named `Command1` by default. If you elect to rename the buttons (or any control), do so before you add code to the event handlers. If you create the handler first and then rename the control, your code will remain in the original subroutine and not be in the new event handler. It is easier to name the control first than to cut and paste all your code.

Listing 9.1. A form file containing examples of MsgBox.

```
1: Private Sub Command1_Click()
2:     ' Catch result in local variable
3:         Dim I As VbMsgBoxResult
4:         I = MsgBox("Welcome to Valhalla Tower Material Defender")
5:         ' An acceptable style for the function call
6:         ConvertInteger I
7: End Sub
8:
9: Public Sub ConvertInteger(MsgResult As VbMsgBoxResult)
10:     ' Convert the constant to its string name
11:         Dim S As String
12:     Select Case MsgResult
13:      Case vbOKOnly:
14:         S = "vbOKOnly"
15:         Case vbCancel:
16:          S = "vbCancel"
17:         Case vbAbort:
18:             S = "vbAbort"
19:         Case vbRetry:
20:             S = "vbRetry"
21:         Case vbIgnore:
22:             S = "vbIgnore"
23:         Case vbYes:
24:             S = "vbYes"
25:         Case vbNo:
26:             S = "vbNo"
27:         Case Else
28:             S = "(unknown)"
29:         End Select
30:     Text1.Text = S + "= " + Str(MsgResult)
31: End Sub
32:
33: Private Sub Command2_Click()
34:     ' An integer works too, but it is preferable to use
35:         ' the closest matching type of argument
36:         Dim I As Integer
37:     I = MsgBox("Hello, World!", vbOKCancel, "Visual Basic MsgBox Demo")
38:     ' A little better style of function call
39:         ConvertInteger (I)
40: End Sub
41:
42: Private Sub Command3_Click()
43:     ' The best declaration yet: a good variable name and
44:         ' the correct type
45:         Dim MsgResult As VbMsgBoxResult
46:         Const POWER = "I've got the power!"
47:         Const BUTTONS = vbExclamation + vbOKCancel + vbMsgBoxHelpButton
48:     MsgResult = MsgBox(POWER, BUTTONS, "Exclamation", "VBENLR3.HLP", 0)
49:     ' I like this one best. Verbose code is the easiest to understand.
50:         Call ConvertInteger(MsgResult)
51: End Sub
52:
53: Private Sub Command4_Click()
54:     Dim MsgResult As VbMsgBoxResult
55:     Const BUTTONS = vbInformation
56:         Const TITLE = "Information"
57:     MULTI_LINE = "Bodacious!" + Chr(13) + Chr(10) + "A powerful function"
58:     MsgResult = MsgBox(MULTI_LINE, BUTTONS, TITLE)
```

```
59:    Call ConvertInteger(MsgResult)
60: End Sub
```

Table 9.1 describes the available predefined button constants. You are free to create combinations in addition to those listed in the table; simply assign the summation of those you want to use to a constant or variable argument.

Table 9.1. A list of predefined button constants.

Constant	Value	Definition
vbOKOnly	0	Displays the OK button only.
vbOKCancel	1	Combines OK and Cancel.
vbAbortRetryIgnore	2	Combines Abort, Retry, and Ignore.
vbYesNoCancel	3	Used for asking a yes, no, or never mind question.
vbYesNo	4	Used when the answer must be yes or no.
vbRetryCancel	5	Used to cancel or retry the last operation.
vbCritical	16	Displays the critical icon.
vbQuestion	32	Displays the question icon. (Help refers to this as the *warning query.*)
vbExclamation	48	Displays an exclamatory icon for statements or warnings.
vbInformation	64	Displays the information icon, represented by a blue i in a text bubble.
vbDefaultButton1	0	Makes the first button the default (the one selected if you immediately press Enter). This is referred to as *having the focus.*
vbDefaultButton2	256	Gives the second button the focus by default.
vbDefaultButton3	512	Gives the third button the focus.
vbDefaultButton4	768	Makes the fourth button the focus, in case you have a button-happy dialog.
vbApplicationModal	0	Makes the dialog modal within this application; the user must respond before continuing in the program.
vbSystemModal	4096	Makes the dialog system modal; the user must respond before doing anything else in any program. (Using this is ideal in installation or utility programs.)
vbMsgBoxHelpButton	16384	Adds a help button.
vbMsgBoxSetForeground	65536	Puts the message box in the foreground.
vbMsgBoxRight	524288	Aligns the text on the right.
vbMsgBoxRtlReading	1048576	Makes the text appear as right-to-left for Hebrew and Arabic language systems.

You don't need to memorize the possible constant values for the buttons argument of the MsgBox function because a complete list is available when you need it. Place the cursor in the second position of the function (after the first comma), click the right mouse button, and select List Constants from the speed menu. Figure 9.2 shows the dialog displayed using the button combination vbExclamation + vbOKCancel + vbMsgBoxHelpButton in Line 47.

FIGURE 9.2.

The exclamation icon and three buttons in the message box.

Using the title Argument

Applying information for the prompt, buttons, and title arguments for the MsgBox function can convey the meaning of your message more clearly. The title argument appears in the window caption area of the message box. (In Figure 9.2, the title is Exclamation.)

The title argument is as easy to use as prompt. If you forget the argument, the default title is the name of the project. If you want to include the title and use the default vbOKOnly button, simply leave the second argument empty:

```
MsgBox "Prompt", , "Title"
```

You can also include the default argument:

```
MsgBox "Prompt", vbOKOnly, "Title"
```

Both approaches enable you to avoid getting stuck with the project name as the default title.

Using the Help File and Context Number

If you want to use help for an individual dialog box, include the path and name of a Windows-compatible help file and an integer representing the help context you want displayed. It is imperative that the help file exist. Further, it is imperative that the help file is in the same directory as your executable, it is in a directory defined in your path statement, or the path information is included with the filename.

It is better to store any path information in an .INI file or the Windows 95 Registry rather than include it as code within the application itself. As well as including the help file, you need to include the context identification number. You can use 0 if you want the index dialog to appear. Line 48 in Listing 9.1 demonstrates how to use the last two arguments. Users of your system are less likely to need expensive customer support if you include extensive help resources for the majority of your software. Many excellent programs can facilitate writing Windows help files.

Using the MsgBox Return Argument

If you use the default vbOKOnly button, there is no need to evaluate the return value of the MsgBox. The message box returns an integer so you can store the return value as an integer (as in Listing 9.1, line 36). The specific return type is a vbMsgBoxResult, also an integer. (Listing 9.1, line 3, shows an example of using this type.) It is generally preferable to use the closest match to the exact data type as possible.

> **NOTE**
>
> Some languages, such as C++, are strongly typed. Strongly typed languages require you to match data types exactly. Visual Basic is not a strongly typed language, so you may use a closely matching type. However, using the closest type match possible is preferable because it serves to document the code more clearly. In the event Visual Basic evolves into a more strongly typed language, you and your code will be prepared in advance.

There are two ways to call functions. One way is to simply list the arguments after the function:

```
ConvertInteger I
```

The preferable way to call functions is to wrap the argument list in parentheses:

```
ConvertInteger(I)
```

Using parenthetical grouping indicates clearly that the variables are in fact arguments to the function. Because you must use parentheses when assigning the return value of a function, you should always use them for the sake of consistency.

Table 9.2 lists all the constant names for the values returned by the MsgBox function.

Table 9.2. Defined constants for the vbMsgBoxResult return value of the MsgBox function.

Constant	Value	Definition
vbOK	1	User clicked OK.
vbCancel	2	User clicked Cancel.
vbAbort	3	User clicked Abort.
vbRetry	4	User clicked Retry.
vbIgnore	5	User clicked Ignore.
vbYes	6	User clicked Yes.
vbNo	7	User clicked No.

You can use the return value from the MsgBox function in any evaluation or assignment you can contrive. Often, the MsgBox is used to determine the path the code executes after the message box closes. If you want to capture string data for other than code-path decision making, take a look at the InputBox in the next section.

Using the InputBox Function

The InputBox function enables you to capture user input in the form of a string that is returned from the function. Several of the arguments for the InputBox are the same as those for the MsgBox function.

The syntax of InputBox is

```
InputBox(prompt[, title] [, default] [, xpos] [, ypos] [, helpfile, context])
```

Any arguments in brackets ([]) are optional. You need to supply only the prompt argument at a minimum. The prompt-only InputBox is as plain as the prompt-only MsgBox (see Figure 9.3). Two primary differences between the two default functions are that the InputBox has an input text field so the user can enter text and always has the OK and Cancel buttons. In addition, you might not specify alternative buttons, but a Help button is added if you provide a help file and help context number.

FIGURE 9.3.

An InputBox when only a prompt is supplied.

The prompt, title, helpfile, and context arguments are identical to those for MsgBox. (Refer to the section "Using the MsgBox Function," earlier in this chapter.) Listing 9.2 contains a fragment from Form2.frm in the InputBox.vbp project on this book's CD-ROM.

> **TIP**
>
> If controls are used in code evaluations, it is a good idea to use a good name for the control rather than the default convention of numbering the controls, as in Command1, Command2, and so on. Controls that are used only on a limited basis can maintain the default naming convention. For example, the only command button on a dialog does not need to be renamed btnOK, cdOK, or OKButton; Command1 will suffice.

Listing 9.2. The InputBox function.

```
1: Private Sub Command1_Click()
2:     Command1.Caption = InputBox("New caption?")
3: End Sub
4:
5: Private Sub Label1_DblClick()
6:     Dim S As String
7:         S = InputBox("New label text is", "Change Label", Label1.Caption)
8:         If (Len(S) > 0) Then
9:                 Label1.Caption = S
10:         Else
11:                 MsgBox "User pressed cancel", vbExclamation
12:         End If
13: End Sub
```

Arguments not included in the MsgBox function are default and the Cartesian xpos and ypos. The InputBox function also returns a string. Use the default argument to supply the user with some pre-entered data in the edit field adjacent to the prompt. Supply x and y coordinates if you do not want the dialog to appear centered, which is the default. Finally, you can simply store the return string or evaluate it to an empty string or Len(Str) = 0. (Refer to line 8 of Listing 9.2.) An empty string indicates that the user clicked the Cancel button.

It is up to each individual programmer to determine which message box to use and how it is adorned. You make subjective decisions such as these simply by determining the type of response and how you want the message conveyed. A minimalist approach is best. In software development, often less is more. For simple return values, the MsgBox and InputBox functions are exceptionally flexible. If you need complex data values or the user needs to perform more than one or two steps, you need to learn how to use the Common Dialog control. Refer to Chapter 24, "Leveraging Windows: Using the Common Dialog Control."

Using API Message Functions

The Windows API is comprised of DLLs, or dynamic link libraries. As you might recall, a DLL contains functions and definitions, but unlike executable files, DLLs are not meant to be executed directly. Dynamic link libraries were contrived to provide a common resource for many programs that might need to use the same functions. If not for DLLs, every program that needed Windows message boxes would need to include the code that makes these nifty dialogs possible. This condition is untenable because every program would be roughly the size of Windows plus the new code.

The entire Windows API—which is generally thought of as kernel32.exe, user32.dll, and GDI32.dll—is available to Visual Basic programmers. Generally, it is much easier to use Visual Basic functions without venturing into the API. However, using the API does not have to be difficult and can be easier with a few techniques you will learn in this section.

> **NOTE**
>
> Typically, all the exported functions in DLLs comprise the interface to the DLL. API is a kind of generic reference to functions stored in DLLs. Any Windows programming language is capable of accessing API functions. Often, the hardest part of using API functions is matching the argument data types to the types native to the language. However, you can avoid doing this more than once by defining a Visual Basic version of any API function with exact type arguments and then implementing the Visual Basic version in terms of the API function.

Three USER32.DLL functions offer a little more control than the Visual Basic versions, which are implemented on top of these functions. The three messaging functions and their respective Visual Basic declarations are

```
Declare Function MessageBox Lib "user32" Alias "MessageBoxA" (ByVal hwnd As_
        Long, ByVal lpText As String, ByVal lpCaption As String,_
        ByVal wType As Long) As Long
Declare Function MessageBoxEx Lib "user32" Alias "MessageBoxExA"_
        (ByVal hwnd As Long, ByVal lpText As String,_
        ByVal lpCaption As String, ByVal uType As Long, ByVal wLanguageId As Long)
➥As Long
Declare Function MessageBeep Lib "user32" Alias "MessageBeep"_
        (ByVal wType As Long) As Long
```

This code shows how you declare the functions in a form or module. To use them in a .frm file, you must declare them as private; in other words, prefix the preceding declarations with the identifier private.

A preferable method of using API functions is to declare them in one module. The file WIN32API.TXT in the VB\WINAPI directory contains approximately 16,000 lines of Windows API declarations that you can simply copy. Consider organizing them in reusable modules by category. Once you have a module with the declaration, all you have to do to use those API methods is include the module and call the function.

API functions exist for your use. As a general rule, you should not have to use them for your average programming tasks; however, if you need the greatest amount of flexible control, you might be able to find it at the API level. Listing 9.3 demonstrates the ease with which you can use and call API functions.

> **NOTE**
>
> I intentionally redefined the API function. Implementing a module function enables you to moderate the input values—what they are and how they are examined—prior to calling the API function. For example, in Listing 9.3, I could remove the hWnd parameter on line 5 and pass 0 for the hWnd parameter to the API function.

Listing 9.3. Messages.bas demonstrates how easy it is to use API functions.

```
1: Private Declare Function MessageBox Lib "user32" Alias "MessageBoxA"_
2:     (ByVal hwnd As Long, ByVal lpText As String, ByVal lpCaption 2: As String,
3:⮕ByVal wType As Long) As Long
4: Private Declare Function MessageBoxEx Lib "user32" Alias "MessageBoxExA"_
5:     (ByVal hwnd As Long, ByVal lpText As String, ByVal lpCaption As String,_
6:     ByVal uType As Long, ByVal wLanguageId As Long) As Long
7: Private Declare Function MessageBeep Lib "user32" (ByVal wType As Long)_
8:     As Long
9: Public Function MessageDialog(ByVal hwnd As Long, ByVal Text As String,_
10:     ByVal Caption As String, ByVal MsgType As Long) As Long
11:' Wrapping the function like this enables you to make changes to
12:⮕the interface. For example, you
13:    ' could remove the hWnd requirement, passing 0 making the interface easier.
14:    MessageDialog = MessageBox(hwnd, Text, Caption, MsgType)
15:End Function
```

Listing 9.4 contains an excerpt from Form5.frm in API_Demo.vbp, included on this book's CD-ROM.

Listing 9.4. Calling the API function.

```
1: Private Sub Command1_Click()
2:     Const THIS_CAPTION = "API Message: "
3:     Const AMESSAGE = "API MessageBox Function"
4:     Const ACAPTION = "API MessageBox"
5:     Dim Result As Long
6:     Result = MessageDialog(Form1.hwnd, AMESSAGE, ACAPTION, 3)
7:     Command1.Caption = THIS_CAPTION + Str(Result)
8: End Sub
```

It is easily arguable that defining a function wrapper and implementing the function in terms of the API enables you to take control and eliminates the need for each developer to redeclare the API declaration. The price you pay for direct access to the API function—in this instance bypassing the Visual Basic function—is that you might be removing safeguards that were added to the API function. If you pass some values in Listing 9.4, you do not get any buttons on the dialog, and calling the API locks up Visual Basic. Bypass Visual Basic functions when you need extra control, but ensure that any implicitly stripped safeguards are replaced.

Summary

Message boxes and input boxes can add a dimension to your applications. You can also reach out to the API if needed. The MsgBox can enable you to write programs that request simple integer values that can alter code-path execution. The InputBox function enables you to capture textual information from the program operator.

There are many means of gathering data in a dialog form by creating your own forms or learning about advanced uses of the CommonDialog controls. To learn more about topics related to this chapter, read

- Chapter 6, "Using Form Templates," demonstrates how to use existing form and code for common user-defined dialogs.
- Chapter 8, "Going Beyond Menu Basics," shows you how to add menus at design time and runtime.
- Chapter 13, "Using Windows API Functions," explores using the API in exhaustive detail.
- Chapter 24, "Leveraging Windows: Using the Common Dialog Control," covers advanced details of that control.

PART

III

IN THIS PART

The Code Behind the Pretty Forms

CHAPTER 10

Declaring, Raising, and Handling Events

by Paul Kimmel

IN THIS CHAPTER

Visual Basic's incarnation as an object-oriented language enables you to declare and raise events. In this chapter, you will learn what an event is and how to write event handlers—functions that respond to events. You will learn how to use event declarations and raise events to extend the core object model, which comprises the Visual Basic tools and ActiveX controls.

You will learn to use events related to the mouse and keyboard, system-generated events, and drag-and-drop events. This book's CD-ROM provides examples so that you can quickly take what you learn and begin experimenting with the topics covered in this chapter. Once you have the basics about events, you will look at the object-oriented extensions that enable you to build from Visual Basic's core architecture.

If you are programming in Visual Basic for the first time, this chapter will teach you everything you need to know to successfully use events and event functions. If you are an experienced developer, the first half may well serve you as a perspective overview and the second half will introduce you to newer language features related to event handling.

This chapter discusses

- An overview of the event hierarchy and event functions
- Defining and using mouse and keyboard events
- Using system-generated events
- Providing drag-and-drop capabilities in your applications with drag-and-drop event handlers

Properties and methods are the most important aspects of the object-oriented architecture. Event handling is the third tier, which enables that architecture to work with Windows 95 and Windows NT. Unleashing the power of event handling is one of three of the most important aspects that enable you to begin successfully developing professional software for Windows. From the Windows perspective, events are the single most important topic. Let's begin unleashing that power now.

The Event-Handler Hierarchy

Multitasking operating systems such as Windows must work with many programs running in the same physical memory at one time. Windows acts as a traffic cop. Although the traffic cop is not a passenger in any vehicle in her jurisdiction, she receives the signal first and directs the drivers of each vehicle based on that signal. Windows performs the same role as the traffic cop: It receives keystrokes and mouse clicks and directs the signals to the individual programs. This kind of architecture is called an *event-driven architecture*, and the signals are referred to as *events*. As the driver of an automobile must respond to the direction of the patrolman, a Windows program must respond to events.

I want to make some distinctions at this point. First, a Windows program, unlike a driver traveling on a busy thoroughfare at rush hour, does not have to respond to all direction. You get to selectively choose to ignore or respond to those events that interest you. The only way that you can respond to anything in a computer program is through a function or subroutine.

An event is something that occurs with computer hardware or an operating system, or an event can be raised by a programmer explicitly. Events can arbitrarily be handled or ignored by your programming, depending on what kinds of occurrences you want to respond to. Event handlers are simply functions or subroutines that have the responsibility of responding to events. Typically, Visual Basic uses subroutines for event handlers.

> **NOTE**
>
> You use subroutines for event handlers because you cannot control what the operating system does with a return value from a function. Think of events as commands that you may act upon that do not require a rebuttal.

Creating Event Handlers

You can easily create event handlers for existing components by double-clicking the Visual Basic control. When you double-click the visual control in Form View, you get the default event handler. Each control has a default event defined. The default event is usually the event that is most beneficial to the primary purpose of the control itself. For example, clicking a button is typically what you do with buttons; therefore, the default event for a command button is the `Click` event.

A direct resource for finding the list of events for a particular control also provides a way you can select any event. In the Code View, you can select the control from the Objects combobox on the left and choose from any of its events in the Procedures combobox on the right. (See Figure 10.1. If you are familiar with earlier versions of Visual Basic, note that the comboboxes are no longer labeled Objects and Procs.) From the procedure list, you can identify all the events related to a particular control that are available for handling. Another nice feature of the Procedures combobox is that the bold names denote those procedures that you have defined and coded.

Selecting the name of an already created event places the cursor in that function or defines a new one and places the Code View focus in the new event handler. For example, you can show a splash screen when your application's main `Form_Load` event occurs. You might place whatever code is necessary right in the event handler:

```
Sub Form_Load()
    Call AboutBox.Show( , Me)
End Sub
```

Although this code displays the splash screen, occupying the user while you perform some background initialization, I caution you against writing code like this for two good reasons. The first reason is that it is odd to use the splash screen by calling the `Form_Load` event:

```
Call Form_Load
```

FIGURE 10.1.

The left combobox contains the controls for the focus form; the right combobox contains the event handlers for the selected control.

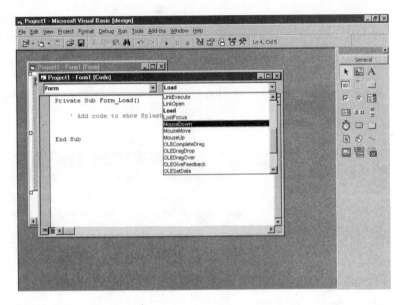

The call works, but outside the context of the load event, it does not make good sense and is not named very well. Secondly, because the code is not self-documenting, it requires comments. *Self-documenting code* is code that describes what it does by how it is named. Form_Load indicates that this subroutine responds to an event, but it doesn't tell you what action it performs. I prefer the following self-documenting, modular code if I have a choice:

```
Sub Form_Load()
    Call ShowSplashForm
End Sub
Sub ShowSplashForm()
    Call AboutBox.Form(, Me)
End Sub
```

The end result is more modular, self-documenting code. Keep in mind that the preceding style represents an ideal. Most of the time, the difference between inexpensive, easily maintainable code and an intractable mess is in a few decisions. Establish a habit of using self-documenting code. In this particular instance, the gains are only modestly significant. What is really gained is reinforcing a good habit instead of a bad one. When you are writing code by the hour, good habits let you focus on the problem and not how you write; the end result may be the difference between success and failure.

Defining User Events and Related Topics

The topics in this section are related to user-defined events. Included is an overview of declaring events, raising events, and using the WithEvents and DoEvents methods. If you are learning Visual Basic programming, feel free to read the remaining sections of this chapter, which will give you plenty of experience, and return to this section after you have finished the rest of the chapter.

Declaring Events

User-defined events are declared and raised in class modules. The purpose of a class module is to define a reusable aggregation of code that solves a particular problem. Declared events act like docking points for variable instances of the class module type. As with built-in controls, many events are available, but each event use is unique. Consequently, you might want to define events for a suite of generalized purposes, allowing the user to pick and choose which ones make sense in a particular context.

To add a class module, select Project | Add Class Module. To declare an event in a class module, simply add a declaration that states the accessibility, followed by the keyword Event and the event name. For example, the declaration of an event named Paint is

```
Public Event Paint()
```

In some function or procedure in the same class, you use the RaiseEvent keyword followed by the event—in the example, Paint—to signal to the code using the class that a Paint event has occurred.

Using RaiseEvent

You use the RaiseEvent statement to signal that any code attached to the event named in the Raise statement should be executed. Suppose that you have a class module with a declared Paint event; raising that event is accomplished in the following manner:

```
RaiseEvent Paint
```

User-defined events enable you to write docking points that users of the class module can attach to execute their code at predefined intervals. The intervals are those times when the event is raised by the class module. Because you do not know in advance what a user of your code might want to do at any given interval, using an event handler enables you to leave it up to him.

Consider a text control's Change event. Some software systems might want to verify that only digit characters were entered into the program. Other programs might want to verify that the text is a correct password. A user-defined event is for those instances where you want to let the user know something happened and also let him decide what to do.

WithEvents

When a compiler reads the code you typed, it needs to resolve names and symbols to particular values and data types. The WithEvents declaration is the way you introduce the name of an event and the owning entity into the module that needs to use it. To use an event named Paint declared in a module Class1, enter the following code in the module that uses it:

```
Private WithEvents AClass As Class1
```

You use the WithEvents clause to associate a variable with its type and events. If a class module declares a Paint event and AClass is defined, a procedure AClass_Paint is recognized as a valid event handler for the class module. The syntax might seem to be an obstacle, but when contrasted with the highly subjective nature of applicable context, the syntax and grammar are pretty easy to learn. It might take you a few tries to get the semantics correct, but the design is arguably correct if the right kinds of reasons exist for applying one tactic over another.

Remember that the `Declare` and `RaiseEvent` statements are used in the class module (`.cls` file), and the `WithEvents` statement and the actual event-handling code are defined in any module that needs to use the class module. The best way to combat the subjectivity issue is by writing code that mimics the code of those who have gone before you successfully.

Yielding Control to Windows Event Processing with DoEvents

Think of Windows as an air traffic control tower. The messaging system is responsible for directing information to the correct application. The probability exists in Windows that one exchange, without intervention, may consume too much time. Consumptive cycles are most likely to occur in tight loops—`for` or `while` loops, for example. To relinquish momentary control to Windows to process other events not related to the current code fragment, insert a call to `DoEvents` to give Windows some breathing room.

Calling `DoEvents` enables events such as Ctrl+C to be processed during the execution of a program. Clearly, a program is perceived as more user friendly if a break combination is received and acted on shortly after the user presses the necessary keys. Candidates for the `DoEvents` procedure are programs or ActiveX controls that are capable of snatching all the available processor cycles in an effort to complete their intended tasks.

The remaining sections provide you with ample opportunity to experiment with a variety of events related to the keyboard, mouse, and operating system. While reading the remaining sections, imagine some events you think might be beneficial.

Handling Mouse Events

I wrote this section as a clear and straightforward way for you to exercise your understanding of mouse events. If you have never used Visual Basic, you will learn in this section everything you need to know about mouse handling, including the relative times at which events occur.

Events other than Visual Basic events are created by the Windows messaging system. Windows uses the rough equivalent of a Visual Basic type (a record in Pascal and a struct in C) and internally recognized constants, which are assigned to an element of the type. The most common means of sending a message is the API `SendMessage` function. Below the API, many events start life as BIOS or other interrupts bottled up as messages, and the end result is that your event is called.

Some messages have constants that directly map to the event being generated. For instance, `WM_LBUTTONDOWN` is defined (refer to `\Program Files\DevStudio\VB\Winapi\WIN32API.TXT`), but you will not find a constant that defines a click message directly. Instead, a click event is usually a combination of a button-down and a button-up event. Although Visual Basic insulates you from messaging at the API level, it is available for your use. Further, you must understand that there exists a correlation between Windows as a messaging operating system and how events are generated. If you want to learn more about advanced levels of Window programming read Chapter 13, "Using Windows API Functions." For now, you will concern yourself with using the event handlers you already have available in Visual Basic.

Handling the `Click` Event

The `Click` event tells you that a `MouseDown` and `MouseUp` cycle was completed. The event handler is an unadorned procedure (that is, it takes no arguments). `Click` is one of the easiest and most useful events you will use. You can move the mouse while pressing, holding, or releasing a mouse button. The control underneath the mouse when you press the mouse button is the one that receives the `Click` event.

If you need to know which button was pressed or released, you write code for the `MouseDown` and `MouseUp` events. Likewise, to uncover the coordinates of the mouse during a click cycle, you use `MouseDown` and `MouseUp`. (Refer to project `UpDown.vbp` on the CD-ROM to experiment with the `Click`, `MouseDown`, and `MouseUp` events.)

The beauty of using events is that once you learn to use an event for one control, you know how to use it for all controls.

Handling the `DblClick`

If you think for a moment, you can imagine designing a `DblClick` event. The `DblClick` event already exists, but as a mental exercise, simply imagine that you use a static variable, set the time of a click, and get the time on a subsequent click. If the interval is arbitrarily short, you consider it a double-click.

NOTE

You may not know it yet, but you can set the interval for double-clicking in the Windows environment. You can manipulate the `DblClick` event interval with `GetDoubleClickTime` and `SetDoubleClickTime`. (Refer to `DblClick.vbp` on the CD-ROM for a demonstration.)

TIP

The add-in API Viewer comes in handy when using API functions. The API Viewer enables you to insert declarations quickly and accurately.

You could implement a double-click event if you were using an abstraction that did not provide you with one. Most controls have `DblClick`. If you are not sure whether a control has the `DblClick` event, check out the context help or the Procedures combobox in Code View. `DblClick` is an unadorned procedure exactly like `Click`, except that two mouse-click events occur in some short period of time.

Handling MouseMove

The `MouseMove` event enables you to track the moment-to-moment movements of the mouse. Imagine that each mouse move is an event, which is derived from a Windows message, and then you can discern the huge amount of messaging that modern processors have to handle. As in a busy airport, expect long lines.

The `MouseMove` event provides the most information about the mouse. The event handler is passed a `Button` integer that tells you which, if any, mouse button is down, a `Shift` parameter that indicates whether an extended key is down, and the x and y Cartesian coordinates of the mouse. Using the `Button` and `Shift` parameters, you can contrive a variety of state combinations, allowing you to extend the variety of key combinations for complex programs.

The `Button` parameter can be 0, `vbLeftButton`, `vbRightButton`, or `vbMiddleButton`. The `Shift` parameter can be `vbShiftMask`, `vbCtrlMask`, or `vbAltMask`. The best way to determine whether particular combinations of buttons or extended keys are down is to use boolean logic, `AND`ing the parameter with the constant. For example, to test whether only the `vbCtrlMask` bit mask is in the `Shift` parameter (the parameters are represented by bit arrays), you write

```
(Shift And vbCtrlMask) > 0
```

Writing the best boolean test is where experience, common sense, or the discrete mathematics you took in college come into play. In the preceding example, you could simply test to see whether `Shift = vbCtrlMask`, but because the `Shift` parameter is bit array, the test does not work if Ctrl and Alt are both pressed. The moral "When in Rome…" in this case suggests that because the bits are packed, you should use boolean logic to test their values.

Handling MouseDown

The `MouseDown` event initiates the `Click` event. The `MouseDown` event passes the event handler the `Button` argument and x and y coordinates. The values of x and y are constrained by the `ScaleHeight`, `ScaleWidth`, `ScaleLeft`, and `ScaleTop` properties of the focus control. The control underneath the mouse when the button is depressed is the control receiving the event. The `Click` event is sent after `MouseUp`, which follows `MouseDown`. The sequence is demonstrated in `UpDown.vbp` on the CD-ROM.

Handling MouseUp

Not that long ago, if you wanted control over the mouse, you would have to write Assembler that would pass a callback function address to Interrupt 51, Function 12. If that sounds really esoteric to you, be glad that Microsoft and Visual Basic have elevated us above the point where you need to know interrupt service routines, function numbers, and how to put values in the AX (accumulator) register.

There was a certain wizardry involved in knowing how to use interrupt vector routines, but for software development to progress, we obviously needed to improve on manipulating processor registers. The signature of the MouseUp event is identical to that of the MouseDown event. The significant difference is that MouseDown happens first.

Handling GotFocus and LostFocus

The GotFocus event is fired when a control becomes the focus control. A control can get the focus when the user tabs from control to control or clicks on a control that previously did not have the focus. LostFocus occurs when the user leaves a control that had the focus. Focus changes can occur through hotkey combinations, tabbing, or mouse clicks.

GotFocus and LostFocus are events that get no arguments. Only controls that have an hWnd property can receive the focus. A form and textbox can receive and lose the focus, but a label control cannot. As you are learning, look for the GotFocus or LostFocus in the procedures combobox; if neither event is there, assume the control cannot be the focus control.

The most common uses for the focus events are pre-processing and post-processing. An example of post-processing is validating the text in a textbox control with a range of valid values.

Using the Mouse for Dragging and Dropping Capabilities

Without the mouse, it is unlikely that dragging and dropping would be meaningful. Dragging and dropping are related to the mouse, but later in this chapter, I provide a section for adding drag-and-drop capabilities to your applications, "Experimenting with Drag and Drop Events."

Using Keyboard Events

Not too long ago, programmers had to use the Interrupt 9 and 25 vectored keyboard services to determine what the user was doing with his keyboard. With events, Microsoft and Visual Basic provide us with a much better way to determine what the user is doing at any given moment. In fact, Windows screams (sort of) if you now try to call interrupt services directly.

The mouse and the keyboard are still the two most important input devices. You learned how to program responses to mouse events in the last section. In this section, you will complement that knowledge by learning how to respond to keyboard events. Some keyboard events are identical to the mouse events with the same names, such as GotFocus and LostFocus, and some keyboard events are analogous to the mouse events, such as KeyDown, KeyUp, and KeyPress. This section is only concerned with the latter category. There is no use in repeating information about GotFocus and LostFocus other than to remind you that the keyboard can also cause a control to receive a change in focus.

Handling the KeyDown Event

The KeyDown event is analogous to the MouseDown event. The distinction is that you need to know the parameters for the event procedure. The first parameter is the KeyCode integer. The KeyCode is the ASCII code and scan code of the key pressed. Pressing the A key causes the KeyCode value to be 65. The second argument is the Shift integer argument. You learned how to use Shift in the section "Handling MouseMove," earlier in this chapter.

The KeyCode can also indicate that the Shift key or F1 key was pressed, for example. If you are examining KeyCode for specific extended keys, use the constants defined in the Visual Basic Object Library. Search for the help topic "Key code constants" for an exhaustive list of KeyCode constants. You can use the constant values immediately; there are no requirements or declarations that must be made prior to using the KeyCode constants.

Handling KeyUp Events

The footprint for the KeyUp event is identical to the footprint for the KeyDown event. KeyUp is analogous to MouseUp. The order for the keyboard events is KeyDown, KeyPress, and KeyUp. (Refer to the sample program Keybd.vbp on this book's CD-ROM, discussed in the section "Using the Change Event," for more details.)

Using the KeyPress Event

Pressing a key generates Interrupts 9 and 22. The job of these two interrupts is to convert a raw character code and scan codes into an ASCII character. For example, pressing the A key could be either a or A, depending on the state of the Shift key or the Caps Lock key.

Fortunately, you do not have to concern yourself with the lower (BIOS) detail any longer. All you are concerned with is that pressing a key generates a KeyDown event, which might be followed by a KeyPress event and winds up the event suite with KeyUp. Pressing any key always generates a KeyDown and KeyUp pair. The KeyPress, however, is only generated if the key was a valid ASCII character and not just an extended code. Therefore, pressing Shift generates KeyDown and KeyUp, in that order. Pressing A generates KeyDown, KeyPress, and KeyUp in that order. The demo program described in "Using the Change Event" and included on the CD-ROM will enable you to experiment with keyboard events and timing issues.

Using the Change Event

The Change, like KeyPress, is only going to be generated if the key pressed causes the Text property to change. Change, like Click, offers no parameters; it is an easy event to use because the fact that it is called tells you all you need to know. If the event is fired, the Text property was changed. You can perform any validation you want when Change is called. Keybd.vbp, in Listing 10.1, enables you to quickly get a feel for when and in what order keyboard events are fired. (The events are put into the LogTextBox control in a LIFO stack.)

NOTE

Line numbers are included in the chapter listings for reference purposes only. You do not use line numbers in the actual programming.

Listing 10.1. Timing for keyboard events.

```
 1: Private Type SYSTEMTIME
 2:    wYear As Integer
 3:    wMonth As Integer
 4:     wDayOfWeek As Integer
 5:     wDay As Integer
 6:     wHour As Integer
 7:     wMinute As Integer
 8:     wSecond As Integer
 9:     wMilliseconds As Integer
10:   End Type
11:
12:   Private Declare Sub GetSystemTime Lib "kernel32"
13: ➡ (lpSystemTime As SYSTEMTIME)
14:
15:   Private Function GetSystemTimeString() As String
16:      Dim T As SYSTEMTIME
17:      Call GetSystemTime(T)
18:      GetSystemTimeString = Str(T.wHour) & ":" & Str(T.wMinute) & ":"
19: ➡ & Str(T.wSecond) & "." & Str(T.wMilliseconds)
20:   End Function
21:
22:   Private Function EndL() As String
23:      EndL = Chr(13) + Chr(10)
24:   End Function
25:
26:   Private Sub Log(ByVal Msg As String)
27:      LogTextBox.Text = Msg & " occurred at " & GetSystemTimeString +
28: ➡ EndL + LogTextBox.Text
29:   End Sub
30:
31:   Private Sub Text1_Change()
32:      Call Log("Change")
33:   End Sub
34:
35:   Private Sub Text1_GotFocus()
36:      Call Log("GotFocus")
37:   End Sub
38:
39:   Private Sub Text1_KeyDown(KeyCode As Integer, Shift As Integer)
40:      Msg = "KeyCode=" & Chr(KeyCode) & ", KeyDown"
41:      Call Log(Msg)
42:   End Sub
43:
44:   Private Sub Text1_KeyPress(KeyAscii As Integer)
45:      Msg = "KeyAscii= " & Chr(KeyAscii) & ", KeyPress"
46:      Call Log(Msg)
47:   End Sub
```

10

DECLARING, RAISING, AND HANDLING EVENTS

continues

Listing 10.1. continued

```
48:
49:  Private Sub Text1_KeyUp(KeyCode As Integer, Shift As Integer)
50:     Msg = "KeyCode = " & Chr(KeyCode) & ", KeyUp"
51:     Call Log(Msg)
52:  End Sub
53:
54:  Private Sub Text1_LostFocus()
55:      Call Log("LostFocus")
56:  End Sub
```

The first 12 lines define the SYSTEMTIME type needed to use the API function GetSystemTime. GetSystemTime enables you to get time at a millisecond granularity. GetSystemTimeString, beginning on Line 14, is a function you might want to copy to a utility module for reusability reasons; the same goes for Endl, starting on Line 20, which returns the carriage-return/line-feed pair, making it convenient to insert multiple lines in a textbox control. The remainder of the listing uses the Log subroutine to create an event log for Text1. If Visual Basic programming is brand new to you, you might want to poke at the program in Listing 10.1 until you are comfortable with the events, relative timing, and order of activity when you press a key on the keyboard.

Of the three key aspects of Windows programming—properties, methods, and events—events are least like the other two. Events are not a part of objects, but without events, objects would not have any direction in a graphical user environment. The next section discusses other events that can be raised by the operating system or the program.

Handling System-Generated Events

So far, you have learned how to write event code and raise user-defined events. Event handlers are functions assigned to respond to messages which signal that an event needs to be raised. The connection that you might not have made is that events are associated with controls as callbacks. A *callback* is a property that is an address of a function. When you create event handlers, what you do not see somewhere in the code is that the address of that function is assigned to a callback property.

In C, C++, and Object Pascal, the use of pointers and addresses is more apparent and prevalent. These three languages have characters that represent pointers and addresses. In some regard, these are the elements that make programming in these languages more challenging. Visual Basic uses long integers when addresses and pointer values are needed. Part of the appeal of Visual Basic is that pointers and addresses are eliminated. You seldom need to worry about the address of something. As I mentioned, assigning event-handling addresses to a callback property is concealed from the Visual Basic developer. The address of a function is the mechanism that makes event handlers possible. Based on that assumption, all that is required is for an entity to refer to the address of a function.

In this section, you are provided with examples that demonstrate system events, such as the Timer event, and other events that you might not have encountered yet.

Using the Timer Event

The timer control is a singularly interesting control. For many years, hooking into Interrupt 28 was the only way a developer could perform an activity each time the hardware clock ticked. Performing time-based tasks is how pop-up programs, screen savers, auto-save features, and simple animation were added to programs. Without the timer, we would have none of those things.

NOTE

The DOS-based PC has an area in low memory called the *interrupt vector table*. The interrupt vector table is an array, or a vector, of 32-bit function addresses. The interrupt vector table is indexed by the interrupt number. Interrupt 28 (or 1C hex) is the 28th 32-bit function address. As with callbacks, you can use the address to call the function. That's exactly what compilers do with all functions—convert them to addresses. Hooking into the vector table meant storing the address at a particular vector and replacing it with the address of your function. If the first thing your function did was call the old function address, the user was none the wiser, and after the original function returned, you could execute some additional code.

It wasn't that hard to accomplish with a little practice, but as with many old tricks, manipulating addresses and pointers tends to be problematic. Microsoft alleviated the potential for misuse by encapsulating the timer tick in a control correctly, so now it is available for everyone's use.

Fortunately, the interrupt is concealed by Windows as a timer and concealed further in Visual Basic as the timer control. The only event is the Timer event. The most important property of the Timer control is Interval, which determines how frequently in milliseconds the Timer event is raised. What activity you decide should be performed in the Timer event is up to you, but some ideas include animation, auto-save features, alarms, or notifications. (For an example of how to use the timer control and the Timer event, refer to the section on the timer in Chapter 21, "Reviewing the Standard Controls.")

Using the Paint Event

Windows raises the Paint event frequently. The Paint event occurs any time a new window is shown, a button is clicked, or an activity affects the appearance of what you see on the screen. A paint message does not send any arguments to Paint event handlers because Microsoft determined that you do not need any parameters. In an object-oriented world, each object capable of handling a Paint event should only be responsible for painting things it can control. Windows has a variety of clipping rules that it uses to determine what is actually displayed on the screen.

One use of the Paint event is to add custom painting to a form. With the PaintEv.vbp project in Chapter 21, you will see that you can add shadow text, as shown in Windows setup programs, to your forms. Each time the form is painted, you must paint the text again, so naturally, the Paint event is a good place for the code.

It would be great if every control had a Paint event, but unfortunately, only a few of the standard controls have it. Included in this short list are the form and the picture box. You can add some really cool custom features, such as shadowed text, using their Paint events. Listing 10.2 from ShdwLbl.vbp on the CD-ROM, demonstrates how you can use the Paint event and a picture box to create a shadow label (shown in Figure 10.2).

Listing 10.2. A Paint event used with a picture box.

```
 1: ' Module1.bas - Reusable module for writing text to the canvas.
 2: Private Declare Function TextOut Lib "gdi32" Alias "TextOutA"
 3: ➥(ByVal hDC As Long, ByVal X As Long, ByVal Y As Long,
 4: ➥ ByVal lpString As String, ByVal nCount As Long) As Long
 5: Private Declare Function SetBkMode Lib "gdi32"
 6: ➥ (ByVal hDC As Long, ByVal nBkMode As Long) As Long
 7: Public Sub CanvasTextOut(ByVal hDC As Long, ByVal X As Integer,
 8: ➥ ByVal Y As Integer, ByVal Text As String)
 9:     Call SetBkMode(hDC, TRANSPARENT)
10:     Call TextOut(hDC, X, Y, Text, Len(Text))
11: End Sub
12:
13: ' Excerpt from Form4.frm
14: Private Sub Picture1_Paint()
15:     Const MSG = "Program Setup"
16:     Length = Len(MSG)
17:     Const YELLOW = &HFFFF&
18:     Picture1.ForeColor = 0
19:     Call CanvasTextOut(Picture1.hDC, 4, 4, MSG)
20:     Picture1.ForeColor = YELLOW
21:     Call CanvasTextOut(Picture1.hDC, 1, 1, MSG)
22: End Sub
```

If the label control had a Paint event handler, it would be much easier to provide special font effects than what's shown in the preceding example. However, because you were provided with Module1.bas, creating shadow effects is pretty easy. The only thing the code in Listing 10.2 doesn't do is enable you to see the result at design time. Lines 1, 2, and 3 declare the API functions for writing to a device context. Lines 5 and 6 set the background mode to transparent and then write the text to the device context (the hDC parameter). Finally, the end result is achieved by making the color selections (Lines 14 and 16) between calls to CanvasTextOut. The shadow effect is created by offsetting the x and y positions of the two disparate writes to the device context.

As mentioned, writing to the canvas is not quite as easy to use as a label, but it is still pretty easy to use. Experiment with the code to see if you can make it more useful and reusable in other contexts. Emulating and improving existing code is an excellent way to improve your knowledge of Windows and your technique.

FIGURE 10.2.

An easily reusable
Paint *event technique*
for special shadow text.

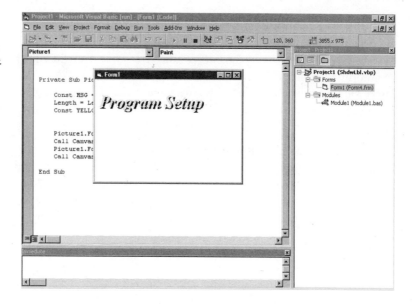

Using Important Form Events

Several important form events are generated at distinct times during the life of an application. From the available form events, I discuss Activate, Deactivate, Initialize, Load, Unload, QueryUnload, Resize, and Terminate. (The previous section discussed the Paint event.) For the remainder of this section, assume that there are no parameters for the event handler unless otherwise specified.

Using Activate and Deactivate

The Activate method is called whenever a form is made the focus form by clicking it, which calls the Show or SetFocus methods. Deactivate is called whenever a form loses focus or Hide is called. Use these two events to perform form-level pre-processing and post-processing. Each time a form loses focus and you want to minimize it or change its z-order, Deactivate is the place to do it. Conversely, the Activate event handler is a good place to add code to maximize a form when it gains the focus. Activate is called before GotFocus, and Deactivate is called after LostFocus; therefore, Activate and Deactivate are the best places to insert early and late processing.

Initializing Forms

The Initialize event occurs before the Load event. Initialize is called when you create a form with the Set command or before the first line of code that uses the form object. Avoid placing initializing code right into the event handler; instead, add one level of indirection and call a function from the Initialize event handler. Creating a slightly more modularized initialize routine makes easier to re-initialize in the event of an error. In other words, you could call the Init routine at any time if you needed.

10

DECLARING,
RAISING, AND
HANDLING EVENTS

Loading and Unloading Forms

By default, the StartUpPosition property of a form is Windows default, or 3. By setting StartUpPosition to Manual—the integer value of 0—you can reduce the time it takes to start a multiform application. A perfect candidate is the form that shows your About information. Users will probably only look at this screen a few times (unless you give them a useful reason for doing otherwise). If the About form is not routinely needed, why should you be willing to pay for its permanent residence in memory?

Postponing the loading of forms that might not be needed frequently enhances your startup time and reduces your program's memory footprint. Generally, both of these results are desirable. (Conversely, leaving frequently opened dialogs in memory might enhance your program because load time is reduced.) If you want to instantiate a form only when it is needed or requested, the Load and Unload form events are for you. Use the Load procedure in the following manner:

```
Load FormName
```

Use the Unload form in the same way: Unload followed by the form name. If you are unloading a form within the form itself, you can use the internal reference Me.

Visual Basic provides a Query_Unload event that enables you to keep the "Are You Sure?" code in one place. Before you unload a form, especially the MainForm, you might want to verify that the user is really sure that he wants to close the form. The Query_Unload event passes two arguments to the event handler. The first is Cancel. Assigning Cancel = True causes the Unload to be aborted, and a value of False—meaning the unload was not canceled—allows the form to be unloaded. Table 10.1 describes all the values that are appropriate for the second parameter, UnloadMode. The UnloadMode value specifies the origin of the close request.

Table 10.1. Constant values for the UnloadMode parameter of QueryUnload.

Name	Value	Description
VbFormControlMenu	0	The Cancel button on the form is the origin of the request.
VbFormCode	1	The form is programmatically unloaded via the Unload command.
VbAppWindows	2	The Windows operating system is being unloaded.
VbAppTaskManager	3	The Windows Task Manager is closing the program.
VbFormMDIForm	4	The MDI child is closing because the program is closing.

A simplified way to set the cancel mode is to assign the comparison of the result of a MsgBox with Yes and No buttons to the Cancel parameter. The code might be written like this:

```
Cancel = MsgBox("Are you sure?", vbQuestion + vbYesNo) = vbNo
```

Surprisingly simple code, isn't it? Small functions and relatively few arguments are characteristic of object-oriented languages. If you have been developing in a structured programming language, these characteristics may take a little getting used to. Quality object code is generally concise and modular, and requires fewer parameters.

Resizing Forms

The `Resize` event is called any time the boundaries of the form change. You can use the `Resize` event to realign or position any controls whose relative size or position is affected by resizing the form on which it resides. For example, in a word processor, you might want the textbox control to use all the available client space of its parent form. If the form were resized, you would naturally want the textbox resized.

A good technique for maintaining the relative position of controls is to use the frame to collect them; then you only have to adjust the frames. If resizing a form requires that subordinate controls be resized, another good technique is to use the `Move` method. The `Move` method takes all four coordinates of the bounding rectangle of the control and reduces the likelihood that multiple paints will occur.

Using the Terminate Event

The `Terminate` event is raised when all the variables that reference the form (or other control) are set to nothing or when `End` is called and no remaining code refers to the form. The `Terminate` method is called after the `Unload` event and can be used for any final processing.

You may want use `Terminate` to ensure that manually loaded DLLs are unloaded, modem connections are closed, or perhaps a database kernel is shut down. If your program spawned subprograms or threads, `Terminate` may be a final opportunity to ensure that any and all cleanup related to those things was performed.

Using the Error Event

The `Error` event occurs during a database-access error or a WinSock error that occurs when your Visual Basic code is not running. In other words, the error is external to code that you have written. The data control, the ActiveX `DBGrid` control, and the Microsoft WinSock control enable you to assign an `Error` event handler. Usually, errors that occur outside your code are out of your control, but in this instance—where database access is concerned—the `Error` event was added to enable you to be notified and regain control of an error condition.

The `Error` event handler has two arguments and one optional argument for database errors and several arguments for WinSock errors. If the event handler is assigned to a data control error, it receives two arguments, the `DataErr` value and a `Response` value. The `DataErr` value is the error code for the error. The `Response` can be `vbDataErrContinue` or `vbDataErrDisplay` (or `0` or `1`). The `vbDataErrContinue` value enables the program to continue, and `vbDataErrDisplay` shows the error message. The syntax of the `Error` event for database controls is

```
Private Sub object_Error ([index As Integer,] DataErr As Integer,
➥response As Integer)
```

In some instances, it is preferable to be proactive. An error-event handler is reactive—the event is raised after the error occurs. You may proactively write code in the event handler, but you must reactively decipher the problem after it occurs. Programming in Windows is complex enough, so it is probably impossible to catch all possible error conditions prior to their occurrence. Error handling allows you to catch all errors after they happen and handle them by deciphering the `DataErr` argument.

A kind of safety-net approach, such as exception handling, works better in the digital world because it is impossible to check for every possible error condition or every possible input value.

Experimenting with Drag and Drop Events

Visual Basic makes dragging and dropping a snap. By default, drag-and-drop controls have their `DragMode` property set to `Manual`. Changing this property to `Automatic` at design time or setting it to `1` at runtime allows your users to visually select elements from one control and drag and drop them into another control. The interpretation of their efforts is context dependent, so it is up to you to write a little code, but all in all, implementing drag-and-drop capabilities is still extremely easy.

Chapter 26 is titled and discusses "Implementing OLE Drag-and-Drop Capabilities in Controls." So that I do not reproduce that material here, I will discuss implementing drag and drop within the same program.

You must make a couple decisions to create the right effect when users drag and drop items from one control to another. Following is a list of items you must consider when implementing drag and drop:

- What is the data type you will drag and drop?
- Between what types of controls will you implement drag and drop?
- Should you display a special cursor when dragging over a receiving control?
- Should you use automatic or manual `DragMode`?
- Will the position of the mouse play any role in what is dragged?
- Will the position of the mouse play any role in how the data is dropped?
- What type of validation will you use on the dropped data?

Although you do not have to make each of these decisions to implement basic dragging and dropping, your intent might not be clear if you do not. Although you must make several decisions, each of them is relatively simple to decide and even easier to implement.

Extracting the Dragged Data

The `DragDrop` event handler gets a reference to the source control. The source control is the control from which the dragging is initiated. The `DragDrop` event handler, shown on line 9 of

Listing 10.3 and included in `DragDrop.vbp` on the CD-ROM, takes a reference to the source control and the x and y coordinates of the drop position. You may use the `TypeOf` command to ascertain the source control type. How you get the data depends on the control type. The example uses a listbox and its `Text` property, dragging and dropping the selected list item to a text control.

Listing 10.3. Automatically dragging and dropping list items to a data field.

```
1: Private Sub List1_GotFocus()
2:     List1.DragMode = 1 'Automatic
3: End Sub
4:  Private Sub List1_LostFocus()
5:     List1.DragMode = 0     ' Manual
6: End Sub
7:  Private Sub Text1_DragDrop(Source As Control, X As Single, Y As Single)
8:     If TypeOf Source Is ListBox Then
9:         If Len(Source.Text) > 0 Then
10:             If (MsgBox("Insert " + Source.Text, vbQuestion + vbYesNo)
11: ➥= vbYes) Then
12:                 Data1.Recordset.AddNew
13:                 Text1.Text = Source.Text
14:             End If
15:             Text1.SetFocus
16:         End If
17:     End If
18: End Sub
```

This small program demonstrates one way to initiate dragging and dropping. The program has a listbox of names. You may drag a name from the listbox control into the textbox control. Dropping a list item into the textbox adds a new record to the dataset and changes the focus to the text control.

Isolating Control Dependencies

The type of control for which you want to initiate dragging and dropping might affect how you implement dragging and dropping. Listing 10.3 uses a listbox control as the source of the drag-and-drop feature. A minor problem exists for automatic drag mode. If `DragMode` equals `Automatic`, clicking and holding the left mouse button initiates dragging and dropping. However, it is also the left mouse click that selects a list item. In automatic drag mode, the listbox control does not get the click, so no item is selected.

In lines 1–3 of Listing 10.3, the code sets drag mode to automatic when the control gets focus. (After the `GotFocus` event is handled, the `DragMode` is set to `Automatic`.) Selecting an item after the control has focus allows you to drag the item from the listbox. Once the control loses focus (in lines 5–7), `DragMode` is reset to `Manual`.

Dragging and dropping can be implemented in a couple other ways, too. For example, you can use the `MouseDown` event to initiate dragging and dropping manually:

```
Private Sub List1_MouseDown(Button As Integer, Shift As Integer, X As Single,
➥Y As Single)
    If (Button = vbRightButton) Then
        List1.Drag 1     ' BeginDrag
    End If
End Sub
```

This MouseDown event handler initiates dragging and dropping programmatically if the mouse button is the right mouse button. A technique to consider in a production application is to track whether the user is using a left-handed or right-handed mouse, thus enabling the algorithm to be implemented on the weak mouse button. A final note: Consider using constant names in place of literals, replacing 1 with a constant indicating that 1 = Automatic drag mode.

Summary

This chapter demonstrates introductory event-handling concepts, leading right on to more challenging concepts such as declaring and raising your own events. Event handling is a primary tier in Windows programming. Without event handlers, your program would be unable to communicate with the operating system.

When defining events, remember to choose only those you want to respond to, and consider implementing the code for your event handler in a separate function. Doing so will ensure that your programs are more modular and extensible. To learn about topics related to events, read the following chapters:

- Chapter 13, "Using Windows API Functions," offers you the entire buffet of available algorithms written by some of the world's best programmers.
- Chapter 16, "Handling Errors," teaches you how to respond to error events.
- Chapter 21, "Reviewing the Standard Controls," offers you an opportunity to employ what you have learned in this chapter in conjunction with the mainstay of VB programming.
- Chapter 26, "Implementing OLE Drag-and-Drop Capabilities in Controls," expands on DragDrop.vbp, showing you how OLE control dragging and dropping can be implemented.

CHAPTER 11

Bits and Bytes About the Program

by Robert Bernavich

IN THIS CHAPTER

Using Standard Modules Instead of Form Modules

Standard modules (.BAS) differ in use from form modules (.FRM) in many ways. The standard module usually contains global variables, functions, and routines that other forms can access throughout an entire project. Suppose that you have a WAIT routine that pauses for a number of seconds. You can easily put that same routine in every one of your forms in the project, but that gets redundant fast. If you place it in the project's standard .BAS module, all the forms can access it and all you need to do is write it once. Of course, you can access a routine from other forms if it is placed in a form module instead of a standard module, but these methods are usually undesirable and can get messy.

If you are careful when you create a .BAS module, you can use the module in many different projects. You just need to remember not to call specific form modules (unless they are also interchanged between projects) or form-specific variables.

One of the more obvious reasons you want to use a form module instead of a standard module is user interaction and communication. A standard module is nothing more than a collection of code that provides nothing for the user to interact with. If you want to display a textbox or command button or even use ActiveX controls, you must use a form module. Although you can easily write and use the standard module's functions and routines in many different projects, you typically confine the form module's code to the project for which it is designed. This is not to say that you can't interchange a form module between projects as easily as a standard module, but you need to be careful not to make calls to external forms or modules that are project specific if this is to be done.

To add a previously created form or standard module to a new project, you simply go to Projects under the File menu, and then choose Add File. After you choose which module to add, it will be added to the current project and will be ready for use.

Again, it is important that, if you are going to do this, the form module or standard module be able to function on its own. There is no use in adding a form module to a project that won't work.

Setting and Getting Properties

The properties of a form or control, as you have learned by now, define how the particular object behaves onscreen and in your project. For example, if you want a form to be a certain height or width, you usually set the properties at design time when the form is created by accessing the form's property box directly.

One of the beauties of Visual Basic is that it lets you set nearly any control or form properties at runtime. If you want the color of a form to change from battleship gray to red, you simply

Bits and Bytes About the Program

CHAPTER 11

185

11

BITS AND BYTES
ABOUT THE
PROGRAM

pass the information to the correct property box in the same way you set a normal variable. The syntax for changing a property is

```
Object.Property = <value you want to set it to>
```

As a Visual Basic developer, you also find it necessary at times to retrieve a property value so you can manipulate it for some reason. The syntax to accomplish this is

```
<Variable> = Object.Property
```

I'll use a real-world example. Suppose you have a form called `frmMAIN`. You want to retrieve `frmMAIN`'s width and display it in a message box. You use the following syntax:

```
Msgbox  frmMAIN.width
```

Now suppose you want to set the width of `frmMAIN` to a certain number. The syntax is

```
frmMAIN.width=5000
```

You can set and retrieve virtually all form and control properties with this method.

Subroutine and Function Procedures

Subroutine and function procedures are blocks of code located in your form, class, or standard module that perform a certain task or event. An example of a subroutine is a `Click` event for a command button.

Subroutines and functions differ in how they are used, and for what purpose. When you call a subroutine procedure, the calling code does not expect to get any type of value back. You would use a subroutine to print text to the screen or perform any other task that does not require a return reply.

If you need to call a procedure and return with a value, you would want to use a function to accomplish this. A function is usually passed variables and then returns with another value possibly indicating success, or any other data. A common task for a function would be passing a set of numbers and using the function to calculate an answer, passing that answer back to the calling code. The following sections go into greater detail on how to use a subroutine and function procedure.

Subroutine Procedures

A subroutine procedure is a piece of modular code that runs and returns to the calling command line *without* returning a value. You can pass to a subroutine a variable that is used in the modular code and defined in the subroutine itself. The following code contains a sample subroutine:

```
Private Sub SampleSub (ByRef MyVar as String)

    Msgbox MyVar

End Sub
```

This simple routine has only a message box that displays whatever string of text you pass to it. The following line of code calls this routine and displays the text `"Test Text"`. When the subroutine is finished executing, the next line of code after the call continues execution:

```
Call SampleSub "Test Text"
```

I break apart the syntax for the subroutine procedure and explain each portion. The header of a subroutine follows:

```
<Scope>  <Type>  <Name> (<ByVal ¦ ByRef> <Variablename> <declaration>)
```

`Scope` can be either public or private. This defines how the procedure is accessed inside the project. If you declare a procedure as private, it can only be used within the module in which it is defined. It cannot be called from outside that module. A procedure declared as public can be accessed from any module within the current project. These two scopes are described later in the chapter.

`Type` is where you define the code as either a subroutine or a function. (You use `Sub` for a subroutine and `Function` for a function.)

`Name` is the name of the subroutine and subsequently what you use in the command line to call it.

`ByVal` or `ByRef` is used when you want to tell the procedure how to handle the variable. The default is `ByRef`, which means that the variable you pass to the procedure can be changed by the procedure itself. If you declare it as `ByVal`, only a copy of the variable is passed to the procedure, and this variable can only be referenced and not changed.

`Variablename declaration` is where you define the variable that was passed to this procedure. The preceding example defined the variable `MyVar` as a string type.

Function Procedures

A function procedure is a piece of modular code that runs and returns to the calling command line *with* an optional returning value. You can pass to a function a variable (or variables) that is used in the modular code and defined in the function itself. The following code contains a sample function:

```
Private Function SampleFunc (ByRef MyNum as Integer) As Integer

    SampleFunc=MyNum + 10

End Function
```

The calling line of code follows:

```
MyValue = SampleFunc 20
```

This function sets the variable `MyValue` equal to the function return value of `SampleFunc`, with `20` as the integer variable to pass. This is the method of calling a function that returns a value. You must call a function this way so the return value can immediately move into a variable.

In the function itself, the function name becomes the variable that returns a value. When you are ready to return to your calling line of code, set the variable to receive the result for `MyValue` (which is `30` in this example).

The header of the function defines the actual name of the function as the integer data type. One other difference between a function and a subroutine is that as a function's name can literally become a variable, it can be given a static scope as well.

What the static scope will do is hold the last value it had in it. Usually, if a variable is declared again (as in the case of a function being called more than once), the variable is reset to empty until a new value can be assigned to it. Declaring a variable as static gets us around this problem. Even though we declare it again, a static variable will retain its previous value.

Optional Typed Arguments

When you call a procedure, you must provide data with the call as shown in the subroutine and function examples *if* a `Variablename` declaration is defined. If there are no `Variablename` declarations in the procedure itself (for example, `Private sub TestSub()`), you do not need to pass a variable to the procedure when you call it.

In the following sample procedure, you must send data that will occupy the `MyVar` variable when you call the procedure or you get an error:

```
Private Function TestFunction (MyVar as String)
End Function
```

This might pose a problem when you want to call the procedure without passing any data to `MyVar`.

A way around this would be to not add a `Variablename` declaration. But what if you need one sometimes? Sure, you could write two separate procedures, but this is unnecessary.

Microsoft resolved this situation by creating the optional reference. When you add `Optional` before the data type declaration, as shown in the following code, you don't have to pass any data to the procedure. As the name suggests, passing data is optional:

```
Private Function TestFunction (Optional MyVar as String)
End Function
```

When a data type is set as `Optional` and no data is passed in the call, the variable is actually set to the data type variant and the value is empty. In the procedure itself, you can test for missing optional data with the `Ismissing(<VariableName>)` keyword. The following example demonstrates this:

```
Private Function TestFunction (Optional MyVar as String)

    If not Ismissing(MyVar) then
        Msgbox MyVar
    Else
        Msgbox " Variable was not passed to Procedure!"
    End If

End Function
```

> **NOTE**
>
> This code is for demonstration purposes only. If you were to write the actual code, you
> would not want to Messagebox the error to the end user. You would want to error trap it and
> handle it.

It is possible to set a default for the variable, in the event that data is not passed in the call. The
following example illustrates this:

```
Private Function TestFunction (Optional MyVar as String= "Default String" )
End Function
```

If this procedure is called without a variable, the procedure automatically assigns it the string
`"Default String"`.

Public, Private, and Static Scopes

When you define a procedure, you must give it one of two scopes: public or private. That is,
you must tell the compiler what objects in the project have access to the variable or procedure,
depending on their location. When defining a variable or function in your project, you can use
a third scope called *static*.

Private Scope

A private scope sets the variable or procedure to be read only in the module in which it is located. It is not defined outside that module. If you define a subroutine in Form1 as private, only
calls inside Form1 are able to access that procedure. Any other modules that attempt to access it
cause an error because it is not defined for them. A private variable that is used throughout the
entire form is declared in the module's general declaration section.

A private variable can also be confined to a particular procedure, losing its value when the procedure ends.

The syntax for declaring a private variable can be written two ways:

```
Dim <variable name> as <Data Type>
```

```
Private <variable name> as <Data Type>
```

You typically want to use private scope for variables as much as possible. Limiting use of the
variable to only that module keeps things tight and under control. That way, you can also add
the particular module to another project and not worry about declaring variables twice, which
results in an error. Declaring a variable as private will also keep memory use to a minimum.
This is because, as you exit the procedure or form, the variable is removed from memory allo-
cation and cleared.

Public Scope

A public (or global) scope sets the procedure or variable to be read by any module in the project. You can call any publicly declared procedure from any form or module.

A public variable retains its last value even if called in another form or standard module. The public variable was once declared more commonly with the `global` keyword. Although `public` now replaces it, you can still declare a public variable using the `global` keyword, but I do not recommend it. The correct syntax for declaring a variable global to the entire project is

```
Public <Variable Name> as <Data Type>
```

Be careful when you use a global variable. It is usually best to group all global variables together in one standard `.BAS` module, which is easier to manage. As with anything that can be accessed throughout an entire project, you must be cautious that you do not inadvertently change the value of a variable that is critical to another procedure. That is why it is best to localize the variables as much as possible at the procedure or module level with private scope. The best time to use global variables, of course, is when other modules need to share the same variable or data.

Static Scope

When you define a variable at the procedure level (in a subroutine or function), that variable is cleared and reset to an empty value each time you run that procedure from the beginning, or more accurately, each time the variable is declared again.

A way to make your variable retain its last value is to declare it not as private or public, but as static. This way, the variable keeps its last value as long as the current module is not unloaded from memory.

The correct syntax for the variable declaration is

```
Static <Variable Name> as <Data Type>
```

The Friend Function

Sometimes you might want your component's objects to be able to communicate with each other without external interference from your component.

You can use public methods inside a class, but this allows external clients as well as other objects in the class to use the object. If you define the method as private, you limit external access and also stop access from objects inside your component.

The `Friend` function allows objects inside a component to access a private method but makes the method invisible to external access.

What an object does when it declares a "friend" is give its friend access to its private methods and variables for use. This is only a one-way friendship though. Because our Tom object invites Harry to come on over and use any of his private things, it doesn't mean Tom can do the same for Harry unless Harry declares Tom his friend also. In order for a bilateral relationship to occur, both objects need to declare each other as a friend. Otherwise, it is a one-way relationship.

The correct syntax for `Friend` is as follows:

```
Friend    [Sub ¦ Function ¦ Property] procedurename
```

`Friend` can appear only in class modules and can only modify procedure names, not variables or types. It is also not shown in the class's type library because it is invisible to external clients.

Adding Asserts to Verify Parameters

You use an `Assert` method at design time to suspend the code's operation in the same way a breakpoint does, but an assert can be conditional. Asserts are stripped out of the program at compile time, making them a perfect tool for you in debugging your programs. The `Assert` method is part of the debug library.

You will want to use an `Assert` instead of a breakpoint when you do not want to suspend execution of your code at design time unless a certain requirement is met. A breakpoint will stop on the line it is attached to when that line is executed, no matter what the conditions of certain variables are.

You should add asserts when you design your project to verify that a certain parameter was passed. The following example has a form with a button. When the button is pushed, the variable equals either `True` or `False`. If the variable equals `False`, you suspend execution of the program, highlighting the `Assert` command line as if you had placed a breakpoint there:

```
Option Explicit
Dim MyVar As Boolean

Private Sub Command1_Click()

        If MyVar Then
                MyVar = False
        Else
                MyVar = True
        End If

        Debug.Assert MyVar

End Sub
```

Bits and Bytes About the Program

CHAPTER 11

191

11

BITS AND BYTES
ABOUT THE
PROGRAM

The `Assert` method can only check a boolean expression. If you want to check whether a string expression equals a certain value, you write the following code:

```
Option Explicit
Dim MyVar As Boolean
Dim MyString As String

Private Sub Command1_Click()

        If  MyString = "This is a test" Then
        MyVar = False

        Else
                MyVar = True
        End If

        Debug.Assert MyVar

End Sub
```

Summary

This chapter covers the "frame" of Visual Basic 5. Without knowing the difference between the different modules, procedures, variable type declarations, and scopes, you will not get far in your coding efforts. Knowing when to declare a variable or procedure as public, private, or static can save you many headaches later on when you are trying to conserve system resources, as well as debug your code.

Maintaining the relationship between objects, procedures, and variables is a very important skill to develop early on when learning Visual Basic 5. Bad habits are hard to break, so it becomes very important to develop good habits instead.

CHAPTER 12

Data Structures, Collections, and Enumerations

by Mike McMillan

IN THIS CHAPTER

One of the keys to creating successful computer programs is to organize your data so that you can perform operations on the data efficiently. Just as structuring programs in a modular fashion helps you create programs that are easier to understand, structuring data in a modular fashion helps you control the complexity of the problem you are trying to solve.

The data programmers deal with is rarely singular data objects that exist on their own with no relation to other data. Programmers typically work with compound data objects made up of different data types. For example, a human resources system tracks data associated with a company's employees. The kinds of data associated with employee records include items such as name, Social Security number, department, salary, years of employment, date of hire, and so on. This one data object, the employee record, consists of several data types—strings, dates, integers, and currency. These kinds of data are best structured as a group of data types combined into one, larger, compound data type. Visual Basic provides the user-defined type (UDT) to create this data structure.

Other kinds of data are best stored as a higher-level group. For example, the employees in the human resources system can all be grouped together and dealt with as a collection of employees. You can then reference each employee individually without knowing that employee's name. For example, to implement an across-the-board pay increase, a procedure can access the collection of employees and deal with them as a whole. The collection structure in Visual Basic allows the programmer to create this type of grouping.

Sometimes you want to give particular names to data that actually mean something else. For example, if you need to track the days of the week by number, it is easier for someone maintaining a piece of code to see the days named Monday, Tuesday, Wednesday, and so on, rather than 1, 2, 3, 4.... Visual Basic's special data type for this kind of data is the enumeration.

User-Defined Types

Most of the data objects programmers manipulate in their programs are compound in nature. An accounts receivable program tracks customer accounts that consist of many parts—customer name, account balance, terms, address, and so on. If each part of the customer account were kept in a separate variable, keeping track of all the variables of a medium- to large-size project would soon become a nightmare. Visual Basic provides a powerful way to create and work with compound data objects—the UDT.

Creating a User-Defined Type

A UDT is created using the `Type...End Type` statement. To define a UDT to store a customer record in an accounts receivable system, you can write the following code:

```
Type CustRecord
    strName as String
    strAddress1 as String
    strAddress2 as String
    strCity as String
    strState as String
```

```
      strZip as String
      curAccountBalance as Currency
      strTerms as String
      curInvoiceTotal as Currency
End Type
```

UDTs are defined in the global module. Once defined, a UDT can be used in the same way as any other data type. When a new customer is added to the accounts receivable system, you can simply create a variable of the user-defined type:

```
Dim Cust01 as CustRecord
```

Next, to add actual data to the UDT, you use a form called *dotted notation*. This means that each different member of the UDT is combined with the name of the variable you have defined as a UDT with a period:

```
Cust01.Name = "John Smith"
Cust01.Address1 = "3234 W. 25th Street"
Cust01.AccountBalance = 325.37
Cust01.InvoiceTotal = 1425.28
```

Using UDTs

A variable declared as a UDT can be treated in the same way as any other variable. You can assign a variable of user-defined type to another variable, as in

```
TotalOfAllAccounts = TotalOfAllAccounts + Cust01.AccountBalance
```

If you have two variables of the same UDT, you can assign all the member element values of one variable to the other variable in one statement:

```
Cust02 = Cust01
```

Now `Cust02.Name` is `"John Smith"`, `Cust02.Address1` is `"3234 W. 25th Street"`, and so on.

Finally, you can create an array of a user-defined type:

```
Dim Customers(100) as CustRecord
```

Using this technique, the first customer is partially defined as

```
Customers(0).Name = "John Smith"
Customers(0).Address1 = "3234 W. 25th Street"
```

UDTs and Arrays Compared

Unlike arrays, which only store data of the same type and number each data item stored, UDTs can store data of any type and are named for reference. The capability to create and use UDTs greatly increases the expressive power of Visual Basic by giving the programmer the capability to define his or her own data types. The data of the real world does not always fall into nice, clear-cut pieces that fit neatly into the data structures provided by Visual Basic. UDTs allow the programmer to structure data in a way that can more naturally model the problem at hand.

Collections

Another advanced data structure provided by Visual Basic is the collection. A *collection* is an ordered set of items that can be referenced as one unit. The Visual Basic programming environment has many collections that are used to organize its many elements. For example, all the fonts available to the printer, forms, and controls are stored in a collection called Fonts. Because collections are ordered, they can be referenced by number for efficiency. If you want to change the font on the command button of a form, you only have to know the number of the font you want and then you can make the assignment:

```
Command1.Font = 2
```

Collection Properties

Actually, collections only have one property—Count. This property tracks how many items are in the collection. Knowing the count of a collection is useful when you want to perform an operation on all the forms or controls in a project but you aren't sure of the exact number of items in the collection. To change the fonts on all the controls on frmMain, you can write the following For...Next loop:

```
For x = 1 to frmMain.Controls.Count - 1
    frmMain.Controls(x).Font = 2
Next x
```

A variation of this For loop is the For Each...Next loop. You use this type of loop with collections when you want to iterate through each item in the collection. To use this loop, create a variable that will hold each collection object as the loop progresses through the collection. The actual processing is performed on the variable, not on the collection object. Here is a program that puts the name of the font of each control of a form into a listbox:

```
Dim AllControls
For Each AllControls In frmMain.Controls
    List1.AddItem AllControls.Font
Next
```

Another way to loop through a set of controls to change their properties is to use the If...TypeOf construction. If you want to change the font on only the command buttons on frmMain, you can write the following code:

```
For x = 1 to frmMain.Controls.Count - 1
    If frmMain.Controls(x) TypeOf CommandButton Then
        frmMain.Controls(x).Font = 2
    End If
Next x
```

Collection Methods

Visual Basic provides three methods to add, remove, and reference the items in a collection: Add, Remove, and Item.

The Add Method

To add a member to a collection, use the `Add` method, which has the following syntax:

```
object.Add(Item, Key, Before, After)
```

`object` is either a Visual Basic object or one created by the programmer. `Add` is the method that adds an item to the collection. `Key` is an optional argument that is a string expression used to reference the item instead of a positional index. `Before` is an optional argument that marks the position in a collection where the item is to be inserted, as in `before 2` or `before Jones`. `After` is an optional argument that marks the position in the collection where an item is to be deleted, as in `after 2` or `after Jones`.

The arguments to the `Add` method are called *named arguments*. This means that when they are called in the method, they are called by explicitly assigning a value to them, such as

```
myCollection.Add(item := "Item 1", before := 2, after := 0)
```

Named arguments differ from standard function arguments in that named arguments can be in any order because the method has the name to keep straight what value is assigned to what argument. In the preceding example, you could have just as easily written

```
myCollection.Add(after := 0, item := "Item 1", before := 2)
```

The Remove Method

To remove an item from a collection, use the `Remove` method, which has the following syntax:

```
object.Remove index
```

`object` is either an object created by Visual Basic or one created by the programmer. `Remove` is the method that removes an item from the collection. `index` is either the item's positional index in the collection or a key that was specified when the item was added to the collection.

The Item Method

To reference a specific item of a collection, use the `Item` method, which has the following syntax:

```
Object.Item(Index)
```

`Object` is either a Visual Basic object or one created by the programmer. `Item` is the method that references an individual member of a collection. `Index` is either the positional index of the item being referenced or a key that was specified when the item was added to the collection.

`Item` is the default method of a collection, so you do not have to use it when you want to reference an item in the collection, as in

```
Print aCollection(1)
```

This code prints the member of the collection in position 1. The other way to accomplish the same thing is to write

```
Print aCollection.Item(1)
```

Adding and Removing from a Collection

Listing 12.1 shows a program that summarizes adding and removing items from a collection.

Listing 12.1. Adding and removing from a collection.

```
Public Sub CreateEmployees()
    Dim MyEmployees as New Collection
    Dim Msg as String
    Dim x as Integer
    Dim y as Integer
    Dim oneEmp, EmpName, aEmp, EmpList
    Msg = "Please enter an employee name." & chr(13) & _
        "Press Cancel to view a list of employees."
    Do
        EmpName = InputBox(Msg,"Create New Employee")
        oneEmp = EmpName
        If oneEmp <> "" Then
            MyEmployees.Add Item := oneEmp
        End If
        oneEmp = ""
    Loop Until EmpName = ""
    For x = t to MyEmployees.Count
        EmpList = EmpList & x & ": " & MyEmployees(x) & _
        Chr(13)
    Next x
    EmpList = ""
    y = InputBox("Enter the number of the employee to _
        remove.")
    MyEmployees.Remove y
    For x = 1 to MyEmployees.Count
        EmpList = EmpList & x & ": " & MyEmployees(x) _
        & Chr(13)
    Next x
    MsgBox EmpList, ,"New List of Employees"
End Sub
```

Here is an explanation of what is happening in the subroutine. The first line creates a new collection called MyEmployees. The next four lines create variables to be used later in the program. The next line creates a string variable that contains a message to be displayed later in the program. After that, a Do loop prompts the user to enter a new employee name. If the variable oneEmp doesn't contain the empty string, the name is added to the collection in the line:

```
MyEmployees.Add Item := oneEmp
```

This line looks funny because of the assignment operator for collections (:=). The Do loop continues until a blank line is entered by the user.

After the `Do` loop is a `For...Next` loop that creates a string containing the employee names. The program loops through the `MyEmployee` collection, adding the collection item that corresponds with the index number of the `For...Next` loop.

Following the `For...Next` loop is a message that asks the user to enter the number of an employee to remove from the collection. The employee is removed using the collection method `Remove`.

Finally, another `For...Next` loop is created to list the `MyEmployee` collection again after a name has been removed. The list is displayed using the `MsgBox` function.

Enumerations

A third type of data structure provided by Visual Basic is the enumeration. The best way to define an enumeration is by providing an example of one. Suppose you are writing a program that needs to track the day of the week. Many decision points in the program key off of which day of the week it is. The first scheme you imagine is to simply use numbers to represent the days of the week: 1, 2, 3, 4, 5, 6, and 7. This works fine for a small program. For a large, complex program, however, it becomes more difficult for the programmer who wrote the code, or for a programmer who comes in later to maintain the code, to understand what all the 1s and 3s and 5s mean.

A better solution to this problem is to use the names of the days of the week:

```
If DayOfWeek = Monday Then
 txtGreeting.Text = "Sorry!"
End If
```

There can be no confusion over what the variable represents. Providing a way to name numerical values used in a program is an important tool in the battle of code complexity.

The Enum Statement

The statement used to create an enumeration data type is the `Enum` statement. Here is the syntax:

```
[Public¦Private] Enum name
   membername = [constantexpression]
   membername = [constantexpression]
End Enum
```

`Public` is an optional declaration that makes the enum type visible throughout the project. `Private` is an optional declaration that makes the enum type visible only within the module in which it appears.

`Enum` is required to declare the type of the data. *name* is required to give a name to the enum type. *membername* is required to create an element of the enum type.

constantexpression is an optional value that can be given to the *membername*. constantexpression can take any data type, including another enum. If constantexpression is not assigned, the elements of the enumeration are assigned long integer values, starting with 0 and continuing from 1 through as many elements are initialized.

Enum types are always defined at the module level, and they can never be empty.

Here is an enum statement where the *membernames* are assigned values explicitly in the code:

```
Public Enum DaysOfTheWeek
    Monday = 1
    Tuesday = 2
    Wednesday = 3
    Thursday = 4
    Friday = 5
    Saturday = 6
    Sunday = 7
End Enum
```

The other way to do this, though not to the same effect, is to not assign values to the elements, as in

```
Public Enum DaysOfTheWeek
    Monday
    Tuesday
    Wednesday
    Thursday
    Friday
    Saturday
    Sunday
End Enum
```

Now Monday is assigned 0, Tuesday gets 1, and so on. This is the normal behavior of the enum statement. Assigning the values to the elements of the enumerated data type is a small price to pay to get the results you really want. However, as in so many other aspects of programming, there is a way to get around this behavior. If you really want your enumerated values to start with 1 and not 0, you can simply assign the first element the value 1 and Visual Basic will consecutively number the rest of the elements starting with 2.

You can now define the DaysOfTheWeek in this way:

```
Public Enum DaysOfTheWeek
    Monday = 1
    Tuesday
    Wednesday
    Thursday
    Friday
    Saturday
    Sunday
End Enum
```

Of course, the tricks don't have to stop with assigning the first value. Maybe you want the weekend days to have special numbers, signifying their importance in your life. You can define your enumerated type in this way:

```
Public Enum DaysOfTheWeek
    Monday = 1
    Tuesday
    Wednesday
    Thursday
    Friday
    Saturday = 1000
    Sunday
End Enum
```

Can you guess the value of Sunday? Of course, 1001 is correct, but then, some people can't put a value on their weekends.

Using the Object Browser to View Data Structures

Visual Basic provides a handy utility for viewing the data structures you create in your programs through user-defined types and enumerations. This utility is called the Object Browser, and you can find it on the menu bar under View. (See Figure 12.1.)

FIGURE 12.1.

The View menu in the Object Browser.

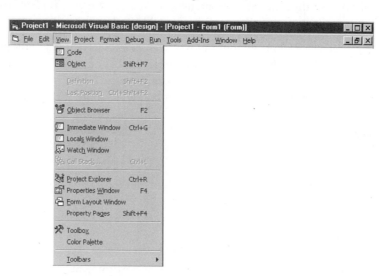

You can also press F2 to view the Object Browser.

When the Object Browser form loads, the object view it defaults to is All Libraries, which is shown in Figure 12.2.

FIGURE 12.2.

The Object Browser's default view.

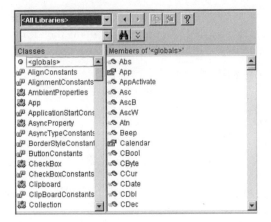

Below the comboboxes are two listboxes: The box on the left holds the classes of the project and the box on the right holds the members of each class. In this case, you can consider a class to be the same thing as an object. Every object that is available to you through Visual Basic is visible in the Classes listbox.

By highlighting a class or object, you can view the properties, methods, and events that are available to that object. Of course, each type of object (such as a listbox control or a printer object) has a different set of properties, methods, and events available to it. Nevertheless, any object available through Visual Basic is visible in the Object Browser.

The default view is All Libraries, but you can narrow your view to just the project you are working on by clicking the listbox with All Libraries in it. The available libraries then appear in the listbox and you can select the one you want. Figure 12.3 shows the selections available in this example, including Project1, the project that holds some of the examples from this chapter.

FIGURE 12.3.

Selecting a library to view.

The other selections in the listbox include

stdole	Standard OLE controls
VB	Objects in the Visual Basic environment
VBA	Objects in the Visual Basic for Applications environment
VBRUN	Objects in the Visual Basic runtime environment

Because you are mostly concerned with what objects are defined in your project, select Project1 for this example.

When you select `Project1`, the objects that have been defined for `Project1` at this point are displayed in the Classes listbox. Figure 12.4 shows that four classes have been defined so far in `Project1`:

`globals`	
`Chapter13`	The name of the default form
`CustRecord`	A user-defined type
`DaysOfTheWeek`	An enumeration

FIGURE 12.4.

The Object Browser, displaying objects from the `Chapter13` *project.*

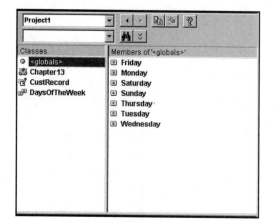

In the Members listbox are the properties, methods, and events or whatever have been defined as members for the object that is highlighted in the Classes listbox. Notice that the members of the `globals` object look conspicuously like the members of the enumeration `DaysOfTheWeek`. Because the enumeration has a global scope, the members of the enumeration display as members of the `globals` object. If other objects had been defined with a public scope, their members would display in the Members listbox also.

To display the members of the other objects, click the object in the Classes listbox. For example, when you click `CustRecord`, the Members listbox displays the elements of the `CustRecord` UDT. (See Figure 12.5.) If you click the `DaysOfTheWeek` selection, the Members listbox displays the enumeration defined for `DaysOfTheWeek`.

You can go directly from the Object Browser to the code that defines the object by double-clicking the object. Figure 12.6 displays the Code window with the cursor placed on the `CustRecord` UDT after double-clicking `CustRecord` in the Object Browser.

FIGURE 12.5.

The Object Browser displaying the CustRecord *UDT.*

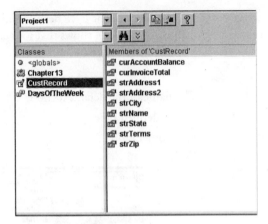

FIGURE 12.6.

The CustRecord *UDT in the Code window.*

Another way to move to the Code window of an object is to right-click the mouse with the object or one of its members highlighted in the Object Browser. Right-clicking brings up a floating menu like the one in Figure 12.7.

From this menu, if you press View Definitions, you go to the Code window for the highlighted selection.

Two other important selections from the floating menu are Group Members and Show Hidden Members. When Group Members is checked, the properties of an object are grouped together, the methods of an object are grouped together, and the events of an object are grouped together. Otherwise, the properties, methods, and events of an object are displayed in alphabetical order.

FIGURE 12.7.

*The Object Browser
floating menu.*

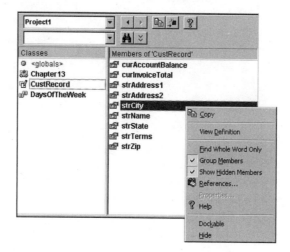

When Show Hidden Members is checked, information marked as hidden in the type library is displayed. These items are displayed in light gray type.

Summary

Visual Basic 5 provides strong support for creating data structures for your programming requirements. Providing support for data structures is very important because the capability to create easy-to-understand data structures to solve complex programming problems is one of the keys to successful computer programming.

Visual Basic provides three major data structures for the programmer:

- ■ User-defined types
- ■ Collections
- ■ Enumerations

This chapter shows how you can use these data structures to organize complex data into simple structures that can then be used to solve the problem at hand.

Using Windows API Functions

by Mike McMillan

IN THIS CHAPTER

The Visual Basic programming environment is a very powerful platform for creating Windows applications. Sometimes, however, you will want to extend the features of Visual Basic to do things that are possible in the Windows environment but are not directly supported by Visual Basic.

An example of extending Visual Basic is printing angled, or slanted, text. In the Visual Basic environment, all text is displayed horizontally, usually within the confines of a textbox or some other control. If you want to display text at any angle other than 45 degrees, you have to call a Windows function that is located in the Windows Application Programming Interface (API).

The Windows Application Programming Interface is a set of several hundred Windows functions that are located in a set of files called dynamic link libraries (DLLs). You can make a function from the Windows API available to your Visual Basic program by "declaring" the function to be callable from your program. You can then use the Windows API function as you do any built-in Visual Basic function or function you have written yourself.

This chapter covers the following topics concerning using the Windows API:

- The set of dynamic link libraries and what they are used for
- How to include Windows API functions in your programs—the `Declare` statement
- The syntax and data types of the `Declare` statement
- How to use the API Text Viewer program
- Examples of using Windows API functions in your applications
- How to use Windows API callbacks

The Windows API Library Files

The library (DLL) files that make up the Windows API are located in the `Windows\System` subdirectory. These files are found on every PC that is running Windows, so you don't have to worry about including them if you create a set of setup disks for distribution.

The three major Windows DLLs are `USER32.DLL`, `KERNEL32.DLL`, and `GDI32.DLL`. Several smaller DLLs are known as extension DLLs and provide functions in addition to those found in the three major DLLs:

```
COMDLG.DLL

DLLLZ32.DLL

VERSION.DLL

APIGID.DLL

COMCTL32.DLL

MAPI32.DLL
```

```
NETAPI32.DLL

ODBC32.DLL

WINMM.DLL
```

Figure 13.1 details the relationship between the three major DLLs and the Windows operating system.

FIGURE 13.1.

The relationship of the major DLLs to the Windows operating system

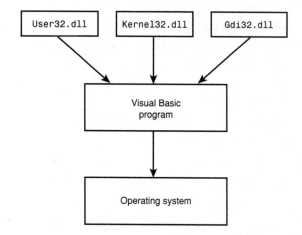

The following sections discuss in some detail what each DLL is responsible for and their constituent functions.

USER32.DLL

The USER32.DLL library file contains functions that relate to managing the Windows environment, such as

■ Handling messages between windows

■ Managing cursors

■ Managing menus

■ Handling other non-display functions

The following list outlines some of the functions of the USER32 library:

GetCursorPos retrieves a cursor's position.

SetWindowPos sets a window's position and z-order.

GetParent returns the handle to a parent window.

GetActiveWindow returns a handle to the active window.

SendMessage sends a message to a window.

GDI32.DLL

The GDI32.DLL library file (the Graphics Device Interface library) contains functions that help manage output to different devices, especially the screen. Following are some of the functions in GDI32:

BitBlt copies a bitmap between two device contexts.

DeleteObject deletes an object from memory.

RoundRect draws a rectangle with rounded corners.

SelectObject selects an object into a device context.

StretchBlt sets the mode for bitmap stretching.

KERNEL32.DLL

The KERNEL32.DLL library contains functions that manage the low-level operating system functions. These functions include

- Memory management
- Task management
- Resource handling
- File and directory management
- Module management

Here are some of the functions in the KERNEL32 library:

GetSystemDirectory returns the path of the Windows system directory.

GetTempFileName creates a temporary file.

GetModuleFileName returns the filename for a module.

GetVersion returns the versions of DOS and Windows.

The Extension DLL Libraries

The extension DLLs are libraries added to Windows when the functionality of Windows has changed in some way, usually with the addition of new features to the operating system. Instead of rewriting the operating system when a new feature is added, a new DLL added to the system includes the functions that add the new feature to the operating system. For example, when Microsoft added multimedia capabilities to Windows, it created a new DLL that includes the multimedia functions, WINMM.DLL.

The major extension libraries that are a part of Windows are

- COMCTL32.DLL, which implements the new Windows common controls that are part of Windows 95 and Windows NT 4.0.
- MAPI32.DLL, which implements the functions that let any application work with electronic mail.

■ NETAPI32.DLL, which implements a set of functions that let applications access and control networks.

■ ODBC32.DLL, which implements a set of functions that let applications work with databases that are ODBC-compliant. ODBC stands for open database connectivity.

■ WINMM.DLL, which implements a set of functions that access the operating system's multimedia capabilities.

These are the library files and extensions to the Windows operating system you will call when you write programs that access the Windows API. Once you learn how to call these libraries from your Visual Basic applications (the subject of the next section), you can tap the full power of the Windows environment.

Declaring a Windows API Function

You include a Windows API function in your Visual Basic programs by using the Declare statement to "declare" the function to be a part of your program. The Declare statement is added to the declarations sections of a code window in either a standard module or a form. If the Declare statement is added to a standard module, the function is considered Public and can be called from anywhere in your applications. If the Declare statement is added to the declarations sections of a form, the function is local to that form and can only be called within that form. In this latter case, you must precede the declaration with the Private keyword.

The syntax of the Declare statement depends on whether the procedure you call returns a value. If the procedure does return a value, you use the Function form of the Declare statement:

```
Declare Function publicname Lib "libname" [Alias "alias"] [(([ByVal] variable _
[As Type] [,[ByVal] variable [As Type]]...])] As Type
```

If the procedure does not return a value, you use the Sub form of the Declare statement:

```
Declare Sub publicname Lib "libname" [Alias "alias"] [(([ByVal] variable _
[As Type] [,[ByVal] variable [As Type]] ...])]
```

Here is an example of calling a Windows API function using the Function form of the Declare statement from a standard module. This function returns the handle of the currently active window on a desktop:

```
Declare Function GetActiveWindow Lib "User32" () As Integer
```

Here is an example of calling a Windows API function using the sub form of the Declare statement from the declarations section of a form. This Windows API function moves the referenced window and changes its size:

```
Private Declare Sub MoveWindow Lib "User32" (ByVal hWnd As _
    Integer, ByVal X As Integer, ByVal Y As Integer, ByVal _
    nWidth As Integer, ByVal nHeight As Integer, ByVal _
    bRepaint As Integer)
```

The two sample Windows API function calls only had integer argument types. However, many more data types are used in calling Windows API functions. Some of these data types are standard Visual Basic data types, but some of the data types you must use are based on the C data types and can be tricky to use for a programmer who doesn't have experience in C. The next sections cover in more detail the structure of the Declare statement's arguments, including how the arguments are passed to the Windows API and the legal data types for Declare statement arguments.

Passing Arguments by Value and by Reference

You can pass arguments to a function by value or by reference. Passing an argument by value means that a copy of the argument is sent to the function. For example, you can create a function called Dble that doubles a number passed to it and use it in the following program fragment:

```
x = 12
NewX = Dble(x)
```

The value of x that is passed to the function Dble is a copy of the variable, not the actual variable itself. Passing arguments by value means that the function cannot change the value of the actual argument because it is actually working with a copy of the argument.

Passing an argument by reference means that the function is actually passing a 32-bit pointer to the memory address where the value of the argument is stored. When an argument is passed to a function by reference, it is possible for the function to actually change the value of the argument because the function is working with the actual memory address where the argument's value is stored and not just a copy of the argument's value.

Here is an example that demonstrates how a subroutine can change an argument passed to it by reference. First, here is a subroutine that very simply changes the argument passed to it to something else:

```
Private Sub ChangeArg(x as Integer)
    x = 1212
End Sub
```

Now here is a Main() subprocedure that calls the ChangeArg subroutine:

```
Public Sub Main()
    Dim x As Integer
    x = 144
    MsgBox "The number is: " & x
    ChangeArg x
    MsgBox "The number is now: " & x
End Sub
```

The first MsgBox function displays the number 144, and the second MsgBox function displays the number 1212. The actual value of the variable x has been changed by the subroutine, all because the argument to it was passed by reference.

This discussion of passing arguments by value or by reference is not just an esoteric lesson in the theory of programming languages. The functions that make up the Windows API expect its arguments to be passed either by value or by reference. It is up to you, the programmer, to know the proper way to pass arguments to a particular function. If you pass an argument by value when the function expects the argument to be passed by reference, or vice versa, the function will receive the wrong type of data and will probably not work correctly.

Visual Basic, by default, passes arguments to functions by reference. It is not necessary then, when writing a Declare statement, to explicitly pass an argument to the function using the ByRef keyword. When passing arguments by value, however, you must explicitly use the ByVal keyword.

Some Windows API functions that require more than one argument might have some arguments that must be passed by value and some arguments that are passed by reference. In this case, you have to use ByVal for the arguments passed by value, but you can use the ByRef keyword or leave it out for arguments passed by reference.

The following code shows an example of a Declare statement that declares a function which requires arguments passed by value and by reference:

```
Declare Function CascadeWindow% Lib "user32" (ByVal hwndParent As _
    Long, ByVal wHow As Long, lpRect As RECT, ByVal cKids As Long, _
    lpKids As Long)
```

Two of the arguments to this function, lpRect and lpKids, are passed by reference, whereas the other arguments are passed by value.

Declare Statement Argument Data Types

The functions that make up the Windows API are written in C. The data types that C accepts are often similar to the data types of Visual Basic, but in some cases there are significant differences between the data types of the two languages. Not having a clear understanding of these differences can lead to Windows API function calls that don't work properly or don't work at all in some cases. The following sections discuss the most common data types the different Windows API functions expect and how they are declared in Visual Basic.

INTEGER

The INTEGER data type is used for 16-bit numeric arguments that correspond to the C data types short, unsigned short, and WORD. Arguments of INTEGER data type are passed by value. Arguments that take the INTEGER data type are usually written as (ByVal *argument* As Integer) or (ByVal *argument*%).

LONG

The LONG data type is used for 32-bit numeric arguments that correspond to the C data types int, unsigned int, unsigned long, BOOL, and DWORD. LONG data type arguments are passed by value. LONG data type arguments are usually written as (ByVal *argument* As Long) or (ByVal *argument*&).

STRING

The Windows API functions expect the LPSTR C data type, which is a pointer to characters. In C, a string is an array of characters. STRING data type arguments are passed by value. STRING data type arguments are usually written as (ByVal *argument* As String) or (ByVal *argument*$). When a string parameter is passed to a Windows API function, the string is supposed to be passed as a pointer to a null terminated string, which is a string with a last character with the ASCII value 0. Visual Basic automatically converts a string passed by value to this type of string by adding a null termination character.

STRUCTURE

Some Windows API functions expect their arguments to be a STRUCTURE type. A STRUCTURE in C is the equivalent to a user-defined type (UDT) in Visual Basic. UDT data type arguments are passed by reference. UDT data type arguments are usually written as (*argument* As UDT), as in (myRect As RECT), where RECT is a UDT that defines a rectangle structure which is very common in controlling windows with the Windows API.

ANY

Some Windows API functions accept more than one data type for the same argument. If you want to be able to pass more than one data type with the argument, use the ANY data type. The ANY data type is passed by reference. ANY data type arguments are usually written as (*argument* As Any).

These are the major data types you will encounter when calling Windows API functions. I need to cover some other aspects of the Declare statement before you look at some examples of actually using the Windows API in a program.

Using Aliases

Some Windows API functions are named using characters that are illegal in Visual Basic. A very common example is the underscore, as in _lopen. Trying to reference this name in Visual Basic generates an error because of the underscore character. The way around this is to "alias" the name in the Declare statement. For example, to use the _lopen function, the following Declare statement will work:

```
Declare Function lopen Lib "kernel32" Alias "_lopen" _
(ByVal lpPathname As String, ByVal ireadWrite As Long) As Long
```

The Windows API function _lopen is renamed lopen so that it is recognized as a legal name in Visual Basic. The Alias keyword lets Visual Basic know that the function it is really working with is _lopen.

Another use of the Alias keyword is to change the name of a function, usually for readability reasons. For example, the GetWindowDesc$ function might be renamed WinDesc through the use of the Alias keyword.

Using Ordinal Numbers as Function Names

Sometimes a Windows API function can be named with its ordinal number rather than a more descriptive text name. Using an ordinal number requires less system resources, so it is slightly more efficient than using a text name.

If you want to refer to a function by its ordinal number, use the Alias keyword to refer to the number, as in

```
Declare Function GetWindowsDirectory Lib "kernel32" Alias "#432" _
  (ByVal lpBuffer As String, ByVal nSize As Long) As Long
```

NOTE

To find the ordinal number of a Windows API function, you must use a utility program such as Dumpbin.exe, which is included with Microsoft Visual C++.

The API Text Viewer

As you have probably surmised by now, creating a Declare statement that gets the right Windows API function and declares it using the proper syntax and data types is not the easiest thing to do. Starting with Visual Basic 4, Microsoft included with the Visual Basic distribution a utility program to help with finding the right API function and declaring it legally and properly within an application—the API Text Viewer. The API Text Viewer, or just the API Viewer, separates three different aspects of calling API functions—constants, declares, and types—into groups that can be viewed together. You can then select an item from the group, and the proper syntactical form is displayed in the API Viewer. You can then take the form and cut and paste it directly into your application. This helps ensure that you do not have a mistake in a Declare statement or a Constant declaration.

The API Viewer is found in the same program group as Visual Basic. If you select Start | Programs | Microsoft Visual Basic 5.0 from the Windows 95 taskbar, the first selection is the API Text Viewer. Selecting it displays the API Viewer form on the screen, as in Figure 13.2.

FIGURE 13.2.
The API Viewer form.

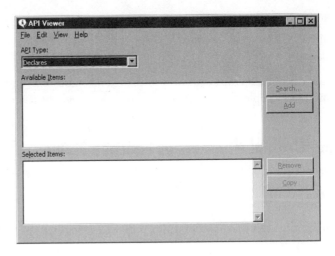

The first selection to make on this form is the API type you want to view. There are three types available:

- Declares
- Constants
- Types

These three API types are stored in a text file called Win32api.txt. When you select one of the types from the API Type listbox, that section of the Win32api text files is loaded.

To load the text file, select File | Load Text File from the API Viewer menu. Then select the Win32api file from the dialog box that appears. Figure 13.3 shows the API Viewer form after the Win32api text file is loaded.

FIGURE 13.3.
The API Viewer form displaying declare API types from the Win32api text file.

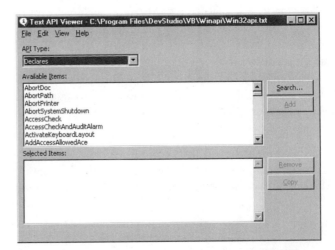

NOTE

After the `Win32api` text file loads, a dialog box pops up, asking if you want to convert the text file to a database (`.MDB`) file. Converting the text file to a database file enables the API types to load faster. Once you do this, you select Load Database File instead of Load Text File from the File menu.

The API functions are loaded into the Available Items listbox in alphabetical order. To select a function to view, double-click the item. It is then displayed in the Selected Items textbox. Figure 13.4 shows the `GetWindowTextLength` function displayed in the Selected Items textbox.

FIGURE 13.4.

The function `GetWindowTextLength` *displayed in the API Viewer.*

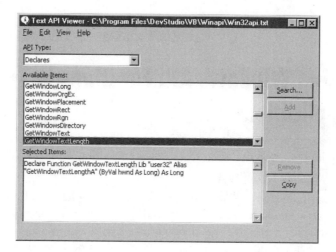

Once you select a `Declare` statement to view, you can copy it to the Clipboard by clicking the Copy button located to the right of the Selected Items textbox. Once the text is on the Clipboard, you can easily paste it into your Visual Basic application.

When selecting an available item, you can also click the Search button to the right of the Available Items listbox. A dialog box opens and you can enter the prefix of a string as the search string to find. Figure 13.5 shows the search dialog box and a search string entered in the textbox.

When you click OK, if the function you are searching for is found, it is highlighted in the Available Items listbox. You can then double-click the item to add it to the Selected Items textbox, or you can click the Add button. The `Declare` statement is added to the Selected Items textbox and you can copy it to the Clipboard.

13

USING WINDOWS
API FUNCTIONS

FIGURE 13.5.

The search dialog box.

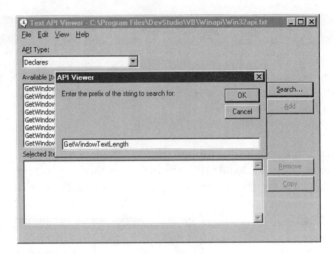

Using Windows API Functions in Your Applications

There are many ways to use the Windows API functions in your applications. One set of API functions you will use often when you start writing advanced Windows applications is API functions that deal with getting information about a window or set of windows.

Every window in the Windows operating system is identified by a handle. The desktop window has a handle, a Visual Basic form displayed in an application has a handle, and even the controls on a form, which are themselves actually windows, have a handle. You can gather a lot of information about the windows in your application once you get the handle of the window that interests you.

To get the handle of the active window on your desktop, you need to use the function GetActiveWindow. This function returns the handle of the active window. To use this function in your application, add the following line to a standard module:

```
Declare Function GetActiveWindow Lib "user32" () As Integer
```

With this function declared, you can now add code to your application to call the function. For example, to use this function in a simple application, create a form with one command button on it. Add the following code to the command button's Click event:

```
Dim hWindow As Integer
hWindow = GetActiveWindow
MsgBox "Active Window Handle: " & Str$(hWindow)
```

When you run this application and click the command button, you see the message box shown in Figure 13.6.

FIGURE 13.6.
*Getting the handle of
the active window.*

After you get the handle of a window, you can use that information to do other things with the windows on your desktop using the Windows API. For example, to make a window the active window, you can pass its handle to the `SetActiveWindow` function, which makes the window associated with the window handle it is passed the active window.

The `Declare` statement for `SetActiveWindow` is

```
Declare Function SetActiveWindow Lib "user32" (ByVal hWnd As Long) As Long
```

You can add this function to your code to make a window the active window:

```
Dim X as Long
X = SetActiveWindow(hWindow)
```

The argument `hWindow` is the handle of a window, which was acquired through another Windows API function such as `FindWindow`. The variable `X` is used because `SetActiveWindow` returns the handle of the previously active window and you must set up a variable to receive that value.

The preceding examples give only a hint of the power of the Windows API functions. Every aspect of the Windows environment, from the Windows environment to handling hardware such as printers and disk drives, can be controlled to a greater or lesser extent using Windows API functions. Taking the time to learn these functions can help you gain greater control over your applications' environment, and you can often achieve significant efficiency gains using the API functions in your applications.

13

USING WINDOWS
API FUNCTIONS

CAUTION

When writing Windows API functions, be sure to save your work often because it is easy to crash your system and lose your work if one of your API functions goes awry. In fact, many programmers set up their Visual Basic environment to prompt them to save the project every time they run it.

How to Use Windows API Callbacks

The Windows API functions include several functions called *enumeration functions*. An example of a Windows API enumeration function is `EnumWindows`. `EnumWindows` provides a list of the handles of all parent windows in the Windows environment. It does this by sending the list to a user-defined function that handles the list in some way, say by adding the list to a listbox control. For this to work, Visual Basic must be able to call the user-defined function within the Windows API function—in this case, `EnumWindows`. The technique to do this is called a *callback*.

To perform a callback, a function pointer that points to the memory address where the function is stored must be in the argument list of the Windows API function. Previous versions of Visual Basic did not have a feature to allow this, but Visual Basic 5.0 has the `addressof` keyword, which provides a function with the memory address of the function that is associated with the keyword. The `addressof` keyword is formed in this way:

```
addressof aFunction
```

`aFunction` is the name of the function `addressof` points to.

To use the function as part of a callback, it must be called from the Windows API function. The following code shows an example of using a callback to list the windows enumerated by the `EnumWindows` function:

```
Dim S As Long
Dim aVal As Long
aVal = 10
S = EnumWindows(addressof ListProc, aVal)
```

This example sends the enumerated windows handle list to a procedure `ListProc`, which handles the list in some way. This function returns a `Long` value, which is nonzero if the function is successful or `0` if the function is not successful. The argument `aVal` can be any `Long` value of the programmer's choosing, which does nothing but fill out the argument list for the function.

Summary

The Windows API function library provides the Visual Basic programmer with all the power available from the Windows platform. Every aspect of Windows, from the desktop environment to the hardware environment, can be controlled with one or more API functions. However, using the API functions can be difficult for a number of reasons, most of which revolve around the fact that the functions themselves are written in C and are not always compatible with Visual Basic. Many Visual Basic programmers are afraid to use the API functions because of this difficulty. However, by spending the time to learn the syntax of the API functions you want to call, you can avoid the unexpected results and system crashes that have given the Windows API a bad name around Visual Basic circles. Using the API Text Viewer program can also help you get a handle on the complexity of the API functions.

Working with Arrays

by Mike McMillan

IN THIS CHAPTER

The most fundamental data structure in Visual Basic is the array. Arrays are used in many computer programs because they are easy to implement and very efficient. Arrays are also fundamental because they resemble how memory is structured in virtually all computer systems.

Many computer applications, such as databases and spreadsheets, are conceptually based on the array. A database table, for example, can be thought of as an array of rows and columns. The rows are the field names of the database, and the columns are where the data that goes in the fields is stored.

A spreadsheet is an even more direct representation of an array. The rows and columns of a spreadsheet correspond directly to the rows and columns that make up a multidimensional array.

Arrays are used primarily to store data of a similar kind and to perform operations on that data. An example of this is matrix mathematics. A matrix is, quite simply, a multidimensional array that stores related data (numbers). The matrix is then used as a basis to perform operations for calculating statistics, for example. One operation that is often performed on a matrix is a matrix transpose. A transpose of a matrix is performed by writing the columns of a matrix as rows. If you have a very small matrix A defined as

```
1 2 3
4 5 6
7 8 9
```

the transpose of matrix A is

```
1 4 7
2 5 8
3 6 9
```

At the end of this chapter, you will develop a program that can perform the transpose of a matrix.

An Overview of Arrays

An array is a set of values, stored contiguously in memory, of the same data type. Because arrays hold values of the same data type, you have to declare the array's data type when you create it. An array can be declared any legal data type, including an array of user-defined types and an array of objects. If you declare an array to be of variant type, then each item in the array can be any legal data type.

> **NOTE**
>
> Even though a variant can store any data type, it is itself a single data type. An array declared as a Variant can store any and all data types because that is the definition of Variant. Many newcomers to Visual Basic get this concept confused because they are used to being able to store only one type of data in an array.

Figure 14.1 shows three arrays storing different data types: integer, string, and variant.

FIGURE 14.1.
Three arrays of different data types.

```
(0   1   2   3   4   5   6   7   8   9)
```

An array of integers

```
("Visual Basic", "Word", "Excel", "PowerPoint")
```

An array of strings

```
(1, "Visual Basic", 2, "Word", 3.125, "Excel")
```

An array of variants

The two kinds of arrays are fixed size and dynamic. As its name implies, a fixed-size array cannot change its size after it has been created. A dynamic array, on the other hand, can change in size after it has been created. I will discuss dynamic arrays in another section.

Fixed-Size Arrays

Arrays can be declared as Public or Private. To make an array Public, declare it in the Declarations section of a module. To declare an array at the module level, declare it as Private in the Declarations section of a module. To create a local array, declare it as Private in any procedure.

Chapter 11, "Bits and Bytes About the Program," discusses scoping of variables, but a little clarification here will help reinforce that lesson. A public array can be accessed from anywhere in the project. A private array can only be accessed from the form module where the array is declared. For example, if in the code section of Form1 you declare a private array, any calls to that array from other forms will not work. However, if you declare a public array in a code module, code from any form in the project can successfully access the array.

Arrays can also be declared using Dim or Static. Arrays, like other variables, have a lifetime during which they retain their value. Arrays declared with Public have a lifetime that lasts as long as the application is running. Arrays that are declared with Dim within a procedure have a lifetime that lasts only as long as the procedure is running. When the procedure quits, the array declared with Dim loses its values. To make a locally declared array retain its value throughout the life of an application, declare it with the Static keyword. The array will then retain its value until the application quits, just as if it had been declared as Public in a code module.

After declaring the scope of an array, you must assign a fixed-size array a size, or number of elements it will hold. This number is called the array's upper bound, and the number can never exceed the range of a Long integer (-2,147,483,647 to 2,147,483,647). An array that is Public and holds 20 integer elements is declared in this way:

```
Public Items(19) As Integer 'A global array of 20 integers
```

Other array declarations for different data types and sizes are described in the following lines:

```
Private Items(49) As String 'A local array of 50 strings
Static Items(29) As Variant 'A local array of 30 variants
Dim Items(9) As Double 'A local array of 10 double precision numbers
```

Notice that the numbers declared as the upper bound are one less than the number of items you actually want in the array. In Visual Basic, the array index starts numbering at 0.

NOTE

If you don't want the array index to start at 0, you can do one of two things:

- Include the statement `Option Base 1` in the `Declarations` section of the global module.
- Explicitly declare the lower bound of the array.

The first option sets the lower bound for all arrays in the project to 1. Do this if you never want an array index to start with 0.

You can explicitly declare the lower bound of an array by using the `To` keyword. An array declaration with an explicit lower bound looks like this:

```
Dim Items(1 To 20) As Integer
```

When explicitly declaring the lower bound of an array, you are not required to set the bound at 1. You can use any integer. If you want the `Items` array to start at 10, for example, you can write

```
Private Items(10 To 20) As Integer
```

The only limitation on setting the lower bound is that the number for the lower bound must be less than or equal to the number for the upper bound. What this means is that it's perfectly legal to declare an array in this way:

```
Dim Items(20 To 20) as Integer
```

There is only one item in this array and its index is 20, but you can assign a value to it and treat it the same as if it were a part of a large group of elements.

Now that I have covered all the details of declaring arrays, here is the formal syntax for declaring an array:

```
(Dim, Static, Public, Private) arrayname([subscripts]) [As datatype]
```

The interpretation of this syntax for the array is as follows:

- An array must be declared as either `Dim`, `Static`, `Public`, or `Private`.
- An array must be given a name, although the choice of the name is up to the developer.

- An array can have a set of subscripts, such as (10,10), but if the array is a dynamic array, it is declared with empty parentheses.
- An array can be declared as a data type if it is not a dynamic array.

Initial Values of Array Items

When you declare an array at any level, the items of the array are initially given a value according to the data type of the array:

- A numeric array variable is initialized to 0.
- A variable-length string array variable is initialized to a zero-length string (" ").
- A fixed-length string array variable is initialized to Empty.
- An array of variants is initialized to Empty.
- Each element of a user-defined type array variable is initialized according to its data type.

Assigning Values to Array Elements

In other computer languages, such as C, you can assign values to an array when the array is first declared. You cannot do this in Visual Basic. The declaration must be done first, followed later in the program with a statement or programming construct that assigns values to the array.

There are two ways to assign values to the individual elements of an array. One way is to explicitly assign them with an assignment statement. For example, if you have declared a string array called Item, you can assign a value to the first element of the array in this way:

```
Item(0) = "Chair"
```

Other elements of the array can be assigned values at the same time or anywhere else in the body of a procedure. However, if you know the values to be assigned to the array elements in advance, it is good programming practice to place the assignment statements at the beginning of a procedure. Placing all your array element assignment statements together makes your code easier to read and makes it clear exactly where to look to find what value was assigned to an array element initially.

The other way to assign values to array elements is to use some sort of looping structure to loop through the array, assigning values to array elements as you go. For example, if you have an array (MultOfFive) that will contain multiples of 5 from 5 to 100, you can write code like this to initialize the array:

```
Temp = 5
For X = 0 To 99
   MultOfFive(X) = Temp
   Temp = Temp + 5
Next X
```

14

WORKING WITH ARRAYS

Another example of initializing an array is to fill an array with the contents of a listbox. The code to initialize the array involves looping through the items of the listbox and assigning an item to an element of the array until there are no more items in the listbox. Here is an example:

```
Dim X as Integer
For X = 0 To lstAList.ListCount
   ListItems(X) = lstAList.List(X)
Next X
```

Extracting Data from an Array

Loops play an important role in array processing. You have seen how to use loops to put data into arrays; loops are also important for extracting data from arrays. For example, here is a code fragment that takes items out of an array (Item) and puts them into a listbox:

```
For X = 0 To 20
   lstAList.additem Item(X)
Next X
```

Multidimensional Arrays

Up to this point, I have discussed arrays that have only one dimension. Not every problem, however, fits into just one dimension. Take the classic example of a course gradebook. One dimension of a course gradebook is the list of students taking the course. The other dimension of the gradebook is the grade the student receives for the course. To store a course grade for each student in the course, you cannot use a single-dimensional array; you have to use a multidimensional array.

A multidimensional array is declared in this way:

```
Dim Algebra(19,19) As String
```

This statement creates an array with 20 rows and 20 columns, or enough storage space to hold the names of 20 students and 20 course grades.

As with single-dimensional arrays, you can explicitly declare the lower bound of multidimensional arrays:

```
Dim Algebra(1 To 20, 1 To 20) As String
```

You are not limited to only two dimensions. You can expand an algebra array of three dimensions by declaring the array as follows:

```
Dim Algebra(19,19,19)
```

The total number of elements that can be stored in this array is 20 times 20 times 20, or 800 elements.

Initializing Multidimensional Arrays

Multidimensional arrays are initialized in much the same way as single-dimensional arrays. However, two loops are usually used because there are two dimensions to initialize. Here is a code fragment to initialize a two-dimensional array that stores the multiples of 2 through 200:

```
Temp = 1
Dim MultOfTwo(1 to 10, 1 to 10) as Integer
For X = 1 to 10
   For Y = 1 to 10
      Temp = Temp * 2
      MultOfTwo(X,Y) = Temp
   Next Y
Next X
```

Notice how the two loops are used. This is called a nested For loop. For each value of X, the program loops through Y 10 times. The end result is a table of values like the array shown in Figure 14.2.

2	4	6	8	10	12	14	16	18	20
22	24	26	28	30	32	34	36	38	40
42	44	46	48	50	52	54	56	58	60
62	64	66	68	70	72	74	76	78	80
82	84	86	88	90	92	94	96	98	100
102	104	106	108	110	112	114	116	118	120
122	124	126	128	130	132	134	136	138	140
142	144	146	148	150	152	154	156	158	160
162	164	166	168	170	172	174	176	178	180
182	184	186	188	190	192	194	196	198	200

FIGURE 14.2.
A multidimensional array of the multiples of 2 to 200.

14

WORKING WITH ARRAYS

Arrays Made Up of Other Arrays

Arrays can hold any data type as long as it is the same data type throughout the array. This requirement is loosened a little when the elements of an array are other arrays. A simple example will make this concept clear.

First, create an array of integers and assign values to some of the elements of the array:

```
Dim SomeInts(20) As Integer
SomeInts(0) = 25
SomeInts(1) = 30
SomeInts(2) = 20
SomeInts(3) = 15
```

Now declare a string array and put some values into it:

```
Dim Items(20) As String
Items(0) = "Chair"
Items(1) = "Couch"
Items(2) = "Bookshelf"
Items(3) = "Bed"
```

Finally, you need to declare a Variant array that will consist of these other two arrays:

```
Dim CombineArrays(2) As Variant
CombineArrays(0) = SomeInts()
CombineArrays(1) = Items()
```

To display an element from each array, you can write

```
MsgBox  CombineArrays (0) (1) 'Displays "30"
MsgBox CombineArrays(1) (2) 'Displays "Bookshelf"
```

This method works because the CombineArrays array is a Variant and can consist of elements of any data type, even other arrays. With a little imagination, you can see how working with arrays of different data types can solve problems that couldn't be solved if you weren't allowed to mix array types within another array.

Dynamic Arrays

Sometimes when working with arrays, you either won't know the maximum size of an array or you won't want to declare an upper bound and perhaps arbitrarily limit the size of an array. In cases such as these, a fixed-size array does not work because once an upper bound is declared in a fixed-size array, that size cannot be changed. Visual Basic provides a useful data structure to deal with this situation: the dynamic array.

Declaring Dynamic Arrays

A dynamic array is an array that can be resized any time after it is declared. To declare a dynamic array, you can use a Public statement or a Dim statement at the module level or use a Private, Dim, or Static statement if you want the array to be local to a procedure. The syntax for declaring a dynamic array is

```
Dim Items() As String
```

Dim can be replaced with any of the other scope-setting keywords I mentioned. Notice that there is an empty dimension list after the array name. This tells Visual Basic that the array is dynamic and will be dimensioned later.

To allocate storage space to the array, use the ReDim statement. You can only use this statement in a procedure because, unlike the Dim and Static statements, the ReDim statement is executable, meaning that ReDim makes the application execute the action of resizing the array at runtime.

To give the array an initial set of elements for storage, you can write

```
ReDim Items(20)
```

You do not have to mention the data type because you have already declared it.

Lower and Upper Bounds of Dynamic Arrays

The syntax that fixed-size arrays follow concerning their lower and upper bounds also applies to dynamic arrays. Every time you redimension an array, you can change the number of elements and the upper and lower bounds of each dimension:

```
Dim Items() As String
    .
    .
    .
ReDim Items(20)
    .
    .
    .
ReDim Items(10)
```

or

```
Dim Items() As String
    .
    .
    .
ReDim Items(5,5)
    .
    .
    .
ReDim Items(10,10)
```

However, the following code is illegal:

```
ReDim Items(5,5,5)
```

Only the number of elements and the lower and upper bounds of each dimension can be changed. The total number of dimensions of a dynamic array cannot be changed.

Preserving the Contents of Dynamic Arrays When Resizing

The ReDim statement, when executed, erases all the current values in a dynamic array. The values are set to the default initialization for the array's data type. For many applications, such as when you want to prepare the array to accept new data or you want to conserve memory, erasing the contents of an array is exactly what you want to do. For other applications, however, the last thing you want to do is lose the values that are already in the array. You can save the

14

WORKING WITH ARRAYS

current values of an array before you resize it by using the `Preserve` keyword with the `ReDim` statement.

Here is a code fragment that puts three items into a dynamic string array:

```
ReDim Items(2)
Items(0) = "Chair"
Items(1) = "Couch"
Items(2) = "Bed"
```

You can increase the size of the array by writing the following statement:

```
ReDim Preserve Items(Ubound(Items) + 10)
```

This statement takes the upper bound `Items`, adds 10 to it, and resets the upper bound to that number, which is 13. Also, the elements in `Items(0)`, `Items(1)`, and `Items(2)` will remain unchanged. Had you not used the `Preserve` keyword, each element would have been set to either `Empty` or the empty string, depending on whether the array was declared as a fixed-length string type or a variable-length string type.

Redimensioning Multidimensional Arrays

The contents of multidimensional arrays can also be retained using the `Preserve` keyword. However, when resizing a multidimensional array, you can change only the upper bound of the last dimension. If you try to change any of the other dimensions, or if you try to change the lower bound of the last dimension, you get a runtime error.

Look at a sample code fragment to see why this is so:

```
Dim Algebra() As String
ReDim Algebra(5,1)
Algebra(0,0) = "Johnny Smith"
Algebra(0,1) = "B"
Algebra(1,0) = "Betty Doe"
Algebra(1,1) = "A"
ReDim Preserve Algebra(2 To 7,2) ' This generates a runtime error
```

The last statement generates a runtime error because by trying to set the lower bound of the first dimension to 2, Visual Basic wants to erase the array elements with a first dimension of 0 or 1. (See Figures 14.3 and 14.4.) Because you used the `Preserve` keyword to save the contents of the array, Visual Basic detects a conflict and issues a runtime error.

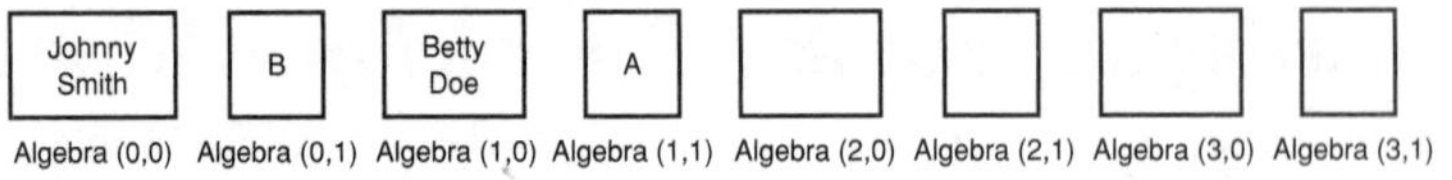

FIGURE 14.3.

The Algebra *array before redimensioning using the* Preserve *keyword.*

Johnny Smith	B	Betty Doe	A					
Algebra (0,0)	Algebra (0,1)	Algebra (1,0)	Algebra (1,1)	Algebra (2,0)	Algebra (2,1)	Algebra (3,0)	Algebra (3,1)	...

FIGURE 14.4.

The error message generated from an attempt to redimension an array using Preserve *outside the bounds of stored data in the array.*

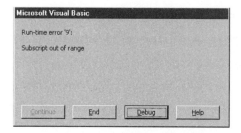

Passing Arrays as Arguments to Functions and Subprocedures

Arrays can serve one more purpose as a data structure. When you need the values of the elements of an array in a function or subprocedure, you can pass the whole array as an argument. You can then have access to the elements of the array in the normal way.

You pass an array to a function or subprocedure in the same way you pass any other argument, except that arrays always must be passed by reference as opposed to by value.

> **NOTE**
>
> By reference (ByRef) indicates that the memory address and not the actual value of the argument is passed. When an address is passed, the argument's value can be changed by the function or subprocedure. If an argument is passed by value (ByVal), then a copy of the argument's value is passed and the actual value cannot be changed. By default, arguments are passed by reference in Visual Basic.

Look at an example of passing an array to a function. First, set up the array:

```
Dim Ints(10) As Integer
For X = 0 to Ubound(Ints) - 1
   Ints(X) = X
Next X
```

Here's the code for the function:

```
Private Function GetElement(ByRef intArray() as Integer, Y as _
   Integer)
   GetElement = intArray(Y)
End Function
Private Sub Command1_Click()
   Dim Message, Title, Default, SomeElement, TheNumber
   Message = "Enter an element number: "
   Title = "Passing an Array to a Function as an Argument"
   Default = "1"
```

14

WORKING WITH ARRAYS

```
    SomeElement = InputBox(Message, Title, Default)
    TheNumber = GetElement(Ints(), Val(SomeElement))
    MsgBox "The value of element " & SomeElement & " is " & _
        TheNumber
End Sub
```

This sample code passes the array and an element number to the function GetElement. The value of GetElement is simply the element located in the position of the number passed to the function.

Versions of Visual Basic before version 4 could not pass arrays as arguments to functions and subprocedures. Being able to pass arrays as arguments to functions and subprocedures is another example of how newer versions of Visual Basic have increased the expressive power of the language.

Transposing a Matrix

As mentioned in the introduction of this chapter, one use of arrays is for storing data in a matrix. A matrix is a row-and-column representation of a set of data. In economics, for example, you can use a matrix to store data on different industries in an economic system.

If you are studying the input and output of different industries in an economy, you can create a matrix known as an input/output matrix. For three industries, you can create a matrix to study the raw materials needs and output of these industries to see which is the most efficient and which is the least efficient or to measure the total output of the system.

For example, if there are three industries in an economic system, industry A, industry B, and industry C, you can measure how much of each other's product they need in order to produce their own products. If industry A needs $.5 of its own product, $.25 of industry B's product, and $.10 of industry C's product, you can arrange this into the first column of a matrix like this:

```
.5     .25    .1
```

If you record the needs of the other two industries, you will come up with this input/output matrix:

```
.50    .42    .23
.25    .00    .47
.10    .63    .05
```

Figure 14.5 displays the matrix with proper labels to identify the parts that make up the input/output matrix, labeled M.

A common operation on a matrix is to transpose the matrix, making the rows be the columns and the columns be the rows. To do this, you must set up the matrix as an array and then perform a series of loops that exchange the rows and columns. Listing 14.1 contains the program.

FIGURE 14.5.
The input/output matrix of an economic system.

User

		A	B	C	
M =	A	.50	.42	.23	Supplier
	B	.25	.00	.47	
	C	.10	.63	.05	

Listing 14.1. Transposing a matrix.

```
Dim M(2, 2) As Double
   M(0, 0) = 0.5
   M(0, 1) = 0.42
   M(0, 2) = 0.23
   M(1, 0) = 0.25
   M(1, 1) = 0#
   M(1, 2) = 0.47
   M(2, 0) = 0.1
   M(2, 1) = 0.63
   M(2, 2) = 0.05
   Dim M1(2, 2) As Double
   For x = 0 To 2
      For y = 0 To 2
         M1(y, x) = M(x, y)
      Next y
   Next x
   For x = 0 To 2
      For y = 0 To 2
        Debug.Print M1(x, y)
      Next y
    Next x
```

In this example, you create a new array, `M1`, to store the results of the transpose. This is easier than copying back into the same array, which is possible but makes the source code look messier.

The results of the transpose are shown in Figure 14.6.

FIGURE 14.6.
The matrix `M` after being transposed.

	.50	.25	.23
M =	.42	.00	.63
	.23	.47	.05

Summary

The array is a powerful data structure, fundamental to the capability to solve problems in Visual Basic. Some of the more powerful features of arrays I examined include

- Using loops to initialize arrays
- Conserving array contents in dynamic arrays with the Preserve keyword
- Passing arrays as arguments to functions and subprocedures

Controlling Program Flow

by Mike McMillan

IN THIS CHAPTER

CHAPTER 15

Programs in Visual Basic are never conceived to be executed in a purely linear manner, where statements are executed one after the other in sequence. Usually, as you write a program to solve a problem, you make decisions based on the data the program receives, and, depending on the data, a certain set of statements is executed. This mode of program execution relies on the capability of Visual Basic to make decisions and control the flow of the program as new data is received. This chapter reviews several sets of statements available for making decisions and controlling program flow.

Programming constructs that control program flow depend on a set of operators that determine what course a control flow statement takes. For example, one of the basic control flow constructs in Visual Basic is the `If...Then` construct. `If...Then` works by making a comparison:

```
If (A > B) Then ...
```

The greater-than sign is one of the comparison operators that are a necessary part of making decisions and controlling program flow in Visual Basic. This chapter explains two sets of operators: comparison operators (such as `<` and `>`) and logical operators (such as `And`, `Or`, and `Not`).

Making Comparisons and Combining Comparisons

Control flow constructs in Visual Basic (and in all computer languages, for that matter) operate by making comparisons between items of data. The comparison is the basis for how the program changes its flow of execution. Comparisons are made using a set of operators called *comparison operators*. Sometimes, for more complex decisions, two or more comparisons must be made at the same time. To do this, comparison operators must be joined using another set of operators called *logical operators*. Together, these operators actually make the decisions that the control flow constructs use to determine which set of program statements is executed.

Comparison Operators

Comparison operators are used to determine the relationship between two objects. You can use comparison operators in three ways, which can be explained by showing the possible syntactical forms of comparison expressions:

```
result = expression1 comparisonoperator expression2

result = object1 Is object2

result = string Like pattern
```

Every comparison expression returns a result, either `True` or `False`. The value of the comparison expression is placed in the *result* variable. Later in this chapter, you will see that with control flow constructs, the value of the comparison expression, instead of being assigned to the *result* variable, is used to determine how the control flow construct executes.

In the first comparison expression, two expressions are compared using a comparison operator. In the second expression, one object is compared to another object to see if the first object Is the same type of object as the second object. The third expression compares a string to a particular pattern of characters to see if the string matches the pattern in some way. (This type of comparison will become clearer when you see an example.)

The comparison operators, when comparing two expressions, can have one of three values, True, False, or Null, depending on the result of the comparison. Table 15.1 shows the list of comparison operators and the conditions that determine their resulting values.

Table 15.1. The comparison operators and their conditions.

Operator	True when	False when	Null when
< (Less than)	expression1 < expression2	expression1 >= expression2	expression1 or expression2 = Null
<= (Less than or equal to)	expression1 <= expression2	expression1 > expression2	expression1 or expression2 = Null
> (Greater than)	expression1 > expression2	expression1 <= expression2	expression1 or expression2 = Null
>= (Greater than or equal to)	expression1 >= expression2	expression1 < expression2	expression1 or expression2 = Null
= (Equal to)	expression1 = expression2	expression1 <> expression2	expression1 or expression2 = Null
<> (Not equal to)	expression1 <> expression2	expression1 = expression2	expression1 or expression2 = Null

The Is and Like operators follow different rules than do the other comparison operators. In comparing two objects, Is evaluates to True if *object1* and *object2* are the same object. The following code fragment demonstrates the Is operator:

```
Dim a As Object
Dim b As Object
Dim c As Object
Dim d As Boolean 'Boolean data types hold either True or False
Set a = Controls!Text1
Set b = a
Set c = Controls!Text2
d = b Is a
```

```
debug.print d 'True will be printed
d = c Is b
debug.print d 'False will be printed
```

The Like operator is more complicated because it is used to test whether *expression1* is matched by a pattern defined in *expression2*. Pattern matching can get very complicated, but if you start out by learning the basic rules, you can quickly learn how to match complex patterns without too much trouble.

The best way to learn pattern matching is to first learn the basic pattern-matching characters. The following shows the characters used in pattern matching and the patterns they match:

?	Matches any single character
*	Matches zero or more characters
#	Matches any single digit
[*charlist*]	Matches any single character in *charlist*
[!*charlist*]	Matches any single character not in *charlist*

The following code shows some examples of how the pattern-matching characters work. By studying these simple examples, you will find it easier to design more complex pattern-matching expressions:

```
MyResult = "Visual Basic" Like "V*" 'Returns True
MyResult = "Visual Basic" Like "V???????????" 'Returns True
MyResult = "VISUAL" Like "v*" 'Returns False
MyResult = "Visual Basic 5" Like "*#" 'Returns True
MyResult = "V" Like "!?" 'Returns False
MyResult = "1" Like "#" 'Returns True
MyResult = "Vi" Like "V[a-z]" 'Returns True
MyResult = "VB" Like "V[a-z]" 'Returns False
```

The sort order for strings relies on the internal binary representations of the characters in Microsoft Windows. The default sort order is A < B < E < Z < a < b < e < z < 0. This is also the default sort order for Visual Basic and is reflected in the Option Compare Binary statement, which tells Visual Basic to do binary sorting. You will use this statement only if you have previously changed the sort order with the Option Compare Text statement.

You can change the sort order by issuing the following statement in a code module: Option Compare Text. This changes the sort order to a case-insensitive order represented by the following sort order (A=a) < (B=b) < (E=e) < (Z=z) < 0.

Logical Operators

For more complex decisions, you can combine comparison operators, as in

```
(A > B) And (B > C)
```

or other such expressions. The connecting operator that compares the comparison expressions is called a logical operator. The two logical operators used most often are Or and And. You use Or to perform a logical disjunction on two expressions; in other words, Or returns True if either one of two expressions is true and returns False if both expressions are false. A simple code fragment illustrates how Or works:

```
Dim A As Integer
Dim B As Integer
Dim MyResult As Boolean
A = 12
B = 10
MyResult = (A > B) Or (B > A)
Debug.Print MyResult
```

This code fragment displays True in the Debug window because the first expression in the comparison (A > B) is true. Here is another code fragment to illustrate how the Or operator works:

```
Dim A As Integer
Dim B As Integer
Dim MyResult As Boolean
A = 10
B = 10
MyResult = (A > B) Or (B > A)
Debug.Print MyResult
```

This code fragment displays False in the Debug window because neither the first expression (A > B) nor the second expression (B > A) is true.

The second logical operator, And, performs a logical conjunction on the two expressions; in other words, And returns True if both expressions are true and returns False if either expression is false. Here is an example:

```
Dim A As Integer
Dim B As Integer
Dim C As Integer
Dim MyResult As Boolean
A = 10
B = 14
C = 9
MyResult = (A < B) And (B > C)
Debug.Print MyResult
```

This code fragment displays True in the Debug window because both the first expression (A < B) and the second expression (B > C) are true. Here is another example:

```
Dim A As Integer
Dim B As Integer
Dim C As Integer
Dim MyResult As Boolean
A = 10
B = 14
C = 9
MyResult = (A > B) And (B > C)
Debug.Print MyResult
```

This code fragment displays False in the Debug window because the first expression (A > B) is false, even though the second expression is true.

For both Or and And, if either expression is Null, the result of the comparison is Null.

Another logical operator is XOR, which is not used as often as Or or And but can be used for certain types of comparisons. You use the XOR operator for logical exclusion, meaning that XOR returns False if both of the expressions are true and returns True if one of the expressions is true and the other one is false. The following code fragment illustrates the use of XOR:

```
Dim A As Integer
Dim B As Integer
Dim C As Integer
Dim MyResult As Boolean
A = 10
B = 14
C = 9
MyResult = (A < B) XOR (C > B)
Debug.Print MyResult
```

This code fragment displays True in the Debug window because only one of the expressions (A < B) is true. Here is another example of XOR:

```
Dim A As Integer
Dim B As Integer
Dim C As Integer
Dim MyResult As Boolean
A = 10
B = 14
C = 9
MyResult = (A < B) XOR (C < B)
Debug.Print MyResult
```

This code fragment displays False in the Debug window because, in this case, both expressions are true and XOR is checking for exclusion, not inclusion.

Figure 15.1 shows the XOR evaluation rules.

FIGURE 15.1.

XOR *evaluation rules.*

Expression 1 evaluates to	Expression 2 evaluates to	The result is
True	True	False
True	False	True
False	True	True
False	False	False

An operator similar to XOR is Eqv, which is the logical equivalence operator. Whereas XOR returns True if either but not both of the expressions is true, Eqv returns True if both of the expressions are true or both false, and returns False if one expression is true and the other expression if false. A sample code fragment illustrates how to use Eqv:

```
Dim A As Integer
Dim B As Integer
Dim C As Integer
Dim MyResult As Boolean
A = 10
B = 14
C = 9
```

```
MyResult = (A < B) Eqv (B < C)
Debug.Print MyResult
```

This code fragment displays True in the Debug window because both expressions are true. Here is another example:

```
Dim A As Integer
Dim B As Integer
Dim C As Integer
Dim MyResult As Boolean
A = 10
B = 14
C = 9
MyResult = (A < B) Eqv (B < C)
Debug.Print MyResult
```

This code fragment displays False in the Debug window because the second expression is false.

If either of the expressions in a XOR or Eqv comparison is Null, the result of the comparison is Null also.

Figure 15.2 outlines the Eqv evaluation rules.

FIGURE 15.2.

Eqv *evaluation rules.*

Expression 1 evaluates to	Expression 2 evaluates to	The result is
True	True	True
True	False	False
False	True	False
False	False	True

Bitwise Operators

Visual Basic has the capability to work with the individual bits that make up the values that are stored in memory. You can use Or, And, XOR, and Eqv to manipulate the bits of the contents of an expression.

Before you can understand the rules of the bitwise operators, you need to understand how Visual Basic stores values in memory. Most people know that computers store information in terms of 0s and 1s—the two digits that make up the binary system. Eight binary digits (bits) make up a byte, which is the unit of storage in which most characters, numbers, strings, and so on are described. For example, an integer value takes 2 bytes (16 bits) of storage space. In the computer, for example, the integer 2 is represented by the following binary number: 0000000000000010. The integer 4 is written in binary as 0000000000000100.

Now you are ready to see how you can use the bitwise operators to manipulate bits. First, look at the bitwise OR. The rules for the bitwise OR look a lot like the rules for the logical Or, but you are working with bits instead of expressions. (See Figure 15.3.)

15

CONTROLLING PROGRAM FLOW

FIGURE 15.3.

Bitwise OR evaluation rules.

Bit in expression 1 is	Bit in expression 2 is	Result is
0	0	0
0	1	1
1	0	1
1	1	1

Now look at a code fragment that uses the bitwise OR:

```
Dim A As Integer
Dim B As Integer
Dim MyResult
A = 5
B = 3
MyResult = A Or B
Debug.Print MyResult
```

This code fragment displays 7 in the Debug window. Figure 15.4 shows the values of A and B in binary form and the result of the bitwise OR.

FIGURE 15.4.

Bitwise OR performed on binary 5 and binary 3.

```
5  = 0101
3  = 0011
─────────
or = 0111
```

Now that you understand how to make comparisons between different data values, you are ready to learn how to use these comparisons with the different program flow constructs Visual Basic provides to change the execution flow of your programs.

Making Decisions

All computer programs, whether written in Visual Basic or some other language, must be able to make decisions about how to deal with data that is processed during the execution of a program. Making decisions becomes a matter of choosing a course to take by evaluating the data. Visual Basic provides a set of decision structures and functions that can test data and perform different operations based on the outcome of the test. These decision structures and functions are

```
If...Then

If...Then...Else

Select Case

Switch

Choose
```

If...Then

You use the If...Then structure to execute one or more statements based on a condition or set of conditions. You can write an If...Then as a statement on one line, or you can write it as a structure using block syntax, where you put each statement to be executed on a separate line. The syntax for an If...Then statement is

```
If condition Then statement
```

The syntax for the If...Then structure is

```
If condition Then
    statement-1
    statement-2
    statement-n
End If
```

> **NOTE**
>
> It is a standard programming practice to indent the statements within a control flow structure. There are many different ways to indent statements, but the most popular way is to tab over once so that each statement is one tab space to the right of the control structure. Keep in mind, however, that Visual Basic doesn't require you to indent your code, and this is done just to make your code easier to read.

Of course, you can execute just one statement in the If...Then structure; in fact, using only one statement in the execution block is the preferred style for structure programming.

The *condition* part of the If...Then structure is usually a comparison of two or more expressions, although it can actually be any expression that evaluates to a numeric value. The *condition* evaluated by Visual Basic must be either True or False. An expression that evaluates to zero is considered False, whereas any non-zero expression is considered True.

In an If...Then statement, if the *condition* evaluates to True, the statement following Then is executed. If the *condition* evaluates to False, nothing happens and the program control reverts to the next statement after the If...Then.

In an If...Then structure, if the *condition* evaluates to True, the statements below the If...Then line are executed. If the *condition* evaluates to False, the program control reverts to the statement immediately following the End If.

Here is an example of an If...Then statement:

```
If AccountBalance < 0 Then Overdrawn = True
```

Here is the equivalent statement written in an If...Then structure:

```
If AccountBalance < 0 Then
    OverDrawn = True
End If
```

If you want to execute more than one statement when *condition* evaluates to True, you must use the If...Then structure:

```
If AccountBalance < 0 Then
    OverDrawn = True
 txtMessage = "Insufficient Funds"
End If
```

If...Then...Else

For more complex decision making, you use the `If...Then...Else` decision structure. This structure allows you to execute one of many different blocks of statements. The syntax of the `If...Then...Else` structure looks like this:

```
If condition1 Then
    [statement block 1]
[ElseIf condition2 Then
    [statement block 2]]
[Else
    [statement block 3]]
End If
```

The flow of the `If...Then...Else` structure proceeds as follows: Visual Basic tests *condition1*. If it is false, the program tests *condition2*. This process repeats until a true condition is found. When a true condition is found, Visual Basic executes the block of statements under the true condition, and program control reverts to the statement following the `End If`. If no condition evaluates to `True`, Visual Basic simply transfers program control to the statement after the `End If`. However, you can include an optional `Else` statement at the end of the structure so that Visual Basic executes the corresponding statement block if all the preceding conditions are false.

It is important to notice that you can have one, many, or no `ElseIf` clauses in an `If...Then...Else`. The following examples will make using `If...Then...Else` easier to understand:

```
If AccountBalance < 0 Then
    OverDrawn = True
ElseIf AccountBalance <= 1000 Then
    OverDrawn = False
    ServiceCharge = True
ElseIf AccountBalance > 1000 Then
    OverDrawn = False
    ServiceCharge = False
Else
    AccountStatus = "Unknown"
End If

If AccountBalance > 1000 Then
    ServiceCharge = False
Else
    ServiceCharge = True
End If
```

You can include as many `ElseIf` clauses in an `If...Then...Else` as you want, but be aware that using more than a few `ElseIf` clauses makes your code harder to read. A more readable way to check a lot of conditions is to use the `Select Case` structure, which is discussed later in this chapter.

Nested If...Thens

You can nest If...Then structures for more complex decision making. When you have more than two or three If...Then structures nested together, however, you can usually rewrite that section of code using If...Then...Else or Select Case. The following code fragment shows an example of a nested If...Then:

```
If AccountBalance > 0 Then
    If AmountToWithdraw > AccountBalance Then
        txtMessage = "Select a lesser amount to withdraw"
    End If
    OverDrawn = False
End If
```

Select Case

An alternative to the If...Then...Else structure for selecting one of many conditions is the Select Case structure. Select Case provides the same functionality as If...Then...Else, but it makes your code more readable when there are several choices.

First, take a look at the syntax of the Select Case structure:

```
Select Case testexpression
    [Case expressionlist1
        [statement block 1]]
    [Case expressionlist2
        [statement block 2]]
    .
    .
    .
    [Case Else
        [statement block n]]
End Select
```

Select Case works by first evaluating *testexpression*. The result of this evaluation is then tested against each Case clause in the structure. If a match is found, each of the statements in the statement block of the Case is executed. You can also add the Case Else clause to execute a block of statements if none of the other Case clauses is successfully matched. After a statement block is executed, program control reverts to the statement after End Select.

The *expressionlist* can be one or more values with multiple values separated by commas. Each statement block has zero or more statements. If more than one Case clause matches the *testexpression*, the program executes the statement block of the first Case that matches, and then control reverts to the statement after End Select.

The following Select Case structure implements a very basic ATM transaction system:

```
Private Sub mnuATM_Click(Index As Integer)
    Select Case Index
        Case 0      ' Withdrawal
            Call Withdrawal
        Case 1      ' Deposit
            Call DispenseEnvelope
```

```
      Case 2      ' Account Balance
         Call DisplayAccountBalance
      Case 3      ' Transfer
         Call TransferChoice
      Case Else
         Call InvalidChoice
   End Select
End Sub
```

Although you can use a `Select Case` structure in place of an `If...Then...Else` structure, `Select Case` acts differently than does `If...Then...Else`. `Select Case` evaluates one expression only at the top of the structure, whereas an `If...Then...Else` structure can evaluate many different expressions in each `ElseIf` clause.

Switch

The preceding decision-making examples you have seen are structures. `Switch` is a function that returns a value or expression based on evaluating a test expression.

The syntax of the `Switch` function is

```
Switch(expr-1, value-1[,expr-2, value-2, ...[,expr-n,value-n]])
```

The two parts to the `Switch` function are the expression and the value. The expression part is a `Variant` expression that evaluates to either `True` or `False`. If the expression evaluates to `True`, the value associated with the expression is returned as the value of the function. If the first expression evaluates to `False` and there are more expressions to test, each expression is evaluated in turn, and the value associated with the first expression that evaluates to `True` is returned. If no expression evaluates to `True`, `Switch` returns a `Null` value.

NOTE

Be careful of undesirable side effects in a `Switch` function. If an expression evaluation leads to a runtime error, even if it is evaluated after an expression evaluates to `True`, the error condition is still flagged.

Here is an example of the `Switch` function:

```
Function SetATMMessage(AccountBalance as Long, AmtToWithdraw as _
   Long)
   SetATMMessage = Switch(AccountBalance < 0, "Insufficient _
   Funds", AccountBalance > 0 And AmtToWithdraw > _
   AccountBalance, "Insufficient Funds", AccountBalance > _
   AmtToWithdraw, "Please take your money")
End Function
```

Choose

A variation of the Switch function is the Choose function. Whereas Switch can test on many expressions, Choose returns a value based on the value of an index that is passed to it. Here is the syntax for the Choose function:

```
Choose(index, choice-1[,choice-2,...[,choice-n]])
```

Choose returns a choice from the list of *choice-1*, *choice-2*,... *choice-n* based on the value of *index*. If the *index* is 1, *choice-1* is returned; if the *index* is 2, the value returned is *choice-2*; and so on.

The index should be a whole number; if the index is not a whole number, it is rounded to the nearest whole number before it is evaluated.

Here is an example of the Choose function:

```
Function MyChoice(Ind as Integer)
    MyChoice = Choose(Ind, "Choice 1", "Choice 2", "Choice 3")
End Function
```

If Ind is 2, then MyChoice is equal to the string "Choice 2".

If the value of Ind is less than 1 or greater than the number of choices, Choose returns Null.

Program Flow Constructs

As I mentioned at the beginning of this chapter, computer programs rarely proceed in a sequential order. You need to be able to make your programs execute certain lines of code more than once in response to some condition. Other times, you need to be able to move from one place in the program to somewhere else to perform a set of instructions. Visual Basic provides two programming constructs to allow control over how your programs flow:

- Looping structures
- Branching structures

Looping Structures

Looping structures give you the capability to execute one or more lines of code repetitively. If you don't know how many times you want to execute a set of statements, the Do...Loop structure is usually the best to use. If you want to process a set of statements a specific number of times, the For...Next structure is what you want. When you want to perform a set of operations on a set of data that is grouped together as an array or object, Visual Basic offers the For Each...Next structure.

Do...Loop

To execute a block of statements an indefinite number of times, use a Do...Loop. The Do...Loop structure evaluates a numeric condition in deciding whether to continue executing. The condition must be able to evaluate to True (nonzero) or False (zero).

The four variations of the Do...Loop structure can be divided into two groups:

- Do...Loops that execute as long as the condition is True
- Do...Loops that execute as long as the condition is False

Do While...Loop

Do While...Loop and its variation, Do...Loop While, execute when the condition evaluates to True. Here is the syntax of the Do While...Loop structure:

```
Do While condition
    statements
Loop
```

When a Visual Basic program encounters a Do While *condition* statement, it first evaluates *condition*. If *condition* is True, the statements immediately following the *condition* are executed. After the last statement is executed, the Loop statement is encountered. Visual Basic then returns to the Do While *condition* line and reevaluates *condition*. As long as *condition* is True, the statements are executed. However, if and when *condition* evaluates to False, the program jumps to the line immediately following the Loop statement and continues executing the rest of the program.

The following procedure allows someone to make withdrawals from an ATM as long as he has enough money in his account:

```
Private Sub Withdrawal(ByRef AccountBalance As Long)
    Dim WDAmount As Long
    Do While AccountBalance > 0
        WDAmount = InputBox "Enter an amount to withdraw: "
        If WDAmount > AccountBalance Then
            AccountBalance = AccountBalance - WDAmount
        Else
            MsgBox "Insufficient funds for this transaction. Enter _
                a smaller amount."
        End If
    Loop
    MsgBox "Insufficient Funds"
End Sub
```

If the AccountBalance is zero or less, the program prints an "Insufficient Funds" message and the Do loop does not execute; otherwise, the Do loop executes until AccountBalance is equal to or less than zero.

A variation of the Do While...Loop structure is Do...Loop While. The Do loop guarantees that the block of statements inside the loop executes at least once. The following code fragment shows the preceding example rewritten with a Do...Loop While structure:

```
Private Sub Withdrawal(ByRef AccountBalance as Long)
    Dim WDAmount As Long
    Do
        WDAmount = InputBox "Enter an amount to withdraw"
        If WDAmount > AccountBalance Then
            AccountBalance = AccountBalance - WDAmount
        Else
            MsgBox "Insufficient funds for this transaction. Enter _
                a smaller amount."
        End If
    Loop While AccountBalance > 0
    MsgBox "Insufficient Funds"
End Sub
```

Do Until...Loop

The second group of Do loops executes the block of statements within the loop as long as the condition is False. As with the Do While...Loop structure, the two variations are Do Until...Loop and Do...Loop Until. Look at the ATM withdrawal example using a Do Until...Loop structure:

```
Private Sub Withdrawal(ByRef AccountBalance as Long)
    Dim WDAmount as Long
    Do Until AccountBalance <= 0
        WDAmount = InputBox "Enter an amount to withdraw"
        If WDAmount > AccountBalance Then
            AccountBalance = AccountBalance - WDAmount
        Else
            MsgBox "Insufficient funds for this transaction. Enter _
                a smaller amount."
        End If
    Loop
    MsgBox "Insufficient Funds"
End Sub
```

In this example, the Withdrawal procedure is executed as long as AccountBalance doesn't fall to zero or less. If AccountBalance does become zero or less, the loop ends and the program displays the message "Insufficient Funds".

Here is the same example again using the Do...Loop Until variation:

```
Private Sub Withdrawal(ByRef AccountBalance as Long)
    Dim WDAmount as Long
    Do
        WDAmount = InputBox "Enter an amount to withdraw"
        If WDAmount > AccountBalance Then
            AccountBalance = AccountBalance - WDAmount
        Else
            MsgBox "Insufficient funds for this transaction. Enter _
                a smaller amount."
        End If
    Loop Until AccountBalance <= 0
    MsgBox "Insufficient Funds"
End Sub
```

Using this structure guarantees that the code within the loop will execute at least one time. If you don't want that to happen, be sure to put the test condition at the top of the loop by using a Do Until...Loop structure.

While...Wend Loops

An alternative to the `Do` loop is the `While...Wend` looping structure. The syntax for the `While...Wend` structure is

```
While condition
    statements
Wend
```

Quite simply, in a `While...Wend` loop, a statement or block of statements is executed while *condition* is `True`, and when *condition* becomes `False`, program control reverts to the line after the `Wend` statement.

The following `While...Wend` loop increments a variable until the variable reaches a certain number:

```
Dim myValue As Integer
myValue = 0
While myValue < 100
    myValue = myValue + 1
Wend
```

For...Next Loops

When you don't know how many times you need to execute a block of statements, the `Do` loop structures are the best to use. When you do know how many times a block of statements should execute, however, the `For...Next` structure is a better choice. Using a counter, a `For...Next` structure executes a block of statements a number of times.

Look at the syntax of the `For...Next` structure to get a better idea of how it works:

```
For counter = start To end [Step increment]
    statements
Next
```

The `For...Next` loop takes three arguments, *counter*, *start*, and *end*, and one optional argument, *increment*. Each of these arguments must be numeric, either a number or a variable with a numeric value.

Here is a simple `For...Next` loop that prints the contents of an array:

```
Private Sub Command1_Click()
    Dim X as Integer
    For X = 0 To Ubound(myArray)
        Debug.Print myArray(X)
    Next X
End Sub
```

To execute the preceding `For...Next` loop, Visual Basic performs the following steps:

1. Set X (*counter*) equal to 0 (*start*).

2. Test to see whether X is greater than the upper bound of `myArray` (*end*).

3. If X isn't greater than *end*, execute the `Debug.Print` command. If X is greater than *end*, revert execution to the line after `Next X`.

4. Increment X by 1 because the default for *step* is 1.

5. Repeat steps 2 through 4 until X is greater than *end*.

You can change the increment amount of the loop by including the *increment* argument. Using the preceding example, if you wanted to print every other element of the array, you could write the new For...Next loop fragment in this way:

```
For X = 0 to Ubound(myArray) Step 2
   Debug.Print myArray(X)
Next x
```

Another variation on the preceding example is to move backward through the array, printing the last items first. Here is the code fragment to do this:

```
For X = Ubound(myArray) To 0 Step -1
   Debug.Print myArray(X)
Next X
```

In this example, the counter moves in a negative direction, starting at the upper bound of the array and moving to the first element index of the array, 0.

For Each...Next Loops

For many applications, you need to be able to loop through all the elements of a group of data, such as an array or an object. Calculating the upper bound of the array or the total number of members in an object unnecessarily adds an extra operation to the program. Visual Basic provides a special For...Next structure to simplify this kind of looping: the For Each...Next structure.

The syntax for the For Each...Next structure looks like this:

```
For Each element In group
   statements
Next element
```

The following sample code fragment loops through all the elements of an array:

```
Dim aElement as Variant
For Each aElement in myArray()
   Debug.Print aElement
Next aElement
```

A For Each...Next loop can operate on any object in your Visual Basic program. For example, you can loop through the Controls collection that groups together all the controls situated on a form using a For Each...Next loop. Here is an example where the Enabled property on all the controls on a form is set to False:

```
Private Function DisableControls(frm as Form)
   Dim myControl as Control
   For Each myControl in frm.Controls
      frm.myControl.Enabled = False
   Next myControl
End Function
```

There are three restrictions to follow when using For Each...Next loops:

- The *element* in a For Each...Next loop that accesses a collection can only be a Variant variable, a generic Object variable, or an object listed in the Object Browser.

- The *element* in a For Each...Next loop that accesses an array can only be a Variant variable.

- You cannot access an array of user-defined types with a For Each...Next loop because a Variant cannot contain a user-defined type.

Exiting Loops

Sometimes in your programs, a condition arises that necessitates exiting a loop early, before the loop ends naturally. Visual Basic provides the Exit statement for exiting loops. You can use the Exit statement with all types of loops, sub procedures, and function procedures.

The following code shows an example of using an Exit statement in a Do loop:

```
Private Sub Withdrawal(ByRef AccountBalance as Long)
    Dim WDAmount As Long
    Do
        WDAmount = InputBox "Enter an amount to withdraw"
        If WDAmount > AccountBalance Then
            AccountBalance = AccountBalance - WDAmount
        Else
            MsgBox "Insufficient funds for this transaction. Enter _
                a smaller amount."
        End If
        If AccountBalance < 0 Then
            Exit Do
        End If
    Loop While AccountBalance > 0
    MsgBox "Insufficient Funds"
End Sub
```

In this example, the condition of the account balance becoming less than zero requires the program to leave the loop, probably so a different procedure can run to handle this situation.

You can use this general form of the Exit statement for the other loop types and sub and function procedures.

With

In an object-oriented programming environment such as Visual Basic, much of what a program does involves checking and setting the properties of objects. For example, based on how a user interacts with a form in your program, the size and location of the controls on the form might have to change. For each control, the set of properties that needs to change must be changed through a block of assignment statements, such as

```
txtUserName.Height = 2500
txtUserName.Width = 2500
txtUserName.Left = 2040
txtUserName.Top = 960
```

Each property is prefaced, quite appropriately, with the name of the control. Fully naming each control, however, can get quite tedious if you must set the properties of many controls during the course of your program. Visual Basic provides a shortcut method that allows you to use the control's name only once: the `With` statement.

The `With` statement allows you to perform a set of operations on a given object without requalifying (using the name of) the object for each operation. The syntax for the `With` statement is

```
With object
    statements
End With
```

You can rewrite the preceding example using the `With` statement in this way:

```
With txtUserName
    .Height = 2500
    .Width = 2500
    .Left = 2040
    .Top = 960
End With
```

CAUTION

One important rule to follow when using the `With` statement is that once you start a `With` block, the object being referenced cannot change. This means you cannot use one `With` statement with a number of different objects.

You can nest `With` statements, but if you do that and you want to reference a member of the object of an outer `With` block in an inner `With` block, you must use a fully qualified reference to that member (the object's name). Here is an example of nesting `With` statements:

```
With OuterObject
    .Height = 200
    .Left = 200
    With InnerObject
        .Height = 300
        .Top = 1000
        OuterObject.Caption = "Outer Object"
        .Caption = "Inner Object"
    End With
End With
```

Do not allow your program to jump into or out of a `With` block. If a statement in a `With` block is executed, but neither the `With` or `End With` statement is executed, your program might generate a runtime error or some sort of unpredictable behavior.

Branching Statements and Structures

In the ancient days of programming, before BASIC became a structured language, the language had a set of statements that transferred (or branched) program control from one part of a program to another. The most famous of these, the GoTo statement, has been vilified in computer programming textbooks for many years now. The problem with branching statements and structures is that in large programs, code that constantly branches from one part of a program to another part and back again quickly becomes hard to read and maintain. As structured programming concepts became more widely taught and practiced, the use of branching constructs became less common.

Today, of course, Visual Basic is a completely structured programming language and has all the modern constructs that generally preclude the necessity of using branching statements and structures. There are, however, certain situations when the use of a branching statement or structure is preferred, and for this reason, combined with the need to stay compatible with other versions of Basic, Visual Basic retains these branching constructs.

The GoTo Statement

The most famous of the branching constructs is the GoTo statement. I already mentioned the problems with GoTo, but in small programs, GoTo can be easier to use than other, more structured constructs. Another, more complicated example of when GoTo might be useful is when you are in a nested loop of some sort and you want to exit all loops at once. A GoTo can take you anywhere in a program you want to go. Programmer, beware!

The GoTo statement transfers control of the program unconditionally to a specified line number or label within a procedure. The syntax of GoTo is very simple:

```
GoTo line
```

Here is a simple example showing how you can use GoTo to branch from one part of a program to another:

```
Sub Command1_Click()
    Dim Number As Integer
    Number = 1
    If Number = 1 Then
        GoTo Line1
    Else
        GoTo Line2
    End If
    Line1:
        txtString = "Number equals 1"
        GoTo End
    Line2:
        txtString = "Number equal something else"
    End:
        Debug.Print "End of program"
End Sub
```

In this procedure, because Number equals 1, the statement associated with Line1 is executed and txtString gets the string "Number equals 1". Then, another GoTo executes and the statement associated with End executes.

GoTo statements are almost always unnecessary. The danger of using GoTos comes into play in large programs where trying to follow the logic of many GoTos can be difficult for the programmer and anyone else who must read the program code. It has also been shown that using the GoTo statement results in programs with more bugs than programs written with more structured programming constructs.

The GoSub...Return Structure

In the early days of BASIC, the language did not have the capability to call functions and subprocedures. Instead, a BASIC programmer had to create subroutines within his program using the GoSub...Return structure. The syntax of the GoSub...Return structure is

```
GoSub line
    statements
    line
        statements
Return
```

The GoSub statement transfers control of the program to the line label used as its argument. A statement or block of statements is executed until the program encounters the Return statement. Control of the program then reverts immediately to the line following the GoSub statement.

The following code fragment shows an example of the GoSub...Return structure:

```
Sub Command1_Click()
    Dim Number As Integer
    Number = 2
    If Number > 0 Then GoSub GreaterThan2
    Debug.Print Number
GreaterThan2:
    Debug.Print "Number is greater than 2"
    Return
End Sub
```

> **NOTE**
>
> A GoSub...Return structure can have more than one Return statement, but the first Return encountered causes the program to transfer control to the line immediately following the GoSub statement.

Although the GoSub...Return structure is perfectly legal to use, in almost every case, you can replace it with a function or subprocedure to ensure more readable code.

The On...GoSub and On...GoTo Structures

The On...GoSub and On...GoTo structures are alternatives to the GoSub...Return and GoTo constructs. You use them when the branching decision must have multiple choices. The syntax for these two structures is

```
On expression GoSub destinationlist
```

```
On expression GoTo destinationlist
```

expression must evaluate to a whole number between 0 and 255, and *destinationlist* is a set of line numbers or line labels separated by commas. If *expression* evaluates to 1, the first line label or line number is where control transfers; if *expression* evaluates to 2, control transfers to the second line number or line label; and so on. If you use the On...GoSub structure, a Return statement transfers control of the program to the line immediately following the On...GoSub. On...GoTo cannot use a Return statement.

Here is an example of On...GoSub:

```
Sub Command1_Click()
    Dim Number as Integer
    Number = 2
    On Number GoSub Equals1, Equals2, Equals3
    Debug.Print Number
Equals1:
    Debug.Print "Number equals 1"
    Return
Equals2:
    Debug.Print "Number equals 2"
Equals3"
    Debug.Print "Number equals 3"
End Sub
```

Here is the same example using On...GoTo:

```
Sub Command1_Click()
    Dim Number As Integer
    Number = 2
    On Number GoTo Equals1, Equals2, Equals3
    Debug.Print Number
Equals1:
    Debug.Print "Number equals 1"
Equals2:
    Debug.Print "Number equals 2"
Equals3:
    Debug.Print "Number equals 3"
End Sub
```

Four things can happen if *expression* evaluates to a number not represented in *destinationlist*:

- ■ If *expression* evaluates to 0, program control reverts to the statement following On...GoSub or On...GoTo.

- ■ If *expression* evaluates to a number greater than the number of items in *destinationlist*, program control reverts to the statement following On...GoSub or On...GoTo.

■ If *expression* is negative, an error is generated.

■ If *expression* is greater than 255, an error is generated.

For situations when an `On...GoSub` or `On...GoTo` seems called for, the `Select Case` structure can provide a more structured way of doing multiple branching.

Summary

All computer programs must have constructs that allow decision making and program control transfer. The decision-making constructs reviewed in this chapter include the following:

■ `If...Then`

■ `If...Then...Else`

■ `Select Case`

■ `Switch`

■ `Choose`

The different kinds of structures and statements you have learned for transferring program control include

■ `Do While...Loop`

■ `Do Until...Loop`

■ `While...Wend`

■ `For...Next`

■ `For Each...Next`

■ `With`

■ `GoTo`

■ `GoSub...Return`

■ `On...GoSub`

■ `On...GoTo`

An important focus of this chapter is how to use decision making and program control transfer in the course of following structured programming techniques. You learned about the statements and structures that do not promote good structured programming practices so that you use them only with caution.

Handling Errors

by Michael C. Amundsen

IN THIS CHAPTER

This chapter covers an important aspect of programming—handling runtime errors. Although you should always work to make sure your program can anticipate any problems that might occur while a user is running your software, you can't account for every possibility. That's why every good program should have a solid error-handling system.

In this chapter, you will learn just what an error handler is and why error handlers are so important. You'll also learn about some of the inner workings of Visual Basic and how that affects error handling.

You'll learn about the difference between local error-handling methods and global error-handling methods. You'll also learn the advantages and disadvantages of each method. You'll see the various types of errors your program is likely to encounter and some guidelines on how to handle each type of error.

You'll also learn about the Err object and the Error collection and how to use these objects to improve the accuracy of error reporting within your application. You'll also learn how to use the Raise method of the Err object to flag errors within custom controls or OLE server objects.

You'll also learn how to create error logs to keep track of errors that occur in your program. You'll learn how to create a trace log to analyze your programs. You'll learn how you can write your programs to turn these features on or off without rewriting program code.

Finally, you'll build an OLE server DLL that contains an improved error handler, an error-logging facility, and a module trace routine. You can use this new OLE server in all your future VBA-compliant programming projects.

Error Handling in General

Error handling is an essential part of any program. No program is complete unless it has good error handling. It is important to write your programs in a way that reduces the chances that errors will occur, but you won't be able to think of everything. Errors do happen! Well-designed programs don't necessarily have fewer errors; they just handle them better.

Writing error handlers is not difficult. In fact, you can add consistent error handling to your program by adding only a few lines of code to each module. The difficult part of writing good error handlers is knowing what to expect and how to handle the unexpected. You'll learn how to do both in this chapter.

Adding error handling to your program makes your program seem much more polished and friendly to your users. Nothing is more annoying—or frightening—to a user than to see the screen freeze up, hear a startling beep, or watch the program (and any file your user had been working on) suddenly disappear from the screen entirely. This only needs to happen a few times before the user vows never to use your program again.

Error Handling in Visual Basic

Writing error handlers in Visual Basic is a bit trickier than in most computer languages. There are several reasons for this. First, Visual Basic is an *event-driven* language model, rather than *procedure-driven* like most computer languages. Second, Visual Basic uses a call stack method that isolates local variables. When you exit the routine, you can lose track of the values of internal variables, which can make resuming execution after error handling difficult. Third, in Visual Basic, all errors are local. If an error occurs, it's best to handle it in the routine where the error occurred, which means you must write a short error handler for each routine in your Visual Basic program.

NOTE

Technically, Visual Basic does allow the use of a global error handler. However, after Visual Basic travels up the procedure stack to locate the error handler, it can't travel back down the stack to resume execution after the error is corrected. (This is typical of most object-oriented languages.) For this reason, I highly recommend using local error handlers in your Visual Basic programs.

The Built-in Visual Basic Error Objects

Visual Basic 5 has two built-in objects that you can use to track and report errors at runtime. The Err object is a built-in object that exists in all Visual Basic programs. This object contains several properties and two methods. Each time an error occurs in the program, the Err object properties are filled with information you can use within your program.

The second built-in object that helps in tracking errors is the Error object and Errors collection. These are available to any Visual Basic 5 program that has loaded one of the Microsoft data access object libraries. The Error object is a child object of the DBEngine. You can use the Error object to get additional details on the nature of the database errors that occur in your program.

WARNING

The Error object is only available if you have loaded a Microsoft data access object library. If you attempt to access the Error object from a Visual Basic program that does not have a Microsoft data access object library loaded, you receive an error.

The advantage of the Error object over the Err object is that the Error object contains more information about the database-related errors than the Err object. In some cases, back-end database servers return several error messages to your Visual Basic application. The Err object only reports the last error received from the back-end server. However, the Errors collection can report all the errors received. For this reason, it is always a good idea to use the Error object when you are working with Visual Basic database applications.

Working with the Err Object

Visual Basic 5 has a built-in object called the Err object. This object has all the information about the most recent error that occurred within the running application space.

> **WARNING**
>
> There is a bit of confusion regarding the Err keyword in Visual Basic. Visual Basic 5 still supports the outdated Err and Error functions, but I do not advise you to use them in your programs. In some rare cases, the values reported by the Err and Error functions are not the same as those reported by the Err object. Throughout this chapter, when I mention Err, I am referring to the Err object, not the Err function.

The Err object has several important properties. Table 16.1 shows these properties and explains their use.

Table 16.1. The properties of the Err object.

Property	Type	Value
Number	Long	The actual internal error number returned by Visual Basic.
Source	String	Name of the current Visual Basic file in which the error occurred. This could be an EXE, a DLL, or an OCX file.
Description	String	A string corresponding to the internal error number returned in the Number property, if this string exists. If the string doesn't exist, Description contains Application-defined or object-defined error.
HelpFile	String	The fully qualified drive, path, and filename of the Help file. You can call this help file to support the reported errors.
HelpContext	Long	The Help file context (topic) ID in the help file indicated by the HelpFile property.
LastDLLError	Long	The error code for the last call to a dynamic-link library (DLL). This is available only on 32-bit Microsoft platforms.

When an error occurs in your Visual Basic program, the Err object properties are populated with the details of the error. You can inspect these values during your program execution and, if possible, use Visual Basic code to correct the error and continue the program.

For example, once an error occurs, you can inspect the properties of the object using the following code:

```
Msgbox "<" & CStr(Err.Number) & "> " & Err.Description & "[" & Err.Source & "]"
```

After the error occurs and the Err object properties are updated, the Err object values do not change until another error is reported or the error handling system is re-initialized.

> **NOTE**
>
> The error-handling system is re-initialized each time a procedure exit or end occurs or when the special error-handling keywords Resume or On Error are executed. You'll learn more about these keywords in the section "Using Resume to Exit the Error Handler" later in this chapter.

If the error that was reported has an associated help file and help context ID, these properties are also filled in. You can use the HelpFile and HelpContext properties of the Err object to display an online help topic to explain the error condition to the user.

If your application calls a dynamic-link library (DLL), you might be able to use the LastDLLError property of the Err object to get additional information about an error that occurred in a DLL. This property is only available on the 32-bit platform and might not be supported by the DLL you are calling.

Working with the Error Object and the Errors Collection

In addition to the built-in Err object, Visual Basic 5 also has a built-in Error object for database errors. This object is a child object of the DBEngine object. For this reason, you can only access the Error object if you loaded a Microsoft data access object library. (Select Project | References from the main menu.)

The primary advantage of the Error object is that it can report additional error information not included in the standard Err object mentioned earlier. Many times, your database application will need to depend on external processes such as ODBC data connections or OLE server modules. When an error occurs in these external processes, they might report more than one error code back to your Visual Basic application.

The Err object is only able to remember the most recent error that is reported. However, the Error object (and its associated Errors collection) can remember all the errors reported by external processes. That is why it is a good idea to use the Error object for reporting errors in all your Visual Basic database programs.

The properties of the Microsoft data access Error object are almost identical to the properties of the Visual Basic Err object. The only difference is that the Error object does not have the optional LastDLLError property. Therefore, the calling convention for the Error object is basically the same as that for the Err object:

```
Msgbox "<" & CStr(Error.Number) & "> " & _
   ➥Error.Description & "[" & Error.Source & "]"
```

Although the Error and Err objects are quite similar, there is one major difference worth noting. The Err object stands alone, but the Microsoft data access Error object belongs to the Errors collection. This is very important when dealing with back-end database servers, especially when your Visual Basic program is connected to databases via the Open Database Connectivity (ODBC) interface. When an error occurs during an ODBC transaction, the Err object always returns the same error message, ODBC failed. However, the Errors collection often contains more than one error message that can tell you a great deal more about the nature of the problem. You can retrieve all the error information by enumerating all the Error objects in the Errors collection. Listing 16.1 shows how that can be done.

Listing 16.1. Enumerating the Errors collection.

```
Dim objTempErr as Object
Dim strMsg as String
For Each objTempErr In Errors
    StrMsg = "<" & CStr(objTempErr.Number) & "> "
    StrMsg = strMsg & objTempErr.Description
    StrMsg = strMsg & " in [" & objTempErr.Source & "]" & vbCrLf
Next
Msgbox strMsg
```

The code in Listing 16.1 creates a single line of text (strMsg) that contains all the error messages reported by the back-end database server. You'll learn more about using both the Err and Error objects in the next section.

Creating Your Own Error Handlers

Before getting into the details of using the Err and Error objects in your Visual Basic programs, take a look at a basic error handler in Visual Basic. Error handlers in Visual Basic have three main parts:

- The On Error Goto statement
- The error-handling code
- The exit statement

The On Error Goto statement appears at the beginning of the sub or function. This is the line that tells Visual Basic what to do when an error occurs, as in the following example:

```
On Error Goto LocalErrHandler
```

In the preceding code line, every time an error occurs in this sub or function, the program immediately jumps to the `LocalErrHandler` label in the routine and executes the error-handling code. The error-handling code can be as simple or as complex as needed to handle the error. A very simple error handler just reports the error number and error message:

```
LocalErrHandler:
    MsgBox CStr(Err.Number) & " - " & Err.Description
```

In the preceding code example, as soon as the error occurs, Visual Basic reports the error number (`Err.Number`) and the error message (`Err.Description`) in a message box.

The third, and final, part of a Visual Basic error handler is the exit statement. This is the line that tells Visual Basic where to go after the error handler is done with its work. There are four different ways to exit an error-handling routine:

- Use the `Resume` keyword to return to the location in the program that caused the error in order to re-execute the same instruction.

- Use the `Resume Next` keywords to resume execution at the Visual Basic code line immediately following the line that caused the error.

- Use the `Resume label` keywords to resume execution at a specified location within the routine that caused the error. This location could be anywhere within the routine—before or after the line that caused the error.

- Use the `Exit Sub` or `Exit Function` keywords to immediately exit the routine in which the error occurred.

Which exit method you use depends on the type of error that occurred and the error-handling strategy you employ throughout your program.

Now that you have the basics of error handling covered, you can write some error-handling routines.

Creating a Simple Error Handler

To start, write a simple error-handling routine to illustrate how Visual Basic behaves when errors occur. Start a new Standard EXE project in Visual Basic 5. Add a single command button to the default form. Set its `Name` property to `cmdSimpleErr` and its `Caption` property to `Simple`. Now add the code in Listing 16.2 behind the command button.

Listing 16.2. Writing a simple error handler.

```
Private Sub cmdSimpleErr_Click()
    '
    ' a simple error handler
    '
    On Error GoTo LocalErr  ' turn on error handling
    '
    Dim intValue As Integer ' declare integer
```

continues

Listing 16.2. continued

```
    Dim strMsg As String     ' declare string
    intValue = 10000000      ' create overflow error
    GoTo LocalExit           ' exit if no error
    '
    ' local error handler
LocalErr:
    strMsg = CStr(Err.Number) & " - " & Err.Description ' make message
    MsgBox strMsg, vbCritical, "cmdSimpleErr_Click"  ' show message
    Resume Next  ' continue on
    '
    ' routine exit
LocalExit:
    '
End Sub
```

Save the form as BASICERR.FRM, and save the project as BASICERR.VBP. Then execute the program and click the command button. You'll see the error message displayed on the screen. (See Figure 16.1.)

FIGURE 16.1.

Displaying the results of a simple error handler.

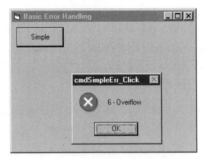

The example in Listing 16.2 exhibits all the parts of a good error handler. The first line in the routine tells Visual Basic what to do in case of an error. Notice that the name for the error-handling code is given as LocalErr. You'll see that every local error handler written in this chapter is called LocalErr. Next, the routine declares an integer variable and then purposely loads that variable with an illegal value. This causes the error routine to kick in.

The error routine is very simple. It is a message that contains the error number and the associated text message. The routine then displays that message along with the warning symbol and the name of the routine that is reporting the error.

The next line tells Visual Basic what to do after the error is handled. In this case, Visual Basic resumes execution with the line of program code that immediately follows the line that caused the error (Resume at the Next line).

When Visual Basic resumes execution, the routine hits the line that tells Visual Basic to go to the exit routine (Goto LocalExit). Notice again the naming convention for the exit routine. All exit jump labels in this chapter are called LocalExit.

Handling Cascading Errors

What happens if you get an error within your error routine? Although it isn't fun to think about, it can happen. When an error occurs inside the error-handling routine, Visual Basic looks for the next declared error routine—an error routine started in the previous calling routine using the On Error Goto *label* statement. If no error routine is available, Visual Basic halts the program with a fatal error.

As an example, add a new button to the BASICERR project and create a cascading error condition. Set the button's Name property to cmdCascadeErr and its Caption property to Cascade. First, create a new subprocedure called CreateErr. Then enter the code from Listing 16.3.

Listing 16.3. Coding the CreateErr routine.

```
Public Sub CreateErr()
    '
    ' create an internal error
    '
    On Error GoTo LocalErr
    '
    Dim strMsg As String
    Dim intValue As Integer
    '
    intValue = 900000 ' create an error
    GoTo LocalExit ' all done

LocalErr:
    strMsg = CStr(Err.Number) & " - " & Err.Description
    MsgBox strMsg, vbCritical, "CreateErr"
    '
    Open "junk.txt" For Input As 1 ' create another error
    Resume Next
    '
LocalExit:
    '
End Sub
```

You'll notice that this routine is quite similar to the code from Listing 16.2. The biggest difference is in the lines of code in the error-handling portion of the subroutine. Notice that Visual Basic attempts to open a text file for input. Because this file does not currently exist, this causes an error.

Now add the code from Listing 16.4 to the cmdCascadeErr_Click event. This is the code that calls the CreateErr routine.

Listing 16.4. Coding the cmdCascadeErr routine.

```
Private Sub cmdCascadeErr_Click()
    '
    ' create an error cascade
    '
```

continues

Listing 16.4. continued

```
On Error GoTo LocalErr
'
Dim strMsg As String
'
CreateErr ' call another routine
GoTo LocalExit ' all done
'
LocalErr:
    strMsg = CStr(Err.Number) & " - " & Err.Description
    MsgBox strMsg, vbCritical, "cmdCascadeErr"
    Resume Next
'
LocalExit:
'
End Sub
```

Save the program and run it to see the results. When you first click the command button, you see the error message that announces the overflow error. Notice that the title of the message box indicates that the error is reported by the CreateErr routine. (See Figure 16.2.)

FIGURE 16.2.

Reporting the error from CreateErr.

When you click the OK button in the message box, you'll see another error message. This one reports an Error 53 File not Found message, which occurred when CreateErr tried to open the nonexistent file. (See Figure 16.3.)

FIGURE 16.3.

Reporting the File not found *error.*

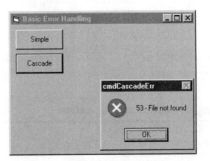

Here's the important point. Notice that the second error message box tells you that the error is reported from the `cmdCascadeErr` routine—even though the error occurred in the `CreateErr` routine! The error that occurred in the `CreateErr` error-handling routine could not be handled locally, and Visual Basic searched upward in the call stack to find the next available error handler to invoke. This action by Visual Basic can be a blessing and a curse. It's good to know that Visual Basic uses the next available error-handling routine when things like this happen, but it's also likely to cause confusion for you and your users if you are not careful. For all you can tell in this example, an error occurred in `cmdCascadeErr`. You must keep this in mind when you are debugging Visual Basic error reports.

It is also worth mentioning that if you use the `Resume Next` keyword (see the section "Using Resume Next to Exit the Error Handler"), the execution begins *after* the call to `CreateErr` and not where the error actually occurred. This can be very confusing and, in some cases, might actually compound the error by executing invalid code in some other routine!

Using Resume to Exit the Error Handler

The simplest method for exiting an error handler is the `Resume` method. When you exit an error handler with the `Resume` keyword, Visual Basic returns to the line of code that caused the error and attempts to run that line again. The `Resume` keyword is useful when you encounter an error that the user can easily correct, such as attempting to read a disk drive when the user forgets to insert a disk or close the drive door. You can use the `Resume` keyword whenever you are confident that the situation that caused the error has been remedied, and you want to retry the action that caused the error.

Modify the BASICERR project by adding a new button to the project. Set its `Name` property to `cmdResumeErr` and its `Caption` property to `Resume`. Now add the Visual Basic code in Listing 16.5 behind the new button's `click` event.

Listing 16.5. Using the Resume keyword.

```
Private Sub cmdResumeErr_Click()
    '
    ' show resume keyword
    '
    On Error GoTo LocalErr
    '
    Dim intValue As Integer
    Dim strMsg As String
    '
    intValue = InputBox("Enter an integer:")
    GoTo LocalExit

LocalErr:
    strMsg = CStr(Err.Number) & " - " & Err.Description
    MsgBox strMsg, vbCritical, "cmdResumeErr"
    Resume ' try it again
    '
LocalExit:
    '
End Sub
```

Save and run the project. When you click the Resume button, you are prompted to enter an integer value. If you simply click the Cancel button or the OK button without entering data (or if you enter a value that is greater than 32,767), you invoke the error handler and receive an error message from Visual Basic. (See Figure 16.4.)

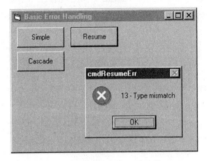

When you click the OK button, Visual Basic redisplays the input prompt and waits for your reply. If you enter another invalid value, you see the error message, and then you see the prompt again. This is the Resume exit method in action. You can't get beyond this screen until you enter a valid value.

This can be very frustrating for your users. What if they don't know what value to enter here? Are they stuck in this terrible error handler forever? Whenever you use the Resume keyword, you should give your users an option to ignore the error and move on or cancel the action completely.

Using Resume Next to Exit the Error Handler

Using the Resume Next method to exit an error handler allows your user to get past a problem spot in the program as if no error had occurred. This is useful when you use code within the error handler to fix the problem or when you think the program can go on even though an error is reported.

Deciding whether to continue the program even though an error is reported is sometimes a tough call. It is usually not a good idea to assume that your program will work fine even though an error is reported. This is especially true if the error that occurs is related to physical devices (missing disk, lost communications connection, and so on) or file errors (missing, corrupted, or locked data files, and so on). The Resume Next keywords are usually used in error-handling routines that fix any reported error before continuing.

To illustrate the use of Resume Next, add a new command button to the project. Set its Name property to cmdResumeNext and its Caption property to Next. Now enter the code in Listing 16.6 behind the button's click event.

Listing 16.6. Using the Resume Next keywords.

```
Private Sub cmdResumeNextErr_Click()
    '
    ' show use of resume next
    '
    On Error GoTo LocalErr
    '
    Dim intValue As Integer
    Dim strMsg As String
    Dim lngReturn As Long
    '
    intValue = InputBox("Enter a valid Integer")
    MsgBox "intValue has been set to " + CStr(intValue)
    GoTo LocalExit
    '
LocalErr:
    If Err.Number = 6 Then ' was it an overflow error?
        strMsg = "You have entered an invalid
            ➥ integer value." & vbCrLf
        strMsg = strMsg & "The program will now set the
            ➥ value to 0 for you." & vbCrLf
        strMsg = strMsg & "Select YES to set the
            ➥ value to 0 and continue." & vbCrLf
        strMsg = strMsg & "Select NO to return to enter a new value."
        '
        lngReturn = MsgBox(strMsg, vbCritical + vbYesNo, "cmdResumeNextErr")
        If lngReturn = vbYes Then
            intValue = 0
            Resume Next
        Else
            Resume
        End If
    Else ' must have been some other error(!)
        strMsg = CStr(Err.Number) & " - " & Err.Description
        MsgBox strMsg, vbCritical, "cmdResumeNext"
        Resume
    End If
    '
LocalExit:
    '
End Sub
```

In Listing 16.6, you added a section of code to the error handler that tests for the anticipated overflow error. You explain the options to the user and then give the user a choice of how to proceed. This is a good general model for error handling that involves user interaction. Tell the user the problem, explain the options, and let the user decide how to go forward.

Notice also that this routine includes a general error trap for those cases when the error is not caused by an integer overflow. Even when you think you have covered all the possible error conditions, you should always include a general error trap.

Save and run this project. When you click the Next command button and enter an invalid value (that is, any number greater than 32,767), you see the error message that explains your options. (See Figure 16.5.)

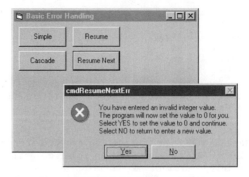

Using Resume *label* to Exit an Error Handler

Sometimes you need your program to return to another spot within the routine to fix an error that occurs. For example, if you ask the user to enter two numbers that you will use to perform a division operation, and it results in a divide-by-zero error, you want to ask the user to enter both numbers again. You might not be able to simply use the Resume statement after you handle the error.

When you need to force the program to return to a specific point in the routine, you can use the Resume *label* exit method. The Resume *label* method enables you to return to any place within the current procedure. You can't use Resume *label* to jump to another sub or function within the project.

Modify the BASICERR project to include an example of Resume *label*. Add a new command button to the project. Set its Name property to cmdResumeLabelErr and its Caption property to Resume Label. Now, place the code in Listing 16.7 behind the click event.

Listing 16.7. Using the Resume *label* keywords.

```
Private Sub cmdResumeLabelErr_Click()
    '
    ' show resume label version
    '
    On Error GoTo LocalErr
    '
    Dim intX As Integer
    Dim intY As Integer
    Dim intZ As Integer
    '
cmdLabelInput:
    intX = InputBox("Enter a Divisor:", "Input Box #1")
    intY = InputBox("Enter a Dividend:", "Input Box #2")
```

```
        intZ = intX / intY
        MsgBox "The Quotient is: " + Str(intZ), vbInformation, "Results"
        GoTo LocalExit
        '
LocalErr:
    If Err = 11 Then       ' divide by zero error
        MsgBox CStr(Err.Number) & " - " & Err.Description, _
        ➥ vbCritical, "cmdResumeLabelErr"
        Resume cmdLabelInput ' back for more
    Else
        MsgBox CStr(Err) & " -" & Error$, vbCritical, "cmdLabel"
        Resume Next
    End If
        '
LocalExit:
        '
End Sub
```

Save and run the project. Enter 13 at the first input box and 0 at the second input box. This causes a Divide by zero error, and the error handler takes over from there. You see the error message shown in Figure 16.6 and then you are returned to the line that starts the input process.

FIGURE 16.6.
Viewing the divide-by-zero error message.

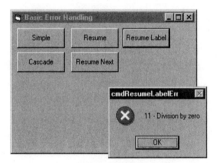

Using the Exit or End Method to Exit an Error Handler

Sometimes an error occurs and there is no good way to return to the program. A good example of this type of error can occur when the program attempts to open files on a network file server and the user forgot to log on to the server. In this case, you need to either exit the routine and return to the calling procedure, or exit the program completely. Exiting to a calling routine can work if you write your program to anticipate these critical errors. Usually, it's difficult to do that. Most of the time, critical errors of this type mean you should end the program and let the user fix the problem before restarting the program.

Add one more button to the BASICERR project. Set its Caption property to End and its Name property to cmdEndErr. Enter the code in Listing 16.8 behind the cmdEnd_Click event.

Listing 16.8. Using the End keyword.

```
Private Sub cmdEndErr_Click()
    '
    ' use End to exit handler
    '
    On Error GoTo LocalErr
    '
    Dim strMsg As String
    Open "junk.txt" For Input As 1
    GoTo cmdEndExit
    '
LocalErr:
    If Err.Number = 53 Then
        strMsg = "Unable to open JUNK.TXT" & vbCrLf
        strMsg = strMsg & "Exit the program and check your INI file" & vbCrLf
        strMsg = strMsg & "to make sure the JUNKFILE setting is correct."
        MsgBox strMsg, vbCritical, "cmdEnd"
        Unload Me
    Else
        MsgBox Str(Err) + " - " + Error$, vbCritical, "cmdEnd"
        Resume Next
    End If
    '
LocalExit:
    '
End Sub
```

In Listing 16.8, you add a check in the error handler for the anticipated File not Found error. You give the user some helpful information and then tell him you are closing the program. It's always a good idea to tell the user when you are about to exit the program. Notice that you did not use the Visual Basic End keyword; you used Unload Me. Remember that End stops all program execution immediately. Using Unload Me causes Visual Basic to execute any code placed in the Unload event of the form. This event should contain any file-closing routine needed to safely exit the program.

Save and run the project. When you click the End button, you see a message box explaining the problem and suggesting a solution. (See Figure 16.7.) When you click the OK button, Visual Basic ends the program.

FIGURE 16.7.

Showing the error message before exiting the program.

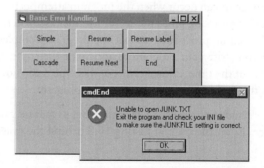

Using the `Err.Raise` Method to Create Your Own Error Conditions

Many times it is not practical or desirable to display an error message when an error occurs. Other times, you might want to use the error-handling capabilities of Visual Basic 5 to your own advantage by creating your own error codes and messages. You can do this using the `Raise` method of the `Err` object. Using the `Raise` method allows you to alert users (or other calling applications) that an error has occurred, but gives both you and the user additional flexibility on how the error is handled.

The `Raise` method takes up to five parameters:

- `ErrorNumber` is a unique number identifying the error that just occurred.
- `ErrorSource` is the code module that generated the error.
- `ErrorDescription` is the text message associated with the error.
- `HelpFile` is the help file that contains support information on the error.
- `HelpContextID` is the ID number of the help topic associated with this error.

When you raise your own errors, you are required to report an error number. This number can be any unique value you want. If you use a number already defined as a Visual Basic error, you'll automatically get the `ErrorDescription` and any associated `HelpFile` and `HelpContextID` information as well. If you generate your own unique number, you can fill in the other parameters yourself. It is recommended that you use the `vbObjectError` constant as a base number for your own error codes. This guarantees that your error number will not conflict with any Visual Basic errors.

Below is a typical call to use the `Err.Raise` method:

```
'
LocalErr:
    ' trouble with file stuff!
    Err.Raise vbObjectError + 1, "errHandler.LogError",
    ➥ "Can't write log file [" & errLogFileName & "]"
'
End Sub
```

It is especially important to use this method for marking errors when you are coding ActiveX DLL servers. Because servers can run at a remote location on the network, you cannot be sure that users will ever see any error dialog you display. Also, remember that even if the DLL is running on the local PC, error dialog boxes are application-modal. No other processing occurs until the dialog box is dismissed. You'll learn to use the `Err.Raise` method when you create your `errHandler` object library in the section "Creating Your Error-Handling OLE Server" later in this chapter.

So far, you have seen how to build a simple error handler and the different ways to exit error handlers. Now you need to learn about the different types of errors that you will encounter in your Visual Basic programs and how to plan for them in advance.

Types of Errors

To make writing error handlers easier and more efficient, you can group errors into typical types. These error types can usually be handled in a similar manner. When you get an idea of the types of errors you can encounter, you can begin to write error handlers that take care of more than one error. You can write handlers that take care of error types.

There are four types of Visual Basic errors:

- **General file errors** are errors you encounter when you are attempting to open, read, or write simple files. This type of error does not include errors related to internal database operations (read/write table records).

- **Physical media errors** are errors caused by problems with physical devices—errors such as unresponsive communications ports or printers and low-level disk errors (`Unable To Read Sector` and so on).

- **Program code errors** are errors that appear in your programs due to problems with your code. Errors include `Divide by zero`, `Invalid Property`, and other errors that can only be corrected by changing the Visual Basic code in your programs.

- **Database errors** are errors that occur during database operations, usually during data read/write or data object create/delete operations.

Each of these types of errors needs to be handled differently within your Visual Basic programs. You'll learn general rules for handling these errors in the following sections.

General File Errors

General file errors occur due to invalid data file information such as a bad filename, data path, or device name. Usually the user can fix these errors and the program can continue from the point of failure. The basic approach to handling general file errors is to create an error handler that reports the problem to the user and asks for additional information to complete or retry the operation.

In Listing 16.9, the error handler is called when the program attempts to open a control file called `CONTROL.TXT`. The error handler then prompts the user for the proper file location and continues processing. Start a new Standard EXE project (`ERRTYPES.VBP`) and add a command button to the form. Set its `Caption` property to `Control` and its `Name` property to `cmdControl`. Also, add a `CommonDialog` control to the project. Enter the code in Listing 16.9 into the `cmdControl_Click` event.

Listing 16.9. Adding code to the cmdControl_Click event.

```
Private Sub cmdControl_Click()
    '
    ' show general file errors
    '
    On Error GoTo LocalErr
    '
```

16

HANDLING
ERRORS

```
    Dim strFile As String
    Dim strMsg As String
    Dim lngReturn As Long
    '
    strFile = "\control.txt"
    '
    Open strFile For Input As 1
    MsgBox "Control File Opened"
    GoTo LocalExit
    '
LocalErr:
    If Err.Number = 53 Then ' file not found?
        strMsg = "Unable to Open CONTROL.TXT" & vbCrLf
        strMsg = strMsg & "Select OK to locate CONTROL.TXT" & vbCrLf
        strMsg = strMsg & "Select CANCEL to exit program."
        '
        lngReturn = MsgBox(strMsg, vbCritical + vbOKCancel, "cmdControl")
        '
        If lngReturn = vbOK Then
            CommonDialog1.filename = strFile
            CommonDialog1.DefaultExt = ".txt"
            CommonDialog1.ShowOpen
            Resume
        Else
            Unload Me
        End If
    Else
        MsgBox CStr(Err.Number) & " - " + Err.Description
        Resume Next
    End If
    '
LocalExit:
    '
End Sub
```

Save the form as FRMERRTYPES.FRM and the project as PRJERRTYPES.VBP. Now run this project. When you click the Control button, the program tries to open the CONTROL.TXT file. If it can't be found, you see the error message. (See Figure 16.8.)

FIGURE 16.8.

Displaying the File not found *error.*

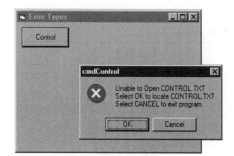

If the user selects OK, the program calls the CommonDialog control and prompts the user to locate the CONTROL.TXT file. It can be found in the same folder that contains the source code for this chapter's directory. (See Figure 16.9.)

FIGURE 16.9.

Attempting to locate the CONTROL.TXT *file.*

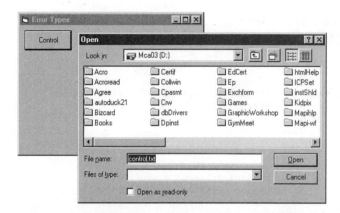

> **TIP**
>
> Notice the use of the CommonDialog control to open the file. Whenever you need to prompt users for file-related action (open, create, save), you should use the CommonDialog control. This is a familiar dialog for your users, and it handles all the dirty work of scrolling, searching, and so on.

Table 16.2 lists errors that are similar to the File not Found error illustrated in Listing 16.9. Errors of this type usually involve giving the user a chance to re-enter the filename or reset some value. Most of the time, you can write an error trap that anticipates these errors, prompts the user to supply the corrected information, and then retries the operation that caused the error.

Table 16.2. Common general file errors.

Error Code	Error Message
52	Bad filename or number
53	File not found
54	Bad file mode
55	File already open
58	File already exists
59	Bad record length

Error Code	Error Message
61	Disk full
62	Input past end of file
63	Bad record number
64	Bad filename
67	Too many files
74	Can't rename with different drive
75	Path/File access error
76	Path not found

In cases when it is not practical to prompt a user for additional information (such as during initial startup of the program), it is usually best to report the error in a message box. Then give the user some ideas about how to fix the problem before you exit the program safely.

Physical Media Errors

Another group of common errors is caused by problems with physical media. Unresponsive printers, disk drives that do not contain disks, and downed communications ports are the most common examples of physical media errors. These errors might, or might not, be easily fixed by your user. Usually, you can report the error, wait for the user to fix the problem, and then continue with the process. For example, if the printer is jammed with paper, all you need to do is report the error to the user and then wait for the OK to continue.

Add another button to the PRJERRTYPES.VBP project to display an example of physical media error handling. Add a new command button to the project. Set its Caption property to &Media and its Name property to cmdMedia. Enter the code in Listing 16.10 into the cmdMedia_Click event.

Listing 16.10. Trapping media errors.

```
Private Sub cmdMedia_Click()
    '
    ' show handling of media errors
    '
    On Error GoTo LocalErr
    Dim strMsg As String
    Dim lngReturn As Long
    '
    ' open a file on the a drive
    ' an error will occur if there
    ' is no diskette in the drive
    '
    Open "a:\junk.txt" For Input As 1
    Close #1
```

continues

Listing 16.10. continued

```
    GoTo LocalExit
    '
LocalErr:
    If Err.Number = 71 Then
        strMsg = "The disk drive is not ready." & vbCrLf
        strMsg = strMsg + "Please make sure there is a diskette" & vbCrLf
        strMsg = strMsg + "in the drive and the drive door is closed."
        '
        lngReturn = MsgBox(strMsg, vbCritical + vbRetryCancel, "cmdMedia")
        '
        If lngReturn = vbRetry Then
            Resume
        Else
            Resume Next
        End If
    Else
        MsgBox Str(Err.Number) & " - " & Err.Description
        Resume Next
    End If
    '
LocalExit:
    '
End Sub
```

In Listing 16.10, you attempt to open a file on a disk drive that has no disk (or has an open drive door). The error handler prompts the user to correct the problem and allows the user to try the operation again. If all goes well the second time, the program continues. The user also has an option to cancel the operation.

Save and run the project. When you click the Media button, you should get results that look like those in Figure 16.10.

FIGURE 16.10.

The results of a physical media error.

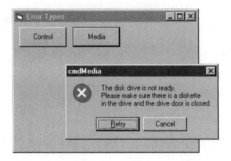

Program Code Errors

Another common type of error is the program code error. These errors occur as part of the Visual Basic code. Errors of this type cannot be fixed by users and are usually due to unanticipated conditions within the code itself. Error messages such as Variable Not Found, Invalid

16

`Object`, and so on are a mystery to most of your users. The best way to handle errors of this type is to tell the user to report the message to the programmer and close the program safely.

Database Errors with the Data Control

A common type of error that occurs in database applications is the data-related error. These errors include those that deal with data type or field size problems, table access restrictions including read-only access, locked tables due to other users, and so on. Database errors fall into two groups. Those caused by attempting to read or write invalid data to or from tables, including data integrity errors, make up the most common group. The second group includes those errors caused by locked tables, restricted access, or multiuser conflicts.

In most cases, all you need to do is trap for the error, report it to the user, and allow the user to return to the data entry screen to fix the problem. If you use the Visual Basic data control in your data forms, you can take advantage of the automatic database error reporting built into the data control. As an example, put together a simple data entry form to illustrate some of the common data entry-oriented database errors.

Start a new Visual Basic Standard EXE project to illustrate common database errors. Add a data control, two bound input controls, and two label controls. Use Table 16.3 as a reference for adding the controls to the form. Refer to Figure 16.11 as a guide for placing the controls.

FIGURE 16.11.

Laying out the DataErr *form.*

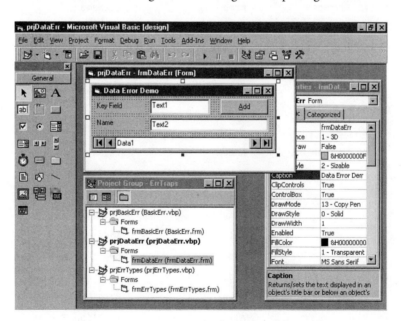

Table 16.3. Controls for the `frmDataErr` form.

Control	Property	Setting
VB.Form	Name	frmDataErr
	Caption	Data Error Demo
	ClientHeight	1335
	ClientLeft	60
	ClientTop	345
	ClientWidth	4665
	StartUpPosition	3 'Windows Default
VB.CommandButton	Name	cmdAdd
	Caption	&Add
	Height	375
	Left	3300
	Top	60
	Width	1215
VB.TextBox	Name	txtName
	DataField	Name
	DataSource	Data1
	Height	315
	Left	1500
	Top	540
	Width	3015
VB.TextBox	Name	txtKeyField
	DataField	KeyField
	DataSource	Data1
	Height	375
	Left	1500
	Top	60
	Width	1515
VB.Data	Name	Data1
	Align	2 'Align Bottom
	Caption	Data1
	Connect	Access

Control	Property	Setting
	DatabaseName	errordb.mdb
	Height	360
	RecordSource	Table1
	Top	975
	Width	4665
VB.Label	Name	lblName
	Caption	Name
	Height	255
	Left	120
	Top	540
	Width	1215
VB.Label	Name	lblKeyField
	Caption	Key Field
	Height	255
	Left	120
	Top	120
	Width	1215

The only code you need to add to this form is a single line behind the Add button. Place the following code behind the `cmdAdd_Click` event:

```
Private Sub cmdAdd_Click()
   Data1.Recordset.AddNew
End Sub
```

Now save the new form as `DATAERR.FRM` and the project as `DATAERR.VBP`. When you run the project, you can test the built-in error trapping for Microsoft data controls by adding a new, duplicate record to the table. Click the Add button, then enter `KF109` in the `KeyField` input box and click one of the arrows on the data control to force it to save the record. You should see a database error message that looks like the one in Figure 16.12.

Are you surprised? You didn't add an error trap to the data entry form, but you still got a complete database error message! The Visual Basic data control is kind enough to provide complete database error reporting even if you have no error handlers in your Visual Basic program. Along with the automatic errors, the data control also has the `Error` event. Each time a data-related error occurs, this event occurs. You can add code in the `Data1_Error` event to automatically fix errors, display better error messages, and so on.

FIGURE 16.12.

*A sample Microsoft
data control error
message.*

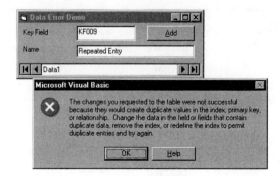

Modify the program a bit to show how you can use the `Data1_Error` event. First, add a `CommonDialog` control to your form. Then edit the `DatabaseName` property of the data control to read `C:\ERRORDB.MDB`. Next, add the code from Listing 16.11 to the `Data1_Error` event.

Listing 16.11. Coding the Data1_Error event.

```
Private Sub Data1_Error(DataErr As Integer, Response As Integer)
    '
    ' add error-trapping for data errors
    '
    Dim strFileName As String
    '
    Select Case DataErr
        Case 3044 ' database not found
            MsgBox "Unable to locate data file",
            ➥ vbExclamation, "Database Missing"
            '
            CommonDialog1.DialogTitle = "Locate ERRORDB.MDB"
            CommonDialog1.filename = "ERRORDB.MDB"
            CommonDialog1.Filter = "*.mdb"
            CommonDialog1.ShowOpen
            Data1.DatabaseName = CommonDialog1.filename
            '
            Response = vbCancel ' cancel auto-message
    End Select
    '
End Sub
```

Notice that the code in Listing 16.11 checks to see if the error code is **3044**. This is the error number that corresponds to the "database missing" message. If the **3044** code is reported, the user sees a short message and then the file open dialog, ready to locate and load the database. Finally, notice the line that sets the `Response` parameter to `vbCancel`. This step tells Visual Basic not to display the default message.

> **TIP**
>
> Usually, it is not a good idea to attempt to override the default error handling of the data control with your own database errors. As long as you use the Visual Basic data control, you do not need to add database error-trapping routines to your data entry forms. The only time you need to add error-related code is when you want to perform special actions in the Error event of the data control.

You need to add one more little bit of code to complete this error trap. Add the following line of code to the `Form_Activate` event:

```
Private Sub Form_Activate()
    Data1.Refresh
End Sub
```

This code makes sure the data entry fields on the form are updated with the most recent data from the database.

Now save and run the project. You'll first see a message telling you that the database is missing. (See Figure 16.13.)

FIGURE 16.13.

Custom error message in the Data1_Error *event.*

Next, you'll see the open file dialog wait for you to locate and load the requested database. (See Figure 16.14.)

FIGURE 16.14.

Locating the requested database.

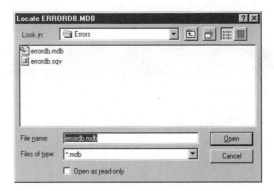

Finally, after you load the database, the data entry screen opens, ready for your input.

Database Errors with Microsoft Data Access Objects

If you use Microsoft data access objects instead of the Visual Basic data control, you need to add error-handling routines to your project. For example, if you want to create a dynaset using Visual Basic code, you need to trap for any error that might occur along the way.

Add the code in Listing 16.12 to the Form_Load event of frmData. This code opens the database and creates a dynaset to stuff into the data control that already exists on the form.

Listing 16.12. Adding code to the Form_Load event.

```
Private Sub Form_Load()
    '
    ' create recordset using DAO
    '
    On Error GoTo LocalErr
    '
    Dim ws As Workspace
    Dim db As Database
    Dim rs As Recordset
    Dim strSQL As String
    '
    strSQL = "SELECT * FROM Table2"
    Set ws = DBEngine.Workspaces(0)
    Set db = ws.OpenDatabase(App.Path & "\ErrorDB.mdb")
    Set rs = db.OpenRecordset(strSQL, dbOpenDynaset)
    Exit Sub
    '
LocalErr:
    MsgBox "<" & CStr(Errors(0).Number) & "> " &
    ➥ Errors(0).Description, vbCritical, "Form_Load Error"
    Unload Me
    '
End Sub
```

The code in Listing 16.12 establishes some variables and then opens the database and creates a new dynaset from a data table called Table2.

> **NOTE**
>
> Notice that instead of the Visual Basic Err object, the DAO Errors collection is used to retrieve the most recent database error. The Errors collection is only available if you have the Microsoft DAO library loaded using the Project | References option from the main Visual Basic 5 menu.

Because there is no Table2 in ERRORDB.MDB, you see a database error when the program runs. The error message is displayed, and then the form is unloaded completely. (See Figure 16.15.)

FIGURE 16.15.

Displaying an error message from the Form_Load *event.*

It is a good idea to open any data tables or files that you need for a data-entry form during the Form_Load event. That way, if there are problems, you can catch them before data entry begins.

Creating Your Error-Handling OLE Server

In the previous sections, you created several error handlers, each tuned to handle a special set of problems. Although this approach works for small projects, it can be tedious and burdensome if you have to put together a large application. Also, after you've written an error handler that works well for one type of error, you can use that error handler in every other program that might have the same error. Why write it more than once?

Even though Visual Basic requires error traps to be set for each sub or function, you can still create a generic approach to error handling that takes advantage of code you have already written. In this section, you'll write a set of routines that you can install in all your Visual Basic programs—the error-handling OLE server. This OLE server will offer some generic error-handling capabilities along with the capability to log these errors to a disk file and to keep track of the procedure call stack. These last two services can be very valuable when you encounter a vexing bug in your program and need to get additional information on the exact subroutines and functions that were executed before the error occurred.

To build the new error-handling OLE server, you need to start a new Visual Basic ActiveX DLL project. Name the default class module errHandler and set the project name to prjErrHandler. You also need to add a BAS module and a form to the project. The form acts as the new customized error dialog box. The BAS module holds a new user-defined type and some API definitions that are used with the customized error dialog box.

Building the errHandler Class

Building the errHandler class involves several steps. First, add some code to the general declaration section of the Class object. (See Listing 16.13.)

Listing 16.13. Adding code to the declaration section of the errHandler class.

```
Option Explicit
'
' error types
Enum errType
    erritem = 0
```

continues

Listing 16.13. continued

```
      errcoll = 1
End Enum
'
' return/option values
Enum errReturn
    errExit = 0
    errresume = 1
    errNext = 2
    errselect = 3
End Enum

'
' handler storage
Private errDefRtn As errReturn
Private errDefType As errType
'
```

The first two items in the declaration section define enumerated types. This special kind of user-defined type is a mix between a standard user-defined type and a public constant. Enumerated types make it easy to write well-documented code. Along with the enumerated types, you see two private variables declared for local use.

Next, you need to add some declaration code to the BAS module in your DLL project. This code defines a special custom data type that you can use to control the display of your custom error dialog box. The errHandler DLL allows you to access any possible help topics associated with the error messages, too. For this reason, the BAS module contains the WinHelp API declaration, which is used on the custom dialog box. Open the BAS module, set its Name property to modErrHandler, and enter the code in Listing 16.14 into the general declaration section of the module.

Listing 16.14. Adding code to the general declaration section of the modErrHandler BAS module.

```
Option Explicit

'
' define dialog data type
Public Type errDialog
    Message As String
    Buttons As Variant
    Title As String
    HelpFile As String
    HelpID As Long
    Return As Long
End Type
'
Public udtErrDialog As errDialog
'
' declare winHelp API
Declare Function WinHelp Lib "user32" Alias "WinHelpA" (ByVal hwnd As Long, _
  ByVal lpHelpFile As String, _
```

```
  ByVal wCommand As Long, _
  ByVal dwData As Long) As Long

Public Const HELP_CONTEXT = &H1
Public Const HELP_QUIT = &H2
```

That's all that you need to add to the modErrHandler. Next, you need to add code to the Initialize event of the errHandler class module. Add the code from Listing 16.15 to the
Class_Initialize event.

Listing 16.15. Adding code to the Class_Initialize event of the errHandler class.

```
Private Sub Class_Initialize()

    ' set starting values
    errDefRtn = errExit
    errDefType = errItem

    udtErrDialog.Buttons = ""
    udtErrDialog.HelpFile = ""
    udtErrDialog.HelpID = -1
    udtErrDialog.Message = ""
    udtErrDialog.Return = -1
    udtErrDialog.Title = ""

End Sub
```

This errHandler class has two public properties—the DefaultAction and DefaultType properties. These defaults were set in the Initialize event and can be overridden by setting the prop-
erties at runtime. Create the DefaultAction property (using Tools | Add Procedure) and add
the code from Listing 16.16 into the Property Let and Property Get routines.

**Listing 16.16. Defining the Property Let and Property Get routines for the DefaultAction
property.**

```
Public Property Get DefaultAction() As errReturn

    ' return default

    DefaultAction = errDefRtn

End Property
Public Property Let DefaultAction(ByVal vNewValue As errReturn)

    ' verify parm and store

    If vNewValue >= errExit Or vNewValue <= errselect Then
        errDefRtn = vNewValue
    End If

End Property
```

Note that the data type for the property is errReturn. This is one of the enumerated types defined in the declaration section of the class module. Next, create the Property Let and Property Get routines for the DefaultType property and enter the code from Listing 16.17 into the project.

Listing 16.17. Coding the Property Let and Property Get routines for the DefaultType property.

```
Public Property Get DefaultType() As errType
    '
    DefaultType = errDefType
    '
End Property
Public Property Let DefaultType(ByVal vNewValue As errType)
    '
    If vNewValue >= errcoll Or vNewValue <= erritem Then
        errDefType = vNewValue
    End If
    '
End Property
```

Finally, you're ready to write the main error-handling method. You can call this method from any VBA-compliant program. You pass the Visual Basic Err object (or database Errors collection) along with a few optional parameters that can control the behavior of the message dialog box. After the method is finished, a value is returned. You can use this value to control program flow and error recovery.

Create a new function method in your class module called errHandler and enter the code from Listing 16.18.

Listing 16.18. Coding the errHandler function.

```
Public Function errHandler(objErrColl As Variant,
    ➥ Optional intType As errType, Optional errOption As errReturn,
    ➥ Optional errRefName As String) As errReturn
    ' -----------------------------------------------
    ' produce msg and prompt for response
    '
    ' inputs:
    '    objErrColl  - DAO collection -OR- VBA Err object
    '    intType     - errType enum that describes objErrColl (coll or item)
    '    errOption   - errReturn enum sets dialog behavior
    '    errRefName  - string to reference caller
    '
    ' returns:
    '    errExit     - end program
    '    errResume   - try again
    '    errNext     - skip to next line
    ' -----------------------------------------------
    '
    Dim strMsg As String
    Dim strTitle As String
    Dim rtnValue As errReturn
    '
```

```
    ' retrieve action option
    If IsMissing(errOption) Then
        errOption = errDefRtn
    End If
    '
    ' retrieve reference name
    If IsMissing(errRefName) Then
        errRefName = ""
    Else
        errRefName = " from " & errRefName
    End If
    '
    ' build full message
    strMsg = errMsg(objErrColl, intType)
    '
    ' write it out, if allowed
    If errLogFlag = True Then
        LogError strMsg
    End If
    '
    ' evaluate things
    Select Case errOption
        Case errExit
            udtErrDialog.Title = "Exiting Program"
            udtErrDialog.Message = strMsg
            udtErrDialog.Buttons = Array("&Exit")
            frmErrDialog.Show vbModal
            rtnValue = errExit
            '
        Case errresume, errNext
            udtErrDialog.Title = "Error Message" & errRefName
            udtErrDialog.Message = strMsg
            udtErrDialog.Buttons = Array("&OK")
            frmErrDialog.Show vbModal
            rtnValue = errOption
            '
        Case Else
            udtErrDialog.Title = "Error Message" & errRefName
            udtErrDialog.Message = strMsg
            udtErrDialog.Buttons = Array("&Cancel", "&Retry", "&Ignore")
            frmErrDialog.Show vbModal
            rtnValue = udtErrDialog.Return
    End Select
    '
    ' give it back
    errHandler = rtnValue
    '
End Function
```

The code in Listing 16.18 calls a support function (errMsg) and a dialog box (frmErrDialog). You need to code these two remaining objects before you can test your error handler. Create a new function (errMsg) in the class module and enter the code from Listing 16.19 into the project.

Listing 16.19. Adding the errMsg support function.

```
Public Function errMsg(objErrColl As Variant, intType As errType) As String
    '
    ' build and return complete error msg
    '
    Dim strMsg As String
    Dim objItem As Error
    '
    strMsg = ""
    '
    If intType = errcoll Then
        For Each objItem In objErrColl
            strMsg = strMsg & "<" & CStr(objItem.Number) & "> "
            strMsg = strMsg & objItem.Description
            strMsg = strMsg & " (in " & objItem.Source & ")." & vbCrLf
        Next
    Else ' intType= errItem
        strMsg = "<" & objErrColl.Number & "> "
        strMsg = strMsg & objErrColl.Description
        strMsg = strMsg & " (in " & objErrColl.Source & ")"
        '
        udtErrDialog.HelpFile = objErrColl.HelpFile
        udtErrDialog.HelpID = objErrColl.HelpContext
    End If
    '
    errMsg = strMsg
    '
End Function
```

The main job of the errMsg routine is to build a complete error message for display to the user. To do this, errMsg needs to know whether the object that was passed was a single VBA Err object or the DAO Errors collection. That is why the errType parameter is included in the call. Also note that the errMsg method is declared as a Public method. You can call this method from your Visual Basic 5 programs, too. That way, even if you don't want to perform all the error-handling operations, you can use errMsg to get an improved error message for your use.

Coding the frmErrDialog Form

The last main piece of the errHandler class is a custom dialog box to display the error message and get input from the user. Often, you want to do more than just display the message and let the user click OK. You might ask them to retry the same process or ask if they want to ignore the error and continue. This dialog box not only displays the message and gives you an opportunity to get a response from the user, but it also allows you to provide an optional Help button to give the user greater support in discovering how to resolve the encountered error.

With the prjErrHandler project still open, add a form to the project. Use Table 16.4 and Figure 16.16 as guides in laying out the form.

Table 16.4. Control table for the `frmErrDialog` form.

Control	Property	Setting
VB.Form	Name	frmErrDialog
	BorderStyle	3 'Fixed Dialog
	Caption	Error Report
	ClientHeight	1755
	ClientLeft	45
	ClientTop	330
	ClientWidth	5460
	ControlBox	0 'False
	MaxButton	0 'False
	MinButton	0 'False
	ShowInTaskbar	0 'False
	StartUpPosition	2 'CenterScreen
VB.TextBox	Name	txtErrMsg
	BackColor	&H80000000&
	Height	1035
	Left	900
	Locked	-1 'True
	MultiLine	-1 'True
	ScrollBars	2 'Vertical
	Top	120
	Width	4395
VB.CommandButton	Name	cmdBtn
	Caption	&Help
	Height	315
	Index	3
	Left	4080
	Top	1320
	Visible	0 'False
	Width	1215

continues

Table 16.4. continued

Control	Property	Setting
VB.CommandButton	Name	cmdBtn
	Caption	&Ignore
	Height	315
	Index	2
	Left	2760
	Top	1320
	Visible	0 'False
	Width	1215
VB.CommandButton	Name	cmdBtn
	Caption	&Retry
	Height	315
	Index	1
	Left	1440
	Top	1320
	Visible	0 'False
	Width	1215
VB.CommandButton	Name	cmdBtn
	Caption	&OK
	Height	315
	Index	0
	Left	120
	Top	1320
	Visible	0 'False
	Width	1215
VB.Image	Name	Image1
	Height	600
	Left	120
	Picture	intl_no.bmp
	Stretch	-1 'True
	Top	120
	Width	600

FIGURE 16.16.

Laying out the frmErrDialog *form.*

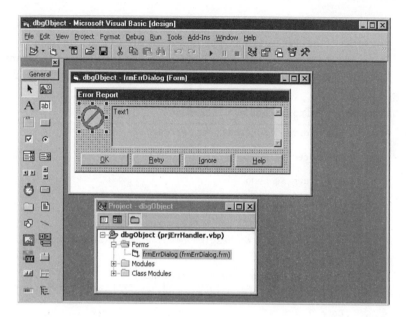

Be sure you build the command buttons as a control array and that you set their Visible properties to False. You'll write code to arrange and enable these buttons as needed at runtime.

You need to code only two events for this form. The Form_Load event handles most of the dirty work. Listing 16.20 shows the code that you should add to the Form_Load event.

Listing 16.20. Coding the Form_Load event of the frmErrDialog form.

```
Private Sub Form_Load()
    '
    Dim intBtns As Integer
    Dim intLoop As Integer
    '
    txtErrMsg = udtErrDialog.Message
    Me.Caption = udtErrDialog.Title
    '
    intBtns = UBound(udtErrDialog.Buttons)
    For intLoop = 0 To intBtns
        cmdBtn(intLoop).Caption = udtErrDialog.Buttons(intLoop)
        cmdBtn(intLoop).Visible = True
        cmdBtn(intLoop).Top = Me.ScaleHeight - 420
        cmdBtn(intLoop).Left = 120 + (1300 * intLoop)
    Next
    '
    ' check for help file
    If udtErrDialog.HelpFile <> "" Then
        cmdBtn(3).Visible = True
        cmdBtn(3).Top = Me.ScaleHeight - 420
        cmdBtn(3).Left = 120 + (1300 * 3)
    End If
    '
End Sub
```

The code in Listing 16.20 first sets the dialog caption and message box. Then, based on the properties of the udtErrDialog type, the buttons are arranged on the form. The only other code that you need to add to this form is the code that goes behind the command button array. Place the code from Listing 16.21 in the cmdBtn_Click event of the form.

Listing 16.21. Coding the cmdBtn_Click event.

```
Private Sub cmdBtn_Click(Index As Integer)
    '
    ' return user selection
    '
    Dim lngReturn As Long
    '
    Select Case Index
        Case 0
            udtErrDialog.Return = errExit
            lngReturn = WinHelp(Me.hwnd, udtErrDialog.HelpFile, HELP_QUIT, &H0)
            Unload Me
        Case 1
            udtErrDialog.Return = errresume
            lngReturn = WinHelp(Me.hwnd, udtErrDialog.HelpFile, HELP_QUIT, &H0)
            Unload Me
        Case 2
            udtErrDialog.Return = errNext
            lngReturn = WinHelp(Me.hwnd, udtErrDialog.HelpFile, HELP_QUIT, &H0)
            Unload Me
        Case 3
            lngReturn = WinHelp(Me.hwnd, udtErrDialog.HelpFile,
            ➥ HELP_CONTEXT, udtErrDialog.HelpID)
    End Select
    '
End Sub
```

The code in Listing 16.21 allows the user to select the command button appropriate for the moment. If the user clicks the Help button, the properties from the udtErrDialog type are used to fill in the parameters of the WinHelp API call.

That's all the code you need to create your errHandler ActiveX DLL. Save the project and then compile it (with File | Make prjErrHandler.dll). If it compiles without error, you are all set for a quick test!

Testing the ErrHandler Object Library

Start a new Visual Basic 5 Standard EXE project. Set the form name to frmTest and the project name to prjTest. Add a data control and a command button to the form. Refer to Figure 16.17 in laying out the form.

Next, you need to add a reference to the error-handler object library to your project. Select Project | References and locate and add the prjErrHandler DLL. (See Figure 16.18.)

FIGURE 16.17.

Laying out the frmTest *form.*

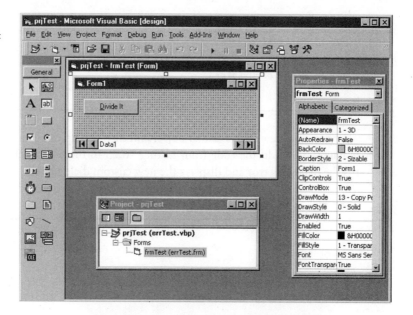

FIGURE 16.18.

Adding the error-handler object library to the project.

Now you can add a bit of code to the form that sets up the error handler and then causes an error to be handled. First, add the following line to the general declaration section of the form. This declares the object that contains the error handler:

```
Option Explicit
'
Public objErr As Object
```

Next, add the code from Listing 16.22 to the Form_Load event of the project.

Listing 16.22. Coding the Form_Load event.

```
Private Sub Form_Load()
    '
    Data1.DatabaseName = "junk"
    Set objErr = New errHandler
    '
End Sub
```

This code creates the new error-handler object and then sets up the data control with a bogus database name. Now add the code from Listing 16.23 to the Data1_Error event. This code intercepts the database error and displays the new custom dialog box.

Listing 16.23. Trapping the data-control error.

```
Private Sub Data1_Error(DataErr As Integer, Response As Integer)
    '
    Dim rtn As Long

    Response = 0
    rtn = objErr.errHandler(Errors, errcoll)
    '
End Sub
```

Save the form (frmTest.frm) and the project (prjTest.vbp) and run the code. You should see your new object library error dialog telling you about the database error. (See Figure 16.19.)

FIGURE 16.19.

The new Error *object library in action.*

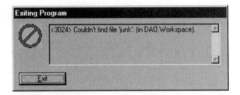

Add some code behind the Command1_click event that creates a divide-by-zero error. The code in Listing 16.24 does just that.

Listing 16.24. Creating a divide-by-zero error in code.

```
Private Sub Command1_Click()
    '
    On Error GoTo Localerr
    Dim rtn as Long
    '
    Print 6 / 0
    '
    Exit Sub
    '
```

```
Localerr:
   rtn = objErr.errHandler(Err, erritem, errresume,
   ➥ "prjTest.Form1.Command1_Click")
   Resume Next
   '
End Sub
```

When you save and run this code, click the command button to see the new error report. You should see that the Help button is active. Click the Help button to see Visual Basic 5 help on dealing with the divide-by-zero error. (See Figure 16.20.)

FIGURE 16.20.

Viewing help on the divide-by-zero error.

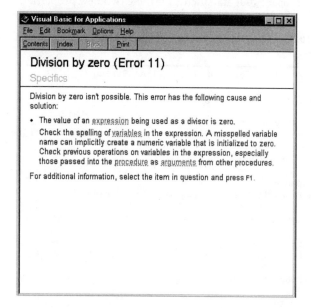

Now add an option that creates an error report file whenever the error handler is activated.

Adding Error Logs to the Error Handler

When errors occur, users often do not remember details that appear in the error messages. It's more useful to create an error log on disk whenever errors occur. This enables programmers or system administrators to review the logs and see the error messages without sitting right next to the user when the error occurs.

To build error-logging features into the existing errhandler class, you need to declare two new properties (LogFileName and WriteLogFlag), create a LogError method to write the errors to a disk file, add some code to the general declarations area and the Class_Initialize and Class_Terminate events, and add a few lines to the errHandler method to call the LogError method.

First, restart the errhandler DLL project and add the following code to the general declaration section of the class module.

```
' logging storage
Private errLogFileName As String
Private errLogFlag As Boolean
```

These lines of code appear at the end of the section. They declare local storage space for the new properties. Now use Tools | Add Procedure to add two new public properties to the class, LogFileName and WriteLogFlag. Listing 16.25 shows the code you need to add to the Property Let and Property Get statements for these two new properties.

Listing 16.25. Coding the Property Let and Get statements for the LogFileName and LogFlag properties.

```
Public Property Get LogFileName() As String

    LogFileName = errLogFileName

End Property
Public Property Let LogFileName(ByVal vNewValue As String)

    errLogFileName = vNewValue

End Property
Public Property Get WriteLogFlag() As Boolean

    WriteLogFlag = errLogFlag

End Property
Public Property Let WriteLogFlag(ByVal vNewValue As Boolean)

    errLogFlag = vNewValue

End Property
```

The LogFileName property holds the name of the disk file that holds the log records. The LogFlag property controls the status of the error logging. If the LogFlag property is set to True, then log records are created. Add the following code to the end of the Class_Initialize event. This sets the default values for the two new properties:

```
errLogFileName = App.EXEName & ".err"
errLogFlag = False
```

Now create a new private sub method called LogError and enter the code from Listing 16.26 into the routine. This is the code that actually creates the log entries.

Listing 16.26. Coding the LogError method.

```
Private Sub LogError(strErrMsg As String)
    '
    ' write error to disk file
    On Error GoTo LocalErr
    '
    Dim intChFile As Integer
    '
    intChFile = FreeFile
    Open errLogFileName For Append As intChFile
        Print #intChFile, Format(Now, "general date")
        Print #intChFile, strErrMsg
        Print #intChFile, ""
    Close intChFile
    '
    Exit Sub
    '
LocalErr:
    ' trouble with file stuff!
    Err.Raise vbObjectError + 1, "errHandler.LogError",
    ➥ "Can't write log file [" & errLogFileName & "]"
    '
End Sub
```

Notice that you added an error handler in this routine. Because you are about to perform disk operations, you need to be ready for errors here too! Notice also that the internal error is not displayed in a message box. Instead, the Raise method of the Err object generates a unique error number and description. This is sent back to the calling application for handling.

> **TIP**
>
> The Visual Basic FreeFile() function returns a number that represents the first available file channel Visual Basic uses to open the data file. Using FreeFile() guarantees that you do not select a file channel that Visual Basic is already using for another file.

All you need to do is add a call to the LogError method from the public errHandler method. Listing 16.27 shows the code you need to add in the routine. Make sure you add these lines of code right after the call to the errMsg function and just before the start of the Select Case statement.

Listing 16.27. Updating the errHandler method.

```
' build full message
    strMsg = errMsg(objErrColl, intType)
    '
    ' write it out, if allowed          '<<< new code
    If errLogFlag = True Then        '<<< new code
```

continues

Listing 16.27. continued

```
        LogError strMsg              '<<< new code
    End If                               '<<< new code
    '
    ' evaluate things
    Select Case errOption
```

That's the end of the code to add logging to the error handler. Save the project and compile the ActiveX DLL. Once the DLL is successfully compiled, close this project and open the test project you built earlier.

Open the Form_Load event of the frmTest form and add two lines to set the LogFileName and WriteLogFlag properties of the errHandler object. Listing 16.28 shows how to modify the code.

Listing 16.28. Modifying the Form_Load event to include error logging.

```
Private Sub Form_Load()
    '
    Data1.DatabaseName = "junk"
    Set objErr = New errHandler
    '
    objErr.WriteLogFlag = True
    objErr.LogFileName = App.Path & "\" & App.EXEName & ".log"
    '
End Sub
```

When you run the project, each error is logged to a file with the same name as the application in the same folder as the application. In the previous example, a file called errTest.log was created in the default folder. Listing 16.29 shows the contents of this error log file.

Listing 16.29. Contents of the errTest.log file.

```
05-Feb-97 5:27:01 AM
<3024> Couldn't find file 'junk'. (in DAO.Workspace).
05-Feb-97 5:27:08 AM
<11> Division by zero (in prjTest)
```

You can easily modify the layout and even the contents of the log reports. You need to change only a few lines of code in the LogError method.

Adding a Module Trace to the Error Handler

The final touch to add to your error-handler library is the option to track and print a module trace. A module trace keeps track of all the modules that are called and the order in which they are invoked. This can be very valuable when you're debugging programs. Often, a routine works just fine when it is called from one module but reports errors if called from another module.

When errors occur, it's handy to have a module trace to examine to help find the source of your problems.

You'll implement the module trace routines as a new `objclass` object in the `prjErrHandler` project. Reload the ActiveX DLL project and add a new class module to the project. Set its `Name` property to `TraceObject` and keep its `Instancing` Property to the default `5 - MultiUse`.

You need two new properties for this object (`TraceFileName` and `TraceFlag`) and a handful of new `Public` methods:

- ▪ `Push` adds a sub or function name to the call list.
- ▪ `Pop` removes a sub or function name from the list.
- ▪ `List` returns an array of all the names on the call list.
- ▪ `Dump` writes the complete call list to a disk file.
- ▪ `Show` displays the complete call list in a message box.
- ▪ `Clear` resets the call list.

First, add the code in Listing 16.30 to the general declarations area of the class module.

Listing 16.30. Declaring the `TraceObject` variables.

```
Option Explicit
'
' local property storage
Private trcFileName As String
Private trcFlag As Boolean
'
' internal variables
Private trcStack() As String
Private trcPointer As Long
```

Next, create the two new `Public` properties `TraceFile` and `TraceFlag` and enter the code from Listing 16.31 into the `Property Let` and `Get` statements for these two new properties.

Listing 16.31. Coding the `Property Let` and `Get` statements for the `TraceFile` and `TraceLog` properties.

```
Public Property Get TraceFileName() As String
'
    TraceFileName = trcFileName
'
End Property
Public Property Let TraceFileName(ByVal vNewValue As String)
'
    trcFileName = vNewValue
'
End Property
Public Property Get TraceFlag() As Boolean
'
```

continues

Listing 16.31. continued

```
    TraceFlag = trcFlag
    '
End Property
Public Property Let TraceFlag(ByVal vNewValue As Boolean)
    '
    trcFlag = vNewValue
    '
End Property
```

Now add the code from Listing 16.32 to the `Class_Initialize` event. This code sets the default values for the two public properties.

Listing 16.32. Coding the `Class_Initialize` event.

```
Private Sub Class_Initialize()
    '
    ' startup stuff
    trcFileName = App.EXEName & ".trc"
    trcFlag = False
    '
End Sub
```

Now it's time to code the various methods you need to manage call tracing in Visual Basic 5. First, create the `Public` sub methods `Push` and `Pop`. These two routines handle the details of keeping track of each function or sub as it is executed. Listing 16.33 shows the code for these two `Public` methods.

Listing 16.33. Coding the Push and Pop methods of the `TraceObject`.

```
Public Sub Push(ProcName As String)
    '
    ' push a proc onto the stack
    trcPointer = trcPointer + 1
    ReDim Preserve trcStack(trcPointer)
    trcStack(trcPointer) = ProcName
    '
End Sub
Public Sub Pop()
    '
    ' pop a proc off the stack
    If trcPointer <> 0 Then
        trcPointer = trcPointer - 1
        ReDim Preserve trcStack(trcPointer)
    End If
    '
End Sub
```

Create another `Public` sub method `Clear` and a `Public` function method `List`. Add the code from Listing 16.34 to the class.

Listing 16.34. Coding the List and Clear methods of the TraceObject.

```
Public Function List() As Variant
    '
    ' return an array of the trace log
    List = trcStack
    '
End Function
Public Sub Clear()
    '
    ' clear off the stack
    trcPointer = 0
    ReDim Preserve trcStack(0)
    '
End Sub
```

> **TIP**
>
> Notice the use of the Variant data type to return an array of items. This is a very efficient way to pass array data among Visual Basic methods.

Create a new Public sub called Dump. This writes the trace list to a disk file. Fill in the method with the code from Listing 16.35.

Listing 16.35. Coding the Dump method of the TraceObject.

```
Public Sub Dump()
    '
    ' write trace log to file
    Dim intFile As Integer
    Dim intLoop As Integer
    '
    intFile = FreeFile
    Open trcFileName For Append As intFile
        Print #intFile, "*** TRACE STACK DUMP ***"
        Print #intFile, "*** DATE: " & Format(Now(), "general date")
        Print #intFile, ""
        '
        For intLoop = trcPointer To 1 Step -1
            Print #intFile, vbTab & Format(intLoop, "000") &
            ➡": " & trcStack(intLoop)
        Next
        '
        Print #intFile, ""
        Print #intFile, "*** EOF"
    Close #intFile
    '
    Exit Sub
    '
LocalErr:
    Err.Raise vbObjectError + 3, "Trace.Dump",
    ➡ "Can't write trace file [" & trcFileName & "]"
    '
End Sub
```

Finally, create the `Public` sub method called `Show` and enter the code from Listing 16.36.

Listing 16.36. Coding the Show method of the TraceObject.

```
Public Sub Show()
    '
    ' show trace log in dialog
    '
    Dim intLoop As Integer
    Dim strMsg As String
    '
    strMsg = ""
    For intLoop = trcPointer To 1 Step -1
        strMsg = strMsg & Format(intLoop, "000")
        strMsg = strMsg & ": "
        strMsg = strMsg & Trim(trcStack(intLoop))
        strMsg = strMsg & vbCrLf
    Next
    '
    MsgBox strMsg, vbInformation, "Trace Stack"
    '
End Sub
```

Notice that the code in Listing 16.36 prints the call array in *reverse* order. This is the conventional way to print trace lists. The top entry shows the most recently executed routine and the bottom entry shows the first routine in this trace.

After adding this last code, save and compile the ActiveX DLL and then load your errTest project. After you load the frmTest form, add the following line of code to the general declarations area of the form:

```
Public objTrace As Object
```

Next, update the Form_Load event as shown in Listing 16.37. This adds use of the trace module to the project.

Listing 16.37. Updating the Form_Load event to include module tracing.

```
Private Sub Form_Load()
    '
    Data1.DatabaseName = "junk"
    '
    Set objErr = New errHandler
    Set objTrace = New TraceObject
    '
    objTrace.Push "Form_Load"
    '
    objErr.WriteLogFlag = True
    objErr.LogFileName = App.Path & "\" & App.EXEName & ".log"
    '
    objTrace.Pop
    '
End Sub
```

16

Note the use of objTrace.Push to add the name of the method to the trace stack. You should do this as soon as possible in the method code. Note the objTrace.Pop line at the very end of the method. This removes the name of the method from the stack just as the method is completed.

Add trace coding to the Command1_click event. Update your form's command1_Click event to match the one in Listing 16.38.

Listing 16.38. Updating the Command1_click event to use module tracing.

```
Private Sub Command1_Click()
    '
    On Error GoTo Localerr
    Dim varList As Variant
    Dim rtn As Long
    '
    objTrace.Push "Command1_Click"
    '
    Print 6 / 0
    '
    Exit Sub
    '
Localerr:
    '
    rtn = objErr.errHandler(Err, erritem, errresume,
    ➥ "prjTest.Form1.Command1_Click")
    '
    objTrace.Show
    objTrace.Pop
    Resume Next
    '
End Sub
```

Save this code and run the project. When you click the command button, you get a trace report on the screen. (See Figure 16.21.)

Figure 16.21.

Viewing the trace message.

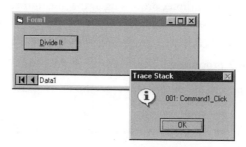

Notice that to add module tracing to a project, you only need to add a .Push line at the start of the routine and a .Pop line at the end of the routine. That is all you need to do in order to update the procedure stack for the program. For this to be really valuable, however, you have to do this for every routine you want to track.

In a real application environment, you don't want to show the procedure stack each time an error is reported. The best place for a stack dump is at exit time due to a fatal error. You should probably use the `TraceFile` option to write the stack to disk instead of displaying it to the user.

Other Error-Handling Options

Now that you have the basics of error handling under your belt, you can continue to add features to the generic error handler. As you add these features, your programs take on a more professional look and feel. Also, using options such as error report logs and procedure stack logs makes it easier to debug and maintain your applications.

Additional features that you can add to your error handler include the following:

- Add the name of the user or workstation address to the reports.
- If you created an error trap for common errors, such as error 53 `File Not Found`, add that recovery code to your generic handler. Now you can count on a consistent handling of common errors without adding code to every project.

Summary

This chapter covers all the basics of creating your own error-handling routines for Visual Basic applications. You learned that an error handler has three basic parts:

- The `On Error Goto` statement
- The body of the error handler code
- The error handler exit

You learned that an error handler has four possible exits:

- `Resume` re-executes the code that caused the error.
- `Resume Next` continues processing at the line immediately following the code line that caused the error.
- `Resume label` continues processing at the location identified by the `label`.
- `Exit` ends processing for the current routine, and `End` exits the program completely.

You learned how to use the `Err.Raise` method to flag errors without resorting to modal dialog boxes.

You learned about the major types of errors that you are likely to encounter in your program:

- General file errors include errors such as `File not Found` and `Invalid Path`. Errors of this type can usually be fixed by the user and then re-attempted. Use `Resume` as an exit for these types of errors.

■ Database errors include errors related to data entry mistakes, integrity violations, and multiuser-related errors, such as locked records. Errors of this type are best handled by allowing the user to correct the data and attempt the operation again. If you use the Visual Basic data control, you do not have to write error handlers; the data control handles them for you. For operations that do not use the data control, you need to write your own error-handling routines.

■ Physical media errors relate to device problems, such as unresponsive printers, downed communications ports, and so on. Sometimes users can fix the problems and continue (such as refilling the paper tray of the printer). Other times, users cannot fix the problem without first exiting the program. It is a good idea to give users an option of exiting the program safely when errors of these types are reported.

■ Program code errors occur due to problems within the Visual Basic code itself. Examples of program code errors include `Object variable not Set` and `For loop not initialized`. Usually, the user cannot do anything to fix errors of this type. It is best to encourage the user to report the error to the system administrator and then exit the program safely.

You also learned that you can declare a global error handler or a local error handler. The advantage of the global error handler is that it allows you to create a single module that handles all expected errors. The disadvantage is that because of the way Visual Basic keeps track of running routines, you cannot resume processing at the point the error occurred once you arrive at the global error handler. The advantage of the local error handler is that you can always use `Resume`, `Resume Next`, or `Resume label` to continue processing at the point the error occurred. The disadvantage of the local error handler is that you need to add error-handling code to every routine in your program.

Finally, you learned how to create an error-handler object library that combines local error trapping with global error messages and responses. The error-handler object library also contains modules to keep track of the procedures currently running at the time of the error, a process for printing procedure stack dumps to the screen and to a file, and a process that creates an error log on file for later review.

Creating Resources and Using the Resource Compiler

by Lowell Mauer

IN THIS CHAPTER

In this chapter, you will learn what a resource file is and what can be included in it. Also, you will learn the reasons you would use a resource file in your application. Once you understand these things, you will learn about the tools that are available from Visual Basic to create a resource file. You will learn about the different keywords used and what they do. Finally, you will see how to include in your Visual Basic application the resource file you have created and how to access the information stored in it.

Understanding Resources

Resources are the presentation data that your application uses. That is to say, no matter what your application does, it uses resources to interact with the user. Resources can be divided into two main groups: string and binary resources. String resources contain text string data such as `"Hello World"` or more realistically, `"Cannot Find Name in Address Book!"`. Binary resources can contain icons, bitmaps, cursors, sounds, videos, or any other data that is usually stored as binary information.

Why Use a Resource File?

Resource files allow you to collect into one central file all the version-specific text, bitmaps, sound, and so on for an application. This information is kept separate from the code, allowing better control over these resources. Resource files are used mostly to give a program the capability to change its strings, pictures, fonts, sounds, and so on, depending on input from the user. A good example of using resource files is when an application is sold in other countries. When an application is used in another country, it should display words and images in that country's language. Instead of rewriting the application for each country, the programmer can have a resource file that contains the different country-specific information and then, depending on input from the user, updates when the program is installed.

What Makes Up a Resource File?

A resource file is a plain text file that consists of

- Preprocessing directives
- Single-line statements
- Multiline statements

By using these commands (discussed later in this chapter) you will be able to take most of your memory-intensive resources and define them in a single resource definition file (`.RC`). Then, with the help of the Resource Compiler, you will compile the resource definition file and the actual resource files into a single binary resource (`.RES`) file.

For more information about the Resource Compiler, see the section "Using the Resource Compiler" later in this chapter.

Creating a Resource File

Because a resource file is nothing more than a simple text file, Notepad or WordPad can be used to create it. However, before you start the text editor, you should have done some homework about the application you are creating this resource file for. What this means is that you need to know most, if not all, of the resources you will be using in the application and which of these you want to include in the resource file. Of course, during the development of the application, you can always add more resources to the definition file and recompile it. The resources that you can include are divided into two types of resources, simple and complex. The simple resources are strings and message tables, and the complex resources are binary resources, such as bitmaps, sounds, and videos.

Starting the Definition File

The best way to understand the workings of a resource definition file is to build one. In this section, you will build a resource definition file that has resources in it from several of the different resource types. This is to give you a good understanding of using them. It will also show you how to use some of the command directives to set variables and flow logic in the definition file when it compiles. Then, after the resource definition file is finished, you'll learn how to compile this information into a finished resource file that Visual Basic can access. Finally, the last section will show you how to include this file into a sample Visual Basic program you will create and then how to access the resources defined within it.

The Definition Building Blocks

As mentioned earlier in this chapter, the resource definition file is created using three main groups of commands and statements. Before creating a definition file, it is a good idea to review these building blocks to understand their meaning.

Preprocessing Directives

Preprocessing directives are used to control what the Resource Compiler will do with the statements included in the definition file. The first directive listed allows you to define variable names and their values to be used later in the file. The remaining directives control which sections of the file will be compiled. The available preprocessing directives are

Directive	Description
#define	Defines a specified name by assigning it a given value.
#elif	Marks an optional block of script that could be compiled.
#else	Marks the final block of script as a series of If statements.
#endif	Marks the end of a conditional block.
#if	Conditionally compiles the script if the expression is true.

continues

Directive	Description
#ifdef	Conditionally compiles the script if a specified name is defined.
#ifndef	Conditionally compiles the script if a specified name is not defined.
#include	Copies the contents of a file into the resource-definition file.
#undef	Removes the definition of the specified name.

Single-Line Statements

Single-line statements define the resources that require only one line of information for the compiler to understand how to create the resource. These statements usually reference files such as bitmaps and icons:

Statement	Description
BITMAP	Defines a bitmap by naming it and specifying its filename.
CURSOR	Defines a cursor by naming it and specifying the file that contains it.
FONT	Specifies the name of a file that contains a font.
ICON	Defines an icon by naming it and specifying the name of the file that contains it.
LANGUAGE	Sets the language for all resources up to the next LANGUAGE statement or to the end of the file. When the LANGUAGE statement appears before the BEGIN in any multiline statement, the specified language applies only to that resource.
MESSAGETABLE	Defines a message table by naming it and specifying the name of the file that contains it.

Multiline Statements

Multiline statements are definitions that require more than one line to fully define the resource. These statements allow you to define complex resources such as the following:

Statement	Description
ACCELERATORS	Defines menu accelerator keys.
DIALOG	Defines a template that an application can use to create dialog boxes.
MENU	Defines the appearance and function of a menu.
RCDATA	Defines data resources to include binary data in the resource file.
STRINGTABLE	Defines string resources. String resources can be loaded from the executable file into the application.

> **NOTE**
>
> For more information on any of the directives or statements used in this chapter, see the RC.HLP file that comes with the Resource Compiler.

Putting the Resources into the File

For the purpose of this chapter, we will add to the resource file the most common resources that are used in an application:

- Stringtable
- Bitmap
- Icon

These should be enough to show you how to create a good resource definition file. To create the definition file, you should use whichever text editor you are most comfortable with. For the purpose of this chapter, the Notepad editor will be used. The first set of statements in the file will define values that will be used later in the file. Enter the following code into the text editor:

```
#define Str_GetName 1
#define Str_GetBirthdate 2
#define Str_DateError 3
#define Str_ExitMessage 4
#define NewIcon 5
#define Open 6
```

This code sets several variables to be used with the following command statements. This allows you to change the ID references without having to search the entire file for each occurrence. The next step is to add the stringtable that will contain the string statements your application will use. In this example, four strings will be created in this file. The first two will be used as labels in the application and the second two will be used as messages for the MsgBox statement. The following code sets these strings you should add this code next in the editor:

```
STRINGTABLE DISCARDABLE
BEGIN
        Str_GetName,      "Please Enter Your Name:"
        Str_GetBirthdate, "Enter Your Birthdate (mm/dd/yy)"
        Str_DateError,    "The date you entered is invalid."
        Str_ExitMessage,  "Okay to Quit?"
END
```

In this code, the option DISCARDABLE means that the resource can be discarded from memory if it's no longer needed.

The following section of code adds an `ICON` and a `BITMAP` resource to the definition file:

```
NewIcon    ICON C:\Temp\Point04.ico
Open       BITMAP C:\Temp\Calendar.bmp
```

Include the code in the definition file using whatever icon and bitmap you want and have available on your computer. Because of an interesting quirk in the Resource Compiler, you should keep the files' paths as short as possible.

Once you have defined all the resources you want in the file, save the file as `RESDEMO.RC` and then close the text editor. You are now ready to compile this definition file into the finished resource file.

Using the Resource Compiler

The Resource Compiler is a DOS-based program that allows you to compile the resource definition file into a `.RES` file. This allows you to use these resources in your Visual Basic application.

To start the Resource Compiler, use the `rc` command. What you need to specify in the command line depends on whether you are compiling resources, adding compiled resources to an executable file, or doing both. The syntax for the Resource Compiler is

```
rc /r [options] definition-file
```

The parameters for the Resource Compiler are

- `/r`—This parameter specifies that the `.RC` file will only be compiled, not linked to any executable.
- `/?`—Displays a list of `rc` command-line options.
- `/fo` *filename*—Uses *filename* for the name of the `.RES` file.
- `/v`—Prints progress messages.
- `/d`—Defines a symbol.
- `/l`—Sets the default language ID in hexadecimal.
- `/i`—Adds a path for `INCLUDE` searches.
- `/x`—Ignores `INCLUDE` environment variables.
- `/c`—Defines a code page used by National Language Support (NLS) conversion.
- `RC file`—Specifies the name of the resource definition file (`.RC`) that contains the names, types, filenames, and descriptions of the resources to be compiled.

To compile the completed definition file and name the compiled version `DEMO32.RES`, you would enter the following command at the DOS prompt:

```
RC /r /fo DEMO32.RES XXXX.RC
```

XXXX is the name of the `.RC` file that you have just created.

> **NOTE**
>
> If the resource file is already in use by your Visual Basic application, you will need to either close your Visual Basic project or remove the .RES file from your project when you re-create the resource file and then add it back.

Including Resource Files in Visual Basic

Now that you have a finished resource file, let's take a look at how to include it in a Visual Basic application and how to use the resources defined in it.

The first thing you need to do is start Visual Basic and create a new project. This application will have command buttons that display each of the strings defined in the resource file, either in a label control or in a message box. There will also be a picture control on the form to display the bitmap in. Finally, the icon will be loaded so that it is displayed as part of the command button that loaded it.

Adding the Controls

Place the PictureBox control, a Label control, and six command buttons on the form as shown in Figure 17.1.

FIGURE 17.1.

Initial placement of the controls on the form.

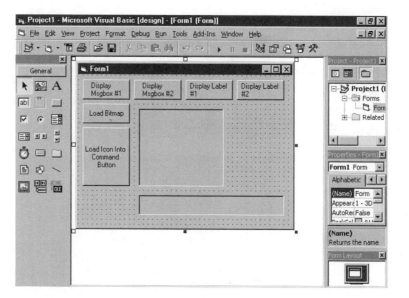

Change the Name and Caption properties of these controls as shown in Table 17.1.

Table 17.1. Setting the correct properties.

Old Name	New Name	Caption	Style
Command1	cmdMsgbox1	Display message box 1	N/A
Command2	cmdMsgbox2	Display message box 2	N/A
Command3	cmdLabel1	Display label 1	N/A
Command4	cmdLabel1	Display label 2	N/A
Command5	cmdBitmap	Load bitmap	N/A
Command6	cmdIcon	Load icon into command button	Graphical
Picture1	picBitmap	N/A	N/A
Label1	lblString	(Blank)	N/A

To have access to the resource file, you need to add it to the project. To do this, right-click on the project window and select the Add option to get the next pop-up menu. Now select Add File to have the Add File dialog box displayed. Locate the resource file that you just created and select it. It will now be displayed in the project window in the group Related Documents (see Figure 17.2).

FIGURE 17.2.

Confirming that the resource file is included in the Visual Basic project.

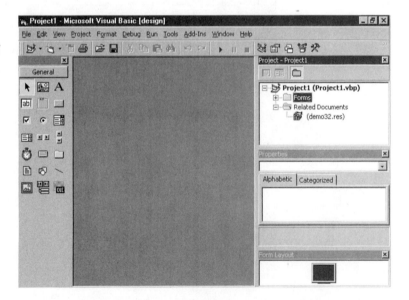

The only thing left to do is to insert the code that accesses the resource file and displays the information.

Visual Basic Resource Commands

Visual Basic has three commands that allow you to retrieve specific resources from the resource file. The syntax of each command is discussed in the following sections.

LoadResString

```
Lblprompt.caption = LoadResString(index)
```

The index parameter is required for the function to work. It can be either an integer value or a string that specifies the identifier (ID) of the data in the resource file.

LoadResPicture

```
PicFrame.Picture = LoadResPicture(index, format)
```

The index parameter is required for the function to work. It can be either an integer value or a string that specifies the identifier (ID) of the data in the resource file.

The format parameter is also required. The value or constant specifies the format of the data being returned, as described here:

Defined Constant	Value	Description
vbResBitmap	0	Bitmap resource
vbResIcon	1	Icon resource
vbResCursor	2	Cursor resource

LoadResData

```
StrHolder = LoadResData(index, format)
```

The index parameter is required for the function to work. It can be either an integer value or a string that specifies the identifier (ID) of the data in the resource file.

The format parameter is also required. The value can be the string name of a user-defined resource. The value or constant specifies the original format of the data being returned, as described here:

Format Value	Description
1	Cursor resource
2	Bitmap resource
3	Icon resource
4	Menu resource
5	Dialog box
6	String resource

continues

Format Value	Description
7	Font directory resource
8	Font resource
9	Accelerator table
10	User-defined resource
12	Group cursor
14	Group icon

Inserting the Code

Once you understand the Visual Basic command that you will be using, the code to use the resources in the resource file is quite easy. Listing 17.1 shows each of the control event routines that are needed to perform the necessary actions in the program.

Listing 17.1. FRMRESOURCE.FRM—Command button `Click` event routines to access the resource file.

```
Private Sub cmdBitmap_Click()
picBitmap.Picture = LoadResPicture(6, vbResBitmap) ' Display the Calendar Bitmap
End Sub

Private Sub cmdIcon_Click()
cmdIcon.Picture = LoadResPicture(5, vbResIcon) ' Display the Point04 Icon

End Sub

Private Sub cmdlabel1_Click()
lblString.Caption = LoadResString(1) ' Display the Str_GetName String
End Sub

Private Sub cmdlabel2_Click()
lblString.Caption = LoadResString(2) ' Display the Str_GetBirthDate String

End Sub

Private Sub cmdMsgbox1_Click()
MsgBox (LoadResString(3)) ' Display the Str_DateError String
End Sub

Private Sub cmdMsgbox2_Click()
MsgBox (LoadResString(4)) ' Display the Str_ExitMessage String

End Sub
```

The first and second command buttons will take the first or second strings, respectively, and use them as the text of a message box. The third and fourth command buttons will display one of two strings in the label on the form. The fifth command button will load the bitmap into the picture box, and the sixth button will add an icon to its own picture property.

Executing the Project

Now that the program is coded, the only thing left to do is test it. When you run the program, it should look similar to Figure 17.3 before you click on any command buttons.

FIGURE 17.3.

The running application before you execute any command buttons.

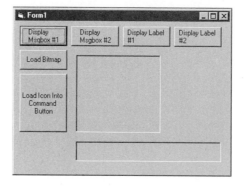

Now click each command button to see what happens. Your application should now look like the one shown in Figure 17.4.

FIGURE 17.4.

A sample program display after you execute all the command buttons.

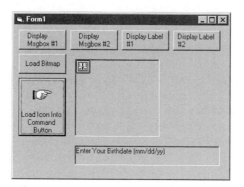

Summary

You have seen what goes into making a resource file and how to use it to make your Visual Basic application much more efficient when it executes. Also, you have seen how to create these resource files using the resource compiler that is included on the Visual Basic 5 CD-ROM.

Reusing and Sharing Components Using the Template Manager and Templates

by John D. Conley III

IN THIS CHAPTER

In previous versions of Visual Basic, it was a hassle to create customized projects and to add regularly used classes and code modules. For customized projects, you had to manually edit the sole default project template file, adding the references to components (OCX and DLL files) and other application files you tended to use over and over again for a particular application architecture. If this architecture changed, you would have to reconfigure the file for the new files. In the situation where you always added the same class, module, or form to a project, you had to do a file lookup in the File dialog, browsing through every directory tree until you found it. With the template services provided in Visual Basic 5, this reuse process is better automated.

What Are Templates?

Templates are groups of components that are saved to a predefined directory structure in the \vb directory when you install your VB environment. You might refer to them as *frameworks*. For instance, an automobile maker would have different car frames (templates) for different classes of cars. Whenever an automobile maker makes a car that is made up of a frame H, the automobile maker simply grabs that frame from its supply of body frames and runs it through the assembly line for that car class. Likewise, templates in VB provide a way for you to reuse components and to add them to projects. *Component*, in this case, refers not only to OCX controls, but to the physical file itself. In other words, the physical representation of every object in our application persists beyond the application in the form of files (otherwise known as components). This clarification may seem trivial, but when you use Visual Modeler (which now ships with Visual Studio Enterprise and the Enterprise Edition of Visual Basic 5), this definition becomes very helpful when designing component models that show the mapping of application objects to the physical file system.

The Benefits of Using Templates

It's probably a well-known fact that Visual Basic 5.0 still does not support inheritance in the classic sense of object-oriented inheritance (if that much). Although you can accomplish the benefits of inheritance through delegation (where a method on a client object simply calls a method of a server object to carry out all its own implementation), using VB templates provides a mechanism for simply inserting whole frameworks of classes into a new project. In addition, Microsoft ships what's called the *Template Manager* to help you with additional automated template reuse for general code, controls, and menus.

Why is reuse so important? Many companies have found that projects developed independently of other enterprise projects seemed to cost the company more in the long run. What's more, it costs companies more money than it's worth to try to dig through tons of code in search of salvageable, freestanding functions. This code mining process doubles where the code is spaghetti code. *Spaghetti code* is a body of programming code that lacks structure and organization and is only understandable to the programmer who created it. Spaghetti code is the most prevalent artifact of the programming process today and has led to many failed projects and monetary waste as a result of the inability to reuse such code. With well-designed class modules, menu controls, and projects readily available in the \Template subdirectory, your managers and clients will enjoy the increased productivity and lower costs that such reuse practices bring about. Each successive project becomes more productive and less costly because reusable classes, components, and projects have been identified and more effectively archived for easier access.

Using Templates for the First Time

It's pretty easy to use templates. The first thing you should do is become familiar with the \Template subdirectory of Visual Basic. Figure 18.1 shows a typical directory structure you'd get when you install Visual Basic (except for Code, Menus, and Controls, which we'll discuss later).

FIGURE 18.1.

For each type of template supported by Visual Basic, there is a corresponding folder (or subdirectory) under \Vb\Template.

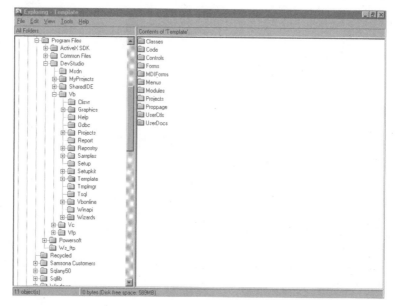

The Template Folders

Each folder under \Template is, in a sense, a type of template you can implement. Thus, you have a the following types of templates as part of your reuse arsenal:

- Class
- Code
- Forms
- MDI forms
- Modules

- Projects
- Proppage (a property page template for your ActiveX controls)
- User controls
- User documents

A View of Templates in VB

When you run Visual Basic, the Projects list of templates displays on the screen by default (see Figure 18.2).

FIGURE 18.2.

A list of project templates displays when you first run Visual Basic.

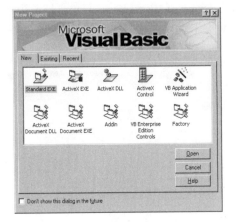

To view this list, simply run Visual Basic the way you normally run it. The New Project dialog displays. Notice the series of project template icons. Now click the Cancel button. We're going to add our own project template using one of the sample projects provided in Visual Basic. Go to the main Visual Basic directory and navigate to the `\Samples\CompTool\Dialer` subdirectory. Copy the files `Dialer.vbp` and `Dialer.frm` to the `\Template\Projects` subdirectory. From the Visual Basic IDE menu, choose File | New. You should see an icon for Dialer, as illustrated in Figure 18.3.

FIGURE 18.3.

Once you add the Dialer project to the `Projects` folder, you can reuse it as a template for future projects.

Double-click the Dialer icon. The Dialer project has now been instantiated into your current VB session. See how easy that is?

If you decide that you don't necessarily need every template type available, you can turn off the ones you don't want. To do so, choose Tools | Options from the menu. This brings up the Options dialog box. Select the Environment tab. You should see a dialog box shown in Figure 18.4.

FIGURE 18.4.

You use the Environ-ment tab to choose which types of templates to reuse.

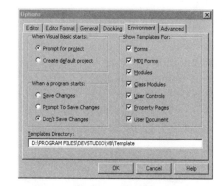

Notice the frame titled Show Templates For: on the right. Every template type is checked, meaning that by default, they are all available. Simply uncheck the ones you don't use and click OK. You might ask why this is important. It really depends on how often you reuse certain types of Visual Basic template items. For instance, if you usually add to your projects new code modules as opposed to existing ones, uncheck the Modules option. This way, when you choose Project Add Module from the menu or right-click on the Project listbox, you bypass the Add Module dialog box and a module is added by default. If you normally add new ones and reuse existing ones, leave the Module option checked.

Becoming Familiar with the Template Manager

In addition to the regular template services provided by the Visual Basic development environ-ment, Microsoft ships an unsupported add-in called the Template Manager. This add-in helps facilitate the reuse of snippets of code, menus that you commonly use, and controls that you often utilize in forms, user documents, and user controls. Once you install Template Manager, a subdirectory under the \Template directory is created for Code, Menus, and Controls. Any code you may have implemented for the menus and controls is preserved, as are the code snippets. When you first install Visual Basic 5, you're not made aware of this tool. In fact, you'd have to browse the installation CD pretty carefully to find it.

18

THE TEMPLATE
MANAGER AND
TEMPLATES

Installing the Template Manager

Although using the Template Manager adds more productivity to your enterprise projects, installing it is rather clumsy (which is perhaps because it is an unsupported tool). And if your licensed copy of Visual Basic was installed by a member of your company's network or software administration team, you'll have to hunt that person down to add the Template Manager. If you reuse menus and controls often, though, it might be worth the hassle.

Locating the Template Manager

The first step in installing this add-in is to get your Visual Basic CD. (If you really need to use Template Manager but don't want to wait several days or weeks before getting the CD from your software administrator, you might be able to get the `tempmgr.dll` file from a colleague in the same environment who already has it. This assumes that both of you have licenses for Visual Basic 5.) With the CD in your CD-ROM drive, browse to `Tools\Unsupprt\Tmplmgr` using Windows Explorer. The directory structure you see should resemble that in Figure 18.5.

FIGURE 18.5.

The folder that contains the Template Manager add-in files is not exactly easy to find, but will have the `tempmgr.dll` *file and the* `Template` *folder.*

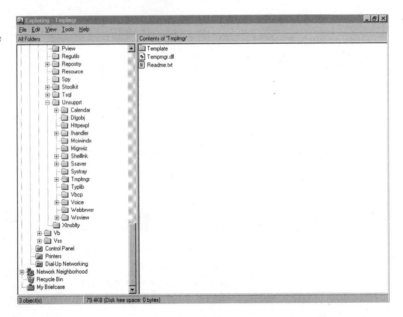

Copy the `Template` folder and the `tempmgr.dll` file to the Visual Basic root directory (where you installed VB). By default, the VB directory is `\Program Files\Vb`. Copying the template folder to the `\Vb` subdirectory adds the `Code`, `Menus`, and `Controls` folders to the existing template folders. The `tempmgr.dll` file is just inserted into the `Vb` directory.

Registering the Template Manager

The next installation step involves registering the add-in. For this, you'll need to use the RegSvr32.exe file. You can find a copy of it in the \Tools\RegUtils directory on your VB5 CD. To make the registration process as simple as possible, copy this executable to the Vb directory. Now bring up the MS-DOS prompt. If you're not familiar with this, click the Start button on the Windows 95 taskbar, move the mouse cursor to Programs, and then move the mouse cursor to and click on MS-DOS Prompt. You should see a dialog that resembles Figure 18.6.

FIGURE 18.6.

Using the MS-DOS Prompt dialog to register your Template Manager add-in.

Make sure the current directory shows the path to your Visual Basic root directory, where you just copied the templmgr.dll file. If is does not, you'll need to use the change directory DOS syntax CD *drive letter*:*directory* to point to the proper directory. Once you've got the right path, you can proceed to issuing the registration command. At the command line in the dialog box, type the following:

```
regsvr32 tempmgr.dll
```

and press the Enter key. You'll hear your computer cranking away, and then it should display a dialog box informing you that the registration process was successful (see Figure 18.7).

FIGURE 18.7.

After you enter the command to register the Template Manager add-in, the system will inform you that the process was successful.

Troubleshooting Installation Problems

If you were not successful, check for common grammatical mistakes that can occur when entering characters on the command line. Once you've corrected the mistakes, try the command again. If you're still not successful, you might try reinstalling Visual Basic or recopying the Template Manager files from your CD. The Template Manager is not supported, so Microsoft might not provide assistance. You might try one of the Visual Basic newsgroups at www.microsoft.com\vb or browse to the numerous Web sites that have Visual Basic content, such as www.samsona.com.

If that were not awkward enough, you're going to have to manually modify your VBADDIN.INI file in the \Windows directory (or wherever you installed your Windows 95 operating system files). If you're not comfortable with modifying initialization files and settings, find someone capable of doing it or simply don't use Template Manager.

The VBADDIN.INI File

The information contained in the VBADDIN.INI file helps Visual Basic load the add-ins supported by (or registered for) the Visual Basic development environment. To modify the VBADDIN.INI file, use Notepad or WordPad. Because of the extra information inserted by more robust word processors, you should not use Word to edit this file. At the end of the file, add the following line:

```
TempMgr.Connect=0
```

Save the revised VBADDIN.INI file and close the word processor. Now you're ready to use the Template Manager. If you already had Visual Basic running, save any existing projects, exit, and restart it.

> **WARNING**
>
> Using Template Manager may consume quite a bit of your memory and cause your Visual Basic session to become corrupt. Before using it, save any work you have opened in other applications and close them.

Using the Template Manager

Let's run the Template Manager. Run Visual Basic. From the menu, choose Add-Ins | Add-In Manager. The Add-In Manager dialog box is displayed (see Figure 18.8).

All the add-ins are listed in alphabetical order, where VB Template Manager is closer to the bottom. Check it by clicking on the checkbox next to VB Template Manager. Click OK.

FIGURE 18.8.

*The Add-In Manager
dialog facilitates the use
of standard and custom
add-ins, such as the
Template Manager.*

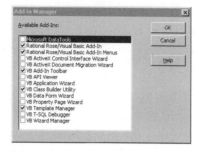

Where Are the Template Manager Services?

Your first temptation might be to choose Add-Ins from the menu to see the Template Manager. Not so fast there, partner. You won't find Template Manager features there. To find the Template Manager services, choose Tools from the menu, leaving the pop-up menu list intact. The Tools submenu pop-up should have items labeled Add Code Snippet, Add Menu, and Add Control Set.

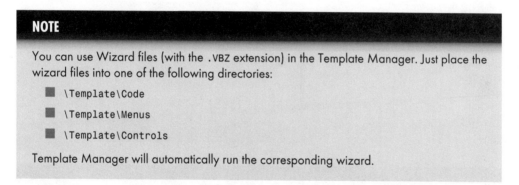

NOTE

You can use Wizard files (with the `.VBZ` extension) in the Template Manager. Just place the wizard files into one of the following directories:

- `\Template\Code`

- `\Template\Menus`

- `\Template\Controls`

Template Manager will automatically run the corresponding wizard.

Using the set of Template Manager tools is pretty easy. If you have a favorite code module you want to reuse, you can add it to the `\Template\Code` directory. Then choose Tools | Add Code Snippet. Of course, you can achieve the same thing with the already existent `\Modules` directory. Just add your code module to the `\Template\Modules` directory. That's why you probably won't get much value out of the Add Code Snippet service.

The Add Control Set Service

The Add Control Set service is not fully functional at this time. If you try to add its default control sets to an existing project, you will very likely encounter errors. The controls will eventually load into the current project, but not before a series of errors pop up. To use this service (when it works properly), add the controls you reuse often to a blank form, and save both the `.FRM` and `.FRX` files to the `\Template\Controls` directory. The Visual Basic Owners' Area of the

Visual Studio 97 on Microsoft's Web site (www.microsoft.com) has a newer version of Template Manager that should address some of these problems, but the Web site has been very busy and I have not had success in downloading it. This new and improved version will ship with subsequent versions of Visual Basic. For now, ignore this service.

The Add Menu Service

Perhaps the most beneficial Template Manager service is the Add Menu service. Of course, if you often reuse the same form that has the menu you want, you can simply place this form in the \Template\Forms directory. However, if you don't reuse the form, but do reuse the menu on the form, save the menu onto a blank form and save this form to the \Template\Menus directory. Be sure to have some code in each menu item. If you don't and you subsequently try to insert a custom menu template onto a new form, you will get an error. But even if you do get this error, you can usually click OK and ignore it. But you'll get this annoying error every time you try to use your custom menus. To use this service, choose Tools | Add Menu from the Visual Basic menu. Figure 18.9 shows the Add Menu dialog box you should see.

FIGURE 18.9.

Using the Add Menu feature to add a reusable menu component to your target form.

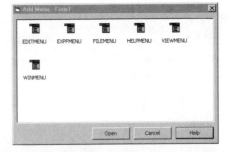

> **NOTE**
>
> Sometimes when you use the Template Manager, you might receive an error stating that no templates could be found. A peculiar trick (prescribed by Microsoft) is to choose Tools | Options from the menu. A dialog box appears. Simply click OK. This forces an update to the Registry.

Understanding Effective Component Reuse Strategies and Standard Interfaces

The Visual Basic environment provides very helpful facilities for reusing many types of custom-developed components (for example, menus, code modules, controls), as mentioned earlier. However, such reuse implementations are of no use if the components being developed are not properly planned and documented. Such planning does not occur magically overnight, but takes time. If you are a developer in a corporate enterprise environment, you won't have nearly as good a list of candidates for reuse on the first project as you would on subsequent projects. Trying to find reusable components during the first project is almost like trying to find the lowest common denominator of several fractions when you only have one fraction. It takes at least two projects to find suitable candidates for reuse, and with each subsequent project, your list of candidates will become finer, focusing on more obvious components that can be reused. A seasoned developer will likely have standard, reusable components in his or her arsenal since such a developer will have already identified reusable components after having worked on many projects. These components will usually be small, specialized components as opposed to bloated, unwieldy, and therefore ineffective components.

In addition to identifying candidates for reuse, you should also spend ample time on designing a proper interface on the components that support interfaces. Such components include class modules, as well as subs and functions in code modules, form modules, and ActiveX controls. An *interface* is the set of public methods (that is, subs and functions) and properties supported by a module. This is different from a module's accompanying *implementation*, which refers to a module's internal way of executing the service offered by the interface. So if you have a method called `displayMessage`, it might have the following interface:

```
Public Sub displayMessage(argString As String)

End Sub
```

and the following implementation:

```
Public Sub displayMessage(argString As String)
    MsgBox argString
End Sub
```

The interface is the name of the sub, `displayMessage`, as well as its argument (`argString`). The single line of code is the implementation. The outside world (that is, those other parts of your application that call this method) does not care how you implement the `displayMessage` interface. It only cares that the sub exists and is functional. So if you change the line of code to read

```
MsgBox "This is great"
```

this is okay, so long as the client expected to see this message. But if you change the name of the method from `displayMessage` to `showMessage`, the client users of the interface won't be too happy (and might take their business elsewhere). That is, when you change your interface, you will lose compatibility with those existing applications that still call `displayMessage`. This becomes especially important when, after you have made a great revision to the newer method, you try to use it in a previous application that still references the old interface. None of the template services in Visual Basic can help you in designing reusable components. The key to reusability, then, is consistency, backward compatibility, and sufficient documentation so that others on a project team can also benefit from reuse.

Summary

In this chapter you have learned what Visual Basic templates are and how they are implemented in the Visual Basic development environment. You have seen the directory structure of the various types of templates, and read some of the key benefits of using templates. You have been introduced to the Template Manager, an important template service add-in that supplements the standard Visual Basic templates. You have learned how to add menus, controls, and project and class templates. Finally, you learned the importance of planning components for reuse and why building well-defined, consistent interfaces is the key to successful component reuse.

File Input and Output Made Easy

by Greg Perry

IN THIS CHAPTER

Files provide long-term storage of your application's data. By learning how to manage your application's files properly, you will better use data files that keep track of data your applications need to monitor.

Visual Basic programmers view file *I/O* (input/output) in different ways depending on their file needs. Some programmers require only short-term simple data files, whereas other programmers need to interface their Visual Basic applications with a database system such as one created with Microsoft Access or Paradox.

This chapter concentrates on simple, non-database data files and explores ways you can integrate such files into your applications. You will see that Visual Basic includes a wide variety of commands and functions that let you manipulate files and directories.

The highlights of this chapter include the following:

- Files come in various formats, and the file formats that your applications access depend on the nature of those files and how your program interacts with them.
- Visual Basic includes several commands and intrinsic functions that let you manage files and directories.
- You can set and read the various file attributes such as the archive and the hidden file attributes. These attribute capabilities let your Visual Basic application read any kind of file that might reside on your system.
- Before you can read from or write to a file, you must prepare that file for access with the Open statement. A subsequent Close statement releases the file for other processes.
- The Write#, Get#, Line Input#, and Input# statements perform simple I/O to and from files.
- When you search for data in a file, fixed-length file records you create with VB's Type statement make the processing go smoothly.

Managing Files

A *file* is a collection of related information. Several kinds of files exist. Here are just a few:

- Data files hold your applications' data.
- Program files contain executable applications.
- Database files contain organized tables that work together to provide information in a predetermined, organized order.
- Visual Basic application files hold form, module, and project descriptions.
- Icon and font files describe icons and fonts on your system.

■ Graphics files describe a picture displayable with a Visual Basic control such as the picture box or image control. You'll often scan these images into your system, download them from an online service, or create them with a paint program.

■ System files hold operating system information needed to make your computer interact properly with its peripherals.

■ Flag files contain indicators that determine how certain applications behave. A flag file is often just a simple, sequential data file.

■ Registry files hold system and application information. Your Visual Basic code should never directly modify the Registry file because system problems could easily appear if you inadvertently changed the Registry.

This chapter is most concerned with the first kind of file, the data file. You'll learn how to manage, create, and delete files.

Although many applications require data files, not every application requires the organized and rigid database files that Visual Basic also supports. Sometimes an application needs to track only a few items of data, and for efficiency reasons, you may decide that simple, non-database text files (often called *flat files*) provide all the external data capabilities you need.

Managing Directories

The concepts you will learn about in this and the next few sections apply to all kinds of files. As most readers of this book already know, PC users organize their files in directories. Directories are often called *folders* in Windows 95 and Windows NT terms. By organizing files that go together in these directory folders, you can easily traverse your disk drives and locate the data you need.

NOTE

In today's world of interconnected, networked, and online computing, your data may be located on a local disk, on a network server's disk, or on a computer in a foreign country. Organizing such massive information into a tree-structured, organized set of drives and directories becomes even more important than in the days when a single floppy disk drive was the standard medium for data.

As a Visual Basic programmer, you can organize the data files your applications create in folders. You might want to create a folder for an application's data files or for various users who log into your password-protected application.

To create a folder, use the MkDir command:

```
MkDir strPath
```

TIP

Fortunately, many of Visual Basic's directory commands have similar commands in MS-DOS. Therefore, if you're familiar with MS-DOS, you will already be somewhat familiar with the VB directory-related commands you will learn about here.

WARNING

Unlike their MS-DOS equivalents, VB's directory-related commands have no abbreviated versions. Therefore, MD is synonymous with MkDir in MS-DOS, but not in Visual Basic.

The *strPath* string argument is the name of the directory folder you want to create. Therefore, if you want to create a new folder named Acctg\Fred in the root directory of the current disk drive, you can do so with the following statement:

```
MkDir "\Acctg\Fred"  ' New in the root directory
```

As with all MS-DOS and Windows drive, path, and file descriptions, you can specify the drive, directory, and filename using uppercase or lowercase characters.

Visual Basic respects the standard tree-structured directory that MS-DOS supports. The initial backslash ensures that the new folder appears in the root directory. If you want to create a new folder in the *current* directory (the directory from which the user ran the application), you omit the initial backslash:

```
MkDir "Acctg\Fred"   ' New in the current directory
```

NOTE

Remember that *folder* and *directory* are terms now used interchangeably.

MkDir always creates the new folder on the current disk drive (the drive that was active when the user started the application). If you want your application to create the folder on a specific disk drive, you should specify that drive in the path:

```
MkDir "d:\Acctg\Fred"   ' New in D's root directory
```

TIP

You can use full network paths to create folders on external, networked disk drives.

If you need to know the current directory to use in a file listbox or to check against a saved directory name, use the intrinsic CurDir() function. CurDir() returns, as a string, the current full directory path. The format of CurDir() is

```
CurDir[(strDrive)]
```

The brackets indicate that the argument is optional; and if you don't specify the argument, you should omit the parentheses. The following statement stores the current directory in the string variable named strMyDir:

```
strMyDir = CurDir    ' Save current directory
```

When you don't specify the drive argument, CurDir() uses the current drive that was active when the user started the application. If you specify a disk drive argument (as a string), CurDir() returns the current directory of the drive you specify:

```
strMyDir = CurDir("E:") ' Save E:'s current directory
```

If you want to change the current directory, use VB's ChDir command:

```
ChDir strPath
```

When Visual Basic executes a ChDir statement, VB changes the current directory to the one you specify with the string argument. The CurDir() function then returns the same directory path. The following statement changes the current directory to the one named \Programs:

```
ChDir "\Programs"
```

> **NOTE**
>
> All of VB's directory- and file-related commands and functions support long filenames that can serve as file and directory names starting in Windows 95.

> **WARNING**
>
> ChDir changes the directory on the current drive or on a different drive if you specify a drive name inside the ChDir argument. ChDir does *not*, however, change the default drive. The current drive always remains the default drive; if you specify a drive name inside ChDir's argument, the statement changes the default directory on that drive, but the current drive remains the default drive.

Use RmDir to remove a directory folder. The folder *must be empty*, or you will receive a runtime error (trappable with an On Error Goto statement). Visual Basic protects you so that you don't inadvertently remove a directory that contains files.

> **TIP**
>
> The `Kill` command, described in the next section, describes how you can erase files from a folder so you can then delete the folder.

Here is the format of `RmDir`:

```
RmDir strPath
```

If you specify a drive inside the `RmDir` command's string argument, you can remove a folder from that disk drive (or even from another computer if you use network notation to designate another computer). The following statement removes the directory named `Temp Files` from the directory named `Data`:

```
RmDir "\Data\Temp Files"
```

Deleting Files

The `Kill` command erases files from any drive or directory. Use `Kill` to erase files from a folder you need to remove. Only after you erase all the folder's files can you then remove the folder with `RmDir`. You can embed the standard MS-DOS wildcard characters, * and ?, to represent multiple characters and single characters.

> **WARNING**
>
> You cannot remove folders with `Kill`; you can only remove files. Do not attempt to erase an open file, or `Kill` will return a runtime error (trappable with `On Error Goto`).

The following command erases all files from the specified directory of drive D:

```
Kill "D:\Acctg\Kim\*.*"
```

Checking for Folders, Files, Volumes, and Attributes

The `Dir()` function lets you check for the presence of a certain file, folder, set of files, set of folders, volume name, or file *attribute* that describes the nature of the file. Here is the format of `Dir()`:

```
Dir[(strPath[, strAttributes])]
```

You *must* specify the first string pathname argument the first time you call `Dir()` from any application. The following statement returns the first file found (in no particular order) that matches the *strPath* wildcard argument:

```
strFound = Dir("C:\*.bat")
```

strFound holds the first file in drive C's root directory that has an extension of bat. If you then called Dir() again (with no argument to indicate that the previous argument is still in effect), strFound holds the next file that contains the extension bat.

> **TIP**
>
> Use a loop to collect all matching files in a string array and sort the array if you need the files in alphabetical order.

Dir() keeps returning filenames until no more matching files are found. When Dir() returns a null string, "", your program knows that no other files remain in that directory that match the argument. You *must* specify an argument once Dir() returns a null string, or Dir() returns a runtime error (trappable with the On Error Goto statement).

Dir() is useful to determine whether a file exists. For example, if you need to create a data file named Orders.Dat if the file does not already exist, you could begin the coding with something like this:

```
If (Dir("Orders.Dat") = "") Then
   ' Put code here to create the file
Else
   ' File already exists
End If
```

Use Dir()'s second argument if you want to collect information about files, paths, drives, or volumes. Table 19.1 lists the possible named constants you can use for the second argument.

Table 19.1. Dir() named constants for the attribute argument.

Attribute	Value	Description
vbNormal	0	A normal file such as a data file
vbHidden	2	A hidden file that does not appear in the directory
vbSystem	4	A system file such as MSDOS.SYS
vbVolume	8	A volume name
vbDirectory	16	A directory (folder)

Suppose you want to know the volume label of drive D. You can find the label with the following Dir() function call:

```
strVolName = Dir("D:", vbVolume)
```

If you wanted to see whether a directory holds additional subdirectories, you could call `Dir()` as follows:

```
If (Dir("*.*", vbDirectory) = "") Then
    ' Directories exist
End If
```

In the same fashion, you can use the `vbSystem` or `vbHidden` named constants to see whether one or more files have the special system or hidden file attributes.

Visual Basic supports yet another function that specifically returns all attribute information for a file. The `GetAttr()` function returns one or more values from Table 19.2. As with any function, `GetAttr()` returns only a single value, but the value is the sum of one or more values from Table 19.2.

Table 19.2. Named constants returned by `GetAttr()`.

Attribute	Value	Description
vbNormal	0	A normal file, such as a data file.
vbReadOnly	1	A read-only file.
vbHidden	2	A hidden file that does not appear in the directory.
vbSystem	4	A system file, such as MSDOS.SYS.
vbDirectory	16	A directory (folder).
vbArchive	32	The file's backup bit is not yet set, so the file has changed since the most recent backup.

To determine exactly which attributes are set if multiple attributes exist for a file, you must use the `And` operator to test for the individual attributes from Table 19.2. For example, the following `If` statement determines whether the file is both a system file and a hidden file:

```
If (GetAttr(strTestFileName) And vbHidden And vbSystem) Then
    ' If logic flows here, file is both hidden and a system file
```

`GetAttr()` returns 0 (false) if the attribute (or attributes) you specify is not set for the file being tested.

Changing File Attributes

Whereas the `GetAttr()` function returns a file's attributes, the `SetAttr` command sets a file's attributes. Here is the format of `SetAttr`:

```
SetAttr strPath, intAttributes
```

The *strPath* argument must specify the file (with an optional path to the file) whose attributes you want to set. *intAttributes* must be one or more of the values from Table 19.3. If you want to set more than one of Table 19.3's attributes for the file, you must add the values together.

As with most of the file-management commands and functions, you cannot set the attributes for a file that's currently open.

Table 19.3. Named constants set with `SetAttr`.

Attribute	Value	Description
vbNormal	0	A normal file, such as a data file (the default).
vbReadOnly	1	A read-only file.
vbHidden	2	A hidden file that does not appear in the directory.
vbSystem	4	A system file such as `MSDOS.SYS`.
vbArchive	32	Resets the file's backup bit so the file appears not to be backed up.

Suppose your application changed the contents of a data file. You can ensure that the file's archive bit is set by coding `SetAttr` like this:

```
SetAttr "C:\Data\MoneyQtr.1", vbArchive
```

Renaming Files and Directories

Use the `Name` statement to rename files and folders:

```
Name strOldName As strNewName
```

You cannot rename files that are currently open, and both names (the old and the new) must reside on the same drive.

The following statement renames a file named `DataCurrent.dat` to `DataOld.dat`:

```
Name "DataCurrent.dat" As "DataOld.dat"
```

TIP

If the path to the old filename differs from the new path, Visual Basic moves the file from the old location to the new directory. You cannot use `Name` to copy files, only to move them. If you want to copy a file to another location, use the `FileCopy` statement, described in the next section.

WARNING

You cannot move folders from one location to another. In addition, the `Name` statement does not support wildcard characters in the old or the new path- or filenames.

19

FILE INPUT AND OUTPUT MADE EASY

Copying Files

Use the `FileCopy` statement to copy one file to another. Here is the format of `FileCopy`:

```
FileCopy strSource, strDestination
```

The `strSource` argument must contain a valid pathname and file, and `strDestination` must contain the target file and the pathname that receives the copy. As with most of the file-related commands and functions, you cannot copy a file that is currently open.

> **TIP**
>
> If your application is about to copy a large file, or any file, to a floppy disk drive, insert code to change the mouse cursor to an hourglass before the `FileCopy` statement so your users will know that the computer is operating and not halted. Change the cursor back to a mouse pointer once the copy operation completes.

Reading a File's Date and Time Stamp

The `FileDateTime()` function returns the date and time (in a `Variant` `Date` data type) when the file was created or last modified. `FileDateTime()`'s only argument is a string expression that holds the file and the optional pathname to the file.

The following statement returns the date and time when the file named `Autoexec.bat` in drive C's root directory was last updated:

```
varLastMod = FileDateTime("C:\Autoexec.bat")
```

Creating, Reading, and Writing Files

Visual Basic cannot create or access a file until you direct Visual Basic to the location of the file. If your user is selecting a file, you can display the File Open dialog box to give the user the capability to change drives, folders, and filenames easily. When your application accesses a file that the user doesn't know about, such as a data file that holds internal and temporary program data, your program must supply the drive, folder, and filename.

> **TIP**
>
> Unless your application creates an internal data file that the user does not need to know about, you almost always display the File Open dialog box to ask the user for the location and name of the file needed. Once your application changes the file, you use the File Save dialog box to save those changes. Chapter 24, "Leveraging Windows: Using the Common Dialog Control," explains how to set up standard File Open and File Save dialog boxes and respond to their results.

Opening Files

The Open statement performs various tasks such as locating a file, making sure that the file exists if needed, and creating some folder entries that manage the file while the file is open. A Visual Basic application always has to open a file, using Open, before the program can create, read, or write data to the file.

Open does for Visual Basic what an open file drawer does for you when you want to retrieve information from a filing cabinet. The Open statement locates the file and makes the file available to Visual Basic. If you want to read a file and the file does not exist, Open returns a runtime error letting you know that the path or filename is incorrect. The error is trappable with the On Error Goto statement.

Here is Open's format:

```
Open strFileName [For Mode] As [#]intFileNumber
```

The *strFileName* must be a string value or variable that holds a filename with an optional path and disk drive. The filename must reside on the default drive or folder unless you specify the full path to the file in *strFileName*.

> **TIP**
>
> Use the CurDir() function described earlier in this chapter if you want to append the currently active folder's name inside the *strFileName* string argument.

The *Mode* value must be a named value from Table 19.4. For completeness, this table contains the two random-access mode values Binary and Random, but these modes are usually better handled by the Visual Basic's database routines that use the special data-bound controls in Visual Basic. *Mode* tells Visual Basic exactly what your program expects to do with the file after Visual Basic opens the file.

Table 19.4. Possible *Mode* values for the Open statement.

Mode	Description
Append	Lets your application add data to the end of the file if the file already exists. If the file does not exist, your application creates the file so that your program can write new data to the file.
Binary	Opens non-text files for input or output and allows for file access at the byte level.

continues

19 FILE INPUT AND OUTPUT MADE EASY

Table 19.4. continued

Mode	*Description*
Input	Opens an existing file so that your program can read data from the file using one of the file-input commands and functions described throughout the rest of this chapter.
Output	Lets your application create a file and write data to the file. If the file does not exist, Visual Basic creates the file. If the file does exist, Visual Basic first erases the existing file and creates a new one under the same name, thereby replacing the original one.
Random	Lets your application open a file for both reading and writing. You don't have to close the file to change direction of the I/O, and you can read the file or write records to the file in any record order.

WARNING

If you open a file for input and the file does not exist, Visual Basic issues a runtime error message. You can trap this error with the On Error Goto statement. As long as you use a standard File Open dialog box to get the file's name and location, Visual Basic never issues an error because the dialog box forces the user to select a file that exists or cancel the selection operation entirely.

TIP

You can use the Dir() function to see if the file exists before you open a file in Open mode. Dir() lets you know if the file exists so that you do not inadvertently overwrite an existing file.

The pound sign, #, is optional, although most Visual Basic programmers do specify the pound sign out of habit. (Some previous versions of the BASIC language required the pound sign.) The *intFileNumber* value represents a number from 1 to 255 and associates the open file with that number.

WARNING

Errors can occur throughout any file I/O operation. The user can leave a floppy disk drive door open, a disk can go bad, a file that your application expects to exist might not exist, or you might attempt to rename a file that's currently open or that does not exist. Always attempt to trap every possible error with the `On Error Goto` command, as many sections of this chapter suggest. If you do not trap and handle such errors inside the program, your users get nasty runtime error messages, and your application appears to be buggy even if the error really occurred due to a user mistake.

After you open a file successfully (assuming that there are no errors), the rest of the program uses file I/O commands and functions to access the file. The file number (sometimes called the *file channel*) stays with the file until you issue a `Close` command that releases the `intFileNumber` and makes the number available to other files.

Assign a unique file number to each file you open. If your application uses multiple files, you can open more than one file within a single application as long as all open files have different file numbers. Each command that accesses one of the files directs its activity toward a specific file using that file's `intFileNumber`. The following `Open` statement creates and opens a data file on the disk drive and associates the file to the file number 1:

```
Open "c:\MyData\Acctg2ndQtr.dat" For Output As #1
```

The `Output` mode indicates that the file is created new with this `Open` statement. If you know that the file already exists and you need to add to that data file, you use the `Append` mode to add to the file with this `Open` statement:

```
Open "c:\MyData\Acct2ndQtr.dat" For Append As #1
```

NOTE

As you can see, the `Open` statement's mode prepares the file for the type of processing your application will perform.

If the `#1` `intFileNumber` argument is in use by another file that you opened earlier in the application, you can assign the open file a different file number:

```
Open "c:\MyData\Acct2ndQtr.dat" For Append As #2
```

Any currently *unused* file number works; you can't associate more than one file at a time to the same `intFileNumber` value.

The following Open statement opens the same file for input. Such a statement is useful if another application needs to use the file's data you recorded in a previous application:

```
Open "c:\MyData\Acct2ndQtr.dat" For Input As #2
```

Locating File Numbers

A useful intrinsic function often used in conjunction with Open is the FreeFile() function. FreeFile() accepts no arguments, so don't type the parentheses after the function name when you use the function. (As is common in books, this chapter keeps the parentheses after FreeFile() when describing the function so you'll know FreeFile() is a function and not a command or method.) FreeFile() returns the next available file number value. For example, if you've already used file numbers 1 and 2 for two open files in an application, the next value returned from FreeFile() is 3.

TIP

Use FreeFile() when you write general-purpose subroutine and function procedures that need to open files. Such procedures often need to be called from more than one routine in an application. Each calling location might open a different number of files at any one time.

FreeFile() is not affected by local and global variable issues. Any procedure can determine the value of the next available file number:

```
intFileNum = FreeFile
```

Subsequent Open (and Close) statements can use the file number FreeFile() returns. No matter how many files are open, the procedure always uses the *next* file number in line to open its file.

WARNING

Do *not* use FreeFile() inside the Open statement like this:

```
Open "c:\MyData.Dat" For Output As FreeFile   ' Bad!
```

Although such a statement will work, you won't know which file number the application associated with the file! Always store the current return value of FreeFile() in a variable and use that variable in the Open statement so subsequent I/O to that file properly locates the file when referencing the file by its file number.

In conclusion, Open associates files using file numbers with which the rest of the program accesses the file. The *Mode* values determine how Visual Basic uses the file. If you want to write to a file, you can't use the Input mode, and if you want to read from a file, you can't use Output or Append.

Closing Files When Finished

VB's `Close` statement closes files you previously opened. `Close` closes a file by writing any final data to the file, releasing the file to other applications, and giving the file's number back to your application in case you want to use that number in a subsequent `Open` statement. Eventually, every program that opens files should close those files.

Visual Basic supports two `Close` statement formats:

```
Close [[#]intFileNumber] [, ..., [#]intFileNumber]

Close
```

The first `Close` format closes one or more open files, specifying the files by the file numbers you used to open the files. The pound sign is optional in front of the file numbers. The second form of `Close` closes *all* files that are currently open. `Close` closes any open file no matter what mode you used to open the file. Even if no files remain open at the time of the `Close`, the second form of `Close` returns no errors.

You can open and close the same file more than once within the same application. If you create a file by opening the file with `Output` mode and then close the file, you can reopen the same file in the same program in `Input` mode to read the file.

> **TIP**
>
> If your application creates critical data files, close the files as soon as your application finishes writing the last value to the file. A power failure can result in a loss of open file data and, even worse, corruption of the entire data file. Although power failures might be rare, you can easily lose power if someone trips over your power cord or knocks a cable loose from the back of your computer. By closing the file as soon as you can, you guard against such loss.

The following statement closes the two open files that were opened and attached to file numbers 1 and 3:

```
Close 1, 3   ' Closes two files
```

The following statement closes all files no matter how many are open:

```
Close   ' Closes ALL files
```

Remember that a single `Close` closes all open files, but you can specify file numbers whenever you need to close one or more files but leave other files open.

If you fail to close one or more files, the operating system closes all open files for you when your program terminates. Relying on the operating system to close open files, however, is messy and consumes resources such as memory and file handles that other applications might need.

Remember that today's computing environments are often networked and are usually *multitasked* (running two or more programs at the same time in different windows). The longer you keep files open that could be closed, the more resources your application takes away from other tasks that need those resources to run efficiently.

> **NOTE**
>
> Visual Basic supplies the `Reset` statement, which performs the same file-closing operation as the second form of `Close`. Most programmers use `Close` and not `Reset` because of `Close`'s mirror-image relationship to `Open`.

Writing to Files with `Write#`

The `Write#` command is perhaps the best command for writing data to an open data file. `Write#` writes data of any data type to a file. Using corresponding input statements that you'll learn in the next section, you can read data that you sent to a file with the `Write#` command.

`Write#` lets you write data of any format to any disk file opened in `Output` or `Append` mode. `Write#` writes strings, numbers, dates, times, Boolean values, constants, and variables in any and all combinations to open disk files. Here is the format of `Write#`:

```
Write #intFileNumber [, ExpressionList]
```

The *intFileNumber* must be a file number associated to a file opened for output. If you don't specify variables or values to write, `Write#` writes a carriage return and line-feed character (an ASCII 13 followed by an ASCII 10) to the file, putting a blank line in the file. If you specify more than one value in the *ExpressionList,* Visual Basic writes that data to the file using the following considerations:

- `Write#` separates multiple items on the same line by adding commas between the values. These files are often called *comma-delimited files.* Many popular programs, such as Microsoft Access and Excel, read such files.

- `Write#` always adds a carriage return and line-feed character to the end of each line written to the file.

- `Write#` adds quotation marks around all strings in the file. The quotation marks make for easy reading of the strings later. The separating commas that appear between written strings never appear inside the quotation marks. If a comma appears inside quotation marks written with `Write#`, the comma is part of the string data being written. (For example, commas often appear inside addresses.)

- `Write#` writes date and time values using the following format:

  ```
  #yyyy-mm-dd hh:mm:ss#
  ```

  If only the date or time appears in the value, the pound signs enclose the date or time.

■ Write# writes #Null# to the file if the data contains a null value (a VarType() return value of 1).

■ Write# writes logical boolean values using the following format:

```
#True#
#False#
```

This format ensures that you can later read those values back into boolean variables.

■ Write# writes nothing when the data value is empty (a VarType() of 0), but does separate even empty values with commas if you write more than one value on a single line. Therefore, each line of data (called a *record*) that you write with Write# always contains the same number of commas to facilitate reading the file later.

The following statement writes five values to the disk file opened on file number 3:

```
Write #3, intAge, blnChecked, curSal, dteEnd, strName
```

This Write# statement writes a single line to the open disk file. The line might look like this:

```
47, #True#, 17423.61, #1-5-1998 14:21:10#, "Mary Sue"
```

If the application contains multiple Write# statements, or if the Write# statement appears inside a loop, a new line writes to file each time Write# executes.

TIP

End the Write# with a semicolon (;) if you want the next Write# to continue on the same line in the data file. As with the Print statement, the semicolon keeps the carriage return from appearing at the end of a written record so that subsequent output can start at the end of the current record.

If you open a file using the Append mode, Write# adds to the end of the file. If the file was opened in Output mode, the first Write# overwrites the file's contents and starts a new file. You can write data to files from variables as well as from controls on the form. Wherever you have data that needs to be written, Visual Basic's Write# command will write that data to a disk file that you open.

Listing 19.1 contains a subroutine procedure that accepts four arrays of four different data types and writes that array data to a disk file named Values.Dat opened in the procedure. Notice that you can use a simple For loop to write large amounts of data to a data file. The fifth argument sent to the subroutine is assumed to contain the total number of elements defined for the arrays so that the procedure can properly step through the entire array.

Listing 19.1. Using `Write#` to write array data to a file.

```
Private Sub WriteData (CNameso As String, CBalc() As
    ➥Currency, CDate() As Variant, CRegion() As Integer)
    ' Writes array data to a file
    Dim intCtr As Integer    ' For loop control

    ' Assumes that each array has the
    ' same number of elements defined
    Dim intMax As Integer
    intMax = UBound(CNames)    ' The maximum subscript
    ' Write intMax lines to the file
    ' with four values on each line
    Open "c:\Mktg.dat" For Output As #1
    For intCtr = 1 To intMax
        Write #1, CNames(intCtr), CBalc(intCtr),
            ➥CDate(intCtr), CRegion(intCtr)
    Next intCtr
    Close #1
End Sub
```

Here are six sample lines from `Mktg.dat` that the program in Listing 19.1 might write:

```
"Adams, H", 123.41, #1998-11-18 11:34:21#, 6
"Enyart, B", 602.99, #21:40:01#, 4
"Powers, W", 12.17, #1999-02-09#, 7
"O'Rourke, P", 8.74, #1998-05-24 14:53:10#, 0
"Grady, 0", 154.75, #1999-10-30 17:23:59#, 6
"McConnell, I", 9502.32, #1999-07-12 08:00:03#, 9
```

The pound signs around the date and time variant values help Visual Basic when you subsequently read the data values back into variant variables. As you can see, the date might have a missing time, or the time might have a missing date. `Write#` still writes as much of the date and time as is available within that variant value.

Reading the Written Data

Visual Basic's `Input#` statement reads data from a file and stores the file's data in your program's variables and controls. `Input#` is the mirror-image statement to `Write#`. Use `Input#` to read any comma-delimited data that you send to a file with `Write#`. The `Input#` statement reads data into a list of variables or controls. Here is the format of `Input#`:

```
Input #intFileNumber [, ExpressionList]
```

Remember that `Input#` needs to be the mirror image of the `Write#` statement that produced the file data. When you write a program that must use data from a data file, locate the program's `Write#` statement that originally created the data file and use that same format for the `Input#` statement.

The following `Input#` statement reads one line of values written with Listing 19.1's `Write#` statement:

```
Input #1, CNames(intCtr), CBalc(intCtr),
        ➥CDate(intCtr), CRegion(intCtr)
```

Detecting the End of File

When reading data from a file, you can very easily cause an error by attempting to read more data than the file holds. For data files that hold data such as customer balances and employee pay values, the number of records varies because you'll add and remove records as transactions take place.

Use the intrinsic Eof() function to test Visual Basic's end-of-file function that senses when an input reaches the end of file. Here is the format of Eof():

```
Eof(intFileNumber)
```

Eof() returns True if the most recent reading of the input file just reached the end of the file, and returns False if the input file still has data left to be read. Most data-input programs loop until the Eof() function returns True. Perhaps the best way to use Eof() is with a Do Until...Loop that follows this general format:

```
Input #1, VariableList      ' Read first record
Do Until (Eof(intFileNumber) = True)
   ' Process the record just read
   Input #1, VariableList    ' Get more data
Loop
```

If there are 0, 1, 10, or 400 records in the file, this format of Do Until keeps reading but stops as soon as the end of file is reached. Many programmers often increment an integer counter variable inside the loop to count the number of records read. The counter is useful later if you're reading the file's data into arrays. If you read file data into arrays, be sure to dimension more than enough array elements to hold the maximum number of records expected.

TIP

You can enhance the efficiency of the code that checks for the end-of-file condition by changing the Do Until test to this format:

```
Do Until Eof(intFileNumber)
```

Comparing against True, as done in the previous code, adds a redundant step because Eof() always becomes its return value of True or False.

Reading Records

Line Input# reads data from open data files. Line Input# reads each *record* of data in the file into a single string variable, whereas Input# reads single values from a record into one or more variables.

Don't specify separate variable names after a Line Input# statement because Line Input# requires a single string value. Line Input# reads data from any file whose lines end with a carriage return and line-feed sequence. (Most file records end this way.)

The `Line Input#` command is simple to use for reading entire records into a single variable. Whereas `Input#` reads each record's values individually, `Line Input#` reads an entire record including all data, commas, quotation marks, and everything else. The string receives the record's contents. Here is the format of `Line Input#`:

```
Line Input #intFileNumber, strVariableName
```

No matter how many record values appear in the file associated with file number 3, the following `Line Input#` statement reads an image of the record into the string variable named `strARecord`:

```
Line Input #3, strARecord
```

Searching Files

All the files created and read in this part of the book are *sequential files*—that is, you must start at the beginning and read or write. The only exception is the append mode, in which you still must write sequentially, one value at a time, from the end of the file until you are through writing data. With sequential files, you do not have the freedom to read or write file data in any order you want. Unlike *random-access files*, if you want to read the 40th record in a sequential file with `Line Input#`, you must first read the first 39 records.

The nature of sequential files makes creating, reading, and writing files simple, but sequential files do not lend themselves to efficient searching. Unlike the database files you can create and work with using data-bound controls, searching for specific information inside sequential files often requires brute-force coding.

> **NOTE**
>
> As mentioned earlier, Visual Basic does support the creation and use of random-access files. Nevertheless, if you have the need for such flexibility, you are much better off using one of Visual Basic's database connections such as the data control or one of the database navigating commands, called *SQL commands*, found in advanced VB language tutorials. The benefit of sequential files is that they are simple to understand and program. As long as your application does not require a lot of data or as long as your application does not require random-access data techniques, the file-navigating tools you learn about in this chapter will work very well.

Suppose you must search a file for a particular value. Although you could read the file's data into variables one value at a time with `Input#`, what if the file were not created using `Write#`? What if the file were not a comma-delimited file but contained a list of data values such as customer name and address information separated by spaces or tab characters?

You can read through the file, from the beginning to the end, searching for the information using a combination of the `Instr()` function and `Line Input#`, as Listing 19.2 illustrates. The string value you want to find in the file is stored in a variable named `strSearch`, already assumed to be declared and initialized. If you want to search for a numeric value, convert that value to a string with the `Str()` function before storing the converted string into `strSearch`, and Listing 19.2 will search for the numeric value.

> **NOTE**
>
> `Instr()` is an intrinsic function that searches a string for a specific value and returns the integer position of the found string (or 0 if the search string does not reside in the target string).

Listing 19.2. Using `Instr()` to locate a string value in a data file.

```
' This code assumes you've already declared and
' initialized all the variables.  The code sets
' the boolean variable named blnRecFound to True
' if the search value (located in strSearch) appears
' anywhere in the file.
blnRecFound = False  ' Stays False until match is found
intFileNum = FreeFile
Open strFile For Input As intFileNum
Do Until Eof(intFileNum)
    ' Read a record into a string variable
    Line Input #intFileNum, strRec
    If Instr(strRec, strSearch) Then
       blnRecFound = True  ' Found it!
    Exit Do   ' No need to look farther
Loop
```

> **TIP**
>
> If you need to know the record number where the search string was found, increment a counter by 1 every time this code reads a new record. When the loop terminates, the record counter variable holds the record number of the matching record, if a match was found according to the value in `blnRecFound`.

Searching with a Key

Of course, you will rarely want to know whether a value exists in a file. More likely, you'll search a file for a *key value* (a unique value that occurs in every record of a file), such as a customer number or a part ID, and then you'll want to locate the information in the record that goes with that key value.

If all your records have the same format and have the same record length, you can use the substring functions, such as Left() and Mid(), to pick off the value you want to examine in the matching record. To ensure that your records have the same format, you must work with fixed-length strings when you originally write the records. Although individual fixed-length strings work fine, you make life simpler if you store all a record's data in a user-defined data type first and then save that data to disk with the Print# statement, as the next section demonstrates.

Making Searches Easier

Programmers often implement fixed record lengths by creating a user-defined data type with the Type declaration statement. As you already know, Type creates a structured collection of data. The following Type statement declares an inventory structure:

```
Type InvRec
   strPartID As String *5
   intQuant As Integer
   curPrice As Currency
   strDesc As String * 15
End Type
```

Remember, InvRec is *not* a variable, but simply declares a new data type. Instead of an integer or a string or a Boolean data type, InvRec is a collection of data types. When you declare a variable of type InvRec, that variable is a multipart variable with four parts. If you declare more than one variable of the data type InvRec, *each variable* consumes the same amount of memory. Therefore, each InvRec variable you write to disk consumes the same record space.

TIP

Declare all user-defined data types in a public module so that all modules within the application can define variables from that data type.

Suppose that you initialize an InvRec variable named typCurrent like this:

```
Dim typCurrent As InvRec
```

You can access each individual value within the variable named typCurrent using the dot operator:

```
typCurrent.strPartID = txtPart.Text   ' Get ID from a text box
```

Assuming that you initialized all the parts of the structure variable named typCurrent, the following code writes the variable to a disk file. You can place this code in a loop along with typCurrent's initialization code to write a set of fixed-length records to disk:

```
intFileNum = FreeFile
Open strFile For Ouput As intFileNum
Print #intFileNum, typCurrent   ' Writes the record
Close #intFileNum
```

This small section of code writes only a single record before closing the file. As mentioned before the code, you actually write more information by putting this code inside a loop. Nevertheless, you can tell from this code that writing fixed-length records is easy. Once you initialize the record variable, the writing of the variable is trivial because you only need to write the record variable. You do not have to write each individual variable within the record as you have to do with four separate variables that reside outside of any record variable.

> **NOTE**
>
> As long as you use fixed record variables declared to be part of a data type created with Type, the file I/O code remains simple. Even if you add or remove items from the record to create a different data file, you don't have to change the actual I/O routine. When you write fixed-length records, you write the record's variable, not the individual members within the variable.

Unlike previous code examples in this chapter, this code uses the Print# statement to write the record to the disk drive, not Write#. Write# is useful for variable-length records because Write#, although less efficient than Print#, separates the file's data items with commas and encloses data inside quotation marks or pound signs, depending on the data type. You need this for-matted, comma-delimited file when you later read the file because each record is not of fixed length, and the commas help your code read the values again properly with Input#. When each record in the file is fixed-length, however, due to the structure with which you defined the record, you should use the more efficient Print# statement.

Print# writes data to a file using the same rules as the Print method you use to write to forms and to the printer. Although Print# supports several formats and lets you combine tabs and spaces with the Tab() and Spc() intrinsic functions, when you write fixed-length records to a file and those records are defined with Type, here's the only Print# format you need to master:

```
Print #intFileNum, recVar
```

recVar is the record variable you want to write. Print# writes the entire variable to the file and automatically places a carriage return and line feed at the end of the record in the file. Instead of using Line Input# or Input# to read the records, however, use Get# and read each record into a variable that's also defined with the same Type statement.

Get# is a command often used with Put# to read and write sequential and random-access data. This chapter focuses on sequential data. Get# reads fixed-length sequential data records written with Print# very well.

Listing 19.3 revisits the file-searching code and shows how you might search a file that holds the fixed-length records created from a Type data type. This listing searches for an inventory record within the inventory file, assuming you have already declared and initialized a variable named strSearchID that holds the part number you're looking for.

Listing 19.3. Looking for a search string using fixed-length records.

```
' This code assumes you've already declared and
' initialized all the variables.  The code sets
' the boolean variable named blnRecFound to True
' if the search value (located in strSearchID) appears
' anywhere in the file.
blnRecFound = False  ' Stays False until match is found
intFileNum = FreeFile
Open strFile For Input As intFileNum
Do Until Eof(intFileNum)
    ' Read a record into a fixed-length variable
    Get #intFileNum, typCurrent
    If (typCurrent.strPartID = strSearchID) Then
        blnRecFound = True  ' Found it!
    Exit Do   ' No need to look farther
Loop
```

> **TIP**
>
> If the key that you're using might contain uppercase and lowercase characters, use either the LCase() or UCase() function to convert the comparison values to the same case so they compare properly.

When this loop terminates, if blnFound is True, the record variable typCurrent holds the inventory record that matches the search part ID. Once you create the fixed-length record file, searching the file becomes extremely trivial. You no longer have to resort to substring functions to pick off the data from the matching record that you need because the file contains a collection of records formatted according to the structured data type. For example, if you want to display the current quantity of the found item on a form, you can use the dot notation to store the quantity in a label control:

```
lblQuantity.Caption = typCurrent.intQuant  ' Display quantity
```

> **TIP**
>
> If you want to create a file that's sorted on an individual value, such as the part ID, you should create an array of record variables, sort the array as in memory, and then write the array to the disk file using a loop.

Summary

This chapter introduces you to the directory- and file-management commands and functions. In addition, you have learned how to create, read, write, and close data files so you can store and update long-term data that your application needs on the disk.

If you've created, removed, and managed directories and files from the MS-DOS prompt, you'll have no trouble mastering Visual Basic's commands and functions that perform similar operations. Often, your applications must create and traverse folders and disk drives, and Visual Basic supplies the tools needed to do just that.

When you need a data file, you must determine the best method to open that file. The method you use to open the file tells Visual Basic how you want to access the file. When you create a file and write to the file with `Write#`, subsequent `Input#` and `Line Input#` statements can read that data back into memory as needed. If you want to search through fixed-length records, first define the data with a `Type` statement. After you write the fixed-length records to a disk file, you can read and search through the data with `Get#`.

In conclusion, I recommend that you follow these optimization tips when handling file input and output:

- Close a file before you attempt to rename, delete, or open the file again within the same program.

- Although the operating system automatically closes files upon program termination, you should explicitly close all files when you are through with them to safeguard the data inside the files.

- Use `On Error Goto` to trap errors throughout your file access. Runtime errors can more easily appear when working with files than at any other time during your application's execution.

- If you must perform extensive searching, sorting, and random-access retrieval and updating of file data, consider using a database system to create the files and using data-bound controls to access that data. Sequential-access files are best reserved for the simple files and applications described in this chapter.

- If you use `Write#` to write data to a file, use `Input#` to read that data back into variables.

- `Line Input#` reads an entire record at once into a string variable, whereas `Input#` reads only a single variable or a variable list.

- Use `Get#` to read fixed-length records from a file whose records are uniform in length. You can more easily retrieve related data when you locate needed records if you defined that data with a `Type` statement before you saved the data to the disk.

19

FILE INPUT AND
OUTPUT MADE
EASY

Printing with Visual Basic

by Greg Perry

IN THIS CHAPTER

CHAPTER 20

When designing this book, the author and editors considered writing about an add-in product included with the Professional and Enterprise Editions of Visual Basic called *Crystal Reports*. This chapter describes printing without the Crystal Reports generator for a couple reasons. Some readers might have the Visual Basic Standard Edition and lack the Crystal Reports feature. They would have been completely left without a way to print described in this entire book. In addition, if you have enough data to justify using Crystal Reports, you probably regularly use a database management system, such as Microsoft Access, that sports much more powerful reporting tools than Visual Basic. Therefore, this lesson concentrates on the fundamental reporting tools that every Visual Basic programmer will need at some time.

This chapter describes how you can integrate the Windows printer driver into Visual Basic applications that you write. Visual Basic communicates with the driver so that you can send text and even graphics to the printer.

The highlights of this chapter include

- Where your application sends printed output
- Which advantages spooled printing provides
- How to use the `Printer` object
- When to use `Printer` methods
- How the `Print` method routes details to your printer

Introducing Printing

Surprisingly, no printer control exists. Unlike most things in Visual Basic, sending output to the printer can be a tedious process. Surprisingly, one of Visual Basic's weaknesses is also its strength: Printing requires that you send a fairly long list of instructions to your printer that describe exactly the way the output is to look. As easily as Visual Basic allows you to add and manage controls, one would think that the printing could be made easier.

Despite the tedium sometimes associated with printing, you will soon see that you can control every aspect of printing, including the font of individual characters that your application sends to the printer. The tedious control needed for printing provides pinpoint accuracy that lets you control all printing details.

> **NOTE**
>
> The *Windows print spooler*, also called the *print queue* or the *printer subsystem*, controls all printed output in Windows.

When your application sends output to the printer, Windows intercepts those printer commands. Rather than sending output directly to the printer attached to your computer, Visual Basic actually sends printed output to the Windows print spooler.

The print spooler determines how all printed output from all Windows programs eventually appears. Therefore, when your Visual Basic application attempts to send printed output directly to the printer, the Windows print spooler intercepts those commands and might change the output before the printer ever sees it.

The Windows print spooler knows how to communicate with any printer supported by Windows. There are hundreds of different kinds of printers now recognized by Windows, and most of these printers require specialized commands. If every program you bought had to provide support for every kind of printer you or your users might own, programs would require even more disk space than they already do. In addition, programs would cost more because each software developer would have to spend time writing the program to produce output onto every kind of printer available.

Rather than require that every software developer support all printers, the Windows print spooler requires that every software developer support only *one* kind of printed output: the kind required by the Windows print spooler. If the applications you write need to produce printed output, Visual Basic produces that output in a form required by the Windows print spooler. Figure 20.1 shows that Visual Basic applications send output directly to the Windows print spooler. The Windows print spooler then converts that output into the individual commands needed by whatever printer is attached to the system.

FIGURE 20.1.

Windows intercepts printer output.

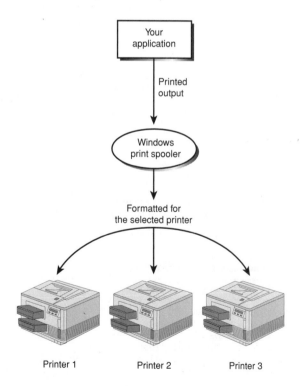

Suppose that you had both a laser printer and a color ink-jet printer attached to your computer. Without the Windows print spooler, you would need to provide two sets of printer commands for every Visual Basic application you wrote. With the Windows print spooler, you need to provide only one generic set of printed output commands. Before running the application, you can use commands available in the Windows print spooler to select one of your two printers. When you run the program, Windows will convert the Visual Basic output into commands needed by whatever printer is selected.

The Windows print spooler simplifies communication with all the various printers. Your Visual Basic application needs only to send output to the Windows print spooler, no matter which kind of printer that output will eventually be directed to. The Windows print spooler knows how to communicate with all Windows-supported printers and converts your Visual Basic application's output to the chosen printer's required format.

Prepare the User for Printing

A user could be caught unaware if your application begins printing without first warning him that the printer must be ready.

Always remind the user to turn on the printer, make sure that the printer has paper, and ensure that the printer is online. If the user's printer is not first turned on and ready with an ample paper supply, he will receive a Windows print spooler error message similar to the one shown in Figure 20.2.

FIGURE 20.2.

The printer is not ready.

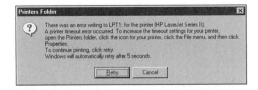

The function procedure in Listing 20.1 provides you with a useful MsgBox() call that you might want to incorporate into your own programs before printing. Of course, if you use common dialog boxes, you don't have to use this message box because the Print common dialog box serves good notice that printing is about to begin.

Listing 20.1. Telling the user about an upcoming print job.

```
Public Function PrReady() As Boolean
    ' Make sure the user is ready to print
    Dim intIsReady As Integer
    intIsReady = MsgBox("Make sure the printer is ready", _
            vbCritical, "Printer Check")
    If (intIsReady = vbCancel) Then
        PrReady = False ' A Cancel press returns a False value
    Else
```

```
        PrReady = True   ' User pressed OK so return True
    End If
End Function
```

Figure 20.3 shows the message box presented by Listing 20.1.

FIGURE 20.3.

*The user can now
prepare the printer.*

After the user reads the message and responds to the message box, the function's return value determines whether the user wants to see the output (assume that he has properly prepared the printer for printing) or cancel the printing. The return value of True or False can be checked as follows from another procedure that prints based on the user's response:

```
If PrReady() Then      ' If function is true...
    Call PrintRoutine  ' then print from sub
End If
```

Introducing the Printer Object

Visual Basic applications send all printed output to a special Visual Basic object called the Printer object. The Printer object supports several property values and methods with which you determine the look of the printed output.

The Printer keyword specifies the Printer object to which your applications will direct all output. There is no printer control in the Toolbox window; all access to the Printer object must take place using Visual Basic code.

The commands that your application sends to the Printer object are generic Windows printer commands. The Windows print spooler converts those generic commands to a specific printer's commands. Therefore, you only worry about what you want printed and let the Windows print spooler worry about how the output is produced.

Throughout this book, when you learned about a new object, such as the Command Button control, you learned about the properties that relate to that object. Before using the Printer object, you should see the properties available for the Printer object so that you'll know what kinds of things you can do with printed output from within Visual Basic. All of the Printer object's properties are listed in Table 20.1.

20

PRINTING WITH VISUAL BASIC

NOTE

In the table, you will see the word *pixel*. A pixel is the smallest addressable point on the screen or printer.

Table 20.1. The `Printer` object's properties.

Property	Description
ColorMode	If 1 (or if set to the `vbPRCMMonochrome` named literal), output prints in monochrome (shades of white and black) even if you use a color printer. If 2 (or if set to the `vbPRCMColor` named literal), output prints in color.
Copies	Specifies the number of copies to print.
CurrentX	Holds the horizontal print column, from the upper-left corner of the page, measured either in twips or by the scale defined by the `ScaleMode` properties.
CurrentY	Holds the vertical print row, from the upper-left corner of the page, measured either in twips or by the scale defined by the `ScaleMode` properties.
DeviceName	The name of the output device, such as a printer driver, to which you want to print.
DrawMode	Determines the appearance of graphics that you draw on the printer.
DrawStyle	Specifies the style of any graphical lines that your application draws.
DrawWidth	Specifies the width of lines drawn, from 1 (the default) to 32767 pixels.
DriverName	The name of the printer driver (do not specify the driver's extension).
Duplex	If 1 (or if set to the named literal `vbPRDPSimplex`), printing will occur on one side of the page. If 2 (or if set to the named literal `vbPRDPHorizontal`), printing will occur on both sides (if your printer supports double-sided printing) using a horizontal page turn. If 3 (or if set to the named literal `vbPRDPVertical`), printing will occur on both sides (if your printer supports double-sided printing) using a vertical page turn.
FillColor	Specifies the color of printed shapes. Determines the shading density for noncolor printed output.
FillStyle	Contains the style pattern of printed shapes.
Font	Returns a font that you can use for setting font attributes.
FontBold	Contains either `True` or `False` to determine whether subsequent printed output will be boldfaced.
FontCount	Specifies the current printer's number of installed fonts.
FontItalic	Holds either `True` or `False` to determine whether subsequent output will be italicized.
FontName	Holds the name of the current font being used for output.

Property	Description
Fonts	Contains a table of values that act as if they were stored in a control array. Fonts(0) to Fonts (FontCount · 1) holds the names of all installed fonts on the target computer.
FontSize	Holds the size, in points, of the current font.
FontStrikeThru	Holds either True or False to determine whether subsequent output will be printed with a strikethrough line.
FontTransparent	Holds either True or False to determine whether subsequent output will be transparent.
FontUnderline	Holds either True or False to determine whether subsequent output will be underlined.
ForeColor	Specifies the foreground color of printed text and graphics. (The paper determines the background color.)
hDC	A Windows device context handle for advanced Windows procedure calls.
Height	Holds the height, in twips, of the current printed page.
Orientation	If 1 (or if set to the named literal vbPRORPortrait), output prints in *portrait mode* (printing occurs down the page). If 2 (or if set to the named literal vbPRORLandscape), output prints in *landscape mode* (printing occurs across the page).
Page	Contains the page number currently being printed and is updated automatically by Visual Basic.
PaperBin	Specifies which paper bin the print job will use. You can search the online help for the PaperBin property for several named literals you can use to specify different kinds of bins.
PaperSize	Specifies the size of paper the print job will use. You can search the online help for the PaperSize property for several named literals you can use to specify different sizes of paper.
Port	Specifies the printer port, such as LPT1:.
PrintQuality	Determines how fine the print quality will appear. If ·1 (or set to the vbPRPQDraft named literal), the printing quality is the lowest, but the print completes quickly. If ·2 (or set to the vbPRPQLow named literal), printing occurs in a low-resolution mode. If ·3 (or set to the vbPRPQMedium named literal), printing occurs in a medium-resolution mode. If ·4 (or set to the vbPRPQHigh named literal), printing is the slowest but is the highest quality.

continues

20

PRINTING WITH
VISUAL BASIC

Table 20.1. continued

Property	Description
ScaleHeight	Specifies how many ScaleMode units high each graphic will be on output.
ScaleLeft	Specifies how many ScaleMode units from the left of the page subsequent printed output will appear.
ScaleMode	Sets the unit of measurement for all subsequent printed output that appears.
ScaleTop	Specifies how many ScaleMode units from the top of the page all subsequent printed output will appear.
ScaleWidth	Specifies how many ScaleMode units wide each graphic will be upon printed output.
TrackDefault	If True, the specified printer changes if you change the default printer at the operating system level. If False, the specified printer remains the same during the program's operation even if the system's default printer changes during the program's execution.
TwipsPerPixelX	Specifies the number of screen twips that each printer's dot (called a *pixel*) height consumes.
TwipsPerPixelY	Specifies the number of screen twips that each printer's dot, or pixel, width consumes.
Width	Holds the size of the page width (measured in twips).
Zoom	Specifies the percentage by which printed output prints. A negative value scales down the output (makes it smaller), 0 requests no scaling, and a positive value scales up the output (makes it larger).

Table 20.1 contains lots of printer properties. Fortunately, you'll use only a few of them for most of your printing needs. The font-related printer properties take care of just about all your printing jobs that are textual in nature.

NOTE

The graphics-related printer properties and methods aren't covered in this lesson. After you master graphics in the next part of this book, you'll be more prepared to understand the graphics-related Printer object's properties. Most of the Printer object's properties are reserved for controlling extremely advanced graphics output. For typical applications, you'll rarely bother to specify any properties because the default values work well for normal reporting requirements.

Unlike most of Visual Basic's control objects, the `Printer` object's methods are much more important than the `Printer` object's property values. Table 20.2 contains a complete list of the methods supported by Visual Basic's `Printer` object.

Table 20.2. The `Printer` object's methods.

Method	Description
Circle	Draws a circle, an ellipse, or an arc on the printer.
EndDoc	Releases the current document, in full, to the print spooler for output.
KillDoc	Immediately terminates the output and deletes the current print job from the print spooler.
Line	Draws lines and boxes on the page.
NewPage	Sends a page break to the printed output so that subsequent output appears on the next page.
PaintPicture	Draws a graphic image file on the printer.
Print	Prints numeric and text data on the printer.
PSet	Draws a graphical point on the printed output.
Scale	Determines the scale used for measuring output.
ScaleX	Converts the printer's width to `ScaleMode`'s measurement unit.
ScaleY	Converts the printer's height to `ScaleMode`'s measurement unit.
TextHeight	Determines the full height of text given in the scale set with `Scale`.
TextWidth	Determines the full width of text given in the scale set with `Scale`.

By far the most widely used `Printer` object methods are `Print`, `EndDoc`, and `NewPage`. Once you master these three methods, you'll rarely need to use any other methods.

The Print Method

The `Printer` object's `Print` method handles almost all printed output. `Print` supports several different formats. With `Print`, you can print messages, variables, constants, and expressions on the printer. The `Print` method is, by far, the most commonly used printing method in Visual Basic. By mastering `Print`, you will have mastered the single most important printing method.

Here is the format of the `Print` method:

```
[Printer.]Print [Spc(n) ¦ Tab(n)] Expression
```

The format makes `Print` look a lot more confusing than it really is, but the portion of the `Print` method that appears to the right of `Print` requires some explanation. The next several sections explain the various options available for the `Print` method.

Printing Literals

The Print method easily prints string and numeric literals. To print a string or numeric literal, place the literal to the right of the Print method. The following methods send the numbers 1, 2, and 3 to the Printer object for output:

```
Printer.Print 1
Printer.Print 2
Printer.Print 3
```

When execution hits these three lines of code, Visual Basic sends 1, 2, and 3 to the Printer object, with each number appearing on subsequent lines. Every Print method sends a carriage return and line feed sequence to the printer. A lone Print method on a line by itself such as the following sends a blank line to the printer:

```
Printer.Print
```

> **WARNING**
>
> Print adds a space before all positive numeric values printed on the page. The space is where an invisible plus sign appears.

The following Print method sends two lines of text to the Printer object:

```
Printer.Print "Visual Basic makes writing programs"
Printer.Print "for Windows easy."
```

When the Windows print spooler gets these two lines of output, the following appears on the printer's paper:

```
Visual Basic makes writing programs
for Windows easy.
```

Printing Variables and Controls

In addition to literals, the Print method prints the contents of variables and controls. The following initializes a string and an integer variable and then prints the contents of the variables on the printer:

```
FirstName = "Charley"
Age = 24
Printer.Print FirstName
Printer.Print Age
```

Here is the output produced by these Print methods:

```
Charley
 24
```

NOTE

Remember that Visual Basic won't send anything to the `Printer` object until the code that contains `Print` executes. You must insert `Print` methods at appropriate places in the code's procedures where printed output is required. For example, if there is a command button labeled `Print Report`, that command button's `Click()` event procedure will contain `Print` methods.

Printing Expressions

If you could print only individual strings, numeric constants, and variables, `Print` would be extremely limiting. Of course, `Print` is not that limited. You can combine literals, variables, and expressions to the right of `Print` methods to produce more complex printed output. The following `Print` method prints 31:

```
Printer.Print 25 + (3 * 2)
```

The expression can contain variables, controls, and constants, like this:

```
Printer.Print sngFactor * lblWeight.Caption + 10
```

If you want to send special characters to the printer, you can do so by using the `Chr()` function. The following expression produces a message that includes embedded quotation marks inside the printed string:

```
Printer.Print "She said, " & Chr(34) & "I do." & Chr(34)
```

When execution reaches the former `Print` method, this is what the print spooler routes to the printer:

```
She said, "I do."
```

NOTE

You wouldn't be able to print the quotation marks without the `Chr()` function. Usually, Visual Basic uses quotation marks to determine where string literals begin and end.

Printing Multiple Values

When you need to print several values on one line, you can do so by separating those values with semicolons and commas. The semicolon forces subsequent values to appear next to each other in the output. The comma forces values to appear in the next print zone.

> **NOTE**
>
> A *print* zone occurs every 14 columns on the page.

The following two messages print on different lines:

```
Printer.Print "The sales were
Printer.Print 4345.67
```

By using the semicolon, you can force these values to print next to each other:

```
Printer.Print "The sales were "; 4345.67
```

The semicolon also acts to keep automatic carriage return and line feed combinations from taking place. The following Print method ends with a trailing semicolon:

```
Printer.Print "The company name is ";
```

The trailing semicolon keeps the printer's print head at the end of the message for subsequent output. Therefore, the subsequent Print statement shown here, no matter how much later in the code the Print appears, would print its output right next to the previous Print's output:

```
Printer.Print lblComName.Caption   ' Finish the line
```

The semicolon is nice for printing multiple values of different data types of the same line. The following Print prints all its data on the same line of output:

```
Printer.Print "Sales: "; curTotsales; "Region:"; intRegNum
```

The comma is still sometimes used to force subsequent values to print in the next print zone. The following Print prints names every 14 spaces on the printed line:

```
Printer.Print strDivName1, strDivName2, strDivName3
```

No matter how long or short each division name is, the next division name will print in the next print zone. The previous Print might produce output similar to the following:

```
North        NorthEast      South
```

When you print lists of numbers or short strings, the comma allows you to easily align each column.

Utilizing the Fonts

Most Windows-compatible printers support a variety of fonts. The font-related properties are often useful for printing titles and other special output messages in special font sizes and styles.

You can add special effects to your printed text by setting the font-modifying properties from Table 20.1. For example, the following code first puts the printer in a boldfaced, italicized, 60-point font (a print size of nearly an inch), and then prints a message:

```
Printer.FontBold = True
Printer.FontItalic = True
Printer.FontSize = 60
Printer.Print "I'm learning Visual Basic!"
```

WARNING

The font properties affect *subsequent* output. Therefore, if you print several lines of text and then change the font size, the text that you've already printed remains unaffected. Visual Basic prints only the subsequent output with the new font.

Better Spacing with Spc() and Tab()

The `Print` method supports the use of the embedded `Spc()` and `Tab()` functions to give you additional control over your program's output. `Spc()` produces a variable number of spaces in the output as determined by the argument you send to it. The following `Print` method prints a total of 10 spaces between the first name and the last:

```
Printer.Print strFirstName; Spc(10), strLastName
```

The argument that you send to the embedded `Tab()` function determines in which column the next printed character appears. In the following `Print`, the date appears in the 50th column on the page:

```
Printer.Print Tab(50), dteDateGenerated
```

As these examples show, if you print values before or after the `Spc()` and `Tab()` functions, you separate the functions from the surrounding printed values using the semicolon.

TIP

`Spc()` and `Tab()` give you more control over spacing than the comma and semicolon allow.

Listing 20.2 contains some code that computes and prints two house-pricing taxation values.

Listing 20.2. Using Spc() and Tab().

```
Tax1 = TaxRate * HouseVal1
Tax2 = TaxRate * HouseVal2

TotalVal = HouseVal1 + HouseVal2
TotTaxes = TaxRate * TotalVal

Printer.Print "House Value"; Tab(20); "Tax"
Printer.Print Format(HouseVal1, "Currency");
```

continues

Listing 20.2. continued

```
Printer.Print Tab(20); Format(Tax1, "Currency")
Printer.Print Format(HouseVal2, "Currency");
Printer.Print Tab(20); Format(Tax2, "Currency")

Printer.Print  ' Prints a blank line
Printer.Print "Total tax:"; Spc(5); Format(TotTaxes, "Currency")
Printer.NewPage
Printer.EndDoc
```

Here is a sample of what you might see after Listing 20.2 executes:

```
House Value     Tax
$76,578.23      $9,189.39
$102,123.67     $12,254.81

Total tax:      $21,444.20
```

The Tab(20) function calls ensure that the second column, which contains the tax information, is aligned. Also, notice that the trailing semicolons let you continue the Print methods on subsequent lines without squeezing long Print method values onto the same line. The code uses Spc() to insert five spaces between the title and the total amount of tax. The last two lines ensure that the printing stops properly.

Starting to Print

The physical printing doesn't begin until all output is released to the print spooler, or until your application issues the EndDoc method.

As you send Print methods to the print spooler via the Printer object, the print spooler builds the page or pages of output but doesn't release that output until you issue an EndDoc method. EndDoc tells the print spooler, "I'm done sending output to you; you can print now."

Without EndDoc, Windows would collect all of an application's output and not print any of it until the application terminates. If you were to write an application that the user runs throughout the day and that prints invoices as customers make purchases, you would need to issue an EndDoc method at the end of each invoice-printing procedure if you wanted each invoice to print at that time.

Listing 20.3 prints a message on the printer and then signals to the print spooler that output is ready to go to paper. Without the EndDoc, the print spooler would hold the output until the application containing the code terminated.

Listing 20.3. Using EndDoc to release printed output.

```
Printer.Print "Invoice #"; invnum
Printer.Print "Customer:"; cust(CCnt); Tab(20); "Final Sales"
Printer.Print "Amount of sale:"; Tab(20); Format(SaleAmt, "Currency")
```

```
Printer.Print "Tax:"; Tab(20); Format(tax, "Currency")
Printer.Print
Printer.Print "Total:"; Tab(20), Format(TotalSale, "Currency")

' Release the job for actual printing
Printer.EndDoc
```

The program containing Listing 20.3's code might continue to run and process other sets of data. The EndDoc method ensures that the output built in the preceding Print methods is all sent to the physical printer immediately. If other Print methods appear later in the program, the print spooler begins building the output all over again, releasing that subsequent output only for an EndDoc procedure or when the application ends.

Page Breaks

When printing to the printer, you must be careful to print at the top of a new page when you want the output to advance one page. The NewPage method forces the printer to eject the current page and begin subsequent output on the next new page.

The Windows print spooler ensures that each printed page properly breaks at the end of a physical page. Therefore, if the printer's page length is 66 lines and you print 67 lines, the 67th line will appear at the top of the second page of output. There are times, however, when you need to print less than a full page on the printer. You can release that incomplete page for printing using the NewPage method (from Table 20.2). To use NewPage, simply apply the NewPage method to the Printer object like this:

```
Printer.NewPage
```

> **NOTE**
>
> Remember that you actually print to the Windows print spooler and that your application's output methods don't directly control a physical printer. Therefore, NewPage tells the print spooler to go to a new page when the print spooler gets to that location in the output.

You have to remember that you're working with printers that support many fonts and font sizes. You can always determine, in advance, how many lines of output will fit on a single page as long as you first check the value of the following formula:

```
intNumLinesPerPage = Printer.Height / Printer.TextHeight("X")
```

As explained in Table 20.3, the Height property determines the height, in twips, of the page, or in whatever measurement value you want to use. The TextHeight property determines the full height of a printed character (including *leading*, which is the area directly above and below characters). TextHeight measures the height in twips if you haven't changed the scale using the ScaleMode property.

For printed reports, you'll rarely use the ScaleMode method. If you have the need to change the scale of measurement, however, you'll have to change the scale back to twips before calculating the number of output lines per page, like this:

```
Printer.ScaleMode = 1
```

ScaleMode accepts the values defined in Table 20.3.

Table 20.3. The ScaleMode values.

Value	Named literal	Description
0	vbUser	A user-defined value
1	vbTwips	Measured in twips (the default)
2	vbPoints	Measured in points
3	vbPixels	Measured in pixels (the smallest unit addressable by your printer)
4	vbCharacters	Measured in characters (120 × 240 twips)
5	vbInches	Measured in inches
6	vbMillimeters	Measured in millimeters
7	vbCentimeters	Measured in centimeters

Listing 20.4 contains code that prints two messages, one per page of printed output.

Listing 20.4. Moving to the top of new output pages.

```
Printer.Print "The Report begins on the next page..."
Printer.NewPage   ' Go to top of new page
Printer.Print "The Campaign Platform"
```

TIP

You can apply the Print method to your form to print directly on the form without using a control. For example, you can print a title on a form named frmAccts with this statement: frmAccts.Print Spc(20); "XYZ, Co.". Although you should use controls as much as possible so that the application's code can rearrange and manage the text on the controls, you should remember to use Print whenever your form needs to hold unchanging text.

Summary

In this chapter you have learned ways you can route output to your printer. Actually, you learned here that all Visual Basic output goes to the Windows print spooler and that the spooler takes care of speaking to your particular printer.

Creating printed output is not always simple. With the exception of printing program listings (which you can do by selecting File | Print from the development environment), printing data can take a while. You must take care of every line and jump to a new page when necessary.

Programming the Easy Way with Controls

IV

PART

Reviewing the Standard Controls

by Paul Kimmel

IN THIS CHAPTER

This chapter offers an overview of the controls you will probably use most frequently. These controls are referred to as the *Standard Controls*. If Visual Basic programming is new to you, you should definitely master the material in this chapter. If you are an experienced Visual Basic user, you are probably busy developing applications for big bucks, but you might want to read this chapter anyway. At a minimum, you will gain a new perspective on familiar material, which might facilitate finding a solution for a particularly intractable problem.

Both the novice and the adept will find detailed coverage of the most commonly used controls and gain experience through the many code examples contained in this chapter. In this chapter, you will see code examples and learn about

- The relationships between the aspects of controls that make them useful: properties, methods, and events
- The Standard Controls in the context of demo programs
- A common subset of properties that will help you learn how to use new controls faster after you have learned the first one
- How to use many of the properties, methods, and events of the Standard Controls

You will acquire the fundamental skills that will hold you in good stead as Microsoft expands its component resources or as you acquire third-party controls to facilitate your development projects. I will begin with a brief overview of the importance of the general aggregate concepts that compose controls.

Reviewing Properties, Methods, and Events

Essentially, objects have evolved in software languages due to shortcomings in the human mind's ability to grapple large chunks of information at one instance. People aggregate, or group, ideas because short-term memory—analogous to a computer's RAM—is only capable of storing roughly a maximum of 7 to 11 pieces of information at an instance. This statistic is demonstrated when you ask someone for a phone number, and the response is a staccato reply of three groups of numbers. We do the same thing with e-mail addresses, Social Security numbers, and long calling-card numbers. (At last count, I dial about 32 numbers for each long-distance phone call, but I think of them as three groups of smaller groups.)

The human mind is drawn to aggregation as iron slivers are drawn to a magnet. For years in software development, developers wrote huge reams of binary-coded lines to solve fairly trivial problems. The first aggregation happened when repetitive binary sets became assembly instructions, which in turn yielded macros that were copied in place of the macro name by the compiler. Further aggregation led to functions, a descendant of the macro. When I began programming, programs were capable of recognizing functions and collections of data. In Visual Basic, a data aggregation is the type; in Pascal, it is the record; and in C, it is the struct.

Reviewing the Standard Controls

CHAPTER 21

383

21

REVIEWING
THE STANDARD
CONTROLS

It is only natural that as the science of software development progresses, we continue to aggregate. It is further likely that we model the real world. The concrete world around us—as opposed to the abstract world—is categorized, and our perception of order is based on classifying things by their capabilities and attributes. It is natural that during our evolutionary course along the path of aggregating to cope with complexity, we cast this view of the physical world on our digital world.

> **NOTE**
>
> Many controls have default properties. The default property is generally the property that captures the primary use of a control. For example, `TextBox`'s primary use is to store text; therefore, the `Text` property is the default. You can modify the default property via the control, as in `Text1.Text = "Hello"` is equivalent to `Text1 = "Text"`. When you do not include a property with its object, the context will determine whether the default property is used.
>
> A word of caution: Software development is not an exercise in clarity. Using default properties can lead to code that is more ambiguous when read by a human.

Controls in Visual Basic use properties to record attributes of controls and methods to define capabilities, much like the concrete world. Events fit into the picture, as in the concrete world, as things that happen to objects. The complete picture of controls is that a control is capable of recording state, having an awareness of its own capabilities, and responding to external occurrences. Perhaps you can see the continuing correlation between developments in software development languages and the creation of black-box entities that are capable of performing a whole series of compound tasks. For the purposes of this chapter, it will suffice that you have an idea of controls as objects that are capable of self-knowledge and responsiveness.

Adding Fit and Finish with Labels and Frames

You may find it odd that I am beginning the intra-chapter journey with fit and finish. Subjectively, you might find that you are developing more aesthetically pleasing applications if you are thinking of aesthetics as early as the first line of code. You will also find the label and frame extremely easy to use. Consequently, you should strive to build your confidence with early successes.

Ironically, the frame is a graphic line box whose purpose is to contrive the appearance of other controls being related by the fact that they are within the proximity of the enclosing frame. The frame, like many controls, has a `Caption` property. The beauty of an object system is that you can learn how to use a property, and it usually plays the same role in every context in which it appears.

The `Caption` property is arguably the most useful property of both the label and the frame. Use the label to display static text; usually the label doesn't respond to user events, although if you need it to react to user action, you can define events for it. (I'll discuss some of those shortly.) The frame's capacity is that of proximal relater. If you put several controls in the frame, the common and accepted understanding is that the controls are interrelated. The `Caption` property is beneficial in that it provides a visual cue about the proximal relationship.

You can assign the `Caption` property in the Properties dialog by pressing F4, selecting the applicable control, and looking in the alphabetic position C. Simply write some text in the edit field to the right of the `Caption` property, and the change is recorded at design time and maintained at runtime unless your code changes it explicitly. To change the `Caption` property with code, simply refer to the object whose `Caption` property you want to change, and concatenate the word `Caption` preceded by a period:

```
Frame1.Caption = "Address"
```

For labels, use the same syntax, but replace the object name on the left side of the period with the label object:

```
Label1.Caption = "City"
```

TIP

You designate a control hotkey by preceding the letter you want to be the hotkey with the ampersand (&). `Label1.Caption = "&Address"` results in a caption of Address.

A distinguishing aspect of the frame, other than the label, is that the frame is capable of containing other controls. To insert a control in the frame, simply select it by clicking once. The frame with the focus is indicated by the dotted line. While the frame is selected, any control you add to the form is inserted in the frame. Additionally, you can move controls into the form by cutting and pasting them. The project `Frame.vbp` is included on the CD-ROM for this book to allow you to begin experimenting with the controls. In the net section, I continue the discussion of controls with the `TextBox` control. Where properties and methods are similar between the controls, this information is brought to your attention.

Using the `TextBox` Control

Labels and frames help organize your forms and provide cues about the individual controls' purposes. Although you can define drag-and-drop events for frames and labels, typically these two controls play a rather innocuous role. If you want to collect input from the user, the simplest and most direct means is to use a textbox with a label prompting the user for the kind of data required.

The textbox is probably the most commonly used control in all Windows programs. Begin by examining examples of properties, methods, and events that apply to the textbox. As you progress, keep in mind that the kinds of exploitive tasks you can easily perform depend on which characteristics are available to the control—in this instance, the textbox.

Textbox Properties

The properties of any control determine the state information a control can record about itself. Properties are data that is contained within the object itself. The Text property is the most important property of a textbox; it determines the string information that can be stored in the textbox. Storing text is the primary function of a textbox, but many other properties assist you in determining the appearance of the textbox. Table 21.1 lists all the properties you can use to modulate the state of any textbox.

> **NOTE**
>
> This chapter intentionally does not contain a table for every control. There would be several pages of tables if this chapter had tables for events, properties, and methods. I included a table at this point to provide a hint at the rich and diverse variety of properties. Two tenets worth remembering are that properties, methods, and events with the same name should behave about the same in all controls, and the context help lets you look them up on-the-fly.

Table 21.1. A complete list of textbox properties.

Name	Data Type	Description
Name	N/A	This object's name; use it to refer to the object in code.
Alignment	Integer	Determines the justification—right, left, or center of the text.
Appearance	Integer	Determines whether the control appears 2-D or 3-D.
BackColor	Long	Determines the canvas, or background, color of the control.
BorderStyle	Integer	With or without a border. (Setting the background color to the form's background color, the BorderStyle to none, and the appearance as flat makes the text look like it is right on the form instead of in a control.)
DataField	String	If connected to a DataSource, this is the field to which the data resolves.

continues

Table 21.1. continued

Name	Data Type	Description
DataSource	String	The table, if any, from which this control resolves data.
DragIcon	Picture	An icon representing the textbox during dragging.
DragMode	Integer	Manual or automatic; determines how and when control dragging begins.
Enabled	Boolean	Determines whether this control can have the focus.
Font	Font	The font used to write the text.
ForeColor	Long	Font color.
Height	Integer	The height in pixels of the control.
HelpContextID	Integer	The help context identification number; Windows uses this number to search a help file.
Index	Integer	Identifies this control in a control array. (See Chapter 25, "Dynamic Control Creation and Indexing.")
Left	Integer	The leftmost pixel's position within the containing control, such as a form.
LinkItem	String	Specifies the data in a destination control in a DDE conversation.
LinkMode	Integer	Identifies the type of a DDEConversation and initiates the conversation. (DDE is dynamic data exchange.)
LinkTimeout	Number	Specifies the time a control waits for a response.
LinkTopic	String	Specifies the source program and the topic in a DDE conversation.
Locked	Boolean	A Boolean value that determines whether the text value can be edited.
MaxLength	Integer	The maximum number of characters in the Text property.
MouseIcon	Picture	Reading or writing the value of a custom icon.
MousePointer	Integer	A Windows constant value representing the pointer.
MultiLine	Boolean	A Boolean value indicating whether the textbox displays multiple lines of a code.

Name	Data Type	Description
OLEDragMode	Integer	A constant integer determining whether you or the control handles an OLE drag-and-drop action.
OLEDropMode	Enumeration	Specifies the value determining how drop operations are handled.
PasswordChar	String	The character used in place of the text you type for passwords.
RightToLeft	Boolean	Meaningful in character sets or languages where text is entered from right to left (such as Hebrew or Arabic).
ScrollBars	Integer	Used to specify None, Vertical, Horizontal, or Both types of scrollbars; especially useful if you use multiline = True. (Check this property for other controls.)
TabIndex	Integer	Determines the tab order relative to other controls.
TabStop	Boolean	A Boolean value indicating whether this control receives the focus when tabbing.
Tag	Integer	A superfluous integer that you can use for any purpose.
Text	String	The string value of this control.
ToolTipText	String	A hint that is displayed when the mouse roams over the control.
Top	Integer	The top, or X, Cartesian coordinate of this control.
Visible	Boolean	Boolean value indicating whether the control can be seen by the user.
WhatsThisHelpID	String	Used to provide Windows "What's This?" help for Windows 95 and Windows NT.
Width	Integer	The visual width of the control.

The key to using properties at all times is to refer to the object by the value in the Name property concatenated with a period and the property you want to evaluate on the right of the period:

```
Text1.Text = "Some Text"
MsgBox Text1.Text
If( Text1.Text = "Some Text") Then
```

Assuming the existence of Text1, this code represents a few of the infinite contexts in which you can use a TextBox control. No matter how you use it, you need the *object.property* format. For the most part, the textbox properties are extremely easy to use. To become proficient, start from the top of the list and work your way down, experimenting with each one.

Textbox Methods

Properties enable you to specify an initial state at design time and modify the state of each object at runtime. The other aspect of objects is their methods, which define the capabilities of objects. These two complementing aspects define the object in two-thirds of its entirety. The remaining third is how the object is capable of responding in the Windows environment. Table 21.2 describes the methods of the textbox.

> **TIP**
>
> Take common, everyday objects in your office and practice categorizing what you are able to observe or know as properties or methods. Identify possible events.

Table 21.2. Methods that compose the textbox.

Method	Description
Drag	Begins, ends, or cancels dragging.
LinkExecute	Signals the destination to perform the operation passed as a command string.
LinkPoke	DDE-transfers the contexts of a label, picturebox, or textbox to the source application.
LinkRequest	Asks a DDE source application to update the label, picturebox, or textbox.
LinkSend	Transfers the image in a picturebox; needed especially for pictureboxes due to the potentially large size of images.
Move	Enables you to specify all four coordinates of a control at once, rather than set them individually.
OLEDrag	Initiates a control's OLE drag-and-drop procedure.
Refresh	Forces the control to repaint.
SetFocus	Gives the control the focus; calls the GotFocus event.
ShowWhatsThis	Displays the "What's This?" help.
Zorder	Changes a control's perceptual z-order.

You can accomplish some methods, such as Move, by setting the Left, Top, Height, and Width properties individually. However, Move was provided because it sets all four values at once before a Windows paint occurs; hence, it was provided for performance. Often, experience with a language helps you implement solutions simply or more efficiently.

Listing 21.1, an excerpt from Form3.frm and TextMove.vbp, demonstrates ways of moving a control. (Form3.frm and TextMove.vbp are included on this book's CD-ROM.) Two means are applied: The first simply sets individual properties that have to do with relative positioning; the second uses the Move method.

> **NOTE**
>
> Line numbers in code listings are used for reference only. You will not need to use line number in actual programs.

Listing 21.1. Properties and methods of a textbox.

```
 1: Private Sub Command1_Click()
 2:     Text1.Top = Text1.Top - Val(Text2.Text)
 3:         If (Text1.Top + Text1.Height < 1) Then
 4:             Text1.Top = Height - Val(Text2.Text)
 5:     End If
 6: End Sub
 7: Private Sub Command3_Click()
 8:     Text1.Left = Text1.Left - Val(Text2.Text)
 9:     If (Text1.Left + Text1.Width < 1) Then
10:             Text1.Left = Width - Val(Text2.Text)
11:     End If
12: End Sub
13: Private Sub Command4_Click()
14:     If (Text1.Left + Val(Text2.Text) < Width) Then
15:             Text1.Move (Text1.Left + Val(Text2.Text))
16:     Else
17:         Text1.Move (1)
18:     End If
19: End Sub
```

> **NOTE**
>
> Listing 21.1 contains a semantic deficit. Use a consistent naming convention within your development team. As an exercise, decide on better names for the command buttons used in this listing. There are several popular notations to choose from, including using complete words and the Hungarian notation, which uses an abbreviated prefix indicating the type. Be consistent.

> **TIP**
>
> One of the best arguments—presented by Rich Battle of Admiral Insurance Company in Cherry Hill, New Jersey—for using the Hungarian prefix is that all controls will be collected in the Properties dialog alphabetically.

Consider this code, which demonstrates how to use properties and the method Move to position a control—in this instance, a textbox. A programmer's job is to take disparate fragments and ideas and exploit the cacophony of chaos, creating an orchestral harmony. When you position each coordinate property (that is, Left, Top, Width, and Height), Windows might try to paint each time; use Move and the paint occurs just once.

Another interesting method you might want to practice using as soon as possible is SetFocus. Calling SetFocus makes the control that called the method the current one for input purposes. You might need to change the focus from that defined in the TabOrder property based on user inputs or conditional results that change the available options. The textbox is a good control for experimentation.

Textbox Events

The notion of an event is something that happens to the program. The user can press a key or click a mouse, and the program that has the focus can receive the event. In other words, a keystroke event can happen to the program, or a mouse event can happen to the program. There are many kinds of events, and it is not necessary to outline them all right now.

> **TIP**
>
> The Nobel physicist, Dr. Richard Feynman, relates in one of his autobiographical works how he conquered the complex language of mathematics. When presented with terms that were meaningless, he applied terms that had a certain ring for him. When he conquered the concept in terms he was comfortable using, he learned to apply the correct term.
>
> You might not like the language of objects. It can be challenging to learn the vernacular and concepts in tandem. Tackle first one and then the other if it helps.

Events are answered by event handlers, but event handlers are simply functions or subroutines. The whole concept quickly steps back into the familiar territory of functions. Table 21.3 outlines the textbox events you need to know throughout this section.

Reviewing the Standard Controls

CHAPTER 21

391

21

REVIEWING
THE STANDARD
CONTROLS

Table 21.3. Textbox events.

Event Name	Description
Change	Occurs when the Text property is modified.
Click	Occurs when the control is clicked with the mouse.
DblClick	Any handler attached to this event is called when you double-click the control.
DragDrop	Called when you release the mouse over the control during a drag operation.
DragOver	Called when the dragged icon enters the air space of the control.
GotFocus	Called when the control first gets the focus.
KeyDown	Called when the key is down.
KeyUp	Called when the key is released.
KeyPress	A key down and key up sequence is a keypress; this event is fired after the key up.
LinkClose	Occurs when a DDE conversation ends.
LinkError	Occurs if a DDE conversation has an error.
LinkNotify	Occurs when the DDE source data changes.
LinkOpen	Occurs during the initiation of a DDE conversation.
LostFocus	Called when the control loses focus.
MouseDown	Called when a mouse key is pressed.
MouseUp	Called when a mouse key is released.
MouseMove	Called anytime the mouse is moved. (This event is fired all the time in Windows.)
OLECompleteDrag	Occurs when a source OLE object is dropped onto a target OLE object.
OLEDragDrop	If the OLEDropMode is set to 1, this event is called when a source object is dropped on a target object.
OLEDragOver	Occurs when one OLE object is dragged over another.
OLEGiveFeedback	Used for feedback after dragging over an OLE object. Use it to set changes in cursors and icons.
OLESetData	Occurs when the Target object calls GetData on the source object's unloaded data.
OLEStartDrag	Called when an OLE drag begins.

The kinds of events a control is designed to handle can make a difference in what the control is capable of doing. Consider Listing 21.2, an excerpt from Form2.frm and PaintEv.vbp (included on the CD-ROM that comes with this book), which uses a form's Paint event, something a textbox does not have. The sample program demonstrates how different events occur at different times. (It also demonstrates how to create shadowed text effects by writing directly to the canvas.) You are encouraged to run this program and identify and understand why things happen and when.

Listing 21.2. The usefulness of events.

```
 1: Private Declare Function TextOut Lib "gdi32" Alias "TextOutA"
 2: ➡(ByVal hdc As Long, ByVal X As Long, ByVal Y As Long, ByVal lpString
 3: ➡ As String, ByVal nCount As Long) As Long
 4: Private Declare Function SetBkMode Lib "gdi32" (ByVal hdc As Long,
 5: ➡ByVal nBkMode As Long) As Long
 6: Private Declare Function GetDC Lib "user32" (ByVal hwnd As Long) As Long
 7:
 8: Private Sub Form_Load()
 9:   Call ShadowText(hdc, 5, 50, "Disappears?")
10: End Sub
11:
12: Private Sub Form_Paint()
13:     Call ShadowText(hdc, 5, 5, "Hello, World!")
14: End Sub
15:
16: Public Sub ShadowText(DC As Long, X As Long, Y As Long, S As String)
17:     ' Make sure the FontTransparent is True
18:     FontTransparent = True
19:     Result = TextOut(DC, X, Y, S, Len(S))
20:     Form1.ForeColor = "&HFFFF"
21:     Result = TextOut(hdc, X + 1, Y + 1, S, Len(S))
22:     Form1.ForeColor = "&H0"
23: End Sub
```

The events determine how you can orchestrate what happens and how. Refer to Table 21.3 and note that there is no Paint event for the textbox. Also note that line 10 has a defined Paint handler, form_paint, for forms. On line 7 of Listing 21.2, the code calls the function ShadowText. That text does not stay on the form because the next time the Paint is called, it overwrites the text that was written to the canvas in the ShadowText function. However, if you build PaintEv.vbp and execute the program, you see that "Hello, World!" in the Paint event handler stays on the canvas always. Why? The reason concerns the events that a particular event function is assigned. Paint is called every time the form is painted, so the "Hello, World!" text remains. You cannot as easily re-create the shadowy text in the same manner for the textbox because it was not designed to respond to the Paint event.

A few good rules to remember from this section are

- The events to which a control responds determine the kind of interaction you can define.
- Many controls can respond to some of the same events, but some events are uniquely defined for only one control.
- Events are external hardware or software occurrences.
- You do not have to write event handlers for every event, just for those events your code needs to perform its tasks.
- Do not place the code directly in the event handler. Write a third function that many events can share, and reuse the code by calling the function.
- Event handlers are functions that respond to those occurrences.

Review the events in Table 21.3, and write simple practice programs that enable you to practice with each of the events. The programs do not have to be long or complicated. Keep them simple so you can focus on one concept at a time.

Using the Listbox

The listbox enables you to manage a collection of strings in an organized manner. It is capable of displaying a list of text horizontally or vertically, encompassing arbitrary rectangular sizes that suit your needs. Properties, methods, and events facilitate the management of a list of strings. An excellent example of the kinds of control data you can manage with listboxes is the FileListBox control. The FileListBox control is a listbox that contains the files in a directory that match a file mask value.

Distinctive Listbox Methods

I mentioned that many controls share a large percentage of methods. It is the distinct methods that separate one control from another. (Keep in mind that it is necessary to have some methods, properties, and events in common because all controls must work commonly within the Windows operating system.)

Table 21.4 contains the methods of note for listboxes. The demo program in Listing 21.3, an excerpt from Form4.frm and ListBox.vbp (on this book's CD-ROM), demonstrates how to use these methods.

Table 21.4. Listbox methods.

Method Name	Description
AddItem	Enables you to insert an item into the listbox object calling the method.
Clear	Removes all items from the calling listbox.
RemoveItem	Remove a single item at a time by specifying its index.

Listing 21.3. Listbox distinct methods and some error handling.

```
 1: Private Sub Command1_Click()
 2:     On Error GoTo ListBoxError
 3:         Call List1.RemoveItem(List1.ListIndex)
 4:         Exit Sub
 5:
 6: ListBoxError:
 7:     Const MSG = "Index Not Found: Select Item Before Deleting"
 8:         Const BAD_ITEM = "Index Not Found"
 9:         Call MsgBox(MSG, vbExclamation, BAD_ITEM)
10: End Sub
11:
12: Private Sub Command2_Click()
13:     List1.Clear
14: Sub
15:
16: Private Sub Form_Load()
17:     Dim I As Integer
18:     For I = 65 To 90
19:         Call List1.AddItem(Chr$(I))
20:     Next I
21: End Sub
22:
23: Private Sub List1_Scroll()
24:     Call MsgBox(List1.List(List1.TopIndex))
25: End Sub
```

The application (shown in Figure 21.1) demonstrates the methods that enable you to program-matically manipulate the List property.

FIGURE 21.1.

ListBox.exe, *which demonstrates fundamental listbox methods.*

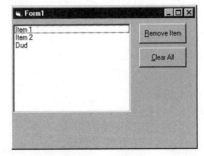

Reviewing the Standard Controls

CHAPTER 21

395

21

REVIEWING
THE STANDARD
CONTROLS

NOTE

Lines 6–9 in Listing 21.3 demonstrate how to use the On Error...Goto error handling provided in Visual Basic. Use this whenever you want to trap generalized errors under any conditions, rather than check beforehand. Line 4 serves as a reminder to call Exit Sub; otherwise, the error-handling code is always executed.

NOTE

Listing 21.3 introduces error handing in the command Click event (lines 1–10). You can make several improvements in the error-handling system. Generally it is better to delegate the error-announcement mechanism to a function instead of right in the error block.

The Err and Erl objects are set when an error occurs. You could create a function that takes these two arguments and creates formatted output from them. In addition, Visual Basic 5 has the Error function, which takes the Err object and returns the error string. The Debug object can be used like this

```
Debug.Print Error(Err)
```

to write the error to the Immediate window. Combining a function indirection and the Error function produces the best results.

In Listing 21.3, line 2 sets up error trapping in case you have a bad index. You can accomplish relatively the same result by checking the listbox ListIndex with an if condition, but error trapping is broad sweeping. If checks are always executed, but exceptional error trapping is executed only when necessary. Error trapping provides a broader kind of coverage against errors.

Line 3 demonstrates the RemoveItem method, and line 4 forces the subroutine to exit. If you forget to exit before the error-trapping code, the error code is always executed. This is never what you want.

Line 13 demonstrates how easy it is to remove all items from a listbox. (The Clear method is called from a command click event handler.) Can you define another way to delete all items? Right—use the RemoveItem method in a loop. It is a good idea to be proactive in finding alternative ways to solve the same problem.

Lines 17–20 use the AddItem method in a For...Loop. You can add items from a file or some other resource. Attaching the listbox to a DataSource and DataField designate that the field is the recipient of any data selection. Lines 23–25 demonstrate using the Scroll event, described in the section "Scrolling the Listbox," later in this chapter.

Distinctive Listbox Properties

In keeping with the theme of the listbox section, this section contains definitions and applications of properties that are more distinctive to the listbox. The listbox's main function is to track a collection of strings. You have seen the methods for doing so; Table 21.5 is a list of properties that facilitate the listbox's characteristic capability to maintain an ordered storehouse of strings.

Table 21.5. Properties characteristic of listboxes.

Property Name	Data Type	Purpose
Columns	Integer	Number of columns used to display the list items.
List	String Array	Contains the strings.
ListCount	Integer	Number of items in the list.
ListIndex	Integer	Current item index.
MultiSelect	Boolean	User can select more than one item.
NewIndex	Integer	Index of the most recently added item.
SelCount	Integer	Count of the selected items.
Sorted	Boolean	Determines whether the list is sorted.
Text	String	The value of the currently selected item.
TopIndex	Integer	The Index property of the topmost visible item.

Painting the listbox as a short rectangle, in conjunction with setting the Columns property, gives you a horizontally oriented listbox. Generally, a listbox is arranged in a vertically aligned style. The MultiSelect and SelCount properties enable you to iterate through multiple selections and process the selected strings. The Sorted property causes the listbox to sort the strings as they are entered or after the fact.

As you might have guessed, both the methods and properties are equally powerful and useful in the management of soft systems. Remember not to discount methods, properties, or events when attempting to solve a new or challenging problem.

Scrolling the Listbox

The listbox has almost all the same events as the textbox. This makes sense because both are used for manipulating strings. The distinction between the two is that the listbox is decidedly a collection of strings, and the textbox is only a collection when the MultiLine property is True.

Use the Scroll event to perform processing when the list is scrolled. From Table 21.5, you learned that the TopIndex indicates which item in the List property is the topmost visible item. Use the Scroll event handler to perform processing while the list is scrolling without any particular selection.

Using Command Buttons

The command button is a simple control with a `Caption` property and one important event. The caption can contain an ampersand, which indicates the hotkey; for example, `&Change` indicates that Alt+C is the hotkey combination for this control. The command button has several events, but the most important is the `Click` event. It is the simplicity of the control that makes it powerful. Responding to a click, the command button can spawn activity from the simplest of user input.

The simple application in the `Command.vbp` project demonstrates how easy it is to use the `Click` event. The application consists of one line of code that calls the OLE `DoVerb` object to initiate the calculator OLE object. You can begin experimenting with the command button and OLE automation by dropping an OLE control on a form, setting the `SourceDoc` to the Windows `Calc.exe` program. Add a command button and use the OLE object to call `DoVerb` on the `Click` event.

Using the Timer Control

The timer control represents the hardware timer in every computer. It enables you to hook into the internal timer in the PC running the program. The `Enabled` property turns the timer on, and the `Interval` property, measured in milliseconds, determines how often the `Timer` event is called. By placing code in the `Timer` event, you can create simple animation with the `PictureBox` and `Image` controls, or with icons. (See the following section, "Using the `PictureBox` and `Image` Controls.") Other ideas for the `Timer` are timeout, autosave, or splash screen delays.

As an example, create a new project and select Project | Add Form. Select the About dialog from the Add Form dialog. Modify the About dialog to contain the text and graphic image for your program. Add a timer to the control. In the `Timer` event, add

```
Close
```

to the event handler. In the application's main form, `Form_Load` event, add code that shows the About dialog. In the About dialog `Form_Load` event, set the `Interval` to five seconds (`Interval = 5000`), enable the timer, and call

```
Call frmAbout.Show(, Form1) ' Form1 or whatever the main form is.
```

which causes the splash screen to display on top of the background screen as it loads. When the `Timer` event occurs, `Hide` or `Unload` the splash form. The demo program is in `Splash.vbp` on the CD-ROM.

Using the **PictureBox** and **Image** Controls

The PictureBox and Image controls provide roughly the same end result: They both display a variety of image formats. The Image control uses fewer resources and paints a little faster than the PictureBox, but it has fewer methods, events, and properties, so it is less flexible.

Both the PictureBox and the Image control can display a variety of image formats, including cursors, bitmaps, icons, metafiles, and JPEG and GIF files. Within the last five years or so, displaying complex graphics has become easier. Using graphic images used to be an arcane art form, requiring the practitioner to write separate algorithms for each of the image formats. Until recently, there was a plethora of books with code examples, mostly in Assembler, that you had to wade through to display graphics in computer programs. Windows and Visual Basic make it easy for you to concentrate on the aesthetic aspect you are trying to achieve, rather than decipher palette information from a binary image file.

An easy and eye-catching use for images is to animate your program's iconic display when on the form or when minimized. (When you log on to the Internet or some other service, Windows 95 animates the Dial-up Networking icon to let you know your connection is active.) Listing 21.4, an excerpt from Form6.frm and Picture.vbp on the CD-ROM, demonstrates just how easy this process is.

Listing 21.4. Simple icon animation using a timer.

```
1: Private Sub Timer1_Timer()
2:     Static A As Integer
3:     A = A Mod 8
4:     Main.Picture = Pix(A).Picture
5:     Form1.Icon = Pix(A).Picture
6:     A = A + 1
7: End Sub
```

Except for the PictureBox controls, this is the entire extent of the program. The activity centers around the timer control's Timer event. Using a static integer, the value of the integer begins as 0 and maintains its value between successive calls to the Timer event handler. Usually local variables are not maintained; defining a variable as static serves this purpose. On the first call to the timer handler, the value A is 0, and it is incremented on each successive call.

> **TIP**
>
> It is preferable to use a static, rather than a global, variable when you want to maintain a value between function calls.

Line 3 uses modulo arithmetic—or remainder division—to ensure that the value is always between 0 and 7. (For example, when A is 8, using the calculation on line 3, you know that 8 Mod 8 equals 0.) The left-hand object Main on line 4 receives the picture from the Pix() array, using the value of A as the index into the control array Pix. (Table 21.6 outlines invaluable PictureBox and Image control properties.) Setting a form's icon to the icon value in the Pix array is what causes the form's icon to be animated. Line 6 increments the images by 1.

Table 21.6. PictureBox and Image control properties.

Property Name	Applies To	Data Type	Description
AutoRedraw	PictureBox	Boolean	Determines whether automatic painting occurs. Use the Paint method if AutoRedraw is False.
AutoSize	PictureBox	Boolean	If False, the image is clipped to the size of the control. Setting AutoSize = True resizes the image to its actual size.
ClipControls	PictureBox	Boolean	If True, the entire image is repainted; if False, only newly exposed images are repainted. False settings result in somewhat faster performance.
DataField	PictureBox	String	Database field containing a picture.
DataSource	PictureBox	String	DataSource where the DataField is defined.
DrawMode	PictureBox	Integer	Determines how the image is drawn in conjunction with the background image. Used for visual effects.
DrawStyle	PictureBox	Integer	Determines the line style for graphics drawing.
DrawWidth	PictureBox	Integer	Determines the width of lines drawn with graphics methods.
FillColor	PictureBox	Long	Determines the color with which shapes are filled.
FillStyle	PictureBox	Integer	Transparent by default, which indicates that the FillColor should be ignored; use this property to specify fill patterns.

continues

Table 21.6. continued

Property Name	Applies To	Data Type	Description
Font	PictureBox	Font	Picturebox's font if you write to the canvas.
FontTransparent	PictureBox	Boolean	If False, the Rect containing the font overwrites the background.
ForeColor	PictureBox	Long	Color of the text.
Height	PictureBox, Image	Integer	Control height, which can be greater than the image height unless AutoSize = True.
Index	PictureBox, Image	Integer	Index if used in a control array.
Left	PictureBox, Image	Integer	Left Cartesian coordinate of the control.
Picture	PictureBox, Image	String	The image. Picture can be an icon, a bitmap, a cursor, a JPEG, or a GIF.
ScaleHeight	PictureBox	Integer	Used to create a custom coordinate scale.
ScaleLeft	PictureBox	Integer	Used for setting left in custom scale.
ScaleMode	PictureBox	Integer	Measurement scale. You might be accustomed to pixels; the default in Visual Basic 5 is twips.
ScaleTop	PictureBox	Integer	Top of the custom scale.
ScaleWidth	PictureBox	Integer	Scaled width.
Stretch	Image	Boolean	Should the image be stretched to fit the Image control frame.
Top	PictureBox, Image	Integer	Top coordinate of the control.
Width	PictureBox, Image	Integer	Width of the control; can be greater than the picture width.

The visual part of the application is completed by placing however many animated frames you want on the form and writing the code in Listing 21.4 in the Timer event. The last step is to set all the images' Visible properties to False for animated icons or all but one to False for

Reviewing the Standard Controls

CHAPTER 21

401

21

REVIEWING
THE STANDARD
CONTROLS

animated graphics. The `Picture.vbp` example is included on this book's CD-ROM. If you installed Visual Basic 5 into the default directory, you can find many graphics provided for you by Microsoft in `\DevStudio\VB\Graphics` (with the moon icons in `.\Icons\Elements`).

With a little experimentation, you can create some interesting effects by orchestrating properties. The optional addition to `Picture.vbp` in Listing 21.5 adds text with a shadow appearance every time there is a full moon.

Listing 21.5. Shadow text on the picturebox's canvas.

```
1:  ' Add this declaration to use the gdi32 API function TextOut.
2:  Private Declare Function TextOut Lib "gdi32" Alias "TextOutA"
3:  ➥(ByVal hdc As Long, ByVal X As Long, ByVal Y As Long,
4:  ➥ByVal lpString  As String, ByVal nCount As Long) As Long
5:      ' Optional Code not listed in the accompanying text.
6:      Const TEXT = "Shadow Moon"
7:      If (A = 4) Then
8:          Main.ForeColor = 0 ' Black
9:              Call TextOut(Main.hdc, 49, 1, TEXT, Len(TEXT))
10:             Main.ForeColor = 255 ' Red
11:             Call TextOut(Main.hdc, 50, 2, TEXT, Len(TEXT))
12:     End If
13:     ' Optional Code End.
```

Table 21.7 contains a complete reference listing of the methods for the `PictureBox` and `Image` controls. You can use the table to easily compare the strengths and weaknesses of the two.

Table 21.7. `PictureBox` and `Image` control methods.

Method	Applies To	Description
Circle	PictureBox	Draws circles in the PictureBox.
Cls	PictureBox	Clears the graphics of images set at runtime only if `AutoRedraw = True`.
Line	PictureBox	Used for line drawing in `PictureBox`.
Move	PictureBox, Image	Moves the control—all four coordinates in one shot, reducing the number of `Paint` messages.
PaintPicture	PictureBox	Paints and positions a picture.
Point	PictureBox	Returns the RGB, or color, value the point specified by the x,y arguments.
PSet	PictureBox	Sets a pixel at the x,y pair specified of the color specified.
Refresh	PictureBox, Image	Repaints the image.

continues

Table 21.7. continued

Method	Applies To	Description
Scale	PictureBox	Defines a coordinate system for the image. The default system is 0,0 for the top-left corner of the control.
ScaleX	PictureBox	Changes the width scale.
ScaleY	PictureBox	Changes the height scale.

In addition to the properties, the methods play a role in how the picturebox or image facilitates solving your software development problem. You can generally think of the Image control as a way to display images down and dirty and quickly. The picturebox provides more properties and methods. Use the picturebox when you need to perform custom graphics, line, and shape drawing. The events specific to these graphic-drawing controls are the Click, Paint, and Resize methods. You can perform the custom text drawing on the Paint event, so any paint message persists the shadow text. It takes some practice to get a feel for the timing and usefulness of the properties, events, and methods particular to any control, including these.

Using Checkboxes and Option Buttons

Checkboxes enable you to offer a way to visually allow users to select a variety of options. The option button is similar, but it is intended for use when you need the user to select only one item from a group of choices. (The shutdown dialog for Windows 95 exemplifies the intended use.)

The simple PizzaNet interface demonstrates the distinction between how option buttons and checkboxes are used. (See Figure 21.2.) The code in PizzaNet.vbp shows that the option buttons are placed in a control array so one Click event handler can be used for the entire group. Typically, you use option buttons when one choice is appropriate and only one can be selected at a time. However, you may use different grouping tactics to allow disparate groups of option buttons; one such tactic is creating a control array. Checkboxes are intended to allow multi-selection input. The Value of an option button can be True (selected) or False (unselected). A checkbox can have one of three states in its Value property: 0 = Unchecked, 1 = Checked, and 2 = Grayed.

As with command buttons, the Click event is the most important event for both of these controls, but you can also catch key and mouse events. In addition, you can assign the DataField and DataSource properties to resolve the value of the checkboxes to a database field. Primarily, you can use these two controls, as in the demo program PizzaNet.vbp, for decision making or control condition checking. Consider the following:

```
If( Option(1).Checked = True ) Then...
If( Option(2).Check = True ) Then...
```

FIGURE 21.2.

The PizzaNet.vbp *demo form shows the distinction between option buttons and checkboxes.*

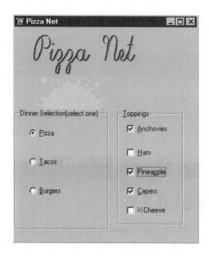

The novice might exhaustively test each button's Value property, but this inhibits extensibility because you would have to add additional checks for each new type of food added. Because you were insightful enough to use a control array, you can use a single Click event handler for the entire array. With one event handler, you can achieve the desired effect—that is, offer toppings for pizzas.

The If...Then...Else...EndIf is extensible. Regardless of the number of items, this Click event handler enables you to display pizza toppings when the pizza is selected and disable them when it is not. Each code line, like time, is money. The actual program created when you compile PizzaNet.vbp uses the boolean evaluation of the index to set the Visible property of the Toppings frame:

```
Frame2.Visible = (Index = 1)
```

Index is compared to 1. If it is 1, the comparison evaluates to True; otherwise, it evaluates to False. This is exactly what you want. For setting simple properties and returning boolean results from functions, using the boolean evaluation as the value can save you time and money. All three code fragments work. You must decide which is appropriate for your purposes.

Using the Combobox

The combobox is the rough equivalent of a textbox and a listbox used in concert. Like the listbox, it contains a list of strings. However, unlike the listbox, which uses the list index to determine the selected item, the combobox stores the selection. The combobox has an iconic arrow; clicking it displays a list of string choices. When you select an item, the drop-down list part of the combobox closes. What is left looks like a textbox. You can read the Text property of the combobox to ascertain the selected string value.

Use a combobox when you need to conserve screen real estate—in other words, when there is not enough room for a large listbox. You must insert the list of strings just as you did with the listbox. You can add the strings into the `List` property at design time or runtime just as you did with the listbox. (Refer to the section "Using the Listbox," earlier in this chapter.)

If you want to use the `DataField` and `DataSource` pair, you still need to fill the list. The difference is that when you select a value, the result, in addition to being recorded in the combobox's `Text` property, is recorded in the current record of the indicated field.

Creating an Open File Dialog with FileList and DriveList

When you have finished this section, you will know how to coordinate properties and events in concert to produce a desired result. This section demonstrates how to create a dialog that is similar to `OpenDialog` with the added twist of viewing graphics. (See Figure 21.3.) By following the sample program, you will get a firsthand look at how using events and properties in concert can produce an effective result with little code. To learn more about the Open dialog, read Chapter 24, "Leveraging Windows: Using the Common Dialog Control."

FIGURE 21.3.

*An Open dialog box
that shows the contents
of picture files.*

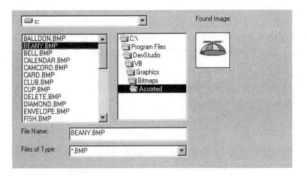

The underlying controls are derived from listboxes, textboxes, and comboboxes. The `FileListBox`, `DirListBox`, and `DriveListBox` demonstrate uses of listboxes. You already know how to use the properties, events, and methods that were incorporated in lieu of their relationship with the listbox.

Listing 21.6 is an excerpt from `Form7.frm` and `PixDlg.vbp`. The `PixDlg` project and `Form7.frm` are included on this book's CD-ROM.

Reviewing the Standard Controls

CHAPTER 21

405

21

REVIEWING
THE STANDARD
CONTROLS

Listing 21.6. FileListBox, DirListBox, and DriveListBox.

```
1: Private Sub Combo1_Change()
2:     File1.Pattern = Combo1.Text
3: End Sub
4:
5: Private Sub Combo1_Click()
6:     File1.Pattern = Combo1.List(Combo1.ListIndex)
7: End Sub
8:
9: Private Sub Dir1_Change()
10:     File1.Path = Dir1.Path
11: End Sub
12:
13: Private Sub Drive1_Change()
14:     Dir1.Path = Drive1.Drive
15: End Sub
16:
17: Private Sub File1_Click()
18:     Text1.Text = File1.filename
19: End Sub
20:
21: Private Sub File1_PathChange()
22:     On Error GoTo IndexError
23:     File1.ListIndex = 0
24:     Text1.Text = File1.filename
25: IndexError:
26:     Text1.Text = ""
27: End Sub
28:
29: Private Sub Text1_Change()
30:     ' Clear the picture
31:     Set Picture1.Picture = LoadPicture()
32:     filename = Dir1.Path + "\" + File1.filename
33:     Select Case Right$(Text1.Text, 3)
34:     Case "CUR", "BMP", "ICO", "WMF"
35:         Set Picture1.Picture = LoadPicture(filename)
36:     End Select
37: End Sub
```

Listing 21.6 shows all the executable code for the picture dialog application (PixDlg.vbp). Fewer than 40 lines of code—but code that acts carefully in concert—produce a reusable artifact that is capable of browsing images before selecting a particular image. The pertinent properties of the controls specific to this chapter are contained in the code listing, so I cover these as I describe the code.

The textbox used for the FileName, the combobox used for the file masks, the DirListBox, the FileListBox, and the DriveListBox are interconnected via Change events. The result is a cascading effect. Line 14 in Drive1_Change connects to the DirlListBox by assigning the value Drive1.Drive to Dir1.Path. Modifying the Path property of the DirListBox invokes the Dir1_Change event, which cascades the drive change through the directory change to the FileListBox by assigning the Path properties of both controls: File1.Path = Dir1.Path in line 10. The end result is achieved when the FileListBox's Change event is called and the FileName property of the FileListBox is assigned to the Text property.

Using this downward cascading of events has the net result of coordinating the moves through the disk system. To be consistent, the image is loaded when the Text1_Change event is called. Lines 29–37 clear the old image and then use LoadPicture to put the image into the picturebox.

> **TIP**
>
> As a general rule, pay for one level of indirection by adding a function that performs the task needed rather than place the code right into the event handler. The event handler can call the function, and so can some other agent.

> **NOTE**
>
> I refer to the distancing of the relationship between the problem-solving code as the loosening of the coupling relationship. Code that is loosely coupled in regard to the graphical user interface generally enhances extensibility and maintainability.

As a qualitative assessment, you can call this down-and-dirty utility a prototype. To enhance reusability and extensibility, it is better to move the function parts of the code outside the event handlers. The net result is that the code is usable in any other context and is not too closely tied to these specific controls and events. For example, lines 29–37 can easily be represented by a function that takes a filename and loads the picture into an Image property. Experiment with the code by loosening the relationship between the code and the controls.

Using Shapes and Lines

The picturebox contains many of the same capabilities as the line and shape controls. If you need professional, custom graphics for an application, these are not the controls for you. Instead, you will want to get high-quality bitmap images and use the PictureBox or Image control. However, if your application needs fundamental drawing capabilities, you can create a wide variety of images with simple lines and shapes. Table 21.8 contains a collection of fundamental properties and methods for the shape and line controls.

Table 21.8. Shape and line control properties and methods.

Name	Type	Applies To	Description
BackColor	Property	Shape	The background color of the control.
BackStyle	Property	Shape	Opaque or transparent background.
BorderColor	Property	Shape, line	Color of the control's frame.

Name	Type	Applies To	Description
BorderStyle	Property	Shape, line	Line style (such as solid, dash, dot, and so on).
BorderWidth	Property	Shape, line	Width of the frame line.
DrawMode	Property	Shape, line	How the image is merged with its background.
FillColor	Property	Shape	The color with which the shape is filled.
FillStyle	Property	Shape	Line styles used for the filler.
Move	Method	Shape	Sets all the properties—Height, Width, Top, and Left—at once.
Refresh	Method	Shape, line	Forces a repaint.
Shape	Property	Shape	Describes the general shape (such as circle, oval, square, and so on).
X1	Property	Line	X-plane or starting x coordinate.
X2	Property	Line	X-plane or ending x coordinate.
Y1	Property	Line	Y-plane or starting y coordinate.
Y2	Property	Line	Y-plane or ending y coordinate.
ZOrder	Method	Shape, line	Adjusts the perception of depth, or Z Cartesian plane.

These controls might be beneficial in creating a drawing or painting program or creating generalized charts or graphics. If you need advanced graphical images, use the Image or PictureBox control. For graphing capabilities, read about MSCHART in Chapter 22, "Moving On to Intermediate Controls."

Using the MaskedEdit Control

The MaskedEdit control is fundamentally a textbox. You already know how to use a textbox (from the section "Using the TextBox Control," earlier in this chapter). The distinction is that the MaskedEdit is a new Microsoft Visual Basic 5 ActiveX control that enables you to define an input mask for the control. Table 21.9 contains the relevant MaskedEdit control properties. Whereas a textbox enables you to enter a string of characters, the MaskedEdit control enables you to define a positional edit mask that fills in mask characters according to the mask rule.

NOTE

If the MaskedEdit control does not appear in the toolbar, select Project | Component and select the Microsoft MaskedEdit Control 5.0 from the Controls tab of the Components dialog. Click Apply.

Table 21.9. MaskedEdit control properties.

Property	Data Type	Description
(Custom)	Property Pages dialog	Enables you to modify the MaskedEdit control in a dialog format at design time. (See Figure 21.4.) Also accessible by clicking a MaskedEdit control and selecting Properties from the right-mouse-click speed menu.
AllowPrompt	Boolean	If True, promptChar is a valid input character.
ClipMode	Integer	Either mskIncludeLiterals or mskExcludeLiterals determines whether the mask literals are included in copy and paste commands.
DataBindings	Object	The property of an object bound to this control.
DataField	String	Field name.
DataSource	String	Name of a database or recordset produced by a SQL statement.
Format	String	The same formatting strings available with the Visual Basic Format function. Use for displaying numbers, dates, times, and text. (On/Off does not work.)
FormattedText	String	Not available at design time. The text without the prompt characters.
Mask	String	The validation mask for this control.
MaskLength	Integer	The maximum length of the input.
PromptChar	Char	The placeholder character; the default is the underscore (_).
PromptInclude	Boolean	Indicates whether the text can contain the prompt character itself.
Text	String	The control's string value (not available at design time), with prompt characters and all.

For an example of how you might apply the control, consider a phone number. A typical U.S. phone number is formatted roughly as (###)###-####. To ensure that the data is entered in the correct or desired format, apply the edit mask. You get the data in the correct format, but your users do not have to type the mask characters (,), and -. Applying the (###)###-#### edit mask ensures that there is always a prefix and a suffix, and an optional area code in the phone number.

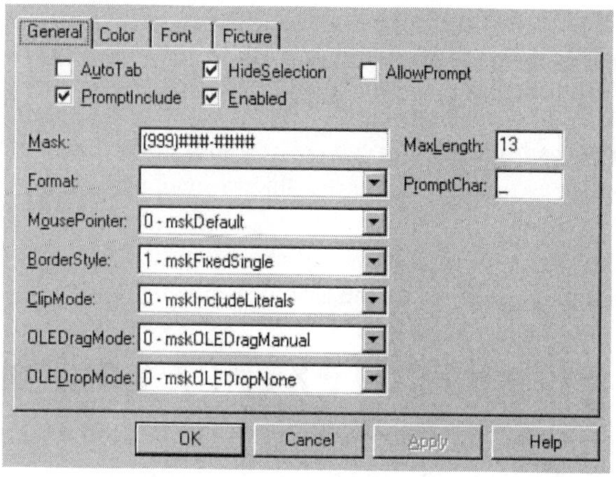

FIGURE 21.4.

The MaskedEdit
*ActiveX control has a
dialog for modifying
properties.*

A good caveat is to use an edit mask wherever possible. Using the edit mask greatly reduces the amount of validation code you have to write to verify user input. The net effect is that you require the user to enter good data but assist them as much as possible to that end; a win-win situation for users and developers. Use the ValidateError event to catch bad input at runtime. Ensuring that your database records always get good data—which is easier to do then fixing bad data—will assist you in keeping your algorithms cleaner because you have to write fewer data-verification checks.

Using the UpDown Control

The UpDown control is an attachable spin control. You can attach it to other controls with the BuddyControl property. Setting the BuddyControl property to another control, such as a TextBox, MaskedEdit, or even a Slider, enables the UpDown button to increment the value of that control. Of course, you must indicate an appropriate property for the UpDown control to manipulate.

Try this example. Attach the UpDown BuddyControl property to a TextBox. Assign the BuddyProperty to the TextBox control's Text property. With the default Increment value of 1, clicking the up button increments the text value by one and clicking the down arrow decrements by one. The alignment of the UpDown control to its buddy is automatic.

For buddy controls with Min and Max values, you must modify the Min and Max values of the UpDown control to coincide with the Min and Max of the BuddyControl. Properties in the UpDown control that you already know how to use are Increment, Min, Max, and Value. Setting SynchBuddy to True causes the UpDown control to synchronize the Value properties of the UpDown control with its buddy. The AutoBuddy boolean property determines whether the UpDown control seeks out a buddy automatically; the Alignment property determines whether the UpDown control appears on the left side of its buddy or on its right; and the Orientation property determines whether the arrow icons are vertical or horizontal.

With the UpDown control, you can create a spin up or down effect on several kinds of controls. Previously, you could spin a TextBox-like control up or down but had to write code and use a scrollbar to create a spinner for other types of controls. You can add the UpDown control by selecting Properties|Components and choosing the Microsoft Windows Common Controls-2 5.0 from the Controls tab of the Components dialog.

Using the RichTextBox Control

The RichTextBox control is a TextBox with added capabilities that allow it to handle *Rich Text Format*, or .RTF files. You can use the Text and Multiline properties in concert to create an .RTF editor. The RichTextBox control enables you to use an extended syntax for text processing. RTF files are commonly used for creating Windows help files.

You can create a poor man's word processor with a few lines of code. (See Figure 21.5.) The EditRTF.vbp project, when compiled, uses the RichTextBox, enabling the user to set fonts; italicize, bold, and underline text; and set different colors. Listing 21.7 contains EditRTF.vbp, an excerpt from Form10.frm. With a little time, you could expand on this project and create a fairly complex word processor.

FIGURE 21.5.

You can easily create a poor man's word processor with the RichTextBox *and* CommonDialog *controls.*

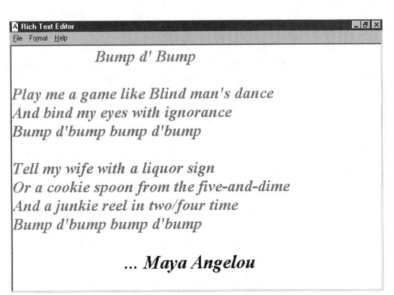

Reviewing the Standard Controls

CHAPTER 21

411

21

REVIEWING
THE STANDARD
CONTROLS

Listing 21.7. A functional word processor.

```
 1: Private Sub Form_Activate()
 2:     RichTextBox1.SetFocus
 3: End Sub
 4:
 5: Private Sub Form_QueryUnload(Cancel As Integer, UnloadMode As Integer)
 6:     If (MsgBox("Are you sure?", vbQuestion + vbYesNo, "Exit Editor")
 7: ➥= vbYes) Then
 8:         Cancel = False
 9:     Else
10:         Cancel = True
11:     End If
12: End Sub
13:
14: Private Sub Form_Resize()
15:     Call RichTextBox1.Move(Me.ScaleLeft, Me.ScaleTop, Me.ScaleWidth,
16: ➥Me.ScaleHeight)
17: End Sub
18:
19: Private Sub mnuBold_Click()
20:     RichTextBox1.SelBold = Not RichTextBox1.SelBold
21: End Sub
22:
23: Private Sub mnuClose_Click()
24:     RichTextBox1.filename = ""
25:     RichTextBox1.Text = ""
26:     RichTextBox1.Refresh
27: End Sub
28:
29: Private Sub mnuColor_Click()
30:     ColorDialog.ShowColor
31:     If (ColorDialog.CancelError = False) Then
32:         RichTextBox1.SelColor = ColorDialog.Color
33:     End If
34: End Sub
35:
36: Private Sub mnuExit_Click()
37:     ' Look "Me" up in the context help.
38:     Unload Me
39: End Sub
40:
41: Private Sub mnuFont_Click()
42:     ColorDialog.Flags = cdlCFBoth
43:     ColorDialog.FontName = RichTextBox1.SelFontName
44:     ColorDialog.ShowFont
45:     If (ColorDialog.CancelError = False) Then
46:         RichTextBox1.SelFontName = ColorDialog.FontName
47:         RichTextBox1.SelFontSize = ColorDialog.FontSize
48:     End If
49: End Sub
50:
51: Private Sub mnuItalics_Click()
52:     RichTextBox1.SelItalic = Not RichTextBox1.SelItalic
53: End Sub
54:
```

continues

Listing 21.7. continued

```
55: Private Sub mnuOpen_Click()
56:     OpenDialog.ShowOpen
57:     If (OpenDialog.CancelError = False) Then
58:         Call RichTextBox1.LoadFile(OpenDialog.filename, 0)
59:     End If
60: End Sub
61:
62: Private Sub mnuSave_Click()
63:     SaveDialog.ShowSave
64:     If (SaveDialog.CancelError = False) Then
65:         Call RichTextBox1.SaveFile(SaveDialog.filename, 0)
66:     End If
67: End Sub
68:
69: Private Sub mnuUnderline_Click()
70:     RichTextBox1.SelUnderline = Not RichTextBox1.SelUnderline
71: End Sub
```

Table 21.10 contains descriptions of the RichTextBox properties and methods. The Menu Designer enables you to create the menu shown in Figure 21.5. (Refer to Chapter 8, "Going Beyond Menu Basics," if you need help in creating the menu.) The remainder of the application can be designed visually with one RichTextBox and three common dialogs on a form. (Chapter 24 provides you with information about the common dialog.)

Table 21.10. RichTextBox properties and methods.

Name	Property/Method	Data Type	Description
BullIndent	Property	Integer	Determines the indent distance if SelBullet is True.
FileName	Property	String	The name of a file loaded into the Text property.
Find	Method		Finds a string in the Text property.
Font	Property	Font	Default text font.
GetLineFromChar	Method		The line number of the line containing the character argument.
HideSelection	Property	Boolean	Indicates whether selected text appears highlighted when the RichTextBox loses focus.
LoadFile	Method		Loads the file argument into the Text property.

Name	Property/Method	Data Type	Description
MaxLength	Property	Integer	Maximum length of the text.
MultiLine	Property	Boolean	If `True`, the `Text` property can display more than one line of text.
RightMargin	Property	Integer	Value of the right margin.
SaveFile	Method		Saves the `FileName` argument to a file.
ScrollBars	Property	Integer	Vertical, horizontal, or both scrollbars.
SelAlignment	Property	Integer	Sets the alignment of the selected text.
SelBold	Property	Boolean	If `True`, the selected text is bold.
SelBullet	Property	Boolean	Bullets the selected paragraphs if `True`.
SelCharOffset	Property	Integer	If `0`, the characters appear on the text baseline; positive values make the selected text superscript, and negative numbers make it subscript.
SelColor	Property	Color	The color of the selected text.
SelFontName	Property	String	Selected text font.
SelFontSize	Property	Integer	Selected font size.
SelHangingIndent	Property	Integer	Depth of hanging indent for the selected text.
SelItalics	Property	Boolean	Selected text is italicized if `True`.
SelPrint	Method		Prints the selected text to the device context argument.
SelProtected	Property	Boolean	Selected text is not modifiable if set to `True`.
SelRightIndent	Property	Integer	Depth of right indentation of selected text.
SelRTF	Property	String	The value of the selected text; use it to modify text in search and replace functionality.

continues

Table 21.10. continued

Name	Property/Method	Data Type	Description
SelTabCount	Property	Integer	Tab count of the selected text.
SelTabs	Property	Integer	Sets the number of tabs in selected text.
SelStrikethrough	Property	Boolean	If True, the selected text has a line through it.
SelUnderline	Property	Boolean	True value underlines the selected text.
Span	Method		Selects text in the control based on a starting and an ending character.
Text	Property	String	The displayed value of the control.

The form's Activate event handler (refer to Listing 21.7) makes the RichTextBox the focus control. Any time you try to exit the program, the QueryUnload event handler verifies that you really want to quit. Setting Cancel to False aborts the closing of the form. You could extend the functionality to verify that any updates to the text are written to a file. Lines 13–16 resize the RichTextBox control when the form is resized.

Several menu items for formatting were added in the Menu Designer. Each of the Click event handlers uses NOT logic to toggle the selection's bold, italic, and underline properties. (See line 18 for an example.) The mnuClose_Click handler clears the FileName and Text properties and refreshes the RichTextBox.

Lines 27–32 use a common dialog to set the color of the SelColor property. Don't forget to check the CancelError property of common dialogs to ensure that the user did not click the Cancel button.

Lines 34–37 execute Unload Me, which sends a message that the QueryUnload event handler receives. (Look up Me in the context-sensitive help; it refers to the enclosing object.)

Lines 39–47 borrow the common dialog used for colors and enable the user to change the FontName and FontSize. You have to set the Flags property before calling ShowFont.

The event handlers mnuOpen_Click and mnuSave_Click use a common dialog and the RichTextBox's LoadFile and SaveFile to provide external file-handling capabilities.

You can use EditRTF.vbp to experiment with the other properties in Table 21.10. Subscripting and superscripting are necessary if you use your rich text editor to create help files. In addition to an RTF file, you need a help compiler to create the binary .HLP files.

Scrollbars and Scrolling

Earlier versions of Visual Basic did not provide a means of visually tracking relative change. In addition to the scrollbar's usual function, it was often used by developers to visually represent some change in value. A good object-based architecture should expose most of the useful artifacts, but earlier extended uses of the scrollbar are now supplanted by more precise or visually appealing controls. The slider in Chapter 22 is a perfect example of such a control.

The two scrollbar controls are the HScrollBar for the horizontal scrollbar and the VScrollBar, or vertical scrollbar. They are separated by their relative visual orientation. Most controls that need scrolling capabilities come with them preattached, and if you need a control to track relative change, refer to the slider and progress bar in Chapter 22.

Clipping Pictures

The PictureClip control enables you to logically slice up a picture into an array of subpictures. By specifying the Rows and Cols properties of a picture, you can treat each section as an individual picture. The sample program enables you to grab slices of the bitmap based on each new position of the mouse. Listing 21.8 contains code for the excerpt from Form11.frm and PicClip.vbp. You can use this method to cut or copy smaller parts of an image from a complete image, and you can see how the zoom capabilities are supported.

Listing 21.8. Clipping on-the-fly.

```
1: Private Sub Form_Initialize()
2:     PictureClip1.Rows = ScaleHeight
3:     PictureClip1.Cols = ScaleWidth
4:     Refresh
5: End Sub
6:
7: Private Sub Form_MouseMove(Button As Integer, Shift As Integer,
8: ➥X As Single, Y As Single)
9:     PictureClip1.ClipX = X
10:    PictureClip1.ClipY = Y
11:        If (X + Picture1.Width >= ScaleWidth) Then
12:             PictureClip1.ClipWidth = ScaleWidth - X
13:    Else
14:             PictureClip1.ClipWidth = Picture1.Width
15:    End If
16:    If (Y + Picture1.Height >= ScaleHeight) Then
17:        PictureClip1.ClipHeight = ScaleHeight - Y
18:    Else
19:        PictureClip1.ClipHeight = Picture1.Height
20:    End If
21:    Picture1.Picture = PictureClip1.Clip
22: End Sub
```

The demo program works by slicing the Rows and Cols properties of the PictureClip control into a matrix with the same number of regions as the form itself. This is accomplished by setting the PictureClip Rows and Cols to the form's ScaleHeight and ScaleWidth. Each X and Y mouse coordinate pair points to an individual, pixel-sized clipping region.

During the MouseMove event, the X and Y positions become the anchor top and left of the clipping region designated by setting ClipY and ClipX equal to X and Y. Finally, the ClipWidth and ClipHeight properties are set to the Width and Height properties of the PictureBox where the clip is shown, producing the sliding snapshot underneath the mouse position.

Load and execute PicClip.vbp from the book's CD-ROM to try it out. Rows, Cols, ClipX, ClipY, ClipHeight, ClipWidth, and Clip—all the pertinent properties and methods of the PictureClip— are demonstrated in the program for you. The most important remaining method is the GraphicCell method; like the Clip method, it returns a picture. However, GraphicCell takes an index argument, which specifies the clipping region. The regions are accessed by counting from 0 the top, leftmost region to Rows * Cols - 1, the extreme right and lowest clipping region—working from top left to bottom right.

Use the demo program to experiment with PictureClip so that you can add to your software development arsenal. You can create some startling effects and offer the greatest versatility when you are able to use all the powerful controls Microsoft has provided for you.

Summary

You will use the Standard Controls more than any other. If you learn how to manipulate properties, methods, and events for the Standard Controls, you will know how to apply these concepts to any control that rolls down the pike.

This chapter discusses several of the controls provided to you as a Visual Basic 5 developer. Seven demonstration programs enable you to experiment and extend your knowledge of labels, frames, and the TextBox, MaskedEdit, and RichTextBox controls. Included in the demo programs on the CD-ROM are other programs that demonstrate some graphics fundamentals and the system timer.

To learn more about controls not covered in this chapter and other topics that are mentioned or introduced, such as common dialogs, read the following chapters:

- Chapter 5, "Designing Forms: Your Look and Feel," will help you with the basics of creating forms and adding controls to them.
- Chapter 6, "Using Form Templates," elaborates on using the template About form.
- Chapter 8, "Going Beyond Menu Basics," shows you how to do some interesting things with menus in your programs.
- Chapter 10, "Declaring, Raising, and Handling Events," gives you the complete scoop on event handling.

- Chapter 16, "Handling Errors," is a must read if you want to write robust, fault-tolerant software solutions.

- Chapter 22, "Moving On to Intermediate Controls," expands on this chapter with more advanced controls.

21

REVIEWING
THE STANDARD
CONTROLS

Moving On to Intermediate Controls

by Paul Kimmel

IN THIS CHAPTER

The controls presented in this chapter represent the mainstay controls that will help you design and develop professional Windows applications. Combined with the controls in Chapter 21, "Reviewing the Standard Controls," completing this chapter will give you an ample repertoire of tools for rapid application development with Visual Basic 5.

This chapter demonstrates controls that require a moderately higher level of understanding and integration to use successfully. The tables, figures, and code listings in the chapter give you the opportunity to unleash the power of these intermediate controls in any domain.

Using the KeyState Control

In computer programming's Jurassic period, programmers had to know the BIOS address where the keyboard state was stored to perform a task as simple as modifying the Caps Lock key state. BASIC programmers had to use the Peek function, passing the address 0x00000417 in hexadecimal, or 1047 decimal, to get a bit-packed integer value containing the extended key state. Here's an example:

```
X = Peek(&H417)
Caps = X And (&H40)        ' Caps = &H40 then caps is set.
```

Once the byte was retrieved into a local variable, the user could mask off different bits to determine which key states were in effect. All these steps required the developer to have an intimate knowledge of the BIOS addresses of IBM-compatible, DOS-based computers and the packed bit arrays stored at these addresses.

Generally, knowledge of esoteric information of this sort was maintained as extemporaneous recall of a few technoids; this information, which was not extensible and was error-prone, inhibited the operating system developer from making changes to the underlying firmware of the operating system. In short, although it was fun to be one of the technoids who knew the information, it was not in the best interest of companies trying to develop software in a timely manner to cope with esoteric chunks of BIOS information.

The MicroHelp KeyState control enables you to easily manage the state of the Caps Lock, Num Lock, Scroll Lock, and Insert keys using a graphical user control with a modifiable boolean value. The Value property enables you to simply toggle or poll the state of a particular extended key. To help you use the KeyState control in your programs, I'll show you where to find it so that you can add it to the toolbox.

Adding the MicroHelp KeyState Control to the Toolbox

The MicroHelp KeyState control is not one of the Standard Controls. You must add the KeyState control to the toolbox to make it available during program development. To add the KeyState control to the toolbox, select Project | Components. On the Controls tab of the Components dialog, check the MicroHelp KeyState Control option and click Apply. To view the KeyState control in the toolbox, select View | Toolbox.

Using the KeyState Properties, Methods, and Events

A control is a small subprogram. Just like the interface and feature set of any program, the interface to a control can help determine a control's acceptance and use among a user community. The interface should be small and complete. Although these rules sound subjective, they are applied regularly in an implicit manner and often can mean life or death to a control. Table 22.1 contains the properties, methods, events, and constants of the KeyState control. The table does not contain an exhaustive list of the KeyState attributes, but outlines only those that make it distinct from other controls.

Table 22.1. Properties, methods, and events for the KeyState control.

Name	Kind	Type	Description
AutoSize	Property	Boolean	If True, the control manages its size; otherwise, the programmer can moderate the control's visual size.
Height	Property	Integer	If the AutoSize property is False, you can resize the KeyState control.
Style	Property	Integer	Set to one of four constants: KeyCapsLock, KeyNumLock, KeyInsert, or KeyScrollLock. This property determines what key state control the instance refers to.
TimerInterval	Property	Integer	A positive number that determines how often the state of the key is scanned. Longer intervals may improve application speed.
Value	Property	Boolean	True toggles the key on. False toggles the key off.
Width	Property	Integer	If AutoSize is False, you can set the visible width.
Change	Event	—	The event is triggered when the Value property changes.
KeyCapsLock	Constant	Integer	Designates a KeyState control as a Caps Lock control.
KeyNumLock	Constant	Integer	Designates a KeyState control as a Num Lock control.
KeyInsert	Constant	Integer	Designates a KeyState control as an Insert control.
KeyScrollLock	Constant	Integer	Designates a KeyState control as a Scroll Lock control.

If you want to keep track of the key states for the Scroll Lock, Caps Lock, Num Lock, and Insert keys, you need to use four KeyState controls. Each one needs the Style property set to the appropriate value. The MicroHelp KeyState control has two aspects to its caption. The first is the name of the style, such as CapsLock or NumLock, and the second is a string, On or Off, which equates to Value = True or Value = False.

You can modify the Value property of the KeyState control in three interconnected ways: changing the Value property, pressing the appropriate physical key at runtime or design time, or setting the Value property programmatically at runtime. The KeyState control is a button that by default has a runtime visual presence. If the default button appearance does not suit the general appearance of your application, remember that you can make the control invisible (Visible = False) and use some other means of displaying the current key state.

Listing 22.1 demonstrates how you can employ an arbitrary second means to track the KeyState. Although the physical appearance of the control might not fit the GUI design scheme for your application, you do not want to reinvent the functionality in the KeyState control. The sample program in Listing 22.1, an excerpt from KeyState.vbp, sets the MhState1 KeyState instance's Visible property to False and ties the state to the CapsLockMenu item. As an optional exercise, consider using a label control to track the various key states. Alternatively, you can complete the exercise with a StatusBar control alone, as you will see in the next section.

> **NOTE**
>
> The line numbers in code listings in this book are used for reference only. Don't type these line numbers in your code.

Listing 22.1. A secondary means of moderating key states.

```
1: Private Sub CapsLockMenu_Click()
2:     CapsLockMenu.Checked = Not CapsLockMenu.Checked
3:     MhState1.Value = CapsLockMenu.Checked
4: End Sub
5:
6: Private Sub Form_Load()
7:     CapsLockMenu.Checked = MhState1.Value
8: End Sub
9:
10: Private Sub MhState1_Change()
11:     CapsLockMenu.Checked = MhState1.Value
12: End Sub
```

Using the StatusBar Control

In this section, you will see how you can use the StatusBar control to track the key states without using the KeyState control. A StatusBar is exactly what it sounds like. Generally, you employ a `StatusBar` to keep track of the state or values that are meaningful to your program. For example, in the word processor used to create this manuscript, it is meaningful to track whether keystrokes will be inserted or will overstrike text. In addition, the `StatusBar` in the word processor tracks the page number, line number, and column number, among other things.

Table 22.2 defines the properties, methods, and events that distinguish the `StatusBar` from other controls. Table 22.3 defines the properties, events, and methods for the `Panels` collection that is contained within `StatusBar`. Many of the newer breed of ActiveX controls, including the `StatusBar`, have custom property editors like the one for the `StatusBar` shown in Figure 22.1.

Table 22.2. Properties, events, and methods for the `StatusBar`.

Name	Kind	Description
Panels	Property	A collection of `StatusBar` panels. (See Table 22.3.)
PanelClick	Event	Passes a reference to the clicked panel object to an event handler.

Table 22.3. Panel properties (elements of the `StatusBar`).

Name	Type	Description
Alignment	Integer	`sbrLeft`, `sbrCenter`, or `sbrRight` defines the alignment of text in each panel.
AutoSize	Integer	`sbrNoAutosize`, `sbrSpring`, or `sbrContents` defines how the `StatusBar` resizes the panel when the form resizes.
Bevel	Integer	`sbrNoBevel`, `sbrInset`, or `sbrRaised` defines how the panel appears in the `StatusBar`.
Enabled	Boolean	Determines whether the panel is enabled or disabled.
Index	Integer	Determines the order of a panel in a panel collection.
Key	String	A unique string that you can use to sort the panel collection.
MinWidth	Integer	Defines the minimum width of the panel object. The individual panel does not resize to a size smaller than the `MinWidth` property.
Picture	String	Points to a bitmap file to be displayed with the control.
Style	Integer	`sbrText`, `sbrNum`, `sbrCaps`, `sbrInsert`, `sbrScroll`, `sbrTime`, `sbrDate`, or `sbrKana` determines the kind of panel. The `sbrText` value is the default; `sbrInsert` and `sbrCaps` are the values used in the `StatusEdit.vbp` project to track those extended keys.

Figure 22.1.

Many ActiveX controls such as the StatusBar *have custom property editors.*

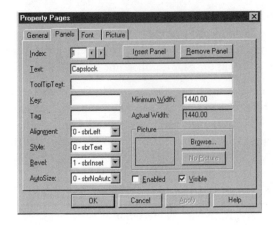

Figure 22.2 displays a modified version of the WinEdit program from Chapter 9, "Using Message Boxes and Input Dialogs." That program, named StatusEdit.vbp in this chapter, is an enhanced version that contains a StatusBar control to help the user. I don't provide an additional code listing here for the StatusEdit program depicted in Figure 22.2 because no additional code was required to add a StatusBar to the program. This is not a detractor; actually, not needing to write code is the most cost-effective solution you can hope for. In fact, not needing to write new code is exactly why object-oriented languages are so powerful.

Figure 22.2.

The StatusEdit program, which is a rich text editor with a status bar.

The StatusBar is capable of screening for changes in the state of the extended keys, such as Caps Lock and Insert. Follow these steps to modify the WinEdit program to create the StatusEdit program:

1. Open the WinEdit.vbp project from Chapter 9.

2. Save the project as StatusEdit.vbp.

3. Press Ctrl+T and select the Microsoft Windows Common Controls 5.0 to add the StatusBar to the toolbox.

4. Double-click the StatusBar to add it to the main form of the project.

5. Modify the `Form_Load` event to encompass the size of the status bar in the resizing of the `TextBox` control. Modify the `Form_Load` event as follows:

```
Call Text1.Move(0, 0, Form1.ScaleWidth, Form1.ScaleHeight -
➥StatusBar1.Height).
```

6. Press F4 to display the Properties dialog for the `StatusBar`.

7. Click the (Custom) property editor button to display the custom property editor as shown in Figure 22.1.

8. In the Property Pages dialog on the Panels tab, set the `Text` of `Index` 1 to `CAPS` and the `Style` to `sbrCaps`.

9. Click the Insert Panel button to add panel 2.

10. Set panel 2's `Text` property to `INS` and the `Style` property to `sbrInsert`.

11. Click Apply to record the changes.

12. Click OK to close the Property Pages dialog.

Press F5 to test `StatusEdit.exe`. By pressing the Insert or Caps Lock keys, you should note an appropriate change in the `StatusBar` panels. Writing code is a lot of fun, but reinventing the wheel is not cost-effective. Reusable ActiveX controls such as the `StatusBar` keep you from doing that.

Using the `TabStrip` Control

The `TabStrip` control is contained in Project | Components | Microsoft Windows Common Controls 5.0. The `TabStrip` control serves the same general purpose as the `TabControl`, which is to collect like data inputs that are applied to a common purpose. (The `TabStrip` control is an ActiveX control that will probably replace the `TabControl` completely in some future implementation of Visual Basic.) You do not have to look too far to find examples of `TabStrip` controls. For example, the word processor used to create this manuscript and the Components dialog in Visual Basic 5.0 have some. (See Figures 22.3 and 22.4.)

Table 22.4 contains descriptions of the attributes of the `TabStrip` control that make it so powerful yet easy to use. The `Tabs` collection is a property of the `TabStrip`; it has its own attributes, which are described in Table 22.5.

Table 22.4. Attributes of the `TabStrip` control.

Name	Kind	Type	Description
MultiRow	Property	Boolean	If `True`, multiple rows are displayed; otherwise, the tabs scroll.
Style	Property	Integer	The possible values are `tabTabs` and `tabButtons`. This property determines whether the tabs appear as tabs or buttons.

continues

Table 22.4. continued

Name	Kind	Type	Description
TabFixedHeight	Property	Integer	If the TabWidthStyle is tabFixed, this property determines the height of each tab.
TabFixedWidth	Property	Integer	If the TabWidthStyle is tabFixed, this property determines the width of each tab.
Tabs	Property	Collection	Indexable collection of all the Tab objects in a TabStrip.
TabWidthStyle	Property	Integer	tabJustified, tabNonJustified, and tabFixed are the three possible values for this property. tabJustified indicates that the tab is wide enough for the caption and is expanded in width to fill available TabStrip width if MultiRow is True. tabNonJustified makes the tab just wide enough for the caption. tabFixed forces all the tabs to be of equal width: the width specified by TabFixedWidth.

FIGURE 22.3.

The Font dialog of Word 97 is a tab control.

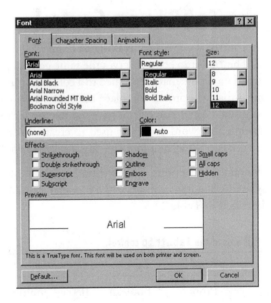

FIGURE 22.4.

The Components dialog of Visual Basic 5.0 is a tab control.

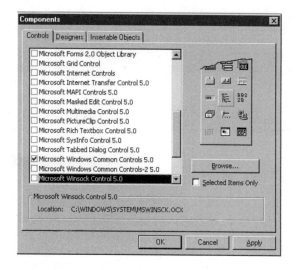

Table 22.5. Attributes of the Tabs collection.

Name	Kind	Type	Description
Caption	Property	String	Tab title.
Height	Property	Number	Height of this tab.
Width	Property	Number	Width of this tab.
Image	Property	String/ Integer	If the value is a string, it is the key to an image in an ImageList control; otherwise, an integer expression is the index of the image in an ImageList control. (See the custom property editor for the TabStrip, as illustrated in Figure 22.5.)
Index	Property	Integer	Each tab keeps its own index value internally.
Key	Property	String	A unique string that can be used for sorting collections or accessing objects in a collection.
Selected	Property	Boolean	Determines whether an object is selected. By setting Selected to True, you make that tab the current tab.
Add	Method	—	A method of the Tabs collection; not an individual object. Used to add an object—in this case, a tab—to a collection.
Clear	Method	—	A collection-level method, clearing all objects in the collection.

continues

Table 22.5. continued

Name	Kind	Type	Description
`Remove`	Method	—	Removes a tab from the collection. Assuming a `TabStrip` object named `TabStrip1`, the `Remove` method syntax to remove tab 1 is `TabStrip1.Tabs.Remove 1`.

FIGURE 22.5.

The Tabs page of the `TabStrip` *custom property editor.*

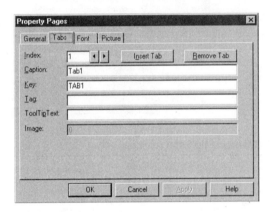

The `TabStrip` demonstration program in Listing 22.2, an excerpt from `TabStripDemo`, gives you an opportunity to experiment with many of the methods and properties of the `TabStrip` control. (See Figure 22.6.)

FIGURE 22.6.

A `TabStrip` *control dynamically designed at runtime in the* `TabStrip` *demo program.*

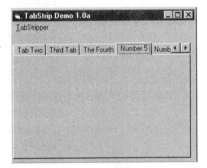

Listing 22.2. Properties and methods of the TabStrip control and tab objects.

```
1: Private Sub AddTabMenu_Click()
2:     Dim Count As Integer
3:     Count = TabStrip1.Tabs.Count + 1
4:     DefaultTabName = "Tab " + Str(Count)
5:     Dim Result As String
6:     Result = InputBox("Enter new tab name:", "Add tab", DefaultTabName)
```

```
 7:
 8:    If (Len(Result) > 0) Then
 9:            ' Demonstrates how to add tabs dynamically
10:                  ' Valid tab indexes are greater than or equal to 1
11:                Call TabStrip1.Tabs.Add(Count, "", Result)
12:    End If
13: End Sub
14:
15: Private Sub ClearAllMenu_Click()
16:    ' Demonstrates how to clear all tabs
17:    Call TabStrip1.Tabs.Clear
18: End Sub
19:
20: Private Sub ExitMenu_Click()
21:    End
22: End Sub
23:
24: Private Sub RemoveTabMenu_Click()
25:    ' Dynamic error handling
26:    On Error GoTo NO_OBJECTS
27:    ' Demonstrates how to remove the current tab object
28:    Call TabStrip1.Tabs.Remove(TabStrip1.SelectedItem.Index)
29:
30:    ' Don't forget to exit sub here or error handler will
31:    ' always fire.
32:    Exit Sub
33: NO_OBJECTS:
34:    ShowError
35: End Sub
36:
37: Private Sub RenameTabMenu_Click()
38:    Dim CurrentIndex As Integer
39:    On Error GoTo NO_OBJECTS
40:    CurrentIndex = TabStrip1.SelectedItem.Index
41:
42:    Dim CurrentName As String
43:    CurrentName = TabStrip1.Tabs(CurrentIndex).Caption
44:    Dim Result As String
45:    Result = InputBox("Enter new tab name:", "Rename Tab", CurrentName)
46:
47:    If (Len(Result) > 0) Then
48:        ' Demonstrates how to rename a tab caption dynamically
49:        TabStrip1.Tabs(CurrentIndex).Caption = Result
50:    End If
51:    Exit Sub
52: NO_OBJECTS:
53:    Call ShowError
54: End Sub
55:
56: Sub ShowError()
57:    MsgBox "Tabs Collection Empty", vbExclamation
58: End Sub
```

Note that in many instances, object and variable instancing is deferred until right before their first use. Look at AddTabMenuClick on Line 1. This is a subjective decision that every programmer must make, but ask yourself, why you are paying for objects before you need them?

Additionally, look at the examples of dynamic error trapping used on Lines 24 and 33. The `On Error GoTo NO_OBJECTS` catches errors that occur in the function that has the statement. It is preferable to use a function to perform the error handling if possible. (I provided the sanity checking so that you could experiment with the demo program relatively error free while you are learning to use the `TabStrip` control.) The TabStrip demo program depicted in Figure 22.6 and contained in Listing 22.2 enables you to experiment with the `SelectedItem` property of the `TabStrip` and the `Count`, `Index`, and `Caption` properties of the tab objects. Tab objects are contained in the `Tabs` collection property of the `TabStrip`. The demo program also enables you to practice using the `Add`, `Remove`, and `Clear` methods of tab objects. The capability to rename a table is added to demonstrate how you can create new algorithms from existing attributes. As an exercise, see if you can add the dynamic capability to add bitmaps to the visual tab.

Marking Change with the ProgressBar and Slider Control

`Slider` and `ProgressBar` are controls that were designed as a means to visually mark some arbitrary change. You have seen these kinds of controls employed in many programs, such as the Windows installation programs. `Slider` and `ProgressBar` are not in the View | Toolbox window by default; you have to select Projects | Components and then choose the Microsoft Windows Common Controls 5.0 to add them to the toolbox. Once added, they can easily be incorporated into any program. The most important aspect of the controls is the set of `Public` attributes they offer to the programmer to modify at design time and runtime. Table 22.6 contains the attributes of both controls; the description outlines which control the attribute describes.

Table 22.6. Slider and ProgressBar attributes.

Name	Kind	Type	Description
Custom	Property Editor	Both	Custom editor enables the user to perform design-time changes to controls in a dialog fashion.
Align	Property	Integer	ProgressBar: vbAlignNone, vbAlignTop, vbAlignBottom, vbAlignLeft, and vbAlignRight constants determine where on the parent control the ProgressBar is aligned.
Appearance	Property	Integer	ProgressBar: Either ccFlat or cc3D, this value determines the visual perception of depth of the ProgressBar.

Name	Kind	Type	Description
LargeChange	Property	Long	Slider: The LargeChange property is tied to the Page Up and Page Down keys. The value of LargeChange determines how much the Value property is incremented when you press Page Up and decremented when you press Page Down.
Max	Property	Number	Both: The maximum value, or 100% mark, of both controls.
Min	Property	Number	Both: The minimum value, or 0% mark, of both controls.
SelectRange	Property	Number	Slider: If True, the Slider can have a selected range.
SelLength	Property	Number	Slider: The SelLength property returns or sets the length of the selection in a Slider control.
SelStart	Property	Number	Slider: SelStart cannot be greater than the Max property. This property determines the anchor point for the selected range.
SmallChange	Property	Number	Slider: The SmallChange is tied to the left and right arrow keys. The left arrow decrements the Value by the SmallChange amount, and the right arrow increments the Value property by the value of SmallChange.
TickFrequency	Property	Number	Slider: Determines the number of ticks per positions in the Slider. With a minimum of 0, a maximum of 100, and a TickFrequency of 5, there are 20 ticks.
TickStyle	Property	Integer	Slider: sldBottomRight, sldTopLeft, sldBoth, and sldNoTicks are valid values for the TickStyle.
Value	Property	Number	Both: The current value, or position relative to Min and Max, of the ProgressBar and Slider controls.

Figure 22.7 shows both the Slider control and the ProgressBar with several different settings of the properties that affect the appearance of the controls. Figure 22.8 displays the output from a demo program that puts the ProgressBar through its paces. The key to using a progress

indicator successfully is tying it to the activity it is measuring. Sometimes an exact match is impossible, and the visual depiction of progress is sufficient enough.

FIGURE 22.7.

The Slider *and* ProgressBar *controls with labels indicating the properties that affected the appearance.*

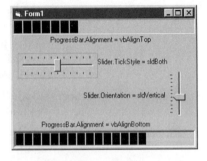

FIGURE 22.8.

A demo program that uses a timer to exercise some of the attributes of a ProgressBar.

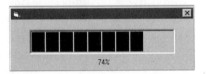

The PBDemo.exe program in Listing 22.3, an excerpt from PBDemo.vbp, demonstrates the Max, Min, and Value properties of the ProgressBar. As you might expect, they are extremely easy to use. The code listing exemplifies a philosophical approach to writing extensible systems. Consider the UpdatePercentComplete method, which is called from Line 19 in the IncrementValue subroutine and the Form_Load event handler. By paying for one level of indirection—that is, adding the function to update the label—you can update the percentage complete. You can think of this as convergence. Convergence enables you to make any changes, such as changing the control that displays the percentage complete or even changing the output device, in one place instead of all over the place. Connectivity points have to diverge, but generally, divergent code everywhere leads to a weaker and less extensible system. Code that demonstrates convergence is code that refers to GUI controls in many places, whereas code that converges conceals the manipulation of GUI controls (or any objects or variables) to a few places.

Listing 22.3. Attributes of the ProgressBar.

```
1: Private Sub Form_Load()
2:    UpdatePercentComplete
3: End Sub
4:
5: Public Sub SetMax(Max As Integer)
6:    ProgressBar1.Max = Max
7: End Sub
8:
9: Public Sub SetMin(Min As Integer)
10:    ProgressBar1.Min = Min
11: End Sub
```

```
12:
13: Public Sub IncrementValue()
14:     If (ProgressBar1.Value < ProgressBar1.Max) Then
15:         ProgressBar1.Value = ProgressBar1.Value + 1
16:     Else
17:         Timer1.Enabled = False
18:     End If
19:     UpdatePercentComplete
20: End Sub
21:
22: Private Function PercentComplete() As Integer
23:     PercentComplete = ProgressBar1.Value / ProgressBar1.Max * 100
24: End Function
25:
26: Private Sub UpdatePercentComplete()
27:     Label1.Caption = Str(PercentComplete) + "%"
28: End Sub
29:
30: Private Sub Timer1_Timer()
31:     IncrementValue
32: End Sub
```

Animating with the Animation Control

After grilling a Microsoft employee on a flight from Seattle to Las Vegas, I can make the distinction between the kind of animation he does in the games department and the kind of animation the Animation control affords you. Professional games and animation use "sprites," clay figures, AVI files playing over background screens, and many other techniques for creating smooth, fast-frame graphics. The Animation control does not help you develop professional games such as Descent or Doom, but it does help you add some moderately interesting animated icons or bitmaps to your application that might be useful in drawing attention to your program or illustrating what operation your program is performing.

Animated graphics can help draw attention to some event that requires user input. Animated graphics may help draw attention to your program in a field of icons, or like the Dial-up Networking icon on the taskbar, it might let you know that you are still connected to the Internet.

The Animation control is capable of displaying *Run-Length-Encoded* (RLE) or uncompressed AVI files. AVI files are capable of storing sound and video, but AVI files for the Animation control cannot have sound in them. The Windows 95 Recycle Bin uses this kind of animation. When you dispose of files, the floating files can be mimicked with the Animation control. When you install Visual Basic 5.0, there are several AVI files (assuming you used the default directory for the Developer Studio) in \Program Files\DevStudio\VB\Graphics\AVIs. Table 22.7 contains the attributes that help you add animation to your applications. Figure 22.9 catches one of the many animations available that you can use in your own programs.

Table 22.7. The Animation control attributes.

Name	Kind	Type	Description
AutoPlay	Property	Boolean	If AutoPlay equals True, the AVI file is played on open.
BackStyle	Property	Integer	Either cc2BackStyleTransparent or cc2BackStyleOpaque, this property determines whether the control uses its BackColor or allows the control it resides on to show through the background.
Center	Property	Boolean	If True, the animation is displayed in the center of the Animation control.
Open	Method	—	Opens an AVI file. If the AVI file contains sound data, an error code (35752) is raised.
Play	Method	—	Takes three integer arguments: the repeat count, the starting frame, and the ending frame.
Stop	Method	—	Stops the AVI animation player.

FIGURE 22.9.

The FileMove.avi *animation in mid-flight.*

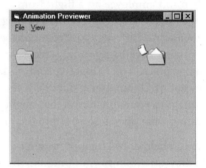

Listing 22.4, an excerpt from AniViewer.vbp, contains a short program that demonstrates how to use the Animation control. You can also use this code for a reusable Animation (AVI) previewer. The program uses the Menu Editor, a common dialog control, an Animation control, and a few short lines of code to complete the job.

Listing 22.4. The Animation control AVI previewer application.

```
1: Private Sub ExitMenu_Click()
2:     End
3: End Sub
4:
5: Private Sub Form_Load()
6:     Const PATH = "C:\Progra~1\DevStudio\VB\Graphics\AVIs\"
7:     CommonDialog1.filename = PATH + "*.AVI"
```

```
 8: End Sub
 9:
10: Private Sub Form_Resize()
11:     Call Animation1.Move(0, 0, Width, Height)
12: End Sub
13:
14: Private Sub OpenMenu_Click()
15:     CommonDialog1.ShowOpen
16:     If (CommonDialog1.CancelError = False) Then
17:         Animation1.Open CommonDialog1.filename
18:     End If
19: End Sub
20:
21: Private Sub PlayMenu_Click()
22:     Const REPEAT_COUNT = 10
23:     Animation1.Play REPEAT_COUNT
24: End Sub
25:
26: Private Sub StopMenu_Click()
27:     Animation1.Stop
28: End Sub
```

Listing 22.4 creates a program that would have been extremely expensive to produce just a few short years ago. The common dialog control used in the application enables the user to search the disk drives for AVI files. The Menu Editor gives you an easy way to add interactive menus, and the Animation viewer does all the rest. For the sample program, I created a viewer. In your application, your goal might be to offer animation to suggest visually the action your program is performing and indicate it is processing. Follow the steps to create the application on your own. If you need help, load the `AniViewer.vbp` sample program from the CD-ROM.

1. With Visual Basic 5.0 loaded, select File | New Project. Choose the Standard EXE from the New Project dialog.

2. Click the Menu Editor toolbar button or press Ctrl+E (the shortcut).

3. Fill out the Menu Editor dialog as shown in Figure 22.10 by adding a File menu with the Open and Exit menu items and a separator bar, and a View menu with the Play and Stop menu items.

4. After closing the Menu Editor, choose File | Open on the Animation Previewer form, and add the code from Lines 15–18 in Listing 22.4.

5. Select the File | Exit and add the statement `End`.

6. Select View | Play and add the code from Lines 22 and 23 in Listing 22.4.

7. Select View | Stop and add `Animation1.Stop` to the Stop menu event handler.

8. Add the remaining code for the `Form_Resize` and `Form_Load` events, copying the code in Listing 22.4.

9. Ensuring that you have an `Animation` control and a common dialog control on the form, test the application by pressing F5.

FIGURE 22.10.

The Menu Editor dialog for the AniViewer.vbp *application.*

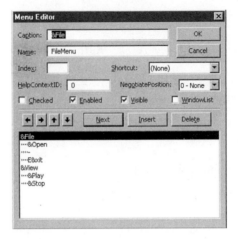

Run the application, stepping through each line of code so that you understand its role. When developing applications with Animation controls, you can reuse the demo application to preview the AVI files to find the right one for your application.

Creating Charts Using the MSChart and Grid Controls

This section demonstrates a basic coordination between the MSChart and Grid controls. The ChartDemo.vbp program demonstrates how to coordinate a matrix of data, such as that in a grid, to produce fundamental charting and graphing. The MSChart and Grid controls are powerful in their own right; Tables 22.7 and 22.8 provide an easy-to-use resource for their attributes.

Grid Control Attributes

You can include the Microsoft Grid control in the toolbox by selecting Microsoft Grid Control from Project | Components. The Grid control is a visual matrix of text-based cell data. (See Figure 22.11.) Several important properties are described in Table 22.8. In addition, Figure 22.12 shows the flexible and easy-to-use custom property editor for the Grid control.

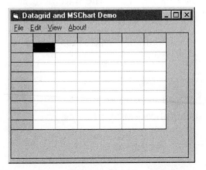

Table 22.8. Microsoft Grid control attributes.

Name	Kind	Type	Description
CellSelected	Property	Boolean	If True, the current Col, Row cell is selected (that is, painted).
Col	Property	Integer	Current column.
Cols	Property	Integer	The number of columns in the grid.
FixedCols	Property	Integer	Number of fixed row cells.
FixedRows	Property	Integer	Number of fixed column cells.
GridLines	Property	Boolean	If True, grid lines are displayed.
Row	Property	Integer	Current row.
Rows	Property	Integer	Number of data rows in the grid.
Text	Property	String	String value of current row, col value.
RowColChange	Event	—	This event is fired when a new cell is clicked.
SelChange	Event	—	This event is fired when the selected cells change.

FIGURE 22.12.

The custom property editor for the Microsoft Grid control.

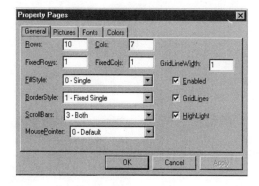

You can use the Row and Col properties of the grid in an iterative loop, in conjunction with the Text property, to access any cell in the grid. An example from the ChartDemo program in Listing 22.5 might appear as follows:

```
Sub InitializeGrid()
     Dim C, R As Integer
     For C = 1 To Grid1.Cols - 1
         For R = 1 To Grid1.Rows - 1
                 Grid1.Col = C
                 Grid1.Row = R
                 Grid1.Text = Str(C * R)
         Next R
     Next C
End Sub
```

The nested loop steps through each of the cells in the grid, setting the Text property of each cell—except, in this case, the labels, column headers, and 0 column and 0 row values, which were intentionally skipped.

MSChart Control Attributes

An MSChart object stores data in a two-dimensional manner. This column-by-row containment of data mirrors the way that other controls such as the Grid control store data, making them an ideal match for storing and visually depicting the grid-stored data. Figure 22.13 shows one of the many possible ways an MSChart control (shown in Figure 22.14) is capable of displaying data. Table 22.9 contains attributes that enable you to display the same data in other graphical ways.

FIGURE 22.13.

An MSChart *control whose properties are set to display a 3-D bar graph.*

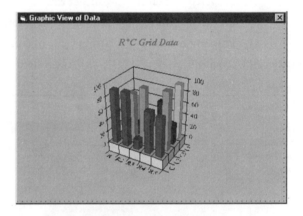

FIGURE 22.14.

The custom property editor for the MSChart *control.*

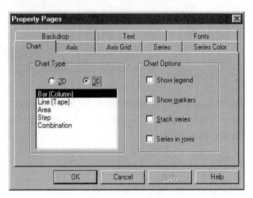

Table 22.9. MSChart control attributes.

Name	Kind	Type	Description
ActiveSeriesCount	Property	Integer	Returns the series count, which is based on the number of columns and the type of the graph.

Name	Kind	Type	Description
AllowDithering	Property	Boolean	If True, it causes the colors to be dithered. Useful for low-quality color monitors.
AllowDynamic Rotation	Property	Boolean	When True, the user can rotate the graph with the cursor. (Hold down the Ctrl key and use the mouse at runtime to rotate the graph.) (See Figure 22.15.)
AllowSelections	Property	Boolean	If True, this property determines that the user can select grid objects, such as series.
Chart3D	Property	Boolean	If True, the chart appears as a three-dimensional chart; otherwise, the chart appears two-dimensional.
ChartData	Property	Array	A two-dimensional variant array from which a chart can extract data.
ChartType	Property	Integer	One of the VtChChartType constants.
Column	Property	Integer	The current chart column.
ColumnLabel	Property	Text	The string value of the current column's label.
ColumnLabelCount	Property	Integer	Determines the number of label levels for a column.
ColumnLabelIndex	Property	Integer	Used to set a column label for columns with more than one label.
Container	Property	Container	The parent container of the chart, either a frame or picture box control.
Data	Property	Integer	The current data point. The current data point is set by changing the Column and Row properties.
DataBindings	Property	Object	Bindable controls such as MSFlexGrid or a Slider control.
DataGrid	Property	DataGrid	A DataGrid object associated with the MSChart control.
Footnote	Property	Object	A Footnote object that contains the attributes of the footnote, including the text.
FootnoteText	Property	String	The text value of the footnote object.
LabelLevelCount	Property	Integer	The number of label levels.

continues

Table 22.9. continued

Name	Kind	Type	Description
Legend	Property	Object	A reference to the Legend object, which contains details about the legend of the chart.
Plot	Property	Object	A reference to a Plot object, which describes the canvas that the chart is drawn upon.
RandomFill	Property	Boolean	Determines whether random data is used to fill the chart.
Repaint	Property	Boolean	Determines whether the chart is repainted whenever the data changes. If you are making several changes, set Repaint to False until all changes are made.
Row	Property	Integer	Current chart row.
RowCount	Property	Integer	Number of rows in each column.
RowLabel	Property	String	Row label text.
RowLabelCount	Property	Integer	Number of row label levels.
RowLabelIndex	Property	Integer	Used to access a row label by index if there is more than one label level.
SeriesColumn	Property	Integer	Get or set the column number for the current series.
SeriesType	Property	Integer	One of the VtCHSeriesType constants found in the help documentation.
ShowLegend	Property	Boolean	Determines whether the legend is visible.
Stacking	Property	Boolean	If True, all series are stacked on top of each other.
TextLengthType	Property	Integer	Either VtTextLengthTypeVirtual or VtTextLengthTypeDevice; choose the former to optimize text printing and choose the latter for printing to the screen.
Title	Property	Object	The object used to manage how the title text is displayed.
TitleText	Property	String	The chart's title.

Name	Kind	Type	Description
EditCopy	Method	—	Copies the current chart to a Windows metafile format and subsequent data to the Windows Clipboard. Use EditPaste to paste the copied picture.
EditPaste	Method	—	Pastes Windows metafile picture or tab-delimited text to a chart.
GetSelectedPart	Method	—	Gets the selected part of a chart.
Layout	Method	—	Forces recalculation of automatic chart values.
SelectPart	Method	—	Sets a selected section of a chart.
ToDefaults	Method	—	Reinitializes the chart to defaults.
TwipsToChartPart	Method	—	Uses x and y coordinates to identify chart parts.
AxisActivated	Event	—	Double-clicking the axis raises this event.
AxisLabelActivated	Event	—	Raised when the user double-clicks an axis label.
AxisLabelSelected	Event	—	Raised when the user clicks an axis label.
AxisLabelUpdated	Event	—	Raised when an axis label has changed.
AxisSelected	Event	—	Raised when the user clicks an axis.
AxisTitleActivated	Event	—	Raised when the user double-clicks an axis title.
AxisLabelSelected	Event	—	Raised when the user clicks the axis label.
AxisTitleUpdated	Event	—	Raised when the axis title has changed.
AxisUpdated	Event	—	Raised when the axis is updated.
ChartActivated	Event	—	Raised when the user double-clicks the chart.
ChartSelected	Event	—	Raised when the user clicks the chart.
ChartUpdated	Event	—	Raised after a chart change has been reflected.
DataUpdated	Event	—	Raised when the data is updated.
DonePainting	Event	—	Raised after a repaint has occurred.
FootnoteActivated	Event	—	Raised when the user double-clicks the footnote.
FootnoteSelected	Event	—	Raised when the user clicks the footnote.

22

MOVING ON TO
INTERMEDIATE
CONTROLS

continues

Table 22.9. continued

Name	Kind	Type	Description
FootnoteUpdated	Event	—	Raised when the footnote has changed.
LegendActivated	Event	—	Raised when the user double-clicks the legend.
LegendSelected	Event	—	Raised when the user clicks the legend.
LegendUpdated	Event	—	Raised when the legend has changed.
PlotActivated	Event	—	Raised when the user double-clicks the chart drawing region.
PlotSelected	Event	—	Raised when the user clicks the chart drawing region.
PlotUpdated	Event	—	Raised when the drawing region of the chart has changed.
PointActivated	Event	—	Raised when the user double-clicks in a data point.
PointLabelActivated	Event	—	Raised when the user double-clicks a point label.
PointLabelSelected	Event	—	Raised when the user clicks a point label.
PointLabelUpdated	Event	—	Raised when a data point label has changed.
PointSelected	Event	—	Raised when the user clicks a data point.
PointUpdated	Event	—	Raised when a data point has changed.
SeriesActivated	Event	—	Raised when the user double-clicks a series.
SeriesSelected	Event	—	Raised when the user clicks a series.
SeriesUpdated	Event	—	Raised when a series has changed.
TitleActivated	Event	—	Raised when the user double-clicks the chart title.
TitleSelected	Event	—	Raised when the user clicks the chart title.
TitleUpdated	Event	—	Raised when the title has changed.

The custom property editor for the MSChart control enables you to experiment with properties at design time to establish the best representation of your dataset. For developers, the custom property editor assists you in learning what those properties are. You might get references to appropriate constant values in the help file or by using the speed menu List Constants item in the Code View. Read the next section for a description and an example of how you can use the MSChart and Grid controls in complementary concert to store and display matrix data.

FIGURE 22.15.

With the AllowDynamicRotation *property set to* True, *the graphic is rotated.*

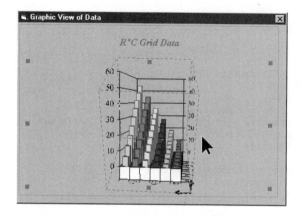

Using the MSChart Control and Grid Control in Concert

The sample program in this section demonstrates several of the attributes of both the MSChart control and the Grid control. The program, created from ChartDemo.vbp on this book's CD-ROM, enables you to modify the code to exercise many of each component's attributes. The program is a fully functional program containing a menu, grid, chart, and even an About dialog. Although the application is trivial, the orchestration of the different pieces demonstrates how you might interconnect similar controls in a real application. (You can run the program at this point by loading and executing ChartDemo.vbp from the CD-ROM.)

The program has a weak association between the Grid control on the main form and a chart on a second form. The association is established in that when the form containing the chart is displayed, the chart is initialized with data from the grid by traversing the individual cells of the grid. Figure 22.16 shows the application with the Chart View in the foreground. Listing 22.5 contains the code for the main form, ChartDemo.frm, and Listing 22.6 contains the code listing for ChartView.frm, containing the chart and the code that pumps data from the grid to the chart.

Listing 22.5. The form containing the grid.

```
1: Private Sub AlignGrid()
2:     Call Grid1.Move(0, 0, ScaleWidth, ScaleHeight)
3: End Sub
4:
5: Sub InitializeGrid()
6:     Dim C, R As Integer
7:     For C = 1 To Grid1.Cols - 1
8:         For R = 1 To Grid1.Rows - 1
9:             Grid1.Col = C
10:             Grid1.Row = R
11:             Grid1.Text = Str(C * R)
12:         Next R
13:     Next C
14: End Sub
```

continues

Listing 22.5. continued

```
15:
16: Private Sub Initialize()
17:     AlignGrid
18:     InitializeGrid
19: End Sub
20:
21: Function Terminate() As Boolean
22:     Terminate = (MsgBox("Are you sure?", vbYesNo + vbQuestion,
23: ➥"Exit Application") = vbYes)
24: End Function
25:
26: Private Sub AboutMenu_Click()
27:     frmAbout.Show 1
28: End Sub
29:
30: Private Sub ChartMenu_Click()
31:
32:     Form2.Show 1
33: End Sub
34:
35: Private Sub ColsMenu_Click()
36:     Dim C As Integer
37:     C = GetNewValue("Enter number of columns")
38:     If (C > 0) Then
39:         Grid1.Cols = C
40:         InitializeGrid
41:     End If
42: End Sub
43:
44: Private Sub ExitMenu_Click()
45:     Unload Me
46: End Sub
47:
48: Private Sub Form_Load()
49:     Initialize
50: End Sub
51:
52: Private Sub Form_QueryUnload(Cancel As Integer, UnloadMode As Integer)
53:     ' If Cancel is True then the application does not terminate,
54:     ' so we have to negate the operation
55:     Cancel = Not Terminate
56: End Sub
57:
58: Private Sub Form_Resize()
59:     AlignGrid
60: End Sub
61:
62: Function GetNewValue(Prompt As String) As Integer
63:     Const TITLE = "Grid Attribute"
64:     Dim result As String
65:     result = InputBox(Prompt, TITLE, "5")
66:     If (Len(result) > 0) Then
67:         GetNewValue = Val(result)
68:     Else
69:         GetNewValue = 0
70:     End If
71: End Function
```

```
72:
73: Private Sub GridOptionsMenu_Click()
74:     MsgBox "Rows=" & Trim(Str(Grid1.Rows)) & " Cols=" & Trim(Str(Grid1.Cols)), _
75:         vbInformation, "Grid Options"
76: End Sub
77: Private Sub RowsMenu_Click()
78:     Dim R As Integer
79:     R = GetNewValue("Enter number of rows")
80:     If (R > 0) Then
81:         Grid1.Rows = R
82:         InitializeGrid
83:     End If
84: End Sub
```

FIGURE 22.16.

The ChartDemo
application.

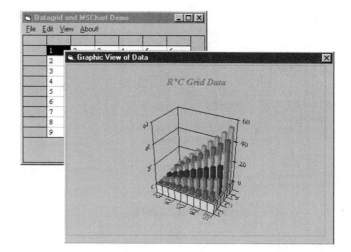

Rather than explain the 83 lines of code in Listing 22.5, I urge you to consider some subjective aspects of software development that will help you be a better developer. An old adage claims that if you want to be good at something, practice with those who have more experience. Not only should you consider reading a lot of text on software development, but you should also read a lot of code. By reading the code, you get ideas that will help you find simpler ways to perform old tasks, and you get alternate perspectives that may be invaluable when solving a new problem. Strive to make your code reusable, extensible, and loosely coupled. In case those terms are new to you, make an effort to make your functions short and reusable with few internal dependencies to outside variables. Consider the function AlignGrid in the preceding code. Why not simply place the one line of code wherever grid resizing is needed? Calling AlignGrid instead of calling Move seems to be a one-to-one replacement.

If you recall the brief discussion of convergence and divergence earlier in this chapter, you know the AlignGrid method is simpler than the Move method. Because you don't have an alignment property for the Grid control, you may need to align the grid in many contexts, such as when resizing the form and initializing the form. In addition, what it means to align the grid can change—as in the example of adding a StatusBar, where you must consider the height of the StatusBar—but the preceding code requires that you make only one change. Take a look at Listing 22.6, which completes the ChartDemo application.

Listing 22.6. The code that pumps data from the Grid control to the MSChart.

```
 1: Function GetColumns() As Integer
 2:     GetColumns = Form1.Grid1.Cols - 1
 3: End Function
 4:
 5: Function GetRows() As Integer
 6:     GetRows = Form1.Grid1.Rows - 1
 7: End Function
 8:
 9: Function GetCellData(Col, Row As Integer) As Integer
10:     Form1.Grid1.Row = Row
11:     Form1.Grid1.Col = Col
12:     GetCellData = Form1.Grid1.Text
13: End Function
14:
15: Sub InitializeChart()
16:     Dim C, R As Integer
17:     With MSChart1
18:         .chartType = VtChChartType3dBar
19:         .ColumnCount = GetColumns
20:         .RowCount = GetRows
21:         For C = 1 To .ColumnCount
22:             For R = 1 To .RowCount
23:                 .Column = C
24:                 .Row = R
25:                 .Data = GetCellData(C, R)
26:             Next R
27:         Next C
28:     End With
29: End Sub
30:
31: Private Sub Form_Load()
32:     InitializeChart
33: End Sub
```

Lines 1–7 compose the GetRows and GetColumns functions. These functions were intentionally written to insulate the capability to extract the number of rows and columns in the data source from where the data resides. These two functions could reside on top of any two-dimensional array, requiring little effort to change the singular implementation of each. Writing these two functions exemplifies a loosening between the coupling of the grid on one form and the chart on another. Lines 15–29 perform the bulk of the work for this form. The code demonstrates how to use the With..End With nested loops and offers you an ideal point to experiment with properties of either the chart or the grid.

Using `MSFlexGrid`

The `MSFlexGrid` is a powerful and versatile grid that enables you to manage complex tabular data. Simple data-management problems can be represented with traditional grids, but consider data where interrelationships between columns are more complex then a one-to-one relationship. The `MSFlexGrid` is the component for you. The `MSFlexGrid` is a read-only control when connected to a `Data` control, but it enables you to sort and merge data whose relationships are anything but mundane.

Microsoft provided you with several good sample programs on the Visual Basic 5 CD-ROM, and the `Flex.exe` program (which you can create by compiling the `\Program Files\ DevStudio\VB\samples\PGuide\ MSFlexGrid\Flex.vbp`) nicely demonstrates the flex grid. The output from the program is a grid browser for `Biblio.mdb`—the Access database also included on the Visual Basic 5 CD-ROM—which demonstrates the flexibility of the Microsoft flex grid.

From Figure 22.17, you may be able to discern that the flex grid is not displaying a symmetric column-by-row matrix of data. This flex grid shows the relationship between authors of books represented by author IDs and the ISBN numbers of the books they have written. Instead of repeating the author identifier for each author, the flex grid displays the author identifier once, adjacent to all the ISBN numbers of the books that author has written: a one-to-many relationship. The demo application also demonstrates the capability of the flex grid to reorganize the data on-the-fly by dragging and dropping the column header.

FIGURE 22.17.

The `ChartDemo` *application.*

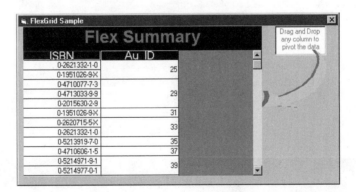

The `Flex.vbp` source resides on your Visual Basic 5 CD-ROM and your hard drive after installing it. I encourage you to read the source code and experiment with the `Flex.vbp` program provided for you by Microsoft. The beauty of learning to use the flex grid is that once you have mastered using the `Data` control and `Grid` control in general, you can use the flex grid. A long, detailed list of properties enables you to micromanage the appearance of the flex grid.

Incorporating the `SysInfo` Control

The `SysInfo` ActiveX control is a canned control that provides you with detailed information about the system where the control is executing. This black-box approach is ideally what object aggregation and ActiveX controls were intended to solve: problems that are repeated in a wide variety of application-development efforts.

`SysInfo` has several properties that enable you to query the control for system information; then, you must format that information in some meaningful format. You can take two courses of action. If your program needs to offer the user the capability to view the system information, or you are offering it as a service, you can simply select Project | Add Form and add the About dialog from the available forms. The About box has a command button whose underlying code executes the `MSINFO32.EXE` program that displays the system information. (See Figure 22.18.) Alternatively, you can use the `SysInfo` control, but you might want to bottle up the information it returns in a reusable and appealing dialog form. Listing 22.7 demonstrates a possible wrapper application that uses the `SysInfo` control to check a laptop's battery life. You can write the program from the listing or load it from this book's CD-ROM.

FIGURE 22.18.

`MSINFO32.EXE` *is executed from the About dialog.*

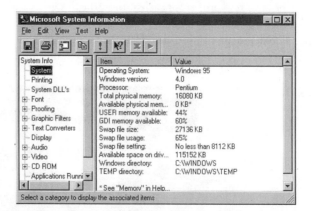

NOTE

Windows enables any operator to gather system information by running `MSINFO32.EXE` or clicking on the System icon in the Windows Control Panel. Remember, *all* code consumes development resources, so ask "What is the added value of providing something users already have?" Defer these kinds of features unless they are free, as is the case with the About dialog, or are absolutely essential to the program's success.

Listing 22.7. The code from `BatteryMeter.exe`.

```
1: Function GetCurrentTime() As String
2:     Dim T
3:     T = TimeSerial(0, 0, SysInfo1.BatteryLifeTime)
4:     GetCurrentTime = Format(T, "h:mm")
5: End Function
6:
7: Function GetPowerStatus() As String
8:     Const LEVEL = "Battery level:"
9:     Select Case SysInfo1.BatteryStatus
10:     Case 1:
11:         GetPowerStatus = LEVEL + " High"
12:     Case 2:
13:         GetPowerStatus = LEVEL + " Low"
14:     Case 4:
15:         GetPowerStatus = LEVEL + " Critical"
16:     Case 8:
17: GetPowerStatus = LEVEL + " Charging"
18:     Case 128:
19: GetPowerStatus = LEVEL + " No Battery"
20:     Case 255:
21:         GetPowerStatus = LEVEL + " Status Unknown"
22:     End Select
23:   End Function
24:
25: Sub UpdatePowerStatus()
26:     Dim Formatted As String
27:     Formatted = GetCurrentTime
28:     Label1.Caption = Formatted + " time remaining"
29:     Label2.Caption = GetPowerStatus
30:     ProgressBar1.Value = SysInfo1.BatteryLifeTime
31: End Sub
32:
33: Private Sub Command1_Click()
34:     End
35: End Sub
36:
37: Private Sub Form_Load()
38:     ProgressBar1.Max = SysInfo1.BatteryFullTime
39:     UpdatePowerStatus
40: End Sub
41:
42: Private Sub SysInfo1_PowerStatusChanged()
43:     UpdatePowerStatus
44: End Sub
```

The Battery Meter demonstrates the versatility of the `SysInfo` ActiveX control. (See Figure 22.19.) `BatteryMeter.exe` puts a `SysInfo` object through some of its paces. Line 3 of the `GetCurrentTime` subroutine uses the `BatteryLifeTime` property to get the remaining battery lifetime. Line 9 uses the `BatteryStatus` property to determine and display the overall battery health. Line 38 gets the `BatteryFullTime` and assigns it to the `Max` property of a `ProgressBar` to visually mark the remaining life of the battery. Finally, Line 42 demonstrates a `PowerStatusChanged` handler. Many other properties and events are pertinent to collecting or tracking other system information. Refer to the online or context-sensitive help for other attributes.

FIGURE 22.19.

`BatteryDemo.exe`
*mimics a laptop battery
meter utility provided
with a Toshiba
400 CS.*

Summary

In this chapter, you learned how to use many controls. Combining them with the controls you learned in Chapter 21, you now have a whole suite of controls that you have practical experience in using. Software development has evolved in large part as a business of using other developers' controls to develop the graphical user interface. Knowing all the attributes of every control is impossible. I hope that by this time, you understand that all controls have a variety of events, properties, and methods (attributes) that make them powerful, error free, and efficient to use. Knowing how to use new controls from an ever-increasing selection of third-party controls will help you develop professional, robust, and cost-efficient software applications.

To learn more about Visual Basic 5 and topics related to the areas discussed in this chapter, read the following chapters:

- Chapter 5, "Designing Forms: Your Look and Feel," offers tips and tricks for creating professional forms.
- Chapter 10, "Declaring, Raising, and Handling Events," shows you how to attach controls to your code.
- Chapter 21, "Reviewing the Standard Controls," demonstrates how to use the Visual Basic mainstay controls.
- Chapter 23, "Using the `ListView`, `TreeView`, and `ImageList` Controls," shows you how to conveniently represent data as lists, trees, or images.

Using the ListView, TreeView, and ImageList Controls

by Lowell Mauer

IN THIS CHAPTER

The ListView and TreeView controls are part of the Windows common controls. These controls allow you to organize data in the same type of format as the Windows Explorer. In this chapter, you will be creating samples of both ListView and TreeView projects. This will show you some of the features of these controls and allow you to understand how they work. Finally, you will combine both controls to create a simple address book application.

When using the ListView and TreeView controls, you will need to have a list of bitmaps available for them to access. You accomplish this by using the ImageList control. The ImageList control is used by several different controls as the repository of icons or bitmaps that will be used in the application.

What Are the ListView, TreeView, and ImageList Controls?

The ListView and TreeView controls are related in that they both give you a way of displaying data as items in a relational format. The ListView control will display the items in one of four different views. You can arrange the data into columns with or without column headings, and you can also display icons and text with the items. Using the ListView control, you can organize the list data items into one of the following views:

- Large icons (standard)
- Small icons
- List view
- Report view

By comparison, a TreeView control displays the data items in a hierarchical list of objects called *nodes*. This control is typically used to display entries in an index, the files or directories on a disk, or any other information that would fit into a hierarchical view. The most common use of both the TreeView and ListView controls can be seen in the Windows 95 Explorer window (see Figure 23.1).

An ImageList control contains a collection of Image objects, each of which can be referred to by its index or key. The ImageList control is not meant to be used alone, but as a central repository to conveniently supply other controls with images. You can use the ImageList control with any control that assigns a Picture object to a Picture property. The ImageList control can be used to supply images for the following controls using certain properties:

- ListView control
- TreeView control
- Toolbar control
- Tabstrip control

You should populate the ImageList control with images before you associate it with another control.

FIGURE 23.1.

The TreeView *and* ListView *common controls are both used in the Windows Explorer interface. The left pane uses the* TreeView, *and the right pane uses the* ListView.

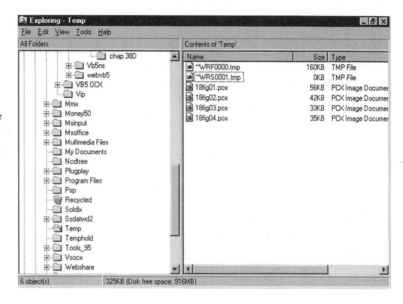

Understanding the ListView Control

The ListView control is similar to a listbox, but with enhanced features that allow you to associate icons with list items in the control. Also, the ListView control allows you to choose from four different views to display the list items.

One way to make the control a bit easier to use is to remember that the ListView needs to have its Icons property set to an ImageList control. The Icons property is used for the large icon images, and the SmallIcon property is for the ImageList control that contains the images for the small icons. The file type of the icons can be either .ico or .bmp.

> **CAUTION**
>
> If you don't set the Icons or SmallIcon property correctly, the associated list graphics will not appear.

Another thing to remember is that if you want to have a report view with resizable column headings, you must create and configure a ColumnHeaders object to be set to the ColumnHeaders properties of the ListView.

Building the ListView Project

The ListView control allows you to display a window that contains a list of information. To illustrate the concepts of using the ListView control, you will create a new Visual Basic project called `ListView`. This project shows you how to display a small list of names and their associated phone numbers in a `ListView` control.

To begin the creation of the project, start a new project in Visual Basic and save it as `LISTVIEW.VBP`. Next, change the name of the default form to `frmAddrBook` and save the form as `FRMADDRBOOK.FRM`.

Once you have created and saved the form and project files, you will need to add several controls to your form. Add `COMCTL32.OCX` to the project by using the Components dialog to add the reference. This will give you access to the `ListView` and `ImageList` controls that you need for the project. Now, add a `ListView` control to the form (see Figure 23.2). To keep it simple, leave the name of the `ListView` control as the default, `ListView1`.

FIGURE 23.2.

The ListView *control after being added to the new form in Visual Basic.*

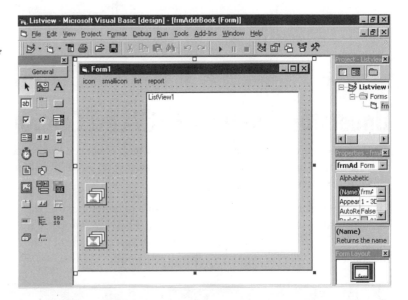

Finally, you will need to add two `ImageList` controls to the form. These controls will be used to hold the large icons and small icons required by the `ListView` control. Again, use the default names of the `ImageList` controls, which are `ImageList1` and `ImageList2`.

Setting the Properties of the `ListView` Control

There are two ways that you can set up the `ListView` control: by using the Properties window and property pages or by adding code to the `Form_Load` routine to set the properties. If you want to set up the `ListView` while you are in the design environment, you can use the property pages shown in Figure 23.3. You will need to set three key properties.

FIGURE 23.3.

*The Property Pages
dialog lets you set the*
ListView *control
properties.*

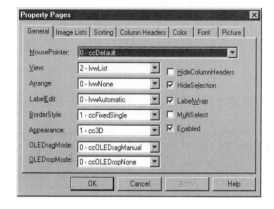

The first property you will need to set is View. This property determines how the list will present information to the user. The View property has four possible values: Icon, SmallIcon, List, and Report.

The next properties you will need to set for the ListView control are the Icon and SmallIcon properties for the ImageList controls that contain the pictures for the large and small icons, shown in the list. If you are using the property pages, you can select the ImageList controls from drop-down lists on the Image List page. These lists will contain all the ImageList controls that are on your form.

When displaying the data as a report, you need to set column headers to label each column of the report. This can be done either by using the Column Headers tab on the ListView property sheet (see Figure 23.4) or by defining a column header object and then adding items to that object, as shown in Listing 23.1. The syntax of this command is

```
Set ColObject = ListView1.ColumnHeaders.Add(,,"Header Text")
```

FIGURE 23.4.

*Using the Column
Headers tab to set the
column header labels to
be used in the report
view.*

You can also set the properties of the ListView control using code when the form is loaded. In the sample project, you will use the code method to set these properties to help you understand the process. To set these properties, insert the code in the Load event for the frmAddrBook form.

Listing 23.1. FRMADDRBOOK.FRM: Using the Load event to set up the ListView control.

```
Private Sub Form_Load()
' Create an object variable for the ColumnHeader object.
    Dim clmX As ColumnHeader

    'Set up the List view in the form
    ListView1.Width = ScaleWidth
    ListView1.Height = ScaleHeight
    ListView1.Top = ScaleTop
    ListView1.Left = ScaleLeft

    'Set up the icons from the image List
    ListView1.Icons = ImageList1
    ListView1.SmallIcons = ImageList2

    ' Add ColumnHeaders.  The width of the columns is the width
    ' of the control divided by the number of ColumnHeader objects.
    Set clmX = ListView1.ColumnHeaders.Add(, , "Name")
    Set clmX = ListView1.ColumnHeaders.Add(, , "Home")
    Set clmX = ListView1.ColumnHeaders.Add(, , "Work")

    'Create a ListItem object.
    Dim itmX As ListItem

    'Add some data setting to the ListItem
    'The first name
    Set itmX = ListView1.ListItems.Add(, , "Microsoft", 1, 1)   'Name
    itmX.SubItems(1) = "206-555-1212"    ' Home.
    itmX.SubItems(2) = "206-444-1212"    ' Work
    'The second name
    Set itmX = ListView1.ListItems.Add(, , "Que Publishing", 1, 1)   'Name
    itmX.SubItems(1) = "317-555-1212"    ' Home.
    itmX.SubItems(2) = "317-444-1345"    ' Work.
    'The third name
    Set itmX = ListView1.ListItems.Add(, , "Sams Publishing", 1, 1)   'Name
    itmX.SubItems(1) = "407-555-1212"    ' Home.
    itmX.SubItems(2) = "407-123-4455"    ' Work.

    ListView1.View = lvwReport ' Set View property to Report.
End Sub
```

The results of Listing 23.1 are shown in Figure 23.5. You can see that this code has used the report format to display the information.

FIGURE 23.5.

The ListView *control, after being set up by your code.*

If you looked carefully at the code in Listing 23.1, you might have noticed that the code not only set up the properties of the ListView control, but also added to the list the items to be viewed. Using code is the only way to set up the list of items. This list is not accessible from the design environment.

In Visual Basic 5, you can use the following defined constants to set the view mode of the ListView control:

- lvwIcon—Displays each item in the list using a large icon and a simple text description.

- lvwSmallIcon—Displays each item in the list using a small icon and a simple text description. The items are listed horizontally.

- lvwList—Similar to the small icon view, except that the items are arranged in a single vertical column.

- lvwReport—Displays each item with a small icon, a text description, and detail information, if it is provided. As with the list view, items are arranged in vertical columns.

You need to perform the following steps to add list items to the ListView control:

1. Create a ListItem object that will be used to add items to the ListView control. Use the following syntax:

   ```
   Dim MyListItem as ListItem
   ```

2. Using the Set statement, add the object to the ListView's ListItems collection:

   ```
   Set MyListItem = ListView1.ListItems.Add(1,"First Name", "Microsoft", 1, 1)
   ```

The syntax for a ListItems Add method is as follows:

```
object.Add(index, key, text, icon, smallIcon)
```

23

LISTVIEW,
TREEVIEW, AND
IMAGELIST

Here are the components of this syntax:

- `object`—Refers to the `ListItems` collection of the `ListItem` object. This is a required parameter.
- `index`—A number used to specify the position in which the `ListItem` object will be inserted into the `ListItems` collection. If you don't set this argument to a value, the `ListItem` is added to the end of the collection. This is an optional parameter.
- `key`—Used to assign a label to the `ListItem` for easier access. This is also an optional parameter.
- `text`—This is the string that you want the `ListItem` to display in the `ListView` window. It is an optional parameter. This argument should not be confused with the `key` argument.
- `icon`—The index number of the image within the `ImageList` that has been assigned to the `ICONS` property of the `ListView` control. An `ImageList` can hold many images. Use this number to select the one you want. This argument is optional.
- `smallIcon`—Similar to the previous argument, `icon`, it is the index number of the image within the `ImageList` that has been assigned to the `SmallIcons` property of the `ListView` control. It is optional. Again, be careful!

> **WARNING**
>
> Remember that for both large icons and small icons, if you forget to fill in a value, no icon will appear in the `ListView` control's icons, small icons, list, or report views.

If you want to add additional information, such as file creation date or file size, to the newly created `ListItem` object, `MyListItem`, you would manipulate the object's `SubItems(Index)` property. Subitems are arrays of strings representing the `ListItem` object's data that are displayed in Report View. For example, you could show the file size and the date last modified for a file. A `ListItem` object can have any number of associated item data strings (subitems), but each `ListItem` object must have the same number of subitems.

Setting Up the `ImageList` Controls

To provide the icons for the `ListView` control, you will need to add `ImageList` controls to your form. In the earlier section "Building the `ListView` Project," you added the two `ImageList` controls needed. All that remains is to add images to the list. To do this, right-click on the first `ImageList` control, `ImageList1`, to display a pop-up menu. Select the Properties item at the bottom of the menu list. This will display the property sheet for the `ImageList` control. Select the Image tab and click the Insert Picture button. Choose the bitmap file `SAVE.BMP` that comes with Visual Basic in `graphics\bitmaps\Offctlbr\Large\Color`. The bitmap is now inserted in `ImageList1` as the first image, as shown in Figure 23.6.

FIGURE 23.6.
Inserting the bitmap
SAVE.BMP *as the first*
image in ImageList1.

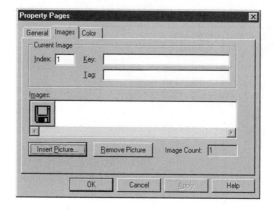

Repeat this process for each additional bitmap you want to add to the ImageList. Then, to add the bitmaps to use as small icons, repeat the appropriate steps for the second ImageList, ImageList2.

Adding a Menu to the ListView Project

To make it easy for you to select different list views of the sample program, you will need to create a menu for the program. Using the Menu Editor, add the menu items shown in Figure 23.7.

FIGURE 23.7.
The menu for
FRMADDRBOOK.FRM, *as*
shown in the Menu
Editor.

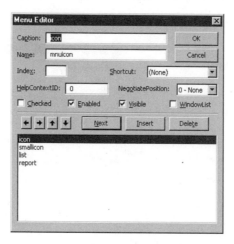

After exiting the Menu Editor, you will need to add code to each menu item to perform the required action. In this case, you need to change ListView's View property, which will modify the ListView display. The code shown in Listing 23.2 uses constants that are included in Visual Basic 5.

Listing 23.2. FRMADDRBOOK.FRM: The menu click events for FRMADDRBOOK.FRM.

```
Private Sub mnuLarge_Click()
    ListView1.View = lvwIcon
End Sub

Private Sub mnuSmall_Click()
    ListView1.View = lvwSmallIcon
End Sub

Private Sub mnuList_Click()
    ListView1.View = lvwList
End Sub

Private Sub mnuDetail_Click()
    ListView1.View = lvwReport
End Sub

Private Sub mnuExit_Click()
    End
End Sub
```

For more information about creating menus, see Chapter 8, "Going Beyond Menu Basics."

Executing the Sample Program

At this point you are ready to run the program. Execute it by either clicking the Run button on the toolbar or pressing the F5 key. Figure 23.8 shows the running program using the Icon View.

FIGURE 23.8.

The Icon View is one of the options in the program.

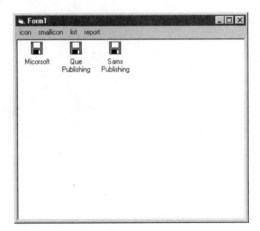

When the project starts, the program initializes the size and location of the ListView control to fill the client area of the form in the Form_Load event. In addition, the ListItem objects (names, home phone numbers, and work phone numbers) for the ListView's ListItem collection are created and added. As each ListItem is added to the ListItems collection, values are assigned to SubItems(1) (the Home column) and SubItems(2) (the Work column) of the ListItem, itmX.

Once the program is running, test the different views of the `ListView` control by selecting from the different options on the program's menu. You can see that the report view is the only view option that displays the subitem information.

Understanding the `TreeView` Control

The `TreeView` control is similar to a `ListView` control because it displays items with a combination of text and graphics, but the `TreeView` control does so by showing items within a tree hierarchy. Given the hierarchical nature of the control, *root, parent,* and *child* are fundamental concepts that must be understood to work with this control. In addition, the `TreeView` control uses the `Node` object extensively. Understanding the `Node` object is a must for effective use of the `TreeView` control.

Understanding Nodes

Nodes are the positions within a tree hierarchy. All `TreeView` controls have nodes, just as all real-life trees have branches. Normally this would seem simple enough. But with `TreeView` controls, it can be a bit confusing. This is because `Nodes` is both a property of a `TreeView` control and an object all by itself.

All trees have branches and all branches of a tree collectively are considered a single property of the tree, the property BRANCHES. The tree has other properties associated with it:

- `Type`—For example, oak or maple
- `Height`—For example, the tree is as tall as my house
- `Location`—For example, the tree is in my backyard

Each of these characteristics is a single property of the tree. Just because a tree has lots of branches does *not* mean that it has lots of `Branch` properties. It has only one property, `Branches`. The property `Branches` has a value that is a collection of individual branches.

Just as a tree has a property `Branches`, a `TreeView` control has a property `Nodes`. The `TreeView` control has only one `Nodes` property, which has a collection of nodes as its value.

Understanding the Root Property

The `Root` property is the top node of any tree hierarchy. Just as the branches of our real-life tree all come from the trunk, which comes from the roots, in the Windows Explorer hierarchy, the Desktop is the root (see Figure 23.1). A root is that from which everything descends.

Working with the Parent Property

A *parent* is an object that has children. A *parent node* is a node that has child nodes, very much like a real-life tree has a branch that contains other branches.

All nodes have parents, but not all nodes are parents. The Parent property of a given Node object reports back who the parent node of that given Node object is. For instance, the value of the Parent property for the node Pontiac is General Motors. The Parent property does not report whether a given node *is* a parent, only if it has a parent.

Working with the Children Property

The Children property returns the total number of children a given node has. To find out whether a node is a parent, you query the Children property using code similar to that shown in Listing 23.3. If the value of the Children property is greater than 0, the node is a parent. For example, if you ask me how many children I have and I report none, you know that I am not a parent.

Listing 23.3. Determining a parent node.

```
Private Sub TreeView1_NodeClick(ByVal MyNode As Node)
    If MyNode.Children = 0 Then
        MsgBox "I have no children, therefore, I am not a parent."
    End If
End Sub
```

Working with the Child Property

The Child property returns the value of the first of the given parent node's descendants. Common sense would say that the Child property should report whether a node is a child. Well, it doesn't. In the node family there is only one Child, and that is the first descending node. All the other nodes that share the child's parent are considered Next or Previous nodes. However, among all the nodes that share the same value for the property, Parent, there is a Firstsibling and Lastsibling.

For example, the nodes Pontiac, Chevrolet, Oldsmobile, Buick, and Cadillac share the same Parent value, General Motors (which is also a node).

The Child of General Motors is Pontiac.

The Next is Chevrolet.

The Next from Chevrolet is Oldsmobile.

The Next from Oldsmobile is Buick.

The Next from Buick is Cadillac.

The Previous from Buick is Oldsmobile.

The Firstsibling is Pontiac.

The LASTSIBLING is Cadillac.

NOTE

One of the best ways to understand nodes is to see the node program code in action. Using the sample code that is included with the online help information for the `TreeView` control is the best way to see how everything operates.

Building the `TreeView` Project

The `TreeView` control lets you display hierarchical data in a tree-like format. The only difference in the analogy is that the root of the `TreeView` control is shown at the top of the list. To illustrate the concepts of the `TreeView` control, you will create a new Visual Basic project that will show you how to display data in the tree format.

To begin the creation of the project, start a new project in Visual Basic and save it as `Treevw.Vbp`. Next, change the default form name to `frmTreeBook` and save it as `frmTreeBook.Frm`. As with the `ListView` project earlier, you will have to add the Windows common controls to your toolbox if they are not already present. You can add the controls using the Components dialog from the Project menu.

After you have added the controls to your toolbox, you can add them to your form. First, add a `TreeView` control to the form and leave the name of the control as the default, `TreeView1` (see Figure 23.9). Next, add an `ImageList` control using the default name, `ImageList1`. This `ImageList` control will contain the bitmaps that the `TreeView` control will use when displaying the data. Finally, add a menu item to allow you to exit the application. Now you are ready to start setting the properties of the control.

FIGURE 23.9.

The `TreeView` *control after being added to the new form in Visual Basic.*

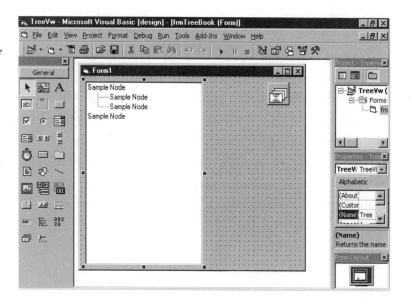

Creating the Code to Set Up the TreeView Control

As was the case in the ListView project, most of the setup for the TreeView control is easier to accomplish through code. However, a few properties can be set in the Properties dialog (see Figure 23.10). Besides standard Windows styles, you can also set the Style, ImageList, and Linestyle properties.

FIGURE 23.10.

The Property Pages dialog lets you set the TreeView control properties.

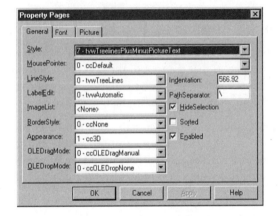

The Style properties determine how the tree information will be displayed. These are the available values:

Value	Description
0 - tvwTextOnly	Text only
1 - tvwPictureText	Image and text
2 - tvwPlusMinusText	Plus/minus and text
3 - tvwPlusPictureText	Plus/minus, image, and text
4 - tvwLinesText	Lines and text
5 - tvwLinesPictureText	Lines, image, and text
6 - tvwLinesPlusMinusText	Lines, plus/minus, and text
7 - tvwLinesPlusMinusPictureText	(Default) Lines, plus/minus, image, and text

The Linestyle property lets you set whether you want the root lines displayed (see Figure 23.11).

Finally, you need to set the ImageList property to the ImageList that you have previously added to the form. The initialization code for the General Motors company TreeView is shown in Listing 23.4. This listing needs to be added to your form as a procedure.

23

LISTVIEW,
TREEVIEW, AND
IMAGELIST

FIGURE 23.11.

The different ways the line styles will be displayed.

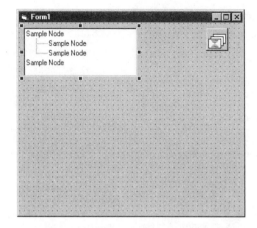

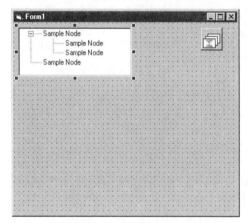

Listing 23.4. FRMTREEBOOK.FRM: The SetCompany procedure displays address book information in the TreeView control.

```
Public Sub SetCompany(t As TreeView)
    '*********************************
    'The sub takes a TreeView as an argument and sets that
    'control to show the Address Books available
    '*********************************
    Dim MyNode As Node
    'Clean out the TreeView control
    t.Nodes.Clear

    'Set the Address Book
    Set MyNode = t.Nodes.Add(, , "A", "Address Book",2)

'Set the Book Types
    Set MyNode = t.Nodes.Add("A", tvwChild, "P", "Personal",1)
```

continues

Listing 23.4. continued

```
    Set MyNode = t.Nodes.Add("A", tvwChild, "B", "Business",1)
MyNode.EnsureVisible

    'Set the Letter Tabs for the Personal Address Book
    Set MyNode = t.Nodes.Add("P", tvwChild, "P1", "ABC")
    Set MyNode = t.Nodes.Add("P", tvwChild, "P2", "DEFG")
    Set MyNode = t.Nodes.Add("P", tvwChild, "P3", "HIJK")
    Set MyNode = t.Nodes.Add("P", tvwChild, "P4", "LMNOP")
    Set MyNode = t.Nodes.Add("P", tvwChild, "P5", "QRST")
    Set MyNode = t.Nodes.Add("P", tvwChild, "P6", "UVW")
    Set MyNode = t.Nodes.Add("P", tvwChild, "P7", "XYZ")
    MyNode.EnsureVisible

    'Set the Letter Tabs for the Business Address Book
    Set MyNode = t.Nodes.Add("B", tvwChild, "B1", "ABC")
    Set MyNode = t.Nodes.Add("B", tvwChild, "B2", "DEFG")
    Set MyNode = t.Nodes.Add("B", tvwChild, "B3", "HIJK")
    Set MyNode = t.Nodes.Add("B", tvwChild, "B4", "LMNOP")
    Set MyNode = t.Nodes.Add("B", tvwChild, "B5", "QRST")
    Set MyNode = t.Nodes.Add("B", tvwChild, "B6", "UVW")
    Set MyNode = t.Nodes.Add("B", tvwChild, "B7", "XYZ")
    MyNode.EnsureVisible

    t.Style = tvwTreelinesPictureText ' Style 4.
    t.BorderStyle = vbFixedSingle
    t.Height = 4455
    t.Width = 4575

End Sub
```

You need to perform the following command in order to add Tree Nodes to the TreeView control. The syntax of the command is as follows:

```
Set MyNode = TreeView1.Nodes.Add("A", tvwChild, "P", "Personal")
```

The syntax for a node's Add method is as follows:

```
object.Add(relative, relationship, key, text, image, selectedimage)
```

Here are the components of this syntax:

- object—Refers to the nodes collection of the TreeView object. This is a required parameter.

- relative—This is the key or index number of a preexisting Node object. The relationship between the new node and this preexisting node is found in the next argument, relationship. This is an optional parameter.

- relationship—This specifies the relative placement of the Node object. This is an optional parameter.

- ■ key—Used to assign a label to the node for easier access. This is also an optional parameter.
- ■ text—The text that appears in the node. This argument is required.
- ■ image—The index number of the image in an associated ImageList control. This is also an optional parameter.
- ■ selectedimage—The index number of the image in an associated ImageList control that is shown when the node is selected. This is also an optional parameter.

The settings to use for the relationship parameter are

Value	Description
0-tvwFirst	The node is placed before all the other nodes at the same level of the node named in relative.
1-tvwLast	The node is placed after all other nodes at the same level of the node named in relative.
2-tvwNext	The node is placed after the node named in relative. This is the default.
3-tvwPrevious	The node is placed before the node named in relative.
4-tvwChild	The node becomes a child node of the node named in relative.

NOTE

If you do not name a Node object in the relative position, the node is placed in the last position of the top node hierarchy.

The final line of code to be added calls the TreeView control's initialization routine, passing the name of the TreeView control. This code should be added to the Form_Load routine:

```
Call SetCompany(TreeView1)
```

Executing the Sample Program

At this point you are ready to run the program. Execute it by either clicking the Run button on the toolbar or pressing the F5 key. Figure 23.12 shows the running program with the TreeView control visible.

When the project starts, the program initializes the TreeView control by calling the routine you added that sets the nodes in the tree. Once the program is running, test the way the TreeView allows you to expand and collapse the different levels of the tree information.

FIGURE 23.12.

Using TreeView *to display structured information.*

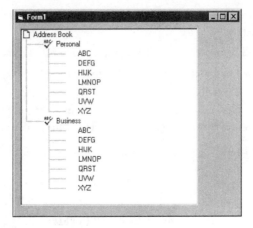

Understanding How the Application Works

The crux of the project TreeView.Vbp is the procedure SetCompany(t as TreeView). When the procedure is called, the TreeView control TreeView1 is passed as an argument. The procedure configures and displays information for TreeView1.

First, the procedure creates a node for the different phone books:

```
Set MyNode = t.Nodes.Add("A", tvwChild, "P", "Personal")
```

The constant tvwChild tells the application to make this new node a child of the node "A".

Then the groups of letters are added as a group node to each phone book node:

```
Set MyNode = t.Nodes.Add("P", tvwChild, "P1", "ABC")
```

Notice that the first argument in the Add method is now "P", which is the unique key of the node of the personal phone book. This is how the "P1" node (which displays "ABC") knows that it is a child of the personal phone book.

Next, the entire phone book node and its children are told to remain expanded (TreeView nodes can be expanded and collapsed) in the line:

```
MyNode.EnsureVisible
```

You can see that there is very little code needed to use a TreeView control (except, of course, for the code that is required to populate the tree with data).

Enhancing Visual Basic Applications Using the TreeView and ListView Controls Together

In this section, you will be combining both the TreeView and the ListView controls into a single application. This application will allow you to choose from two phone books using the TreeView control and display the name and phone numbers for the selected book using the ListView control (see Figure 23.13). You will be able to create this application using the techniques you have learned so far in this chapter.

FIGURE 23.13.

The completed phone book application showing the TreeView *and* ListView *controls.*

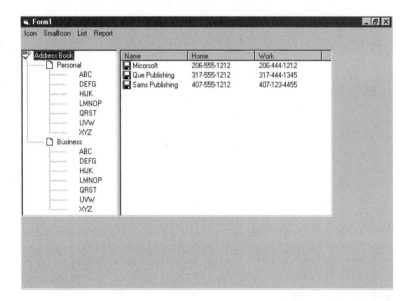

The controls that are used in this application are TreeView, ListView, and ImageList. There will actually be two ListView controls, one for each phone book, and three ImageList controls, one for the TreeView control and two for the ListView controls. In addition, you will be adding several sections of code to initialize the controls and display the appropriate ListView control based on which book node is selected in the TreeView control.

Building the Application

By making use of the TreeView control's methods and events, you will be able to switch the ListView control that is visible to the user. To begin the creation of the project, start a new project in Visual Basic and save it as PHONEBOOK.VBP. Next, change the name of the default form to frmPhoneBook and save the form.

Once you have created and saved the form and project files, you need to add the controls to your form. To get access to the controls you need, add COMCTL32.OCX to the project using the Components dialog. Now, add three ImageList controls and name them TreePics, ListPics1, and ListPics2, respectively. Then, add the TreeView control to the left side of the form and the two ListView controls to the right side of the form, as shown in Figure 23.14. Leave the names of the TreeView and ListView controls as the defaults.

FIGURE 23.14.

Adding the controls to the form.

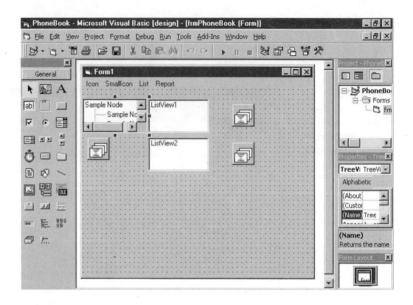

Don't worry about the placement of the controls; you will be setting these properties when the program is loaded.

Setting the Properties

The easiest properties to set are the ImageList properties. Display the Property dialog for each of the ImageList controls and add the following bitmaps to their respective ImageList controls:

TreePics ImageList	Bitmap1
	Bitmap2
ListPics1 ImageList	Bitmap1
ListPics2 ImageList	Bitmap1

These bitmaps can be found in the \VB\Graphics\Bitmaps\Offctlbr\ subdirectory that came with Visual Basic.

Next, you need to set the Icon property for each ListView control to ListPics1 ImageList and the SmallIcon property for each ListView control to ListPics2 ImageList. Then set the ImageList property of the TreeView control to TreePics ImageList. Then, for both ListView controls, set the View property to lvwReport and the TreeView control's Style property to tvwPictureText. This will set the ListView displays to Report View, and TreeView display will show bitmaps next to the node text. Finally, don't forget that you need to create column headers for the Report View of the ListView controls.

> **NOTE**
>
> Remember that you can set the column headers in the Property dialog or within the code.

Adding the Program Logic

The program logic for this application falls into two groups: the code that will initialize the TreeView and ListView controls and the code that will allow you to manipulate the information while the program is running.

To initialize the ListView controls, copy the code from Listing 23.1. The only change that you must make to this code is to duplicate it to initialize the second ListView control (and maybe change the names and phone numbers). Next, to initialize the TreeView control, copy the code from Listing 23.4 and add the following statement to the Form_Load routine:

```
Call SetCompany(TreeView1)
```

Another action that you will take in the Form_Load routine is to set the Width, Height, Top, and Left properties for the TreeView and ListView controls. The settings for each of the controls and the form are shown in Table 23.1.

23

LISTVIEW,
TREEVIEW, AND
IMAGELIST

Table 23.1. Property settings for the form and the controls.

Control	Property	Value
Form	Windowstate	vbMaximized
TreeView1	Height	4200
	Width	2500
	Top	240
	Left	0
ListView1	Height	4200
	Width	5500
	Top	240
	Left	2520
	Visible	True
ListView2	Height	4200
	Width	5500
	Top	240
	Left	2520
	Visible	False
FrmPhoneBook	Windowstate	vbMaximized

Now, if you want to be able to change the `ListView` display style, you should create the menu options shown in Figure 23.6 and add the code from Listing 23.2. Again, remember to duplicate the `ListView1.view` statements to also change the display for the second `ListView` control. Each of the menu events should resemble the following code:

```
Private Sub mnuSmall_Click()
    ListView1.View = lvwSmallIcon
    ListView2.View = lvwSmallIcon
End Sub
```

The last section of code that is needed is the piece that will check which phone book is selected in the `TreeView` control and then make the appropriate `ListView` control visible. This is done by using the `Click` event for the `Node` object. When a node is clicked, you can check the parent for that node to see which phone book should be displayed and then which group is selected. You can then set the properties and the position of the appropriate `ListView` control. The following code performs the described actions:

```
Private Sub TreeView1_Click()
If TreeView1.SelectedItem.Text = "Personal" Then
    ListView1.Visible = True
    ListView2.Visible = False
ElseIf TreeView1.SelectedItem.Text = "Business" Then
    ListView1.Visible = False
    ListView2.Visible = True
ElseIf TreeView1.SelectedItem.Text = "Address Book" Then
    ListView1.Visible = False
    ListView2.Visible = False
End If
End Sub
```

Executing the Program

You are now ready to execute this program. After the program starts, try changing the display of the `ListView`; then, in the `TreeView`, select different groups or the other phone book node. You can see that, given a little more enhancement, you will have a working phone book to use on your computer. By adding database access to add and retrieve the names and phone numbers to display in the list, you would make this program complete. A completed copy of this application is included on the CD-ROM that comes with this book.

Summary

This chapter covers how to make use of the `ListView` and `TreeView` controls from the Windows common controls. In addition, you have seen how the `ImageList` control is used to store the bitmaps that will be used with both the `TreeView` and `ListView` controls. You have also seen how to incorporate both of these controls into a Visual Basic application to allow the user to select the information he needs using a format that he is very familiar with (because it is just like the Windows Explorer).

Leveraging Windows: Using the Common Dialog Control

by Michael C. Amundsen

IN THIS CHAPTER

In this chapter you'll learn how to use one of most versatile controls in your Visual Basic 5 toolbox—the Common Dialog control. This control gives you access to the most commonly used services of the Windows operating system. You'll learn how you can use this single control to provide users access to their own font and color selections and give them the ability to print and perform printer setups and installations. You'll also learn how to use the Common Dialog control to easily open and save files from any available device and to access the built-in help services on the workstation—including the ability to link help files to the various dialogs.

Throughout this chapter, you'll build a sample Visual Basic 5 application that will demonstrate each of the dialogs available to you when you use the Common Dialog control. Each example focuses on a single dialog service (fonts, colors, and so on) and is divided into three parts. The first part of the example shows you the basics of how to access the dialog and get results. The second part shows how, with a little added coding, you can greatly enhance the efficiency and effectiveness of each of the dialogs. The third part of the example shows you how to add advanced options to your dialogs to make them even more customized for your needs.

When you are done with this chapter, you'll know how to unleash the power of one of the most useful controls in your programmer's toolkit. You'll know how to add customized fonts and colors to your dialogs, to provide access to printers, to easily add file open and save dialogs to your applications, and to help users get additional information about your program through the help services available through the Common Dialog control.

What Is the Common Dialog Control?

The Common Dialog control was one of the first controls developed by Microsoft. It was intended to be a single source for all the common services required by every good Windows program. Microsoft wanted to encourage programmers to make all their programs adhere to the Windows look and feel. The company reasoned that one of the best ways to encourage the common interface was to provide ready-made dialogs that handled the most commonly requested services: opening and saving files, setting the fonts and colors, handling printing, and gaining access to online help. To do this, Microsoft created a single control object that contained all these services—the Common Dialog control.

It's Not Like the Others

The Common Dialog control does not behave like most of the other controls that ship with Microsoft Visual Basic. First, it is not an intrinsic control; that is, it is not a built-in part of Visual Basic as are the textbox, label, and other basic controls. When you use the Common Dialog control, you are adding additional disk and memory requirements to your project.

NOTE

Including the Common Dialog control in your project will actually result in two additional
disk files in your installation package: COMDLG32.OCX and COMMMDLG.DLL.

Because the Common Dialog control is not a built-in control, you can use it only after you
have added it to your current project using the Project | Components menu option (see Fig-
ure 24.1).

FIGURE 24.1.

*Adding the Common
Dialog control to the
current project.*

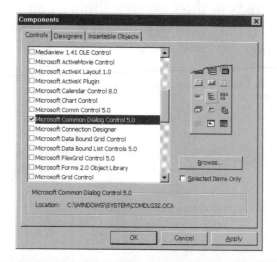

WARNING

You will not be able to access any of the Common Dialog control's methods or properties
unless you first add the component to your current project.

Another unusual thing about the Common Dialog control is that it is invisible at runtime.
Even though you see it on your form at design time, you cannot see it when the program is
actually running. You can't resize the Common Dialog control on the form, either, but because it is invisible while the program is running, its size and location on the form are of no
significance.

Finally, unlike most other controls that have a single purpose (text input, picture display, and
so on), the Common Dialog control actually provides several services. Instead of having a control for fonts, another control for colors, and so on, you can use the Common Dialog control

to handle multiple chores. Although this is handy for programmers, it means that learning to understand and use the Common Dialog control can be a bit harder than learning the other controls. Many of the same properties are used differently depending on the service you are requesting. And some of the properties are ignored completely for one service, but for another service that same property might be required!

You'll learn more about how each service uses the Common Dialog control's properties later in this chapter. First, let's take a quick tour of all the methods and properties of the Common Dialog control.

The Methods of the Common Dialog Control

The Common Dialog control has only a handful of built-in methods. Table 24.1 lists these methods, along with a short description.

Table 24.1. The Common Dialog control's methods.

Method	Description
AboutBox	Displays the About box for this control. Not needed for most programs.
ShowColor	Displays the Color selection dialog. Used to allow users to select a color for painting forms, setting foreground or background colors for controls, and so on.
ShowFont	Displays the Font selection dialog. Used to allow users to select font type, style, and size and, optionally, to indicate underlines, strikethrough, and/or font color.
ShowPrinter	Displays the Printer dialog. Used to allow users to select and install printers, indicate the number of copies to print, specify the starting and ending pages, and so on.
ShowOpen	Displays a File Open dialog box. Used to allow users to navigate any available device and locate and select one or more file objects to load, print, process, and so on.
ShowSave	Displays a File Save dialog box. Used to allow users to indicate the final save name of a file object.
ShowHelp	Provides access to several Windows Help dialogs, including displaying online help text, search dialogs, and other help services.

As you can see from the table, each method gives you access to one of the basic Windows operating-system services. In the sections that follow you'll learn how to use each of these methods to provide easy access to the desired dialog.

The Properties of the Common Dialog Control

Along with the seven methods shown in the table, the Common Dialog control has 36 properties. The property list for the Common Dialog control is a bit daunting at first glance, but is not really as difficult as it appears. First, 10 of the properties are dialog specific; in other words, they are used by only one (in a few cases by two) of the dialog services. Another seven of the properties are part of the standard ActiveX control properties (Name, Index, Tag, and so on). Also, one of the properties (Action) is no longer in use in the current version of the Common Dialog control, but is included for compatibility with earlier versions. That accounts for about half the properties in the list. The other half, however, presents a bit of a challenge. These are properties that are used by more than one dialog and, in some cases, actually have different meanings depending on the dialog in service.

Finally, there is one property that is very versatile: the Flags property. This single value is probably the most-used property of all. It is used to set various control flags that affect the behavior and appearance of the requested dialog. And there are almost 70 different flag values! You'll learn about the various flag values as you learn about each dialog service. For now, review Table 24.2 to get a quick summary of the Common Dialog control's properties and their descriptions. You'll also see a column that indicates the data type for the property and another that shows which dialog method uses the property. The Basic designation in the Methods column indicates that the property is a basic ActiveX control property—one that appears for almost all the ActiveX controls.

Table 24.2. The properties of the Common Dialog control.

Property	Valid Methods	Type	Description
Action	All	Integer	Used to request a dialog. Valid values for this property are 0—No Action. 1—Displays the Open dialog box. 2—Displays the Save As dialog box. 3—Displays the Color dialog box. 4—Displays the Font dialog box. 5—Displays the Printer dialog box. 6—Runs WINHLP32.EXE (Help). Note: This property is no longer in use and is only included for compatibility with earlier versions of the Common Dialog control. Its use is not recommended.

continues

24

USING THE
COMMON DIALOG
CONTROL

Table 24.2. continued

Property	Valid Methods	Type	Description
CancelError	All	Boolean	A value indicating whether an error is generated when the user clicks the Cancel button. If the value is set to True, an error code (32755) is returned when the user clicks the Cancel button on the dialog box.
Color	ShowFont ShowColor	Long	Returns or sets the selected color. This long integer can be set using the built-in RGB() or QBColor() function. You must set the Flag property to cdlCFEffects to include the Color property in the Font dialog.
Copies	ShowPrinter	Integer	Indicates the number of copies that should be printed. This value may be ignored by some printer drivers.
DefaultExt	ShowOpen ShowSave	String	Used to return to set the default extension for reading and writing files—for example, txt or mdb. The value in this property should *not* contain the dot (.).
DialogTitle	All except ShowHelp	String	This string is displayed at the top of the requested dialog box.
FileName	ShowOpen ShowSave	String	Returns or sets the complete name (device, folder, and filename) of the file to write or read. Can be set prior to calling the dialog box to act as a default value.
FileTitle	ShowOpen ShowSave	String	Returns the name of the file (without the device and folder) to read or write. Only works if the Flag property is not set with cdlOFNNoValidate.
Filter	ShowOpen ShowSave	String	Used to set the list of file types displayed in the dialog. Valid format is *description*¦*mask*, where *description* is a friendly string, and *mask* is the file filter to use (for

Property	Valid Methods	Type	Description
			example, "Text Files¦*.txt"). You can string multiple *description¦mask* pairs (such as "Text¦*.txt¦ASCII¦*.asc"). Use the FilterIndex property to set the pair to display as the default selection.
FilterIndex	ShowOpen ShowSave	Integer	A value that indicates which of the *description¦mask* pairs in the Filter property should be used as the default set upon opening the dialog. The first valid value is 1, not 0.
Flags	All	Long	Contains one or more control values that alter the look and behavior of the requested dialog. There are close to 70 different valid values, depending on the requested dialog. Detailed lists that apply to each dialog are included in later sections of this chapter.
FontBold FontItalic FontUnderline FontStrikethru	ShowFont	Boolean	Boolean values that indicate whether the font effect is turned on (True) or off (False). You must set the Flags property to cdlCFEffects to use the FontStrikethru and FontUnderline properties.
FontName	ShowFont	String	Used to return or set the name of the selected font.
FontSize	ShowFont	Integer	Used to return or set the size of the selected font. The selected font determines valid values. The absolute maximum value is 2160.
FromPage ToPage	ShowPrinter	Integer	Used to set or return the starting and ending page numbers to send to the printer. The Flag property must be set to cdlPDPageNums for these properties to be valid.

continues

Table 24.2. continued

Property	Valid Methods	Type	Description
hDC	ShowPrinter	Long	Contains the device context handle of the selected printer. This value can be used in conjunction with Windows API calls.
HelpCommand	ShowHelp	Long	Indicates the type of help service you are requesting. There are 12 valid values for this property. See the section "The Help Services," later in this chapter, for details on how to use this property.
HelpContext	All	Long	A number indicating the help topic to display. Valid numbers are supplied by the author of the help file.
HelpKey	ShowHelp	String	A string indicating the keyword to search for and display in the help file. If an exact match if found, the help topic will be displayed. If more than one topic contains the selected keyword, a list of topics is displayed. If no topic contains the keyword, the keyword list is displayed with the closest match highlighted.
Index	Basic	Integer	Returns the index value that identifies this control in a control array.
InitDir	ShowOpen ShowSave	String	Used to indicate the default directory to use when displaying the Open or Save dialog. If this value is empty, the current directory is used.
Left, Top	Basic	Long	Used to indicate the location of the control on the parent object (usually the form).

Property	Valid Methods	Type	Description
Max, Min	ShowFont ShowPrinter	Integer Integer	For the ShowFonts method, used to indicate the maximum and minimum font size allowable. For the ShowPrinter method, used to indicate the maximum and minimum pages allowed in the FromPage and ToPage properties. If these values are used for the ShowFont method, the Flags property must be set to cdlCFLimitSize.
MaxFileSize	ShowOpen	Integer	Used to set the maximum size of the filename allowed in the ShowOpen dialog. Default value is 256. Minimum value is 1; the maximum is 32,000B. If the Flag property is set to cdlOFNAllowMultiSelect, it is advisable to set this value higher than the 256-byte default.
Name	Basic	String	The internal name of the control object.
Object	Basic	Object	Used for OLE Automation services.
Parent	Basic	Object	Contains the name of the object on which the Common Dialog control resides (usually a form).
PrinterDefault	ShowPrinter	Boolean	Indicates whether the user's settings in the ShowPrinter dialog are saved to the Registry. The default value is True.
Tag	Basic	String	Free-form storage space. Can be used for any type of information required.

24

USING THE COMMON DIALOG CONTROL

As you can see from the table, the Common Dialog control has quite a collection of properties to work with. One of the real challenges of working with the Common Dialog control is learning to use these properties to create effective dialogs. In the sections that follow you'll learn how each dialog can be modified and improved through the use of the proper collection of property settings.

Building the Common Dialog Control Sample Form

Before jumping into the Common Dialog control sample code, let's build a very simple input form. This form will act as the test bed for the various Common Dialog control methods by simulating most of the common operations that every Visual Basic application must deal with and helping you learn how to use the Common Dialog control to provide real-life solutions to common programming challenges.

Laying Out the `cdlSample` Form

First, start a new Visual Basic 5 Standard EXE project. Set the project's `Name` property to `prjCDLSample` and set the default form's `Name` property to `frmCDLSample`. Next, select Project | Components from the main menu of Visual Basic 5 and select Microsoft Common Dialog Control 5 from the list of available components that appears (refer to Figure 24.1).

Once the Common Dialog control has been added to your project, lay out the `cdlSample` form using Table 24.3 and Figure 24.2 as a guide.

> **TIP**
>
> You'll notice that there are several controls that have their `Index` property set. This indicates that these are control arrays. The easiest way to build a control array is to add one control to the form, set all its properties (including the `Index` property), and then use Copy and Paste to add additional controls. This will cut down on typographical errors and speed up the form-design process a great deal.

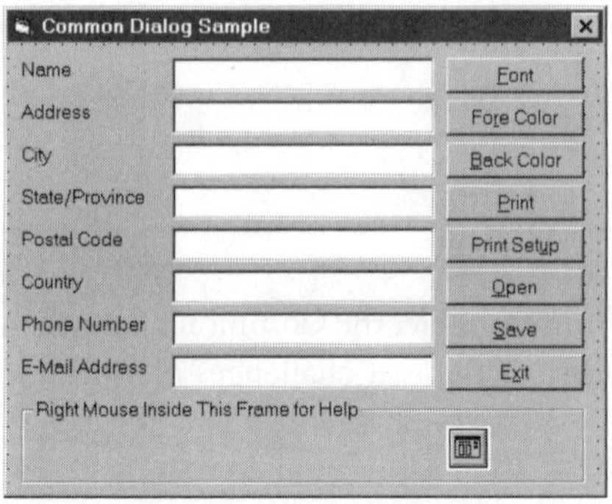

FIGURE 24.2.

Laying out the
cdlSample form.

Table 24.3. The configuration of the controls for the `cdlSample` form.

Control	Property	Setting
VB.Form	Name	frmCDLSample
	BorderStyle	3 'Fixed Dialog
	Caption	Common Dialog Sample
	ClientHeight	3816
	ClientLeft	36
	ClientTop	324
	ClientWidth	5208
MSComDlg.CommonDialog	Name	cdlSample
	Left	3840
	Top	3240
VB.Frame	Name	fraHelp
	Caption	Right Mouse Inside This Frame for Help
	Height	732
	Left	120
	Top	3000
	Width	4932
VB.TextBox	Name	txtField
	Height	288
	Index	7
	Left	1440
	Tag	E-Mail
	Top	2640
	Width	2292
VB.CommandButton	Name	cmdDialog
	Caption	E&xit
	Height	300
	Index	7
	Left	3840
	TabIndex	15
	Top	2640
	Width	1200

24

USING THE
COMMON DIALOG
CONTROL

continues

Table 24.3. continued

Control	Property	Setting
VB.TextBox	Name	txtField
	Height	288
	Index	6
	Left	1440
	Tag	Phone
	Top	2280
	Width	2292
VB.CommandButton	Name	cmdDialog
	Caption	&Save
	Height	300
	Index	6
	Left	3840
	Top	2280
	Width	1200
VB.CommandButton	Name	cmdDialog
	Caption	&Open
	Height	300
	Index	5
	Left	3840
	Top	1920
	Width	1200
VB.TextBox	Name	txtField
	Height	288
	Index	5
	Left	1440
	Tag	Country
	Top	1920
	Width	2292
VB.CommandButton	Name	cmdDialog
	Caption	Print Set&up
	Height	300

Control	Property	Setting
	Index	4
	Left	3840
	Top	1560
	Width	1200
VB.CommandButton	Name	cmdDialog
	Caption	&Print
	Height	300
	Index	3
	Left	3840
	Top	1200
	Width	1200
VB.CommandButton	Name	cmdDialog
	Caption	&Back Color
	Height	300
	Index	2
	Left	3840
	Top	840
	Width	1200
VB.CommandButton	Name	cmdDialog
	Caption	Fo&re Color
	Height	300
	Index	1
	Left	3840
	Top	480
	Width	1200
VB.CommandButton	Name	cmdDialog
	Caption	&Font
	Height	300
	Index	0
	Left	3840
	Top	120
	Width	1200

24

USING THE
COMMON DIALOG
CONTROL

continues

Table 24.3. continued

Control	Property	Setting
VB.TextBox	Name	txtField
	Height	288
	Index	4
	Left	1440
	Tag	Postal Code
	Top	1560
	Width	2292
VB.TextBox	Name	txtField
	Height	288
	Index	3
	Left	1440
	Tag	State/Province
	Top	1200
	Width	2292
VB.TextBox	Name	txtField
	Height	288
	Index	2
	Left	1440
	Tag	City
	Top	840
	Width	2292
VB.TextBox	Name	txtField
	Height	288
	Index	1
	Left	1440
	Tag	Address
	Top	480
	Width	2292
VB.TextBox	Name	txtField
	Height	288
	Index	0

Control	Property	Setting
	Left	1440
	Tag	Name
	Top	120
	Width	2292
VB.Label	Name	lblField
	Caption	E-Mail Address
	Height	252
	Index	7
	Left	120
	Top	2640
	Width	1212
VB.Label	Name	lblField
	Caption	Phone Number
	Height	252
	Index	6
	Left	120
	Top	2280
	Width	1212
VB.Label	Name	lblField
	Caption	Country
	Height	252
	Index	5
	Left	120
	Top	1920
	Width	1212
VB.Label	Name	lblField
	Caption	Postal Code
	Height	252
	Index	4
	Left	120
	Top	1560
	Width	1212

24

USING THE
COMMON DIALOG
CONTROL

continues

Table 24.3. continued

Control	Property	Setting
VB.Label	Name	lblField
	Caption	State/Province
	Height	252
	Index	3
	Left	120
	Top	1200
	Width	1212
VB.Label	Name	lblField
	Caption	City
	Height	252
	Index	2
	Left	120
	Top	840
	Width	1212
VB.Label	Name	lblField
	Caption	Address
	Height	252
	Index	1
	Left	120
	Top	480
	Width	1212
VB.Label	Name	lblField
	Caption	Name
	Height	252
	Index	0
	Left	120
	Top	120
	Width	1212
VB.Menu	Name	mnuHelp
	Caption	&Help
	Visible	0 'False

Control	Property	Setting
VB.Menu	Name	mnuHelpItem
	Caption	&Contents
	Index	0
VB.Menu	Name	mnuHelpItem
	Caption	&Index...
	Index	1
VB.Menu	Name	mnuHelpItem
	Caption	&Help on Help
	Index	2
VB.Menu	Name	mnuHelpItem
	Caption	&Key Word
	Index	3
VB.Menu	Name	mnuHelpItem
	Caption	Help Partial Key
	Index	4
VB.Menu	Name	mnuHelpItem
	Caption	Help Macro
	Index	5

You'll notice that the control list contains a set of menu array controls. It's easy to build menu arrays. Simply set the Name property to the same name as another control and increment the Index property each time you add a new copy of the control (see Figure 24.3).

Figure 24.3.

Building the cdlSample *menu.*

You might also note that the top-level menu control (mnuHelp) has its Visible property set to False. That is because you are building a pop-up menu for the form. Pop-up menus do not always appear on the form itself until the user performs the correct sequence of mouse clicks and keystrokes in the right place on the form. In this example, the user will be able to click the right mouse button while the cursor is hovering over the fraCDLSample frame to make the pop-up menu appear.

Also be sure to enter the information in the Tag properties of the text box controls. You'll need that data when you code the ShowSave and ShowOpen dialogs.

After building the Common Dialog control sample form, save the project (prjCDLSample.vbp) and the form (frmCDLSample.frm) before going on to the next section.

Coding the cdlSample Form

Before coding the specific examples, you need to add a bit of code to help the form work correctly. First, add the code in Listing 24.1 to the general declaration section of the form.

Listing 24.1. Coding the general declaration section of the form.

```
Option Explicit
'
' color flags
Enum clrType
    clrFore = 0
    clrBack = 1
End Enum
'
' form-level vars
Dim strHelpFile As String
'
' help context ids for dialogs
Private Const Select_a_Font = 10
Private Const Select_a_Foreground_Color = 11
Private Const Select_A_Background_Color = 12
Private Const Print_the_Data = 13
Private Const Perform_Print_Setup = 14
Private Const Open_the_Data_File = 15
Private Const Save_the_Data_File = 16
```

The enumerated type (clrType) will be used to indicate whether the user wants to apply the color selection as the foreground or the background, whether the strHelpFile string will be used throughout the project to access and display help files, and whether the list of Private Constants are settings that point to specific topics in the help file.

Now add the code from Listing 24.2 to the Form_Load event of the form.

Listing 24.2. Coding the `Form_Load` event.

```
Private Sub Form_Load()

    ' point to sample help file
    strHelpFile = App.Path & "\Help\cdlSample.hlp"
    '
End Sub
```

The code in Listing 24.2 sets the `strHelpFile` variable to the location of the `cdlSample.hlp` help file. You will need to adjust this setting if `cdlSample.hlp` is stored somewhere else on your machine.

> **NOTE**
>
> The `cdlSample.hlp` document is a compiled Windows help file. It was built using a help compiler tool in conjunction with Microsoft Word 97. Although the MS Help Compiler ships with Visual Basic 5, creating Windows help files is not covered in this chapter. The Help folder contains all the source code for the help file. If you know how to use the MS Help Compiler, you can use these source file files to create your own custom help files.

Now add the code from Listing 24.3. This is the code that will pop up the help menu each time the user clicks the right mouse button inside the frame control at the bottom of the form.

Listing 24.3. Coding the Help menu's PopUp event.

```
Private Sub fraHelp_MouseDown(Button As Integer, Shift As Integer,
    ➥ X As Single, Y As Single)
    '
    ' respond to right mouse over form
    '
    If Button = vbRightButton Then
        PopupMenu mnuHelp
    End If
    '
End Sub
```

Next you need to add several custom methods to the form. In this first stage, you'll add the new methods, but you will not add any Visual Basic code to them. This creates a set of stub methods that you will fill in later.

> **TIP**
>
> *Stub methods* are short entries that declare the methods but contain no working code. Stub methods are great for building large systems where you don't have all the details worked out, but need to have the method declared so that other routines work without errors.

24

USING THE
COMMON DIALOG
CONTROL

To add new methods to the form, select Tools | Add Procedure from the menu bar, fill in the method name in the dialog, and click OK (see Figure 24.4).

FIGURE 24.4.

Adding a new method to the form.

Using the information in Table 24.4, create the six methods needed for the cdlSample project.

Table 24.4. Adding custom methods to the form.

Method Name	Parameters
SetFont	
SetColor	clrFlag as clrType
SetPrint	
SetPrintSetup	
ReadData	
SaveData	

After adding the methods, you need to locate the SetColor method and add the parameter declaration to the method. When you're done, it should look like the following code sample:

```
Public Sub SetColor(clrFlag As clrType)
End Sub
```

The last set of code you need to add to the basic form is shown in Listing 24.4. This is the code that translates the command-button clicks into code that executes the proper custom methods.

Listing 24.4. Coding the cmdDialog_Click event.

```
Private Sub cmdDialog_Click(Index As Integer)
    '
    ' handle cdl selections
    '
    Select Case Index
        Case 0 ' font
            Call SetFont
```

```
        Case 1 ' fore color
            Call SetColor(clrFore)
        Case 2 ' back color
            Call SetColor(clrBack)
        Case 3 ' print
            Call SetPrint
        Case 4 ' print setup
            Call SetPrintSetup
        Case 5 ' open
            Call ReadData
        Case 6 ' save
            Call SaveData
        Case 7 ' exit
            Unload Me
    End Select
    '
End Sub
```

That's all the setup code you need to add. Now you're ready to start coding the Common Dialog control's demonstration routines. Be sure to save the form (`frmCDLSample.frm`) and the project (`prjCDLSample.vbp`) before you continue with the chapter.

The Font Dialog

The first Common Dialog control demonstration routine you'll create is the one that shows how you can add custom font selections to your projects. In this example, you'll add some code to the `SetFont` custom method. This code will execute the `ShowFont` method of the Common Dialog control and then use the information from the dialog to alter the fonts on the demonstration form.

The Basic ShowFont Example

Locate the `SetFonts` custom method you created earlier and enter the code from Listing 24.5. This will set up the Common Dialog control to handle a call to the `ShowFont` method and then use the resulting selections to alter the fonts used on the sample form.

Listing 24.5. Coding the basic ShowFont example.

```
Public Sub SetFont()
    '
    ' set font for entire screen
    '

    ' in case control does not support the property
    On Error Resume Next
    '
    ' for local loop
    Dim ctlTemp As Control
    Dim lngFlags As Long
    '
```

continues

Listing 24.5. continued

```
    ' ignore user cancels
    cdlSample.CancelError = False
    '
    ' set some flag values
     lngFlags = lngFlags + cdlCFBoth ' use both screen and printer fonts
    cdlSample.Flags = lngFlags ' move to property
    '
    ' show font screen
    cdlSample.ShowFont
    '
    ' set all controls to user selection
    For Each ctlTemp In Me.Controls
        ctlTemp.FontName = cdlSample.FontName
        ctlTemp.FontSize = cdlSample.FontSize
        ctlTemp.FontBold = cdlSample.FontBold
        ctlTemp.FontItalic = cdlSample.FontItalic
        ctlTemp.FontUnderline = cdlSample.FontUnderline
        ctlTemp.FontStrikethru = cdlSample.FontStrikethru
        ctlTemp.ForeColor = cdlSample.Color
    Next
    '
End Sub
```

The code in Listing 24.5 sets the CancelError property to False so you won't get an error message if the user clicks the Cancel button on the dialog box. The next section of code sets the Flag property to indicate that you want to see both screen and printer fonts in the list of available fonts. Then it executes the call for the ShowFonts dialog.

The next section of code does not execute until the user closes the Fonts dialog. This code takes the settings from the dialog and copies them to every control on the form.

Save and execute the project. When you click the Font button, you should see a dialog that looks like the one in Figure 24.5.

FIGURE 24.5.

Viewing the Font dialog.

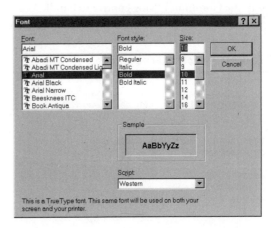

Some Added Settings for the Font Dialog

You might have noticed that the code in Listing 24.5 copies the Underline, Strikethru, and Color properties from the Common Dialog control to the controls on the form, but the Font dialog has no options displayed for these features. In order to see these added special font effects, you need to include additional values in the Flag property.

In fact, there are several possible values for the flag that can be useful in creating an effective Font dialog. Modify the code for the SetFont method so that it matches the code shown in Listing 24.6.

Listing 24.6. Some added settings for the Font dialog.

```
Public Sub SetFont()
    '
    ' set font for entire screen
    '

    ' in case control does not support the property
    On Error Resume Next
    '
    ' for local loop
    Dim ctlTemp As Control
    Dim lngFlags As Long
    '
    ' ignore user cancels
    cdlSample.CancelError = False
    cdlSample.Min = 8 ' minimum font size
    cdlSample.Max = 12 ' maximum font size
    '
    ' set some flag values
    lngFlags = cdlCFApply ' add apply button
    lngFlags = lngFlags + cdlCFHelpButton ' show help button
    lngFlags = lngFlags + cdlCFEffects ' allow colors/underline/strikethru
    lngFlags = lngFlags + cdlCFBoth ' use both screen and printer fonts
    lngFlags = lngFlags + cdlCFForceFontExist ' must select an available font
    lngFlags = lngFlags + cdlCFLimitSize ' control min/max size
    cdlSample.Flags = lngFlags ' move to property
    '
    ' show font screen
    cdlSample.ShowFont
    '
    ' set all controls to user selection
    For Each ctlTemp In Me.Controls
        ctlTemp.FontName = cdlSample.FontName
        ctlTemp.FontSize = cdlSample.FontSize
        ctlTemp.FontBold = cdlSample.FontBold
        ctlTemp.FontItalic = cdlSample.FontItalic
        ctlTemp.FontUnderline = cdlSample.FontUnderline
        ctlTemp.FontStrikethru = cdlSample.FontStrikethru
        ctlTemp.ForeColor = cdlSample.Color
    Next
    '
End Sub
```

Note the addition of a number of new `Flag` settings and the inclusion of the `Min` and `Max` properties to limit the size of the fonts available to the user. Save and run the project. When you click the Font button, you should see something like the dialog in Figure 24.6.

FIGURE 24.6.

Viewing the modified Font dialog.

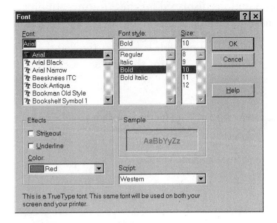

The Font Dialog's Flag Settings

The flag settings you see in Listing 24.6 are not all the possible settings. Because the Font dialog can be used to set both screen and printer fonts, there are a number of flag settings you can use to limit the types of fonts shown in the dialog. Table 24.5 lists all the valid values for the `Flag` property when you are calling the `ShowFont` method of the Common Dialog control.

Table 24.5. Valid `Flag` values for the `ShowFont` method.

Constant	Value	Description
cdlCFANSIOnly	&H400	Specifies that the dialog box allows only those fonts that use the Windows character set. If this flag is set, the user won't be able to select a font that contains only symbols.
cdlCFApply	&H200	Enables the Apply button in the dialog box.
cdlCFBoth	&H3	Causes the dialog box to list the available printer and screen fonts. The `hDC` property identifies the device context associated with the printer.
cdlCFEffects	&H100	Specifies that the dialog box enables strikethrough, underline, and color effects.
cdlCFFixedPitchOnly	&H4000	Specifies that the dialog box selects only fixed-pitch fonts.

Constant	Value	Description
cdlCFForceFontExist	&H10000	Specifies that an error message box is displayed if the user attempts to select a font or style that doesn't exist.
cdlCFHelpButton	&H4	Causes the dialog box to display a Help button.
cdlCFLimitSize	&H2000	Specifies that the dialog box selects only font sizes within the range specified by the Min and Max properties.
cdlCFNoFaceSel	&H80000	Indicates that no font name has been selected.
cdlCFNoSimulations	&H1000	Specifies that the dialog box doesn't allow graphic device interface (GDI) font simulations.
cdlCFNoSizeSel	&H200000	Indicates that no font size was selected.
cdlCFNoStyleSel	&H100000	Indicates that no style was selected.
cdlCFNoVectorFonts	&H800	Specifies that the dialog box doesn't allow vector-font selections.
cdlCFPrinterFonts	&H2	Causes the dialog box to list only the fonts supported by the printer, as specified by the hDC property.
cdlCFScalableOnly	&H20000	Specifies that the dialog box allows only the selection of fonts that can be scaled.
CdlCFScreenFonts	&H1	Causes the dialog box to list only the screen fonts supported by the system.
cdlCFTTOnly	&H40000	Specifies that the dialog box allows only the selection of TrueType fonts.
cdlCFWYSIWYG	&H8000	Specifies that the dialog box allows only the selection of fonts that are available both on the printer and onscreen. If this flag is set, the cdlCFBoth and cdlCFScalableOnly flags should also be set.

Many of the Flag values are mutually exclusive, and some work in partnership. You can experiment with the various values to arrive at a Font dialog that fits your needs.

An Advanced Font Dialog

When you ran the last example, you might have noticed that clicking the new Help button on the Font dialog did not result in any helpful information. This is because you, as the programmer, must supply the help information for the button. Setting some of the help-related properties of the Common Dialog control before you execute the ShowFonts method does this.

The code in Listing 24.7 shows the SetFont method with additional code that sets the help values and allows the user to get customized help information when the Help button is clicked. Change your SetFont code to match the code in Listing 24.7, and then save and run your project.

Listing 24.7. Adding custom help to the Font dialog.

```
Public Sub SetFont()
    '
    ' set font for entire screen
    '

    ' in case control does not support the property
    On Error Resume Next
    '
    ' for local loop
    Dim ctlTemp As Control
    Dim lngFlags As Long
    '
    ' ignore user cancels
    cdlSample.CancelError = False
    cdlSample.Min = 8 ' minimum font size
    cdlSample.Max = 12 ' maximum font size
    '
    ' set some flag values
    lngFlags = cdlCFApply ' add apply button
    lngFlags = lngFlags + cdlCFHelpButton ' show help button
    lngFlags = lngFlags + cdlCFEffects ' allow colors/underline/strikethru
    lngFlags = lngFlags + cdlCFBoth ' use both screen and printer fonts
    lngFlags = lngFlags + cdlCFForceFontExist ' must select an available font
    lngFlags = lngFlags + cdlCFLimitSize ' control min/max size
    cdlSample.Flags = lngFlags ' move to property
    '
    ' set help topic for button
    cdlSample.HelpFile = strHelpFile
    cdlSample.HelpCommand = cdlHelpContext
    cdlSample.HelpContext = Select_a_Font
    '
    ' show font screen
    cdlSample.ShowFont
    '
    ' set all controls to user selection
    For Each ctlTemp In Me.Controls
        ctlTemp.FontName = cdlSample.FontName
        ctlTemp.FontSize = cdlSample.FontSize
        ctlTemp.FontBold = cdlSample.FontBold
        ctlTemp.FontItalic = cdlSample.FontItalic
        ctlTemp.FontUnderline = cdlSample.FontUnderline
```

```
        ctlTemp.FontStrikethru = cdlSample.FontStrikethru
        ctlTemp.ForeColor = cdlSample.Color
    Next
    '
End Sub
```

Now when you run the project, you can click the Help button and see customized help on how to use the control (see Figure 24.7).

FIGURE 24.7.
Viewing the Font dialog's Help information.

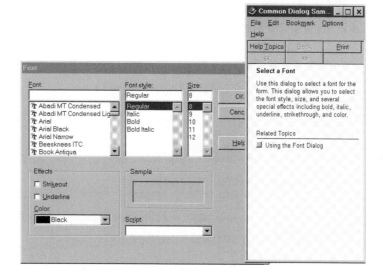

Now that you've completed the Font dialog example, you're ready to move on to the next Common Dialog control dialog: the Color dialog.

The Color Dialog

The Color dialog is used to collect information about color selections from the user. You can use this information to set the foreground or background color of any control, including any lines you might draw on the background of the form itself. In this example, you'll add code that will reset either the foreground or background colors of all the controls on the form.

The Basic Color Dialog Example

Locate the SetColor method you added earlier and enter the code shown in Listing 24.8. This code simply starts the Color dialog and, on return, copies the selected color to either the ForeColor or BackColor property of the form's controls.

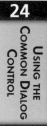

Listing 24.8. Coding the basic Color dialog example.

```
Public Sub SetColor(clrFlag As clrType)
    '
    ' set color for entire form
    '

    '
    ' in case object does not support colors
    On Error Resume Next
    '
    ' for local loop
    Dim ctlTemp As Control
    Dim lngFlags As Long
    '
    ' ignore user cancel
    cdlSample.CancelError = False
    '
    ' show color set
    cdlSample.ShowColor
    '
    ' set all controls w/ user selection
    For Each ctlTemp In Me.Controls
        If clrFlag = clrFore Then
            ctlTemp.ForeColor = cdlSample.Color
        Else
            If TypeOf ctlTemp Is TextBox Then
                ctlTemp.BackColor = vbWhite ' force inputs to white
            Else
                ctlTemp.BackColor = cdlSample.Color ' use selected color
            End If
        End If
    Next
    '
    ' set form w/ user selection
    If clrFlag = clrFore Then
        Me.ForeColor = cdlSample.Color
    Else
        Me.BackColor = cdlSample.Color
    End If
    '
End Sub
```

After adding this code, save and run your project. When you click the ForeColor or BackColor button, you should see a dialog that looks like the one in Figure 24.8.

FIGURE 24.8.

*Viewing the basic
Color dialog.*

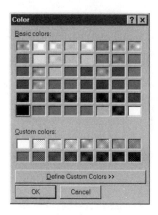

Some Added Settings for the Color Dialog

You can add a few `Flag` values to improve the Color dialog. Modify your `SetColor` code to
match the code in Listing 24.9.

Listing 24.9. Some added settings for the Color dialog.

```
Public Sub SetColor(clrFlag As clrType)
'
    ' set color for entire form
'


'
    ' in case object does not support colors
    On Error Resume Next
'
    ' for local loop
    Dim ctlTemp As Control
    Dim lngFlags As Long
'
    ' ignore user cancel
    cdlSample.CancelError = False
    lngFlags = cdlCCFullOpen ' show full color palette
    lngFlags = lngFlags + cdlCCHelpButton ' display help button
    lngFlags = lngFlags + cdlCCRGBInit ' preset the color
    cdlSample.Flags = lngFlags ' move to property
'
    ' set starting color
    If clrFlag = clrFore Then
        cdlSample.Color = Me.ForeColor
    Else
        cdlSample.Color = Me.BackColor
    End If
'
    ' show color set
    cdlSample.ShowColor
'
    ' set all controls w/ user selection
```

continues

24

USING THE
COMMON DIALOG
CONTROL

Listing 24.9. continued

```
For Each ctlTemp In Me.Controls
    If clrFlag = clrFore Then
        ctlTemp.ForeColor = cdlSample.Color
    Else
        If TypeOf ctlTemp Is TextBox Then
            ctlTemp.BackColor = vbWhite ' force inputs to white
        Else
            ctlTemp.BackColor = cdlSample.Color ' use selected color
        End If
    End If
Next
'
' set form w/ user selection
If clrFlag = clrFore Then
    Me.ForeColor = cdlSample.Color
Else
    Me.BackColor = cdlSample.Color
End If
'
End Sub
```

Notice that, along with new Flag property settings, the code in Listing 24.9 also copies the current color (foreground or background) into the Color property *before* executing the ShowColor method.

When you save and run the project this time, you'll see an expanded Color dialog when you click the ForeColor or BackColor button (see Figure 24.9).

FIGURE 24.9.

Viewing the expanded Color dialog.

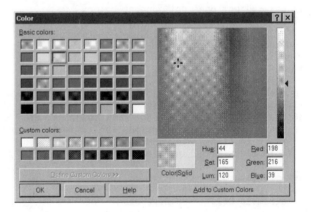

The Color Dialog Flag Settings

There are only four possible Flag property settings for the Color dialog. (See Table 24.6.)

Table 24.6. Valid Flag property settings for the Color dialog.

Constant	Value	Description
cdlCCFullOpen	&H2	Displays the entire dialog box, including the Define Custom Colors section.
cdlCCHelpButton	&H8	Causes the dialog box to display a Help button.
cdlCCPreventFullOpen	&H4	Disables the Define Custom Colors command button and prevents the user from defining custom colors.
cdlCCRGBInit	&H1	Sets the initial color value for the dialog box.

WARNING

Due to a typographical error, the help file that ships with some copies of Visual Basic 5 incorrectly identifies the cdlCCFullOpen constant as cdCClFullOpen and the cdlHelpButton constant as cldShowHelp. Be sure to use the correct constants when setting the Flag value.

Adding Help to the Color Dialog

Finally, you can use the help-related properties to establish a custom help topic for the Help button that appears on the Color form. Modify your SetColor method to match the code in Listing 24.10 and then save and run the project.

Listing 24.10. Adding help to the Color dialog.

```
Public Sub SetColor(clrFlag As clrType)
    '
    ' set color for entire form
    '


    '
    ' in case object does not support colors
    On Error Resume Next
    '
    ' for local loop
    Dim ctlTemp As Control
    Dim lngFlags As Long
    '
    ' ignore user cancel
    cdlSample.CancelError = False
```

24

USING THE
COMMON DIALOG
CONTROL

Listing 24.10. continued

```
    lngFlags = cdlCCFullOpen ' show full color palette
    lngFlags = lngFlags + cdlCCHelpButton ' display help button
    lngFlags = lngFlags + cdlCCRGBInit ' preset the color
    cdlSample.Flags = lngFlags ' move to property
    '
    ' set starting color
    If clrFlag = clrFore Then
        cdlSample.Color = Me.ForeColor
    Else
        cdlSample.Color = Me.BackColor
    End If
    '
    ' set help topic for button
    cdlSample.HelpFile = strHelpFile
    cdlSample.HelpCommand = cdlHelpContext
    If clrFlag = clrFore Then
        cdlSample.HelpContext = Select_a_Foreground_Color
    Else
        cdlSample.HelpContext = Select_A_Background_Color
    End If
    '
    ' show color set
    cdlSample.ShowColor
    '
    ' set all controls w/ user selection
    For Each ctlTemp In Me.Controls
        If clrFlag = clrFore Then
            ctlTemp.ForeColor = cdlSample.Color
        Else
            If TypeOf ctlTemp Is TextBox Then
                ctlTemp.BackColor = vbWhite ' force inputs to white
            Else
                ctlTemp.BackColor = cdlSample.Color ' use selected color
            End If
        End If
    Next
    '
    ' set form w/ user selection
    If clrFlag = clrFore Then
        Me.ForeColor = cdlSample.Color
    Else
        Me.BackColor = cdlSample.Color
    End If
    '
End Sub
```

Notice that the SetColor method sets the help topic to match either the foreground or background color change request.

Be sure to save your form (frmCDLSample.frm) and project (prjCDLSample.vbp) before continuing.

The Print Dialog

You can use the ShowPrinter method to display the Print dialog. This dialog allows users to select (or install) a printer and set the print range, the number of copies, and the collate option. You can also allow (or remove) a Print To File checkbox. In this example, you'll display the dialog and then, using the selected settings, send data to the printer for output.

The Basic Print Dialog

Locate the SetPrint method you built earlier and add the code from Listing 24.11 to it. This code gets the user's selections and then sends a copy of the data to the attached default printer.

Listing 24.11. Coding the basic Print dialog.

```
Public Sub SetPrint()
    '
    ' handle call for a print run
    '
    On Error GoTo SetPrintErr ' trap for errors
    '
    ' some local  vars
    Dim ctlTemp As Control
    Dim lngFlags As Long ' use to hold control flags
    '
    ' don't ignore user cancel
    cdlSample.CancelError = True
    '
    ' show print selection dialog
    cdlSample.ShowPrinter
    '
    ' send header to the print device
    Printer.Print "Common Dialog Sample Printout" ' title
    Printer.Print Now() ' date
    Printer.Print "" ' empty line
    '
    ' print data
    For Each ctlTemp In Me.Controls ' loop through controls
        If TypeOf ctlTemp Is TextBox Then ' text box?
            Printer.Print ctlTemp.Tag; "="; ctlTemp.Text ' write it out
        End If ' ctlTemp=Textbox
    Next ' ctlTemp
    '
    Printer.EndDoc ' end of job
    Exit Sub
    '
SetPrintErr:
    '
End Sub
```

Notice in the code that the CancelError property has been set to True for the first time. When sending data to another device (printer, disk drive, FTP location, and so on), it's best to allow the user to cancel the job if he desires.

When you save and run the project and click the Print button, you'll see a dialog that looks like the one in Figure 24.10.

FIGURE 24.10.

Viewing the basic Print dialog.

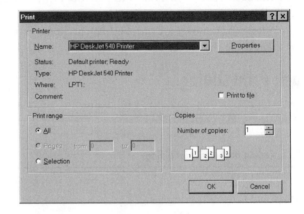

Some Added Settings for the Print Dialog

You can greatly improve the Print dialog by including some additional settings for the Common Dialog control's properties. Modify your version of the SetPrint example to match the one shown in Listing 24.12.

Listing 24.12. Some added settings for the Print dialog.

```
Public Sub SetPrint()
    '
    ' handle call for a print run
    '
    On Error GoTo SetPrintErr ' trap for errors
    '
    ' some local  vars
    Dim ctlTemp As Control
    Dim lngFlags As Long ' use to hold control flags
    '
    ' don't ignore user cancel
    cdlSample.CancelError = True
    '
    ' handle various flag options
    'lngFlags = cdlPDUseDevModeCopies ' let printer decide if
      ➥ multi-copies are allowed
    'lngFlags = lngFlags + cdlPDHelpButton ' show help button for user
    'lngFlags = lngFlags + cdlPDPageNums ' allow page num option
    'lngFlags = lngFlags + cdlPDNoSelection ' disallow selection option
    'lngFlags = lngFlags + cdlPDHidePrintToFile ' hide print to file flag
    'cdlSample.Flags = lngFlags ' move flags to cdl property
    '
    ' show print selection dialog
    cdlSample.ShowPrinter
    '
    ' send header to the print device
```

```
Printer.Print "Common Dialog Sample Printout" ' title
Printer.Print Now() ' date
Printer.Print "" ' empty line
'
' print data
For Each ctlTemp In Me.Controls ' loop through controls
    If TypeOf ctlTemp Is TextBox Then ' text box?
        Printer.Print ctlTemp.Tag; "="; ctlTemp.Text ' write it out
    End If ' ctlTemp=Textbox
Next ' ctlTemp
'
Printer.EndDoc ' end of job
Exit Sub
'
SetPrintErr:
'
End Sub
```

The `cdlDevModeCopies` setting will check the printer to see if it supports multiple-copy printing. If it does, the Number of copies spinner is displayed. If the printer does not support multiple copies, the spinner control is removed from the form.

When you save and run your example and click the Print button, you should see a dialog like the one in Figure 24.11.

FIGURE 24.11.

Viewing the modified Print dialog.

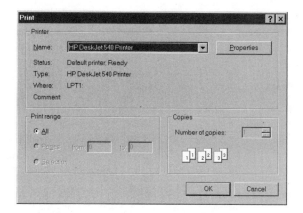

You should notice that the Print to file, Number of copies, and Collate items have been disabled or removed completely. This was done using the `Flags` settings.

Be sure to save your work before continuing.

The Flag Settings for the Print Dialog

The Print dialog has a number of valid `Flag` property settings. Study Table 24.7 for a review of the valid values.

Table 24.7. The `Flag` settings for the Print dialog.

Constant	Value	Description
cdlPDAllPages	&H0	Returns or sets the state of the All Pages option button.
cdlPDCollate	&H10	Returns or sets the state of the Collate checkbox.
cdlPDDisablePrintToFile	&H80000	Disables the Print To File checkbox.
cdlPDHelpButton	&H800	Causes the dialog box to display the Help button.
cdlPDHidePrintToFile	&H100000	Hides the Print To File checkbox.
cdlPDNoPageNums	&H8	Disables the Pages option button and the associated edit control.
cdlPDNoSelection	&H4	Disables the Selection option button.
cdlPDNoWarning	&H80	Prevents a warning message from being displayed when there is no default printer.
cdlPDPageNums	&H2	Returns or sets the state of the Pages option button.
cdlPDPrintSetup	&H40	Causes the system to display the Print Setup dialog box rather than the Print dialog box.
cdlPDPrintToFile	&H20	Returns or sets the state of the Print To File checkbox.
cdlPDReturnDC	&H100	Returns a device context for the printer selection made in the dialog box. The device context is returned in the dialog box's hDC property.
cdlPDReturnDefault	&H400	Returns the default printer name.
CdlPDReturnIC	&H200	Returns an information context for the printer selection made in the dialog box. (An information context provides a fast way to get information about the device without creating a device context.) The information context is returned in the dialog box's hDC property.

Constant	Value	Description
CdlPDSelection	&H1	Returns or sets the state of the Selection option button. If neither cdlPDPageNums nor cdlPDSelection is specified, the All option button is in the selected state.
CdlPDUseDevModeCopies	&H40000	If a printer driver doesn't support multiple copies, setting this flag disables the Number of copies spinner control in the Print dialog. If a driver does support multiple copies, setting this flag indicates that the dialog box stores the requested number of copies in the Copies property.

Accessing the Print Setup Dialog

You can use one of the Flag settings to force the ShowPrinter method to display only the Print Setup options. This is a great way to add support for the Print Setup menu options you see in almost all programs.

Locate and select the SetPrintSetup method you added earlier and enter the code from Listing 24.13.

Listing 24.13. Coding the SetPrintSetup routine.

```
Public Sub SetPrintSetup()
    '
    ' handle print setup dialog
    '
    ' set some properties
    cdlSample.CancelError = False
    cdlSample.Flags = cdlPDPrintSetup
    '
    ' set help topic for button
    cdlSample.HelpFile = strHelpFile
    cdlSample.HelpCommand = cdlHelpContext
    cdlSample.HelpContext = Perform_Print_Setup
    '
    ' show the dialog
    cdlSample.ShowPrinter
    '
End Sub
```

24

USING THE
COMMON DIALOG
CONTROL

After adding this code, save and run your project. When you click the Print Setup button, you should see a dialog that looks like the one in Figure 24.12.

FIGURE 24.12.

Viewing the Print Setup dialog.

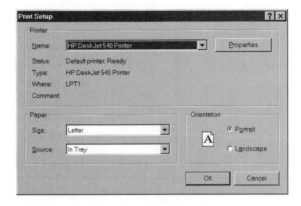

The File Save and File Open Dialogs

The File Save dialog and its counterpart, the File Open dialog, are probably the two most frequently used services of the Common Dialog control. Like the ShowPrint method, the ShowOpen and ShowSave methods do not actually perform the requested file operation. Their only role is to present an efficient dialog for collecting the filename to use when reading and writing data files.

In this example, you'll first create a routine that uses the File Save dialog to collect a filename and then save data from the input controls on the form to the selected file. Then you'll build a routine that uses the File Open dialog to collect a filename and then read the stored data into the form's input controls.

Using the File Save Dialog

The File Save dialog is used to prompt the user for the location and name of the file to use as the target in a data-saving operation. It is important to remember that the File Save dialog does not actually save any data—it just prompts the user for a valid filename. Your program must handle the actual saving of the data. The techniques used to save data to the disk are as varied as the number of data formats you can find on your machine. In this example, you'll be saving simple text data. For this you can use a few built-in Visual Basic keywords to open and write to (and read from) the file.

The Basic File Save Dialog

Unlike the previous dialogs, a number of properties should be set for this dialog *before* you invoke the ShowSave method. These properties will allow you to assist the user in determining the default location, file type, and other key parameters needed to safely save the data to disk.

One of the more important of these properties is the `Filter` property. This property establishes the suggested file types to use when displaying information in the File Save dialog. The `File` property is a string that has the following format:

`description¦mask`

`description` represents a friendly word or phrase that describes the type of file—for example, `Text Files` or `Bitmaps`. `mask` represents the actual filter used when selecting files from the current directory for display in the dialog list. For example, to force the dialog to display only text files, you would set the `mask` portion of the string to `"*.txt"`. To display only bitmap files, the mask would be set to `"*.bmp"`.

The code in Listing 24.14 shows a very basic example of the File Save Common Dialog control operation. Locate the `SaveData` method you built earlier and add this code to the method.

Listing 24.14. Coding the basic File Save example.

```
Public Sub SaveData()

    ' save the data from the form to a file

    On Error Resume Next ' ignore errors

    Dim ctlTemp As Control ' for reading text boxes
    Dim lngFlags As Long ' for dialog flags
    Dim strFileName As String ' for file name to write

    ' set dialog properties
    cdlSample.CancelError = False
    cdlSample.DialogTitle = "Save Data Dialog"
    cdlSample.DefaultExt = "txt"
    cldSample.InitDir = App.Path ' start looking in the application's path
    cdlSample.Filter = "ASCII File(*.asc)¦*.asc¦Comma Separated
    ➥Values(*.csv)¦*.csv¦Text File(*.txt)¦*.txt"
    cdlSample.FilterIndex = 3 ' which item to show

    strFileName = ""
    cdlSample.ShowSave ' show the save dialog
    strFileName = cdlSample.filename ' get returned filename

    ' if it's a good name, write the data as requested
    If Len(strFileName) <> 0 Then ' a good file?
        Open strFileName For Output As #1 ' open the file
        For Each ctlTemp In Me.Controls ' loop through controls
            If TypeOf ctlTemp Is TextBox Then 'a text box?
                Print #1, ctlTemp.Tag&; ","; ctlTemp.Text
            End If ' ctlTemp=TextBox
        Next ' ctlTemp
        Close #1 ' close open file
    End If ' strFileName<>""

End Sub
```

24

USING THE COMMON DIALOG CONTROL

Note the use of the `Filter` and `FilterIndex` properties. This will force the dialog to display only the files that have `.txt`, `.asc`, or `.csv` as their file extension. Which files are displayed is determined by the `FilterIndex` property. Because `FilterIndex` is set to 3, only the `.txt` files will be displayed when the dialog starts. Users can use the drop-down listbox to change the `FilterIndex` (see Figure 24.13).

FIGURE 24.13.

Modifying the `FilterIndex` *property of the Save Data dialog.*

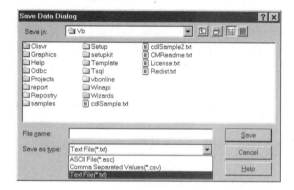

Now save and run the project. Fill in each of the fields on the form with some data and then click the Save button. You'll see a dialog pop up, much like the one shown in Figure 24.13. Enter a filename and click Save. This will copy the data from the form into the file you selected.

NOTE

A sample file called `cdlSample.txt` is included with the sample code on the CD-ROM. You can read this file with Windows `Notepad.exe` to see how it looks. You can compare this file with the one you wrote to make sure your program is working properly.

Some Added Settings for the File Save Dialog

There are a number of `Flag` values you can use with the File Save and File Open dialogs. The code in Listing 24.15 shows the most useful flags for the File Save dialogs. Modify your code to match this listing.

Listing 24.15. Some added settings for the File Save dialog.

```
Public Sub SaveData()

    ' save the data from the form to a file


    On Error Resume Next ' ignore errors

```

```
Dim ctlTemp As Control ' for reading text boxes
Dim lngFlags As Long ' for dialog flags
Dim strFileName As String ' for file name to write
'
' set dialog properties
cdlSample.CancelError = False
cdlSample.DialogTitle = "Save Data Dialog"
cdlSample.DefaultExt = "txt"
cdlSample.Filter = "ASCII File(*.asc)¦*.asc¦Comma Separated Values(*.csv)
  ➥ ¦*.csv¦Text File(*.txt)¦*.txt"
cdlSample.FilterIndex = 3 ' which item to show
'
' set some flag values
lngFlags = cdlOFNHelpButton ' add help button
lngFlags = lngFlags + cdlOFNCreatePrompt ' confirm file creates
lngFlags = lngFlags + cdlOFNHideReadOnly ' don't show read-only check
lngFlags = lngFlags + cdlOFNOverwritePrompt ' confirm overwriting existing file
lngFlags = lngFlags + cdlOFNPathMustExist ' confirm valid path
cdlSample.Flags = lngFlags
'
strFileName = ""
cdlSample.ShowSave ' show the save dialog
strFileName = cdlSample.filename ' get returned filename
'
' if it's a good name, write the data as requested
If Len(strFileName) <> 0 Then ' a good file?
    Open strFileName For Output As #1 ' open the file
    For Each ctlTemp In Me.Controls ' loop through controls
        If TypeOf ctlTemp Is TextBox Then 'a text box?
            Print #1, ctlTemp.Tag&; ","; ctlTemp.Text ' write tag and value
        End If ' ctlTemp=TextBox
    Next ' ctlTemp
    Close #1 ' close open file
End If ' strFileName<>""
'
End Sub
```

You'll notice that the `Flag` settings have been added to force the dialog box to automatically do a number of handy things:

- Confirm the creation of a new file
- Hide the Read-Only checkbox
- Confirm file overwrites
- Make sure the entered path (folder) already exists

Now when you save and run the project, you'll see a much friendlier dialog box that confirms your selection.

Adding Help to the File Save Dialog

The code in Listing 24.16 shows you how to add help support for the File Save dialog. Keep in mind that you need to have the custom help file already built, and you must also have the exact context ID value for the topic that relates to the File Save dialog. Of course, your program might call the File Save dialog in more than one place. You can create as many custom help topics as you need, and link the Common Dialog control to the help topic appropriate for the current file-save operation.

Listing 24.16. Adding custom help to the File Save dialog.

```
Public Sub SaveData()
    '
    ' save the data from the form to a file
    '

    On Error Resume Next ' ignore errors
    '
    Dim ctlTemp As Control ' for reading text boxes
    Dim lngFlags As Long ' for dialog flags
    Dim strFileName As String ' for file name to write
    '
    ' set dialog properties
    cdlSample.CancelError = False
    cdlSample.DialogTitle = "Save Data Dialog"
    cdlSample.DefaultExt = "txt"
    cdlSample.Filter = "ASCII File(*.asc)¦*.asc¦Comma Separated Values(*.csv)
      ➥ ¦*.csv¦Text File(*.txt)¦*.txt"
    cdlSample.FilterIndex = 3 ' which item to show
    '
    ' set some flag values
    lngFlags = cdlOFNHelpButton ' add help button
    lngFlags = lngFlags + cdlOFNCreatePrompt ' confirm file creates
    lngFlags = lngFlags + cdlOFNHideReadOnly ' don't show read-only check
    lngFlags = lngFlags + cdlOFNOverwritePrompt ' confirm overwriting existing file
    lngFlags = lngFlags + cdlOFNPathMustExist ' confirm valid path
    cdlSample.Flags = lngFlags
    '
    ' set help topic for button
    cdlSample.HelpFile = strHelpFile
    cdlSample.HelpCommand = cdlHelpContext
    cdlSample.HelpContext = Save_the_Data_File
    '
    strFileName = ""
    cdlSample.ShowSave ' show the save dialog
    strFileName = cdlSample.filename ' get returned filename
    '
    ' if it's a good name, write the data as requested
    If Len(strFileName) <> 0 Then ' a good file?
        Open strFileName For Output As #1 ' open the file
        For Each ctlTemp In Me.Controls ' loop through controls
            If TypeOf ctlTemp Is TextBox Then 'a text box?
                Print #1, ctlTemp.Tag&; ","; ctlTemp.Text ' write tag and value
            End If ' ctlTemp=TextBox
        Next ' ctlTemp
        Close #1 ' close open file
    End If ' strFileName<>""
    '
End Sub
```

Using the File Open Dialog

The code for the File Open dialog is almost identical to the code you used for the File Save dialog. In fact, you could easily use one dialog to perform both tasks because you are only retrieving a filename in each case. However, the File Open dialog's default button has a caption of Open, while the default button for the File Save dialog is set to Save.

NOTE

Although you can customize almost every aspect of the File Save and File Open dialogs (dialog titles and so on), you cannot change the captions of the command buttons in the dialogs.

In this section you'll create a routine that can read the data created in the SaveData method and copy it into the form to display.

The Basic File Open Dialog

Listing 24.17 shows the basic form of the File Open dialog. Just as you did with the File Save dialog, you need to set a few parameters before starting the dialog. Locate the ReadData method you created earlier and add the code shown in Listing 24.17.

Listing 24.17. Coding the basic File Open dialog.

```
Public Sub ReadData()
    '
    ' read data from file and load form
    '

    On Error Resume Next ' ignore errors
    '
    Dim ctlTemp As Control ' for text boxes
    Dim strField As String ' for field tag
    Dim strValue As String ' for field value
    Dim lngFlags As Long ' for dialog flags
    Dim strFileName As String ' for read file name
    '
    ' set dialog properties
    cdlSample.CancelError = False
    cdlSample.DialogTitle = "Read Data Dialog"
    cdlSample.DefaultExt = "txt"
    cdlSample.Filter = "ASCII File(*.asc)|*.asc|Comma Separated Values(*.csv)
    ➡ |*.csv|Text File(*.txt)|*.txt"
    cdlSample.FilterIndex = 3 ' which item to show
    '
    ' do the dialog action
    strFileName = ""
    cdlSample.ShowOpen ' show dialog
    strFileName = cdlSample.filename ' get selected file
    '
```

continues

24

Listing 24.17. continued

```
    ' if it's a good name, load the data
    If Len(strFileName) <> 0 Then
        Open strFileName For Input As #1 ' open the file
            Do Until EOF(1) ' read until no more records
            Input #1, strField, strValue ' read a line
            For Each ctlTemp In Me.Controls ' loop thru controls
                If ctlTemp.Tag = strField Then ' a match?
                    ctlTemp.Text = strValue ' fill it in
                    Exit For ' skip the rest
                End If ' if tag=strfield
            Next ' next ctlTemp
        Loop ' until EOF(1)
        Close #1 ' close the open file
    End If ' if strFileName<>""
    '
End Sub
```

By this time, most of this code should look very familiar. You can see that the `DialogTitle` property has been changed, but all the rest of the Common Dialog control–related code is identical to the File Save dialog request.

Save and run the project, and then click the Open button. You'll see a dialog that waits for you to select a file to read (see Figure 24.14).

FIGURE 24.14.
Using the File Open dialog.

Some Added Settings for the File Open Dialog

The real difference between the File Save and File Open dialogs is in the `Flag` settings. Whereas the `Flag` settings for the File Save dialog are focused on confirming the overwrite of an existing file, the File Open dialog has settings that will automatically confirm that the file actually exists.

Alter your `ReadData` method to match the code in Listing 24.18. Then save and run the project to test the effects of the new flag settings.

Listing 24.18. Some added settings for the File Open dialog.

```
Public Sub ReadData()
    '
    ' read data from file and load form
    '

    On Error Resume Next ' ignore errors
    '
    Dim ctlTemp As Control ' for text boxes
    Dim strField As String ' for field tag
    Dim strValue As String ' for field value
    Dim lngFlags As Long ' for dialog flags
    Dim strFileName As String ' for read file name
    '
    ' set dialog properties
    cdlSample.CancelError = False
    cdlSample.DialogTitle = "Read Data Dialog"
    cdlSample.DefaultExt = "txt"
    cdlSample.Filter = "ASCII File(*.asc)¦*.asc¦Comma Separated Values(*.csv)
    ➥ ¦*.csv¦Text File(*.txt)¦*.txt"
    cdlSample.FilterIndex = 3 ' which item to show
    '
    ' set some flag properties
    lngFlags = cdlOFNHelpButton ' show help button
    lngFlags = lngFlags + cdlOFNFileMustExist ' must be a real file
    lngFlags = lngFlags + cdlOFNHideReadOnly ' don't show read-only box
    lngFlags = lngFlags + cdlOFNLongNames ' allow long file names
    lngFlags = lngFlags + cdlOFNPathMustExist ' path must already exist
    cdlSample.Flags = lngFlags ' move it into the property
    '
    ' do the dialog action
    strFileName = ""
    cdlSample.ShowOpen ' show dialog
    strFileName = cdlSample.filename ' get selected file
    '
    ' if is't a good name, load the data
    If Len(strFileName) <> 0 Then
        Open strFileName For Input As #1 ' open the file
            Do Until EOF(1) ' read until no more records
            Input #1, strField, strValue ' read a line
            For Each ctlTemp In Me.Controls ' loop thru controls
                If ctlTemp.Tag = strField Then ' a match?
                    ctlTemp.Text = strValue ' fill it in
                    Exit For ' skip the rest
                End If ' if tag=strfield
            Next ' next ctlTemp
        Loop ' until EOF(1)
        Close #1 ' close the open file
    End If ' if strFileName<>""
    '
End Sub
```

Adding Help to the File Open Dialog

As with all the other dialogs, you can easily add a custom help topic to the File Open dialog, too. Listing 24.19 shows how this can be done.

Listing 24.19. Adding custom help to the File Open dialog.

```
Public Sub ReadData()
    '
    ' read data from file and load form
    '

    On Error Resume Next ' ignore errors
    '
    Dim ctlTemp As Control ' for text boxes
    Dim strField As String ' for field tag
    Dim strValue As String ' for field value
    Dim lngFlags As Long ' for dialog flags
    Dim strFileName As String ' for read file name
    '
    ' set dialog properties
    cdlSample.CancelError = False
    cdlSample.DialogTitle = "Read Data Dialog"
    cdlSample.DefaultExt = "txt"
    cdlSample.Filter = "ASCII File(*.asc)¦*.asc¦Comma Separated Values(*.csv)
➡ ¦*.csv¦Text File(*.txt)¦*.txt"
    cdlSample.FilterIndex = 3 ' which item to show
    '
    ' set some flag properties
    lngFlags = cdlOFNHelpButton ' show help button
    lngFlags = lngFlags + cdlOFNFileMustExist ' must be a real file
    lngFlags = lngFlags + cdlOFNHideReadOnly ' don't show read-only box
    lngFlags = lngFlags + cdlOFNLongNames ' allow long file names
    lngFlags = lngFlags + cdlOFNPathMustExist ' path must already exist
    cdlSample.Flags = lngFlags ' move it into the property
    '
    ' set help topic for button
    cdlSample.HelpFile = strHelpFile
    cdlSample.HelpCommand = cdlHelpContext
    cdlSample.HelpContext = Open_the_Data_File
    '
    ' do the dialog action
    strFileName = ""
    cdlSample.ShowOpen ' show dialog
    strFileName = cdlSample.filename ' get selected file
    '
    ' if is't a good name, load the data
    If Len(strFileName) <> 0 Then
        Open strFileName For Input As #1 ' open the file
            Do Until EOF(1) ' read until no more records
            Input #1, strField, strValue ' read a line
            For Each ctlTemp In Me.Controls ' loop thru controls
                If ctlTemp.Tag = strField Then ' a match?
                    ctlTemp.Text = strValue ' fill it in
                    Exit For ' skip the rest
                End If ' if tag=strfield
            Next ' next ctlTemp
        Loop ' until EOF(1)
        Close #1 ' close the open file
    End If ' if strFileName<>""
    '
End Sub
```

After modifying your ReadData method, save and run the project. Now when you click the Open button and then click the Help button, you'll see online help on how to use the Open button of the form (see Figure 24.15).

FIGURE 24.15.

Viewing the custom help for the File Open dialog.

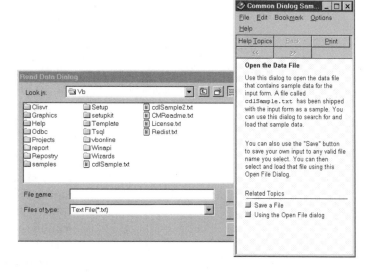

The Flag Settings for the File Open and File Save Dialogs

As mentioned earlier, there are lots of possible values for the Flag property when you are requesting the ShowOpen or ShowSave method of the Common Dialog control. Table 24.8 lists the possible values, their types, and their descriptions.

Table 24.8. Valid Flag values for the File Open and File Save dialogs.

Constant	Value	Description
cdlOFNAllowMultiselect	&H200	Specifies that the File Name listbox allows multiple selections. The user can select more than one file at runtime by pressing the Shift key and using the up-arrow and down-arrow keys to select the desired files. When this is done, the FileName property returns a string containing the names of all selected files. The names in the string are delimited by spaces.

continues

Table 24.8. continued

Constant	Value	Description
cdlOFNCreatePrompt	&H2000	Specifies that the dialog box prompts the user to create a file that doesn't currently exist. This flag automatically sets the cdlOFNPathMustExist and cdlOFNFileMustExist flags.
cdlOFNExplorer	&H80000	Uses the Explorer-like Open A File dialog box template. Works with Windows 95 and Windows NT 4.0.
cdlOFNExtensionDifferent	&H400	Indicates that the extension of the returned filename is different from the extension specified by the DefaultExt property. This flag isn't set if the DefaultExt property is Null, if the extensions match, or if the file has no extension. This flag value can be checked when closing the dialog box.
cdlOFNFileMustExist	&H1000	Specifies that the user can enter only names of existing files in the File Name text box. If this flag is set and the user enters an invalid filename, a warning is displayed. This flag automatically sets the cdlOFNPathMustExist flag.
cdlOFNHelpButton	&H10	Causes the dialog box to display the Help button.
cdlOFNHideReadOnly	&H4	Hides the Read Only checkbox.
cdlOFNLongNames	&H200000	Indicates that long filenames are valid.
cdlOFNNoChangeDir	&H8	Forces the dialog box to set the current directory to what it was when the dialog box was opened.
cdlOFNNoDereferenceLinks	&H100000	Specifies to not dereference shell links (also known as shortcuts). By default, choosing a shell link causes it to be dereferenced by the shell.

Constant	Value	Description
cdlOFNNoLongNames	&H40000	Indicates that long filenames are *not* valid.
cdlOFNNoReadOnlyReturn	&H8000	Specifies that the returned file won't have the Read Only attribute set and won't be in a write-protected directory.
cdlOFNNoValidate	&H100	Specifies that the common dialog box allows invalid characters in the returned filename.
cdlOFNOverwritePrompt	&H2	Causes the Save As dialog box to generate a message box if the selected file already exists. The user must confirm whether to overwrite the file.
cdlOFNPathMustExist	&H800	Specifies that the user can enter only valid paths. If this flag is set and the user enters an invalid path, a warning message is displayed.
cdlOFNReadOnly	&H1	Causes the Read Only checkbox to be initially checked when the dialog box is created. This flag also indicates the state of the Read Only checkbox when the dialog box is closed.
cdlOFNShareAware	&H4000	Specifies that sharing-violation errors will be ignored.

That's all there is to the File Open and File Save dialogs. Be sure to save your project (prjCDlSample.vbp) and form (frmCDlSample.frm) before you move on to the last coding section in this chapter.

The Help Services

The last type of service that the Common Dialog control provides to programmers is access to the Windows Help system. If you've been working through the examples in this chapter, you know that there are several properties that can be used to attach help files and specific topics to a dialog. These same properties (along with a few others) can be used to make direct calls to the Windows Help system. You can use these calls to display a help topic, a search dialog, a help contents page, or other help-related services.

In this section you'll learn how to use the Common Dialog control to gain easy access to help files and the functions of the Windows Help system.

Demonstrating Common Dialog Control Help Services

The process of gaining access to the Windows Help system involves one more step than the other Common Dialog control services. Along with the call to the ShowHelp method, you also need to set the HelpCommand property to tell the Common Dialog control which form of Help service you would like to access.

The code in Listing 24.20 shows the most common help service requests. Locate the mnuHelpItem_Click event and add the code from Listing 24.20 to your form.

Listing 24.20. Coding the Common Dialog control help example.

```
Private Sub mnuHelpItem_Click(Index As Integer)
    '
    ' handle help requests
    '
    Dim strPartialKey As String
    '
    cdlSample.HelpFile = strHelpFile
    '
    Select Case Index
        Case 0 ' contents page
            cdlSample.HelpCommand = cdlHelpContents
        Case 1 ' index page
            cdlSample.HelpCommand = cdlHelpIndex
        Case 2 ' help on help
            cdlSample.HelpCommand = cdlHelpHelpOnHelp
        Case 3 ' helpkey
            cdlSample.HelpCommand = cdlHelpKey
            cdlSample.HelpKey = "font"
        Case 4 ' helppartialkey
            strPartialKey = InputBox("Enter a search word:",
            ➥ "Help Partial Key", "font")
            cdlSample.HelpCommand = cdlHelpPartialKey
            cdlSample.HelpKey = strPartialKey
        Case 5 ' help command (macro)
            cdlSample.HelpCommand = cdlHelpCommandHelp
            cdlSample.HelpKey = "about()"
    End Select
    '
    cdlSample.ShowHelp
    '
End Sub
```

As you can see from Listing 24.20, there are several possible service options for the ShowHelp method. cdlHelpContents and cdlHelpIndex both return the default contents page of the associated help file. The cdlHelpHelpOnHelp setting provides an online tutorial on how to use the help system. `cdlHelpKey` and `cdlHelpPartialKey` each make calls to the search capabilities of the Windows Help engine. The last request (`cdlHelpCommandHelp`) actually allows you to run a help macro from within your Visual Basic program. In this example, you are calling the about() macro, which will display the Windows Help About screen.

After entering the code from Listing 24.20, save and run the project. To test the help features of the Common Dialog control, click the right (alternate) mouse button over the frame at the bottom of the form. You'll see a menu pop up. Select an item from the menu to see the related help service (see Figure 24.16).

FIGURE 24.16.

Viewing the pop-up help menu.

The Flag Settings for the ShowHelp Method

Even though the `ShowHelp` method does not present a consistent dialog as do the other Common Dialog control methods, you can still have some control over how the help services are presented by modifying the `HelpCommand` property of the Common Dialog control.

> **WARNING**
>
> It is important to remember that the constants that control the behavior of the help services are not applied to the `Flags` property. All help-related settings are passed in the `HelpCommand` property.

Table 24.9 shows all the possible values for the `HelpCommand` property of the Common Dialog control.

Table 24.9. Valid values for the `HelpCommand` property.

Constant	Value	Description
cdlHelpCommandHelp	&H102	Executes a Help macro.
cdlHelpContents	&H3	Displays the Contents topic in the current help file.
cdlHelpContext	&H1	Displays help for a particular topic.
cdlHelpContextPopup	&H8	Displays a topic identified by a context number.
cdlHelpForceFile	&H9	Creates a help file that displays text in only one font.
cdlHelpHelpOnHelp	&H4	Displays help for using the Help application itself.
cdlHelpIndex	&H3	Displays the index of the specified help file (same as `cdlHelpContents`).
cdlHelpKey	&H101	Displays help for a particular keyword.
cdlHelpPartialKey	&H105	Calls the search engine in Windows help.
cdlHelpQuit	&H2	Notifies the Help application that the specified Help file is no longer in use.
cdlHelpSetContents	&H5	Designates a specific topic as the Contents topic.
cdlHelpSetIndex	&H5	Sets the current index for multi-index help.

Summary

In this chapter you have learned how to add the Common Dialog control to your Visual Basic 5 projects and how to use that control to gain access to common Windows services, including

- `ShowColor`, which displays the Color dialog.
- `ShowFont`, which displays the Font dialog.
- `ShowPrinter`, which displays the Print dialog.
- `ShowOpen`, which displays a File Open dialog.
- `ShowSave`, which displays a File Save dialog.
- `ShowHelp`, which provides access to several Windows Help dialogs.

You also learned that there are a number of properties of this control and many special `Flag` values you can use to improve the effectiveness of the program.

Dynamic Control Creation and Indexing

by Paul Kimmel

IN THIS CHAPTER

CHAPTER 25

Being able to add controls at runtime adds a measure of dynamism to your Windows applications. Dynamically added controls, or controls added at runtime, are powerful controls you can add after the user has begun using the program. Adding dynamic controls affords you the ability to answer programmatic questions that haven't been asked yet. It also enables you to answer programmatic problems for which you know the possible answers. A development tool is a perfect example. Consider Visual Basic. Microsoft knows that you will want to use its controls. It offers you the toolbox, and as a user, you can orchestrate the assemblage of the controls. A development tool is probably the most extreme solution because it is generically defined for solving any problem. Within the realm of dynamic solutions, Visual Basic is a complex example, but perhaps you will need to define a data management program that allows the user to add fields on-the-fly. How will you support added fields programmatically? This chapter shows you how.

The other side of this coin is the ability to reuse code. Consider a collection of similar controls that can basically share the same algorithm, perhaps with minor differences. Would you want to write an algorithm 50 times simply because the control is different? Generally, no. Usually what you want to do is share the common algorithm. Control arrays enable you to do that. A control array enables you to specify controls as part of an array; when controls are part of an array, they will share event handlers in common. The control index will enable you to pivot on the minuscule differences in code.

Combining dynamic controls with control arrays offers the best of both worlds. Dynamic controls enable your program to do a little jig in step with your end users' needs; the control array enables you to easily manage the pool of dynamically created controls. In this chapter you will learn how to create and use dynamic controls and control arrays by reading and referring to the following topics:

- The mechanics of defining control arrays.
- Determining when a control array is best and how to maximize it.
- How to use control array properties and methods.
- Examples of creating forms on-the-fly.

If you have never created control arrays or dynamic controls, this chapter is a must-read. If you are an old hand at Visual Basic programming, you will find examples and demonstrations in this chapter that will help you hone your skills.

Creating Control Arrays

Visual Basic 5 is a powerful Windows development tool. It was designed by programmers for programmers. The reason the obvious has been restated for you is that sometimes it is easy to forget when you are struggling to learn something new that the tool you are learning, or learning better, was designed to be easy to learn. When you are a little bit stuck, sometimes the easiest way you can think of to perform a task should be the first thing you try. This rule applies to control arrays, as you will see in a minute.

A control array, like any other array, is an array of a data type. Every array has an upper and a lower bound, and it is a collection of some data type. The difference between a control array and an integer array, or any other array, is the data type. An array of controls is so powerful because you are using the array to organize the pool of controls in contiguous memory. As with all arrays elements, you can access every control in the array by indexing each element of the array. The intuitive part of using a control array lies in how easy it is to define an array of controls. Simply put, if you perform an Edit | Copy, followed immediately by an Edit | Paste, Visual Basic will ask you if you want to make a control array (see Figure 25.1).

Try this simple example. Open Visual Basic 5. Select View | Toolbox if the toolbox is not showing. Double-click on the command button in the toolbox. While the command button is still selected—denoted by the solid squares surrounding the button—select Edit | Copy, followed by Edit | Paste. The dialog shown in Figure 25.1 will be displayed. Clicking Yes will create a control array with two buttons in the array.

FIGURE 25.1.

The dialog that asks whether you want to create a control array.

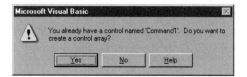

Pros and Cons of Using Control Arrays

A control array will reduce the amount of code you have to write if several controls of the same type can share the same algorithm. Consider a slide viewer program. Perhaps the program displays a zoomed-in view of several images shown on the same form. You might solve the problem by creating a form, inserting the image on the form, and showing the form as a modal dialog. The only thing that changes in the scenario is the actual image. The object being the only thing that is different is a classic example of when to use a control array.

Consider the alternative. While many controls on a form are of the same type, none of them share the same code, even remotely. Creating a control array under these circumstances adds complexity and you gain nothing. For every control array, you immediately add the complexity of determining—by the index—which control was involved. Thus, at a minimum, you will need a case statement or multiple `if` conditionals to determine which controls in the array were involved.

> **TIP**
>
> It is a good idea to pay the cost of a single function indirection by always placing event code in a well-named function. Doing so will enable you to call the function outside the context of an event, and your code will have a greater degree of modularity and semantic correctness.

The end result is that for the small overhead in determining the actual control that invoked an event handler, you could ultimately reduce the amount of code by a factor of the number of controls in the array. The result can be dramatic. As mentioned earlier, this will add complexity to the event handler, but all you should really ever have in an event handler is a function call to the code that solves the task. Read the next section for examples of creating and using control arrays.

Using a Control Array

The saying "take care of the pennies, and the dollars will take care of themselves" can be used as an analogy for software development. Take care of the discrete aggregations, and the modules will take care of themselves. Too often you may come across code where simple principles have been ignored. Often the reason is that the developer may have tried to quantify the benefit of a technique in a single context, such as one function. It is an understatement to say that positive techniques will have an accumulatively positive effect.

The `ControlArray.vbp` example demonstrates a small but fundamental usage of a control array. The program shown in Figure 25.2 enables the user to click on any of the pictures, presenting an expanded view of the bitmap. The code in Listing 25.1 is straightforward. What is important to note is that one code fragment works for an arbitrarily large number of controls (although the example demonstrates just four controls).

FIGURE 25.2.

A bitmap slide viewer created with a `PictureBox` *control array.*

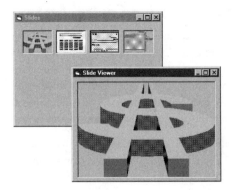

Listing 25.1. A bitmap slide viewer using one event for an arbitrary number of bitmaps.

```
Private Sub Picture1_Click(Index As Integer)
    Form2.Picture1 = Picture1(Index)
    Form2.Show Modal
End Sub
```

Listing 25.1 uses the `Index` argument of this one event handler to distinguish which control in the array of `PictureBox` controls was clicked, assigns a picture to the view form's picture, and displays the form modally. It is evident that the amount of code saved is proportionate to the number of controls in the array.

FIGURE 25.3.

A single control with focus on the Properties dialog; note the index reference in the control combobox.

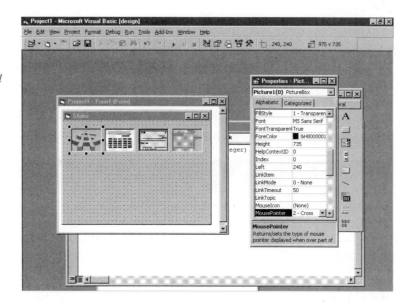

Keep in mind while you are developing that small distinctions in techniques can have magnified results over the lifetime of a program. A good demo program provided by Microsoft, demonstrating button control arrays, is the use of the `Toolbar` control in the `VisData` example in `c:\Program Files\DevStudio\VB\Samples\VisData`. (The directory may be different, depending on what path you specified when installing your copy of Visual Basic 5.)

Finally, remember that creating a function that performs a task is another good way to minimize the number of times you have to write the same algorithm and maximize your effort. Consider using a control array when the algorithm is the same for a set of similar controls, as the `ControlArray.vbp` example does, and always consider distancing the implementation of an algorithm from an event handler by at least one level of indirection. Read the next section for a closer examination of event handling for control arrays.

Designing Event Handlers for Control Arrays

Event handlers are generally associated with a single control. The importance of this is that when you are writing code for a control, the event handler provides the context. For example, there is clearly a distinction between the `Click` event for a form and one for a `PictureBox` control. The naming convention used—*controlname_eventname*—for event handlers also suggests the owner of the control. Hence, context determines which control will originate an event. The only way to determine the originator in a control array is by examining the `Index` argument. Consider the slight differences between a `Click` event handler for a `PictureBox` control and one for a `PictureBox` array:

```
' Click for a PictureBox array
Private Sub Picture1_Click(Index As Integer)
End Sub
```

```
' Click for PictureBox that is not in an array
Private Sub Picture2_Click()
End Sub
```

The distinction is purely in the argument count and type. `Picture1` is the name of a `PictureBox` array; therefore, it will have an `Index As Integer` argument. The `Index` argument is directly beneficial when you want to call methods of the control or manipulate inherent properties. `Index` is secondarily important when you want to perform disparate activities related to a particular control, and `Index` is used to selectively determine the control that raised the event.

TIP

It is strongly suggested that any array indexing be prefixed with array bounds checking. This is mitigated in the context of a control array event handler. Why? The event is raised internally and will only be raised by a valid control. Therefore, the index is guaranteed to be valid.

In a control array the name of the control is actually the name of the array, and the control is actually referred to by using the array and index pair. The following are pseudo-code examples depicting how the index can be used to determine the caller. Given a control array with fewer than three controls, you might use an `If...Then...Else...Endif` test to determine the control and the action. For control arrays with three or more controls, it is more desirable to use a `case` statement.

NOTE

Don't be lulled into complacency when using a case statement. Insist that all code in case statements greater than one line be indirectly implemented via a function call. Doing so will keep the purpose of the case distinct from the action required, and thus easier to read.

You know how to create control arrays at design time and associate event handlers with arrayed controls. In the next section you will see examples demonstrating how to create controls at runtime, reasons you might want to do so, and how predefined event handlers are associated with dynamic control arrays.

Creating Controls Dynamically

There are two kinds of control creation. The first is design-time control creation. When referring to creating a control at design time, we are referring to painting a control on a form from the toolbox. The program is not running, and the developer adds the control. Runtime creation, on the other hand, refers to adding a control to an existing form and control array programmatically while the user or tester is executing the program. Obviously, adding controls at design time is how many Windows programs are conceived. Generally only a comparatively small number of controls are added dynamically, but the end result can be a program that is perceived to be flexible and user friendly.

Visual Basic makes it extremely easy to dynamically add controls as part of a control array. `CommandArray.vbp` in Listing 25.2, illustrated in Figure 25.4, demonstrates the ease with which dynamic controls can be added.

Listing 25.2. CommandArray.vbp—Adding controls on-the-fly is as straightforward as this example.

```
1: Private Sub Command1_Click(Index As Integer)
2:     Static I As Integer
3:     I = I + 1
4:     Load Command1(I)
5:     Command1(I).Left = Command1(I - 1).Left + 20
6:     Command1(I).Top = Command1(I - 1).Top + 20
7:     Command1(I).Caption = "Clone" + Str$(Index)
8:     Command1(I).Visible = True
9:     Call Command1(I).ZOrder(0)
10: End Sub
```

FIGURE 25.4.

*Command buttons
added dynamically
demonstrate the steps
required to add
controls.*

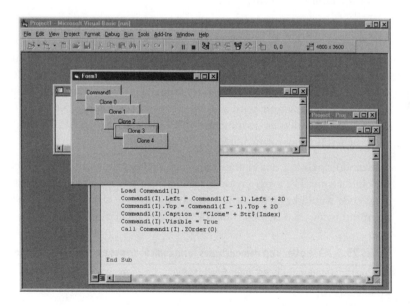

This brief listing demonstrates the simplicity with which controls can be added at runtime. The following is a brief summary of how this code adds controls dynamically. At design time a `CommandButton` control was painted on the form and given an index of `0`. The preceding two steps create a `CommandButton` array. Arbitrarily, and for simplicity, the code to add additional buttons was placed in the `Click` event handler. You can choose to add housekeeping code almost anywhere that suits your purposes. To keep track of the most recent addition to the `CommandButton` array named `Command1`, a `Static` integer was used. Line 3 in Listing 25.2

increments the integer, ensuring a unique Index property value. The Load command on line 4 dynamically creates the button, and lines 5 through 9 ensure that the button is visible and distinct from the 0th button created at design time. The control is created when the Load command is executed, but the control is equally useless to the programmer if it is not distinct.

Instantiating Forms at Runtime

A special kind of control that can be created dynamically is the MDI (or multiple-document interface) style document. Software applications such as spreadsheets use MDI to share the code from one form among many instances. Consider a Microsoft Excel spreadsheet document. The cells and related code that make Excel work are the same among all worksheets, regardless of the number of worksheets in use. The only difference is the data in the sheets. Setting the MDIChild property of a form to True enables you to designate a child as an MDI document.

The implication is that you may have many copies of the same form open, and they will all behave differently except for the data that is placed in them. MDI child forms are ideal candidates for control arrays. The array structure enables you to centrally manage the forms, regardless of the number of forms in use.

A classic example of an MDI application is provided in \DevStudio\VB\Samples\PGuide\ MDI\MDINote.vbp (see Figure 25.5) provided with Visual Basic 5. Prior to MDI and Windows, text editors and word processors were designed to display one text document at a time. The MDINote.vbp example shipped as a sample program with Visual Basic 5 demonstrates how easy it is to use MDI and how easy it is to manage MDI child documents using a control array. The MDI child itself is a form with a TextBox control (see Figure 25.6). In addition to the TextBox control, the form has its own menu, which, because it is an MDI child form, will be merged with the MDI form, or the parent form.

The module mdinote.bas contains the code that has the form array, which in turn manages all the child forms. The program looks simple, but there is a significant amount of code involved. That code would be greater if it were not for control arrays and MDI. Browse the brief fragment in Listing 25.3, which is followed by an explanation.

Listing 25.3. MDINote.vbp demonstrates form control arrays and MDI document applications.

```
1: Public Document() As New frmNotePad      ' Array of child form objects
2:
3: Sub FileNew()
4:     Dim fIndex As Integer
5:     ' Find the next available index and show the child form.
6:     fIndex = FindFreeIndex()
7:     Document(fIndex).Tag = fIndex
8:     Document(fIndex).Caption = "Untitled:" & fIndex
9:     Document(fIndex).Show
10:     ' Make sure the toolbar edit buttons are visible.
11:     frmMDI.imgCutButton.Visible = True
12:     frmMDI.imgCopyButton.Visible = True
13:     frmMDI.imgPasteButton.Visible = True
14: End Sub
```

FIGURE 25.5.

The MDINote.vbp *project provided with Visual Basic 5 demonstrates how to use a control array with MDI child forms.*

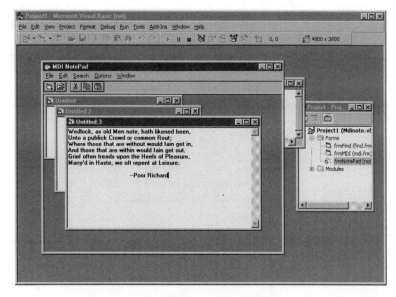

FIGURE 25.6.

notepad.frm *is the MDI child form that is capable of having multiple instances.*

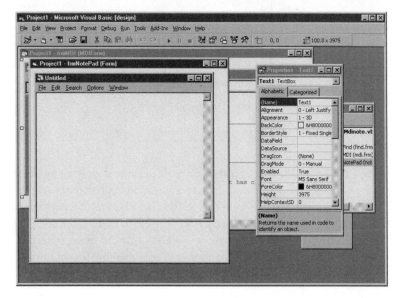

> **NOTE**
>
> Figure 25.7 shows the listboxes that are displayed as you type statements. The listboxes contain objects and constructs that are valid in a given context. This level of attention to detail makes it a challenge to make mistakes. The listboxes that appear can be toggled off and on by selecting Tools | Options. On the Editor tab of the Options dialog, check Auto List Members to enable or uncheck to disable.

FIGURE 25.7.

The option Tools | Options | Auto List Members enables you to select a contextually correct construct or member visually.

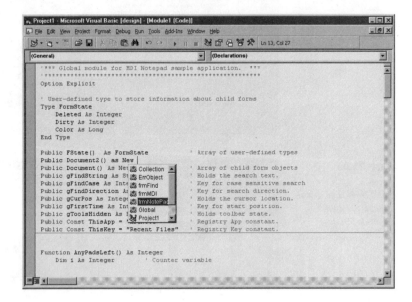

Line 1 in Listing 25.3 declares the public form control array using the New command. The use of the keyword New enables implicit object creation, and memory will be allocated the first time the object is used. The object in this context is each of the frmNotePad documents in the array. Line 6 calls FindFreeIndex, defined in this program to manage the document array. FindFreeIndex returns an available index or ReDims the array if more space is needed. The remaining lines manipulate the form specified by fIndex. The remaining line of note, line 9, calls Show, which performs an implicit Load and makes the form visible.

Using Control Array Properties

Control arrays have four properties distinct from the properties of the controls in the array. Where individual controls are concerned with properties such as Caption, Top, Left, or DataSource, the control array has Count, Item, LBound, and UBound. These are discussed in turn.

The `Count` property tells you how many items are in the control array. You can use the `Count` property for loop control. For example (assuming the `Option Base` default of `0`), the following code fragment demonstrates how you might iterate through all controls given a control array named `Data1`:

```
Dim I As Integer
For I = 0 to Data1.Count - 1
' Shows all record sets in a Data control array
    MsgBox Data1(I).RecordSet
Next I
```

The `Item` property is the default property. `Item` enables you to refer to a specific item in the control array by specifying the index. As it is the default property, both

```
Command1.Item(number)
```

and

```
Command1(number)
```

refer to the same object. The `LBound` and `UBound`—lower bound and upper bound, respectively—are included because you cannot use the functions with the same name to perform these tests. For example, given an array of integers

```
Dim I(10) As Integer
```

testing it with either `UBound` or `LBound` in the following manner:

```
If( UBound(I) > 1000 ) Then
    ' perform some action
End If
```

is syntactically correct. The same test cannot be performed on a control error. Hence this:

```
' Syntax error
If( UBound(Command1) > 5 ) Then
    ' perform some action
End If
```

where `Command1` is defined as a control array, is syntactically incorrect. The correct way to perform the equivalent test for either the lower or upper bound is

```
Command1.LBound
```

or

```
Command1.UBound
```

provided that `Command1` is a control array. A control array name refers to all the controls in an array. Using an index specifies a specific element—a control—in the array.

25

Creating Data Controls Dynamically

You may write dynamic and extensible database programs by using what you have learned thus far and applying it to the Data control. The Data control can also be designated as a control array. By simply specifying an Index value for a single Data control, you designate that name as a Data control array. The actual control you placed on the form becomes the 0th element of the control array. In short, by specifying an Index property for a single Data control, Data1 the control becomes Data1 the control array and Data1(0) is the control on the form.

Dynamic data controls can have many applications. Suppose you want to manage several recordsets at once. A Data control array is a great way to do it. Consider the scenario where you want to queue any users' most frequent dynamic SQL queries. Combining the Data control array with DBGrid makes it a snap. Listing 25.4 shows a short demo program that inserts a new Data control into a control array named Data1. (The program compiled from DataArray.vbp is illustrated in Figure 25.8.)

Listing 25.4. A Data control array.

```
1: Public Sub AddNew()
2:     Const SQL = "Select CustomerID From Customers"
3:     Dim I As Integer
4:     I = Data1.Count
5:     DBGrid1.ClearFields
6:     Load Data1(I)
7:     Set Data1(0).Recordset = Data1(0).Database.OpenRecordset(SQL)
8:     DBGrid1.ReBind
9: End Sub
10:
11: Private Sub AddDataSourceMenu_Click()
12:     Call AddNew
13: End Sub
```

FIGURE 25.8.

A short program demonstrating a control array of Data controls.

Listing 25.4 provides another example of a control array. With what you already have learned about control arrays in this chapter you can easily contrive uses for Data control arrays. Intentionally, each time the user clicks Query | Add Datasource in the sample program DataArray.exe, the same SQL statement is pushed to the front of the control array. With minor modifications

you could easily insert a SQL query from user inputs and list all previously entered queries. To further your understanding of Visual Basic, Data controls, and control arrays, try these exercises:

■ Use the InputBox function to enable the user to specify the SQL statement or table name.

■ Add a menu item that allows the user to see all the recordsets in the Data control array. Use the Count property to iterate through the Data control.

■ Add menu items to display and execute the most recently added recordsets.

■ Add an option to enable the user to save the recordsets in the Data control array to and from text files.

> **NOTE**
>
> To insert the Microsoft Data Bound Grid Control, check the component in the Components dialog accessed by selecting Project | Components.

One important aspect of the code in Listing 25.4 is the Load statement in line 6. As with other control arrays, Load creates the control referred to by the index. In line 7 the 0th element is set to an open recordset; the statement used is roughly the same for any Data control whose recordset you want to change at runtime. For the sample program, DBGrid was used. Line 5 in Listing 25.4 resets the Microsoft Databound Grid Control to two empty columns, the default. Line 7 binds the fields in the current record, causing the correct number of columns to be displayed.

Summary

Using control arrays is a means by which you can share code among many like controls. You have learned that given an event handler for a control array, all controls in the array share the same code. Controls can also enable you to easily make your programs more dynamic and extensible by offering your users a way to add controls during the execution and life cycle of their programs.

There are many supporting topics that make using control arrays and dynamic control creation possible. To learn about related topics, read the following chapters:

■ Chapter 2, "Conquering the Integrated Development Environment," shows you how to navigate your way around the Developer Studio.

■ Chapter 5, "Designing Forms: Your Look and Feel," offers professional advice.

■ Chapter 6, "Using Form Templates," helps you maximize reusing forms.

■ Chapter 9, "Using Message Boxes and Input Dialogs," describes useful dialogs and functions that will add a layer of interactivity to your programming projects.

25

DYNAMIC CONTROL CREATION

- Chapter 10, "Declaring, Raising, and Handling Events," is an essential chapter demonstrating how to write the code that responds to the user.
- Chapter 12, "Data Structures, Collections, and Enumerations," offers additional opportunities to experiment with other data structures.
- Chapter 14, "Working with Arrays," gives you ample opportunity to become an expert in using arrays.

Implementing OLE Drag-and-Drop Capabilities in Controls

by Lowell Mauer

IN THIS CHAPTER

Almost every Windows application on your PC has drag-and-drop functionality. Whether you are in a word processor and moving (dragging) a letter, word, or sentence to another location or you are in Explorer and copying a file to another folder, you are using drag and drop.

OLE drag and drop is a more advanced version of the simple drag-and-drop functionality. Instead of dragging one object to another to invoke a section of code, you are moving *data* from one control or application to another control or application. For example, dragging a text file from Windows Explorer into an open Notepad window uses OLE drag-and-drop operations.

In fact, when Microsoft developed the standards for Windows 95, it included OLE drag and drop as one of the features that defines a Windows 95–compliant product. These standards are used to determine whether a new product meets the requirements to be able to display the Windows 95 logo on its packaging and documentation.

In this chapter, you will see what OLE drag and drop is, how it works, and, more importantly, how to use it in a Visual Basic application. You will see how to use OLE drag and drop for something that is useful in an actual application.

What Is OLE Drag and Drop?

OLE drag and drop is probably the most powerful and useful feature that is available to a Visual Basic programmer; it adds the capability to drag text or graphics from one control to another, from a control to another Windows application, or from a Windows application into a control. The new feature of OLE drag and drop allows you to add this functionality to your application.

If you have been coding in Visual Basic for a while, you should be familiar with the standard drag-and-drop capabilities of the controls within a Windows application. All the concepts you learned in order to use the drag-and-drop functions still pertain to the new OLE drag-and-drop functions. The difference is that the OLE drag-and-drop features open your Visual Basic application to any other application that the user has on his PC.

> **NOTE**
>
> Although OLE drag and drop is new to Visual Basic 5, it is already available in most current ActiveX-compliant controls, such as the `RichTextBox` control.

Most Visual Basic controls support OLE drag and drop in some fashion. Depending on the control, you can use OLE drag and drop without any code, or you might need to write some sections of code to support the function you need. The following list outlines the standard and ActiveX controls that are included in the Professional and Enterprise editions of Visual Basic along with the level of OLE drag-and-drop support that they have.

The first group provides full support for the automatic OLE drag-and-drop capabilities. These controls are

- Apex data-bound grid
- Image
- Masked edit box
- Picturebox
- Rich textbox
- Textbox

The second group supports only automatic drag functions. If you need any drop functionality, you must code for it. These controls are

- Combobox
- Data-bound combobox
- Data-bound listbox
- Directory listbox
- File listbox
- Listbox
- List view
- Tree view

The final group supports only manual OLE drag and drop. This requires you to write the code needed to support any drag-and-drop functionality. These controls are

- Data
- Drive listbox
- Checkbox
- Command button
- Frame
- Label
- Option button

TIP

The easiest way to see what OLE drag-and-drop capabilities an ActiveX control has is to load the control and check the properties list. If OLEDragMode and OLEDropMode are listed, the control supports automatic or manual processing.

How Does OLE Drag and Drop Work?

Certain events are triggered whenever an OLE drag-and-drop operation is performed. The events for source control are always generated for both automatic and manual processing. However, events for the target control are generated only during a manual drop operation. Table 26.1 shows which events occur on the drag source and which occur on the drop target.

Table 26.1. OLE source and target events.

Source	Target
OLEStartDrag	OLEDragDrop
OLESetData	OLEDragOver
OLEGiveFeedback	
OLECompleteDrag	

Depending on how you want OLE drag and drop to perform, you generate code for only those events to which you want to respond. For example, you can create an application with a textbox that allows the user to automatically drag data from another application into the textbox. To do this, you simply set the textbox's OLEDropMode property to Automatic. If you want to allow the user to drag the data from the textbox control as well, you just set its OLEDragMode property to Automatic.

If you want to change the mouse cursors or perform different functions based on the button or the Shift key that was pressed, you need to manually respond to the source and target events. Also, if you want to analyze or change the data before it's dropped into the control, you need to use manual OLE drag-and-drop operations. This gives you full control of the drag-and-drop process.

Because you can drag and drop data into many different Visual Basic controls and Windows applications, implementing OLE drag and drop can range in difficulty from straightforward to fairly complex. The easiest method, of course, is dragging and dropping between two automatic objects, whether the object is a Word document or a control in your application that is set to Automatic.

> **NOTE**
>
> Even though many controls support OLE drag and drop, the examples used in this chapter use the textbox control. The textbox control is the simplest control with which to learn drag-and-drop concepts.

Implementing OLE Drag-and-Drop Capabilities in Controls

CHAPTER 26

543

26

IMPLEMENTING
OLE DRAG-AND-
DROP CAPABILITIES

Beginning the Drag

A manual OLE drag-and-drop operation in your Visual Basic application starts when the user drags data from an OLE drag source (such as a textbox control) by selecting and then holding down the left mouse button. The OLEStartDrag event is triggered, and you can then either store the data or simply specify the formats that the source supports. You also need to specify whether copying or moving the data or both is allowed by the source.

Going Over the Target

As the user drags the data over the target, the target's OLEDragOver event is triggered. You can specify what the target will do if the data is dropped there. The three choices are copy, move, and refuse the data. The default is generally set to move, but it could just as easily be set to copy.

Once the drop effect is set, the OLEGiveFeedback event is triggered. You use the OLEGiveFeedback event to give the user feedback on what action is taken when the data is dropped (that is, the mouse pointer changes to indicate a copy, move, or "no drop" action). Figure 26.1 shows the three different mouse pointer icons that come with Visual Basic.

FIGURE 26.1.

Default mouse icons for the OLE drag-and-drop process.

Completing the Drag

When the user drops the data onto the target, the target's OLEDragDrop event is triggered. The target checks the data from the source object to see whether it is the proper data type for the intended target. Depending on the outcome of that check, it either retrieves or rejects the data.

If the data was stored when the drag started, the GetData method retrieves the data. If the data wasn't stored when the drag started, the source's OLESetData event is triggered and the SetData method retrieves the data.

When the data is accepted or rejected, the OLECompleteDrag event is triggered, and the source can then perform the necessary clean-up. If the data is accepted and a move was requested, the source deletes the data.

Automatic or Manual Processing?

Deciding whether to use automatic or manual OLE drag and drop really depends on the type of functionality you allow the user to perform with your application.

With automatic drag and drop, all operations are controlled by Windows and the internal Visual Basic process. You can drag text from one textbox control to another by simply setting the `OLEDragMode` and `OLEDropMode` properties of these controls to `Automatic`. No code is required to respond to any of the OLE drag-and-drop events. When you drag a range of cells from Excel into a Word document, you perform an automatic drag-and-drop operation. Depending on how a given control or application supports OLE drag and drop and what type of data is dragged, automatically dragging and dropping data may be the best and simplest method.

When using manual drag and drop, you manually handle one or more of the OLE drag-and-drop events. Manual implementation of OLE drag and drop may be the better method when you need greater control over each step in the process or you need to provide the user with customized visual feedback. Manual implementation is the only option when a control does not support automatic drag and drop.

It is useful to know the terms for discussing OLE drag-and-drop operations. In a drag-and-drop operation, the object from which data is dragged is called the *source.* The object into which the data is dropped is called the *target.* Visual Basic provides the properties, events, and methods to control and respond to actions affecting both the source and the target. Remember that the source and the target may be in different applications, in the same application, or even in the same control. Depending upon your requirements, you might need to write code for the source, for the target, or both.

Using Automatic OLE Drag and Drop

If the controls you want to use support automatic drag and drop, you can activate the features by setting the control's `OLEDragMode` or `OLEDropMode` properties to Automatic. To see how this works, you are going to create a Visual Basic application that accepts text from a Word document and also allows you to drag text from the application into the Word document. To create this application, follow these steps:

1. Start Visual Basic and open a new project.
2. Place two textboxes on the form and name them `txtDrag` and `txtDrop`.
3. Add two labels, one for each textbox. Enter `Drag from Me` in the caption for one label and place it next to the `txtDrag` textbox. Enter `Drop on Me` in the label caption for the other textbox.
4. Place a command button, `cmdQuit`, on the form and set its caption to `Quit`.
   Your completed form should look like the form displayed in Figure 26.2.
5. In the `cmdQuit_click` routine, enter `END` to terminate the application.
6. To allow data to be dragged from the `txtDrag` textbox, set its `OLEDragMode` property to `Automatic`.
7. To allow data to be dropped into the `txtDrop` textbox, set its `OLEDropMode` property to `Automatic`.

Implementing OLE Drag-and-Drop Capabilities in Controls

CHAPTER 26

545

26

IMPLEMENTING
OLE DRAG-AND-
DROP CAPABILITIES

8. Start the new application and then start Word.

9. In Word, enter some text. Select it and drag it into the Drop on Me textbox. (See Figure 26.3.)

10. Enter some text in the Drag from Me textbox. Select this text and then drag it into the Word document.

FIGURE 26.2.

An automatic drag-and-drop form.

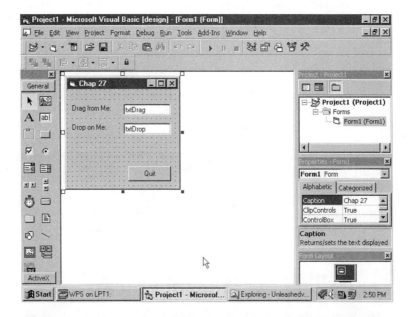

FIGURE 26.3.

An application after drag-and-drop operations.

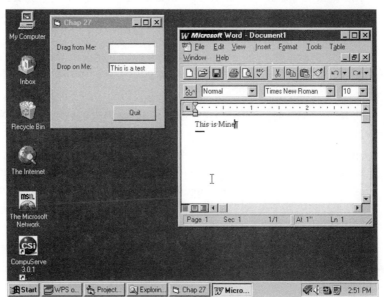

By default, when you drag text from the textbox into a Word document, it is moved rather than copied into the document. To copy the text instead of moving it, you can hold the Ctrl key down while you are dragging the text. This is the default behavior for all objects or applications that support OLE drag and drop. To change this default, you need to use the manual drag-and-drop techniques instead of the automatic process.

Automatic support does have some limitations; some of these limitations are derived from the controls themselves. For example, if you move text from a Word document into a textbox, all the rich text formatting in the Word document is stripped out because the standard textbox control doesn't support this formatting. Similar limitations exist for most controls. The RichTextBox control is the correct control to use for this particular situation.

Modify the previous example by adding a RichTextBox control to the form, and set its OLEDropMode property to Automatic. In the Word document, format some text and then drag it into both the standard textbox and the RichTextBox.

NOTE

When dragging data, you might notice that the mouse pointer shows whether the control it is currently on supports OLE drag and drop for the type of data you are dragging. If it does, the "drop" pointer is displayed; if it doesn't, the "no drop" pointer is displayed.

Controlling the Manual Process

If you want to specify which data formats or drop effects (copy, move, or no drop) are supported, or if the control you want to drag from doesn't support the automatic drag operation, you need to make your OLE drag operation manual.

Starting a manual drag-and-drop operation is done by calling the OLEDrag method. At that time, you can set the allowed drop effects and supported data formats, and if necessary, you can place data into the DataObject object.

You use the OLEDrag method to manually start the drag operation and the OLEStartDrag event to specify the allowed effects and the supported data formats.

Manual OLE drag and drop works the same way as the simple, event-driven drag-and-drop manual operations. With OLE drag and drop, you're not dragging one control to another control to invoke some code; you're moving *data* from one control or application to another control or application. An example of this is when the user drags a range of cells from Excel into the DBGrid control in your application.

The DataObject Object

When working with the simple, event-driven drag and drop, you were always sure of where the data came from. Because it was within the same application, the code could reference the Source variable in the event routine at runtime to access the information. However, when using OLE drag and drop, you do not always know where the data is coming from. The code process must work whether the data is within the same application or from another application, such as Word or Excel. To facilitate this process, Visual Basic provides an object to contain the data being moved, no matter where it comes from.

The DataObject object is the way Visual Basic moves data from the source to the target. It does this by providing the methods needed to store, retrieve, and analyze the data. Table 26.2 lists the property and methods used by the DataObject object.

Table 26.2. The DataObject properties and methods.

Category	Item	Description
Property	Files	Holds the names of files dragged to or from the Windows Explorer.
Methods	Clear	Clears the content of the DataObject object.
	GetData	Retrieves data from the DataObject object.
	GetFormat	Determines if a specified data format is available in the DataObject object.
	SetData	Places data into the DataObject or sets a specified format.

These methods allow you to manage data in the DataObject object only for controls contained in your Visual Basic application. The Clear method allows you to empty the DataObject before setting the object with new information. The Files property allows you to send a list of filenames that can be dropped into a target.

Finally, the SetData and GetData methods use the *data* and *format* arguments to put or get data stored in the DataObject object.

> **NOTE**
>
> Visual Basic can detect only a few data types. If the data being dragged is a bitmap, metafile, enhanced metafile, or text, Visual Basic sets the format. All other formats must be specified explicitly, or an error will occur.

Table 26.3 outlines the constants that are used to specify the format of the data.

Table 26.3. Data type constants.

Constant	Value	Meaning
vbCFText	1	Text
vbCFBitmap	2	Bitmap (.BMP)
vbCFMetafile	3	Metafile (.WMF)
vbCFEMetafile	14	Enhanced metafile (.EMF)
vbCFDIB	8	Device-independent bitmap (.DIB or .BMP)
vbCFPalette	9	Color palette
vbCFFiles	15	List of files
vbCFRTF	-16639	Rich text format (.RTF)

The SetData, GetData, and GetFormat methods use the *data* and *format* arguments either to return the type of data in the DataObject object or to retrieve the data itself if the format is compatible with the target. In following code, data in a textbox was selected and the *format* was specified as text (vbCFText). This information is stored in the DataObject to allow the target control (wherever it is) to retrieve the data:

```
Private Sub txtSource_OLEStartDrag(Data As VB.DataObject, _
AllowedEffects As Long)
Data.SetData txtSource.SelText, vbCFText
End Sub
```

The OLEDrag Method

Just like a simple drag and drop, the OLEDrag method is called from an object's MouseMove event when data is selected by clicking the left mouse button and holding it down to drag the data.

The OLEDrag method's primary purpose is to initiate a manual drag and then allow the OLEStartDrag event to set the conditions of the drag operation.

You must set the OLEDragMode property to Manual and then use the OLEDrag method in order to have manual control over the drag operation. If the control supports manual but not automatic OLE drag, it will not have the OLEDragMode property; however, it will still support the OLEDrag method and the OLE drag-and-drop events.

The OLEStartDrag Event

When the OLEDrag method is called, the control's OLEStartDrag event is triggered. This event is used to specify what drop effects and data formats the source will support.

The OLEStartDrag event uses two arguments to set the supported data formats and indicate whether the data can be copied or moved when the data is dropped.

> **WARNING**
>
> If no drop effects or data formats are specified in the OLEStartDrag event, the manual drag will not start.

The `allowedeffects` argument specifies which drop effects the drag source supports. Listing 26.1 specifies that a move or a copy can be performed when the data is dragged. This argument can be checked in the target control's OLEDragDrop event, and the program can respond based on the settings.

To specify which data formats the source control supports, the *format* argument is set in the OLEStartDrag event. The SetData method is used to set the format of the data. Listing 26.1 also assigns the data format of the DataObject to both text and rich text data.

Listing 26.1. StrtDrag.TXT—code to modify the start drag process.

```
Private Sub rtbSource_OLEStartDrag(Data As _
    VB.DataObject, AllowedEffects As Long)
    AllowedEffects = vbDropEffectMove Or vbDropEffectCopy
    Data.SetData , vbCFText
    Data.SetData , vbCFRTF
End Sub
```

Placing Data into the `DataObject` Object

Data is usually placed into the DataObject object when you begin a drag operation by using the SetData method in the OLEStartDrag event:

```
Private Sub txtSource_OLEStartDrag(Data As VB.DataObject, _
AllowedEffects As Long)
    Data.Clear
    Data.SetData txtSource.SelText, vbCFText
End Sub
```

The preceding code clears the default data formats from the DataObject, specifies the data format of the selected data, and then places that data into the DataObject object.

The `OLEDragOver` Event

The OLEDragOver event is triggered whenever data is dragged over a control. Two important arguments in the OLEDragOver event are the *effect* and *state* arguments. These inform the program of the exact properties and status of the data being dropped.

The *effect* argument of the OLEDragOver event is used to specify what action is taken if the object is dropped. Whenever the effect value is changed, the source's OLEGiveFeedback event is triggered. The OLEGiveFeedback event contains its own *effect* argument, which is used to provide visual feedback to the user. (The mouse pointer is changed to indicate a copy, move, or "no drop" action.) Table 26.4 shows the constants that are used by the *effect* argument of the OLEDragOver event.

Table 26.4. Effect constants.

Constant	Value	Meaning
vbDropEffectNone	0	The drop target cannot accept the data.
vbDropEffectCopy	1	A drop results in a copy. The original data is untouched by the drag source.
VbDropEffectMove	2	The drag source removes the data.
VbDropEffectScroll	&H80000000&	Scrolling is about to start or is currently occurring in the target.

The *state* argument of the OLEDragOver event allows you to respond to the source data entering, passing over, and leaving the target control. For example, when the source data enters the target control, the *state* argument is set to vbEnter.

The *state* argument of the OLEDragOver event specifies when the data enters, passes over, and leaves the target control by using the constants in Table 26.5.

Table 26.5. State constants.

Constant	Value	Meaning
vbEnter	0	The data was dragged within the range of a target.
vbLeave	1	The data was dragged out of the range of a target.
vbOver	2	The data is still within the range of a target, and either the mouse has moved, a mouse or keyboard button has changed, or a certain system-determined amount of time has elapsed.

The following code checks the DataObject object for a data format that is compatible with the target control. If the data is compatible, the *effect* argument tells the source that a move is requested if the data is dropped. If the data is not compatible, the source is informed and a "no drop" mouse pointer is shown:

```
Private Sub txtTarget_OLEDragOver(Data As _
    VB.DataObject, Effect As Long, Button As _
    Integer, Shift As Integer, X As Single, _
    Y As Single, State As Integer)
If Data.GetFormat(vbCFText) Then
    Effect = vbDropEffectMove And Effect
Else
    Effect = vbDropEffectNone
End If
End Sub
```

Providing Customized Visual Feedback

To modify the default visual behavior of the mouse in an OLE drag-and-drop operation, you can insert code in the OLEDragOver event for the target or the OLEGiveFeedback event for the source.

OLE drag and drop provides automatic visual feedback during a drag-and-drop operation. For example, when you start a drag, the mouse pointer changes to indicate that a drag has been initiated. When you pass over objects that do not support OLE drop, the mouse pointer changes to the "no drop" cursor.

The OLEGiveFeedback Event

The source's OLEGiveFeedback event is triggered automatically whenever the *effect* argument of the OLEDragOver event is changed. In this event, you can change the default behavior of the mouse pointer based on the *effect* argument. The OLEGiveFeedback event contains the *effect* and *defaultcursors* arguments. These allow you to check the effects allowed and then modify the default mouse pointers as needed.

The *effect* argument, like the other OLE drag-and-drop events, specifies whether data is to be copied, moved, or rejected. The purpose of this argument in the OLEGiveFeedback event is to allow you to provide customized feedback to the user by changing the mouse pointer to indicate these actions.

The *defaultcursors* argument specifies whether the default OLE cursor set is used. Setting this argument to False allows you to specify your own cursors using the Screen.MousePointer property of the Screen object.

TIP

Specifying custom mouse pointers is unnecessary because the default behavior of the mouse is handled by OLE.

CAUTION

If you decide to specify custom mouse pointers using the OLEGiveFeedback event, you need to account for every possible effect, including scrolling.

The following code example shows how to specify custom cursors (.ICO or .CUR files) for the copy, move, and scroll effects by setting the MousePointer and MouseIcon properties of the Screen object:

```
Private Sub TxtSource_OLEGiveFeedback(Effect As Long, _
        DefaultCursors As Boolean)
```

```
DefaultCursors = False
If Effect = vbDropEffectNone Then
    Screen.MousePointer = vbNoDrop
ElseIf Effect = vbDropEffectCopy Then
        Screen.MousePointer = vbCustom
        Screen.MouseIcon = _
LoadPicture("c:\Program Files\devstudio\vb\icons\copy.ico")
ElseIf Effect = (vbDropEffectCopy Or _
        vbDropEffectScroll) Then
        Screen.MousePointer = vbCustom
        Screen.MouseIcon = _
        LoadPicture("c:\Program Files\devstudio\vb\icons\copyscrl.ico")
ElseIf Effect = vbDropEffectMove Then
        Screen.MousePointer = vbCustom
        Screen.MouseIcon = LoadPicture("c:\Program
➡Files\devstudio\vb\icons\move.ico")
ElseIf Effect = (vbDropEffectMove Or _
        vbDropEffectScroll) Then
        Screen.MousePointer = vbCustom
        Screen.MouseIcon = _
        LoadPicture("c:\Program Files\devstudio\vb\icons\movescrl.ico")
Else
    DefaultCursors = True
End If
End Sub
```

> **WARNING**
>
> You should always reset the mouse pointer in the OLECompleteDrag event if you specify a custom mouse pointer in the OLEGiveFeedback event.

The OLEDragDrop Event

The OLEDragDrop event is triggered whenever the user drops the data onto the target. If data was placed into the DataObject object, it can be retrieved when the OLEDragDrop event is triggered by using the GetData method. The following example retrieves data from the DataObject and places it into the target control. The dragged data is retrieved using the GetData method:

```
Private Sub txtTarget_OLEDragDrop(Data As _
    VB.DataObject, Effect As Long, Button As _
    Integer, Shift As Integer, X As Single, _
    Y As Single)
    txtTarget.Text = Data.GetData(vbCFText)
End Sub
```

You might need to query the DataObject object for the data type that is dropped onto the target. You use the GetFormat method to check whether the data being dropped is compatible with the target. If it is, the drop action is completed.

The following code shows how to perform this action using an If..Then statement to choose which format to process:

Implementing OLE Drag-and-Drop Capabilities in Controls

CHAPTER 26

553

26
IMPLEMENTING
OLE DRAG-AND-
DROP CAPABILITIES

```
Private Sub txtTarget_OLEDragDrop(Data As _
  VB.DataObject, Effect As Long, Button As _
  Integer, Shift As Integer, X As Single, _
  Y As Single)
    If Data.GetFormat(vbCFText) Then
        txtTarget.Text = Data.GetData(vbCFText)
    End If
End Sub
```

If the data was not placed into the `DataObject` object when the `OLEStartDrag` event occurred, the `OLESetData` event is triggered when the target uses the `GetData` method to retrieve source data. The `OLESetData` event allows the source to respond to only one request for a given format of data.

The following code shows the `OLESetData` event responding only to text data:

```
Private Sub txtSource_OLESetData(Data As _
  VB.DataObject, DataFormat As Integer)
    If DataFormat = vbCFText Then
        Data.SetData txtSource.SelText, vbCfText
    End If
End Sub
```

The *effect* argument of the `OLEDragDrop` event specifies how the data was moved to the target when the data was dropped. Whenever this argument is changed, the `OLECompleteDrag` event is triggered for the source control. The source control can then take the appropriate action in its event routine.

The `OLECompleteDrag` event is also triggered if the OLE drag-and-drop operation was canceled. The `OLECompleteDrag` is the last event in the drag-and-drop operation.

The `OLECompleteDrag` Event

The `OLECompleteDrag` event contains only one argument (*effect*), which is used to inform the source of the action that was taken when the data is dropped onto the target.

If a move is specified and the data is dropped into the target, the following code deletes the data from the source control and resets the default mouse pointer:

```
Private Sub txtSource_OLECompleteDrag(Effect As Long)
    If Effect = vbDropEffectMove Then
        txtSource.SelText = ""
    End If
        Screen.MousePointer = vbDefault
End Sub
```

The *button* and *shift* arguments can respond to the state of the mouse buttons and the Shift, Ctrl, and Alt keys. For example, when dragging data into a control, you can allow the user to specify a copy operation by pressing the Ctrl key when dragging the data.

In the following code, the *ctrl* argument of the OLEDragDrop event is used to determine whether the Ctrl key is pressed when the data is dropped. If it is, a copy is performed. If it is not, a move is performed:

```
Private Sub txtTarget_OLEDragDrop(Data As _
    VB.DataObject, Effect As Long, Button As _
    Integer, Shift As Integer, X As Single, _
    Y As Single)
If Shift And vbCtrlMask Then
    txtTarget.Text = Data.GetData(vbCFText)
    Effect = vbDropEffectCopy
Else
    txtTarget.Text = Data.GetData(vbCFText)
    Effect = vbDropEffectMove
End If
End Sub
```

You can use the *button* argument to respond to the various mouse button states. For instance, you might want to let the user move the data by pressing the right mouse button.

Enhancing Visual Basic Applications with OLE Drag and Drop

Now that you have seen what OLE drag and drop is and what it can do, you will create a small Visual Basic application that allows you to drag a text file from Windows Explorer into a textbox.

The following application uses a textbox control and the OLEDragOver and OLEDragDrop events to open a single text file using the Files property and the vbCFFiles data format of the DataObject object.

To create this application, follow these steps:

1. Start a new project in Visual Basic.

2. Add a textbox control to the form. Set its OLEDropMode property to Manual. Set its MultiLine property to True and clear the Text property. Then set its ScrollBars property to Vertical.

3. Add a File | Exit menu item that will end the application. Your application form should look the same as the one in Figure 26.4.

4. Add the following code to open the selected file and move the text into the textbox in your application:

```
Sub DropFile(ByVal txt As TextBox, ByVal strFN$)
Dim iFile As Integer
Dim Str$, strLine$
    iFile = FreeFile
    Open strFN For Input Access Read Lock Read _
    Write As #iFile
    While Not EOF(iFile) And Len(Str) <= 32000
        Line Input #iFile, strLine$
        If Str <> "" Then Str = Str & vbCrLf
        Str = Str & strLine
```

Implementing OLE Drag-and-Drop Capabilities in Controls

CHAPTER 26

555

26

IMPLEMENTING
OLE DRAG-AND-
DROP CAPABILITIES

```
      Wend
      Close #iFile
      txt.SelStart = Len(txt)
      txt.SelLength = 0
      txt.SelText = Str
   End Sub
```

5. Add the following procedure to the OLEDragOver event. The GetFormat method is used to test for a compatible data format (vbCFFiles):

```
Private Sub Text1_OLEDragOver(.....)
   If Data.GetFormat(vbCFFiles) Then
      'inform the source of the action to be taken
      Effect = vbDropEffectCopy And Effect
   End If
   'If the data is not desired format, no drop
   Effect = vbDropEffectNone
End Sub
```

6. Finally, add the following code to the OLEDragDrop event:

```
Private Sub Text1_OLEDragDrop(.....)
'No matter how many files are selected only drop one
   If Data.GetFormat(vbCFFiles) Then
      If Data.Files <> "" Then
         DropFile Text1, vFN
      End If
   End If
End Sub
```

7. Run the application, open the Windows Explorer, highlight a text file, and drop it into the textbox control. The final outcome should look like Figure 26.5.

FIGURE 26.4.

A completed text file example.

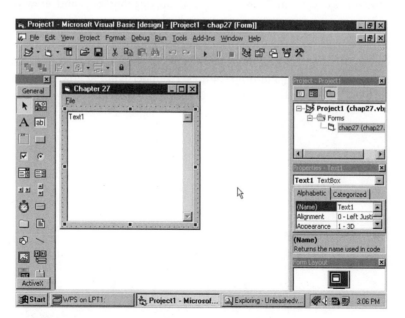

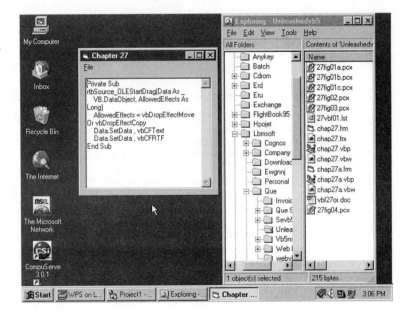

Summary

This chapter shows you how versatile OLE drag and drop really is. By using this feature of Visual Basic, you can use many different applications' data and allow your application to get data from anywhere else and send data back.

You have seen that the OLE techniques are almost the same as the simple, event-driven techniques for drag and drop. The examples in this chapter have shown you only one useful way of using the OLE drag-and-drop features. By understanding how these examples work, you can take the techniques and extend them into your applications.

I

INDEX

MACMILLAN COMPUTER PUBLISHING USA

A VIACOM COMPANY

Technical ----- Support:

If you need assistance with the information in this book or with a CD/Disk accompanying the book, please access the Knowledge Base on our Web site at **http://www.superlibrary.com/general/support**. Our most Frequently Asked Questions are answered there. If you do not find the answer to your questions on our Web site, you may contact Macmillan Technical Support **(317) 581-3833** or e-mail us at **support@mcp.com**.

Visual Basic for Applications Unleashed

Paul McFedries

Combining both power and ease of use, Visual Basic for Applications (VBA) is the common language for developing macros and applications across all Microsoft Office components. With the format of the best-selling *Unleashed* series, users will master the intricacies of this popular language and exploit the full power of VBA. This book covers user interface design, database programming, networking programming, Internet programming, and standalone application creation.

Price: $49.99 USA/$70.95 CAN   *User level: Accomplished—Expert*

ISBN: 0-672-31046-5   *800 pages*

VBScript Unleashed

Brian Johnson

In *VBScript Unleashed*, Web programming techniques are presented in a logical and easy-to-follow sequence that helps readers understand the principles involved in developing programs. The reader begins by learning the basics of writing a first program and then builds on that to add interactivity, multimedia, and more to Web page designs.

Price: $39.99 USA/$56.95 CAN   *User level: Casual—Accomplished—Expert*

ISBN: 1-57521-124-6   *650 pages*

Teach Yourself Database Programming with Visual Basic 5 in 21 Days, Second Edition

Michael Amundsen & Curtis Smith

Visual Basic, the 32-bit programming language from Microsoft, is used by programmers to create Windows and Windows 95 applications. It can also be used to program applications for the Web. This book shows those programmers how to design, develop, and deploy Visual Basic applications for the World Wide Web.

Price: $45.00 USA/$63.95 CAN   *User level: New—Casual—Accomplished*

ISBN: 0-672-31018-X   *1,000 pages*

World Wide Web Database Developer's Guide with Visual Basic 5

Mark Swank, Drew Kittel & Mark Spanik

Written by developers for developers, this advanced guide shows users how to design, develop, and deploy secure client/server databases on the Internet and intranet Web sites using the latest version of Microsoft Visual Basic. This book includes real-world examples and applications for users to implement on their sites.

Price: $59.99 USA/$83.95 CAN   *User level: Accomplished—Expert*

ISBN: 1-57521-276-5   *900 pages*

Teach Yourself Visual C++ 5 in 21 Days, Fourth Edition

Nathan Gurewich & Ori Gurewich

This book merges the power of the best-selling *Teach Yourself* series with the knowledge of Nathan Gurewich & Ori Gurewich, renowned experts in code, who create the most efficient way to learn Visual C++. In just 21 days this book will transform a novice into a knowledgeable programmer. The hands-on approach provides all the training needed to write code in just days.

Price: $35.00 USA/$49.95 CAN　　　*User level: New—Casual*

ISBN: 0-672-31014-7　　　*832 pages*

Visual C++ 5 Unleashed, Second Edition

Viktor Toth

This is the perfect book for advanced Visual C++ programmers. Its 1,100 pages explore the most advanced topics, and its enclosed CD-ROM allows the user to quickly learn by working through the programs in the book. It not only covers Visual C++ 5 and its capabilities, but also teaches LAN programming, OLE, DLLs, OLE automation, and how to update old programs to the new version of Visual C++.

Price: $49.99 USA/$70.95 CAN　　　*User level: Accomplished—Expert*

ISBN: 0-672-31013-9　　　*1,100 pages*

Teach Yourself Microsoft Visual InterDev in 21 Days

Michael Van Hoozer

Using the familiar, day-by-day format of the best-selling *Teach Yourself* series, this easy-to-follow tutorial provides users with a solid understanding of Visual InterDev, Microsoft's new Web application development environment. In no time, users will learn how to perform a variety of tasks, including front-end scripting, database and query design, content creation, server-side scripting, and more.

Price: $39.99 USA/$56.95 CAN　　　*User level: New—Casual—Accomplished*

ISBN: 1-57521-093-2　　　*800 pages*

Visual Basic 5 Developer's Guide

Anthony T. Mann

Visual Basic 5 Developer's Guide takes the programmer with a basic knowledge of Visual Basic programming to a higher skill level. Readers learn how to exploit the new features of the latest version of Visual Basic, in addition to implementing Visual Basic in a network setting and in conjunction with other technologies and software.

Price: $49.99 USA/$70.95 CAN　　　*User level: Accomplished—Expert*

ISBN: 0-672-31048-1　　　*1,000 pages*

Add to Your Sams Library Today with the Best Books for Programming, Operating Systems, and New Technologies

The easiest way to order is to pick up the phone and call

1-800-428-5331

between 9:00 a.m. and 5:00 p.m. EST.
For faster service please have your credit card available.

ISBN	Quantity	Description of Item	Unit Cost	Total Cost
0-672-31046-5		Visual Basic for Applications Unleashed	$49.99	
1-57521-124-6		VBScript Unleashed	$39.99	
0-672-31018-X		Teach Yourself Programming with Visual Basic 5 in 21 Days, Second Edition	$45.99	
1-57521-276-5		World Wide Web Database Developer's Guide with Visual Basic 5	$59.99	
0-672-31014-7		Teach Yourself Visual C++ 5 in 21 Days, Fourth Edition	$35.00	
0-672-31013-9		Visual C++ 5 Unleashed, Second Edition	$49.99	
1-57521-093-2		Teach Yourself Microsoft Visual InterDev in 21 Days	$39.99	
0-672-31048-1		Visual Basic 5 Developer's Guide	$49.99	
		Shipping and Handling: See information below.		
		TOTAL		

Shipping and Handling: $4.00 for the first book, and $1.75 for each additional book. If you need to have it NOW, we can ship product to you in 24 hours for an additional charge of approximately $18.00, and you will receive your item overnight or in two days. Overseas shipping and handling adds $2.00 per book and $8.00 for up to three disks. Prices subject to change. Call for availability and pricing information on latest editions.

201 W. 103rd Street, Indianapolis, Indiana 46290

1-800-428-5331 — Orders   1-800-835-3202 — Fax   1-800-858-7674 — Customer Service

Book ISBN 0-672-31073-2

What's on the
CD-ROM

The companion CD-ROM contains all of the authors' source code and samples from the book, as well as many third-party software products.

Windows 95/NT 4 Installation Instructions

1. Insert the CD-ROM into your CD-ROM drive.
2. From the Windows 95 desktop, double-click on the My Computer icon.
3. Double-click on the icon representing your CD-ROM drive.
4. Double-click on the icon titled SETUP.EXE to run the installation program.
5. The installation program creates a program group with the book's name as the group name. This group contains icons to browse the CD-ROM.

NOTE

If Windows 95 is installed on your computer and you have the AutoPlay feature enabled, the SETUP.EXE program starts automatically when you insert the CD-ROM into your CD-ROM drive.

System Requirements

This CD-ROM contains the Microsoft Visual Basic Control Creation Edition. Some of the features of Visual Basic 5 discussed in this book might not be usable with the Control Creation Edition. The Control Creation Edition is provided to allow you to become familiar with the Visual Basic environment and to create your own ActiveX controls.

The following are the minimum system requirements for the Visual Basic Control Creation Edition:

- A personal computer with a 486 or higher processor
- Microsoft Windows 95 or Windows NT Workstation 4.0 or later
- 8MB of memory (12MB recommended) if running Windows NT Workstation
- The following hard disk space:
    Typical installation: 20MB
    Minimum installation: 14MB
    CD-ROM installation (tools run from the CD-ROM): 14MB
    Total tools and information on the CD-ROM: 50MB
- A CD-ROM drive
- A VGA or higher-resolution monitor (SVGA recommended)

LIMITED WARRANTY

NO WARRANTIES. Microsoft expressly disclaims any warranty for the SOFTWARE PRODUCT. The SOFTWARE PRODUCT and any related documentation is provided "as is" without warranty of any kind, either express or implied, including, without limitation, the implied warranties or merchantability, fitness for a particular purpose, or noninfringement. The entire risk arising out of use or performance of the SOFTWARE PRODUCT remains with you.

NO LIABILITY FOR DAMAGES. In no event shall Microsoft or its suppliers be liable for any damages whatsoever (including, without limitation, damages for loss of business profits, business interruption, loss of business information, or any other pecuniary loss) arising out of the use of or inability to use this Microsoft product, even if Microsoft has been advised of the possibility of such damages. Because some states/jurisdictions do not allow the exclusion or limitation of liability for consequential or incidental damages, the above limitation may not apply to you.

original solely for backup or archival purposes. You may not copy the printed materials accompanying the SOFTWARE PRODUCT.

5. **DUAL-MEDIA SOFTWARE.** You may receive the SOFTWARE PRODUCT in more than one medium. Regardless of the type or size of medium you receive, you may use only one medium that is appropriate for your single computer. You may not use or install the other medium on another computer. You may not loan, rent, lease, or otherwise transfer the other medium to another user, except as part of the permanent transfer (as provided above) of the SOFTWARE PRODUCT.

6. **U.S. GOVERNMENT RESTRICTED RIGHTS.** The SOFTWARE PRODUCT and documentation are provided with RESTRICTED RIGHTS. Use, duplication, or disclosure by the Government is subject to restrictions as set forth in subparagraph (c)(1)(ii) of the Rights in Technical Data and Computer Software clause at DFARS 252.227-7013 or subparagraphs (c)(1) and (2) of the Commercial Computer Software—Restricted Rights at 48 CFR 52.227-19, as applicable. Manufacturer is Microsoft Corporation, One Microsoft Way, Redmond, WA 98052-6399.

7. **EXPORT RESTRICTIONS.** You agree that neither you nor your customers intend to or will, directly or indirectly, export or transmit (i) the SOFTWARE or related documentation and technical data or (ii) your software product as described in Section 1(b) of this License (or any part thereof), or process, or service that is the direct product of the SOFTWARE, to any country to which such export or transmission is restricted by any applicable U.S. regulation or statute, without the prior written consent, if required, of the Bureau of Export Administration of the U.S. Department of Commerce, or such other governmental entity as may have jurisdiction over such export or transmission.

MISCELLANEOUS

If you acquired this product in the United States, this EULA is governed by the laws of the State of Washington.

If you acquired this product in Canada, this EULA is governed by the laws of the Province of Ontario, Canada. Each of the parties hereto irrevocably attorns to the jurisdiction of the courts of the Province of Ontario and further agrees to commence any litigation which may arise hereunder in the courts located in the Judicial District of York, Province of Ontario.

If this product was acquired outside the United States, then local law may apply.

Should you have any questions concerning this EULA, or if you desire to contact Microsoft for any reason, please contact the Microsoft subsidiary serving your country, or write: Microsoft Sales Information Center, One Microsoft Way, Redmond, WA 98052-6399.

c. Separation of Components. The SOFTWARE PRODUCT is licensed as a single product. Its component parts may not be separated for use by more than one user.

d. Rental. You may not rent, lease, or lend the SOFTWARE PRODUCT.

e. Support Services. Microsoft may provide you with support services related to the SOFTWARE PRODUCT ("Support Services"). Use of Support Services is governed by the Microsoft policies and programs described in the user manual, in "online" documentation, and/or in other Microsoft-provided materials. Any supplemental software code provided to you as part of the Support Services shall be considered part of the SOFTWARE PRODUCT and subject to the terms and conditions of this EULA. With respect to technical information you provide to Microsoft as part of the Support Services, Microsoft may use such information for its business purposes, including for product support and development. Microsoft will not utilize such technical information in a form that personally identifies you.

f. Software Transfer. You may permanently transfer all of your rights under this EULA, provided you retain no copies, you transfer all of the SOFTWARE PRODUCT (including all component parts, the media and printed materials, any upgrades, this EULA, and, if applicable, the Certificate of Authenticity), **and** the recipient agrees to the terms of this EULA. If the SOFTWARE PRODUCT is an upgrade, any transfer must include all prior versions of the SOFTWARE PRODUCT.

g. Termination. Without prejudice to any other rights, Microsoft may terminate this EULA if you fail to comply with the terms and conditions of this EULA. In such event, you must destroy all copies of the SOFTWARE PRODUCT and all of its component parts.

3. **UPGRADES.** If the SOFTWARE PRODUCT is labeled as an upgrade, you must be properly licensed to use a product identified by Microsoft as being eligible for the upgrade in order to use the SOFTWARE PRODUCT. A SOFTWARE PRODUCT labeled as an upgrade replaces and/or supplements the product that formed the basis for your eligibility for the upgrade. You may use the resulting upgraded product only in accordance with the terms of this EULA. If the SOFTWARE PRODUCT is an upgrade of a component of a package of software programs that you licensed as a single product, the SOFTWARE PRODUCT may be used and transferred only as part of that single product package and may not be separated for use on more than one computer.

4. **COPYRIGHT.** All title and copyrights in and to the SOFTWARE PRODUCT (including but not limited to any images, photographs, animations, video, audio, music, text, and "applets" incorporated into the SOFTWARE PRODUCT), the accompanying printed materials, and any copies of the SOFTWARE PRODUCT are owned by Microsoft or its suppliers. The SOFTWARE PRODUCT is protected by copyright laws and international treaty provisions. Therefore, you must treat the SOFTWARE PRODUCT like any other copyrighted material except that you may install the SOFTWARE PRODUCT on a single computer provided you keep the

c. Redistributable Components.

(i) Sample Code. In addition to the rights granted in Section 1, Microsoft grants you the right to use and modify the source code version of those portions of the SOFT-WARE designated as "Sample Code" ("SAMPLE CODE") for the sole purposes of designing, developing, and testing your software product(s), and to reproduce and distribute the SAMPLE CODE, along with any modifications thereof, only in object code form provided that you comply with Section c(iii), below.

(ii) Redistributable Components. In addition to the rights granted in Section 1, Microsoft grants you a nonexclusive royalty-free right to reproduce and distribute the object code version of any portion of the SOFTWARE listed in the SOFTWARE file REDIST.TXT ("REDISTRIBUTABLE SOFTWARE"), provided you comply with Section c(iii), below.

(iii) Redistribution Requirements. If you redistribute the SAMPLE CODE or REDISTRIBUTABLE SOFTWARE (collectively, "REDISTRIBUTABLES"), you agree to: (A) distribute the REDISTRIBUTABLES in object code only in conjunction with and as a part of a software application product developed by you that adds significant and primary functionality to the SOFTWARE and that is developed to operate on the Windows or Windows NT environment ("Application"); (B) not use Microsoft's name, logo, or trademarks to market your software application product; (C) include a valid copyright notice on your software product; (D) indemnify, hold harmless, and defend Microsoft from and against any claims or lawsuits, including attorney's fees, that arise or result from the use or distribution of your software application product; (E) not permit further distribution of the REDISTRIBUTABLES by your end user. The following **exceptions** apply to subsection (iii)(E), above: (1) you may permit further redistribution of the REDISTRIBUTABLES by your distributors to your end-user customers if your distributors only distribute the REDISTRIBUTABLES in conjunction with, and as part of, your Application and you and your distributors comply with all other terms of this EULA; and (2) you may permit your end users to reproduce and distribute the object code version of the files designated by ".ocx" file extensions ("Controls") only in conjunction with and as a part of an Application and/or Web page that adds significant and primary functionality to the Controls, and such end user complies with all other terms of this EULA.

2. DESCRIPTION OF OTHER RIGHTS AND LIMITATIONS.

a. Not for Resale Software. If the SOFTWARE PRODUCT is labeled "Not for Resale" or "NFR," then, notwithstanding other sections of this EULA, you may not resell, or otherwise transfer for value, the SOFTWARE PRODUCT.

b. Limitations on Reverse Engineering, Decompilation, and Disassembly. You may not reverse engineer, decompile, or disassemble the SOFTWARE PRODUCT, except and only to the extent that such activity is expressly permitted by applicable law notwithstanding this limitation.

END-USER LICENSE AGREEMENT FOR MICROSOFT SOFTWARE

Microsoft Visual Basic, Control Creation Edition

IMPORTANT—READ CAREFULLY: This Microsoft End-User License Agreement ("EULA") is a legal agreement between you (either an individual or a single entity) and Microsoft Corporation for the Microsoft software product identified above, which includes computer software and may include associated media, printed materials, and "online" or electronic documentation ("SOFTWARE PRODUCT"). By installing, copying, or otherwise using the SOFTWARE PRODUCT, you agree to be bound by the terms of this EULA. If you do not agree to the terms of this EULA, do not install or use the SOFTWARE PRODUCT; you may, however, return it to your place of purchase for a full refund.

Software PRODUCT LICENSE

The SOFTWARE PRODUCT is protected by copyright laws and international copyright treaties, as well as other intellectual property laws and treaties. The SOFTWARE PRODUCT is licensed, not sold.

1. **GRANT OF LICENSE.** This EULA grants you the following rights:

    a. Software Product. Microsoft grants to you as an individual, a personal, nonexclusive license to make and use copies of the SOFTWARE for the sole purposes of designing, developing, and testing your software product(s) that is designed to operate in conjunction with any Microsoft operating system product. You may install copies of the SOFTWARE on an unlimited number of computers provided that you are the only individual using the SOFTWARE. If you are an entity, Microsoft grants you the right to designate one individual within your organization to have the right to use the SOFTWARE in the manner provided above.

    b. Electronic Documents. Solely with respect to electronic documents included with the SOFTWARE, you may make an unlimited number of or electronic form), provided that such copies shall be used and are not republished or distributed to any third party.